Act Like a Man

Act Like a Man

Challenging Masculinities in American Drama

Robert Vorlicky

Ann Arbor
The University of Michigan Press

Copyright © by the University of Michigan 1995
All rights reserved
Published in the United States of America by
The University of Michigan Press
Manufactured in the United States of America
♾ Printed on acid-free paper

1998 1997 1996 1995   4 3 2 1

A CIP catalogue record for this book is available from the British Library.

Library of Congress Cataloging-in-Publication Data

Vorlicky, Robert.
    Act like a man : challenging masculinities in American drama /
Robert Vorlicky.
        p.   cm.
    Includes bibliographical references and index.
    ISBN 0-472-09572-2 (alk. paper). — ISBN 0-472-06572-6 (pbk.: alk. paper)
    1. American drama—20th century—History and criticism.
2. Masculinity (Psychology) in literature. 3. Gender identity in
literature. 4. Sex role in literature. 5. Men in literature.
I. Title.
PS338.M37V67 1995
812'.5409353—dc20   94-38076
                                                                    CIP

Speak what we feel, not what we ought to say.
                                        —Shakespeare, *King Lear*

Acknowledgments

I am fortunate to have as mentors two extraordinary peers—Joseph A. Boone and Una Chaudhuri. Joe and Una gave unselfishly and generously of their time, energy, and intellect throughout the writing of this book. Both scholars have my deepest respect. I can still hear Joe's voice, just as I was about to leave in 1988 for a Fulbright appointment in Zagreb, encouraging me to work on a comprehensive study of male-cast plays for publication. Joe, a longtime friend, remains the ideal colleague: the length to which he has gone to share information, to anticipate problems, to suggest options, and to critique drafts carefully and incisively—always in a genuinely caring way—has surpassed my expectations. He, along with Una, gently urged me on to complete my task. Una, a more recent friend, provided astute criticism at pivotal stages in the writing; her insights, coupled with her enviable patience and loving manner, navigated and calmed this voyager more often than she knows. Her joy of teaching, learning, and living continues to inspire me.

I honor Joe and Una, for their enduring friendship and colleagueship—as well as the memory of my parents, Florence Kiess Vorlicky and William A. Vorlicky, and my childhood friend, William G. Krause—with this book. Also Chlöe, Tom, and Martin Webster, through whom my desire for and faith in new beginnings reside.

The journey to complete *Act Like a Man* has been a challenging one. Along the way, many people—far too many to mention here—have contributed to making the experience a fulfilling one. Yet a long trip can test the best relationships, so to my family—Bill, Jacquie, John, and Beth Vorlicky—and friends a heartfelt "thank you" for your patience and encouragement; you provided me not only with the space to do the work but with the peace of mind to know that our period apart was only temporary.

Michele Souda, Douglas Peine, and David M. Robinson read the manuscript at various stages of its development. I am in awe of the intelligence and skill of this trio. My work has benefited enormously from their comments, and my life is far richer for our years of friendship. My deepest appreciation to David Román for his belief in this study and for his presence at key moments in my life. Also to Michael Mayer for his selfless reassurance and valued opinions. The conversations and adventures remain a source of immense pleasure, as does our passion for the theater.

I am extremely grateful to LeAnn Fields of the University of Michigan Press, for her perseverance and genuine kindness from start to finish. Her professionalism and personal commitment to the book always demanded the best of me, and for that I am truly appreciative. The invaluable advice on shaping and editing the text, from the perceptive, encouraging evaluations by the anonymous outside readers to the meticulous, insightful copyediting by Michigan's staff, is evident throughout. My thanks, in particular, to Christina Milton, Ellen McCarthy, and Eve Trager.

For their guidance on issues of editing and production, my appreciation to Maria Epes and Molly Vaux. To Patricia Faiella, many thanks for keeping what matters most always in (our) sight. I value each of these dear friends for her thoughtfulness and loyalty; I have learned much from them.

This project gained immeasurable support from the Faculty Resource Network at New York University. During my semester as a scholar in residence in NYU's Department of English, I was able to complete much of the necessary research and to connect with faculty members Peggy Phelan (Performance Studies) and Una Chaudhuri (English), each of whom provided the intellectual and creative stimulation that was vital to my moving forward. To them, and to the Faculty Resource Network, I extend profound gratitude. Two summers in residence at Williams College offered me the rare opportunity to think and to write amid the peace and quiet of the Berkshires. My sincere thanks to Tim Cook and Jack Yeager for so many things during those seasons. Their own achievements, personal and professional, are models for me, and our time together in Williamstown is memorable.

Along with the assistance provided by the staff at Sawyer Library, Williams College, I am indebted to those at the Research Division of The New York Public Library for the Performing Arts, Bobst Library at New York University, Memorial Library at the University of Wisconsin–Madison, and, in particular, the Shanahan

Library at Marymount Manhattan College. Henry Blanke, specifically, facilitated endless requests, often under pressing time constraints. For their research assistance, many thanks to Martin Webster, Patricia Faiella, and Steven Frank, who were always available to double check citations, to make phone calls, and to run the quick errands that inevitably surfaced. Several scholars in theater studies were very helpful in advising me on their areas of expertise: Paul K. Jackson (African American plays and playwrights), Randy Barbara Kaplan (Asian American), and David Román (Latino and gay). The works cited and bibliography also were enhanced by input from numerous other individuals and sources; most notably, John Glines, the late Terry Helbing, Beth Rice, Don Shewey, Roberta Uno, Stuart Hecht, Nancy Hellner, Ken Furtado, Newberry Library (Chicago), San Francisco Performing Arts Library and Museum, Schomburg Center for Research in Black Culture (New York), Applause Theatre Books, Dramatists Play Service, and Samuel French.

Among the playwrights whose work I discuss in detail and who responded graciously to requests for further information, I am beholden to Edward Albee, Amiri Baraka, Dick Goldberg, Philip Kan Gotanda, Alonzo Lamont, Jr., Sidney Morris, and Robin Swados. I owe a vast debt to the Non-Traditional Casting Project for their indispensable listing of American playwrights of color and their works. Through the Project's records, I was able to contact many writers who, although unknown to the general public, are actively contributing to the new directions in American theater. Prompted by our correspondence, countless playwrights sent me their unpublished (though often produced) materials. It was a privilege to read their work, and we should all look forward to seeing well-deserved performances of many of them. The spirit of these emerging playwrights and their plays graces this study. And to Michael Feingold, my appreciation for his stimulating criticism and commitment to the world's old and new dramas; his keen intellect and dedication have long invigorated me.

Finally, my sincere gratitude to Ken Corbett and Alan DeLollis, longtime, admired friends whose brotherhood is steadfast. And for their counsel over the years and their confidence in this project and in me, my thanks to Jessica Benjamin, Eve Yunis Peterson, Dick Peterson, Andrea Musher, Ellen Bialo, Marsha Waterbury, Stephen Pickover, Mark Oram, Dale Wall, the late Sam Byers, Elaine Tannenbaum, Sheilah Loebel, Jane Aronson, Michael Cunningham, Gabrielle Cody, Lynda Hart, the Souda family, Jill Weiner, Aubrey Simpson, John and Priscilla Costello, Mary Fleischer, David Linton,

Zoë Kaplan, Patricia McAskin, Daniel Kaizer, Chris Waters, Karen Harris, Michael Cadden, Michael Hinden, Betsy Draine, Susan Stanford Friedman, Doris Kretschmer, my students, the administration of Marymount Manhattan College, and my colleagues in the Fine and Performing Arts Division and the Humanities Division at MMC (in particular, the faculties of Theatre and English).

To all playwrights: I salute you for enriching our theaters and our classrooms with your visions.

Contents

Introduction

Gender, Structure, and Dialogue

This book is about the power that is exercised by, contested by, and occasionally shared by American men. The canon of realist male-cast drama does not merely illustrate and display such power; by repeatedly staging it, this drama transforms it into an active and crucial component of American cultural politics. Thus, American male-cast drama affords a unique perspective on the mutual determinations of dramaturgy and culture, particularly on the relationship of realism to changing gender codes. Precisely because of the absence of women from its otherwise realistic context, the male-cast play embodies a striking, double-edged politics. On the one hand, the choice of realism, which purports to mirror reality, invites the playwright to document the historicity of patriarchal ideology, its dogmas as well as its variations. On the other, unfortunately, it is only the dogmas that have traditionally been privileged in the canon under study. In spite of its place in realist tradition, most variations of American male-cast drama resist the diversity of American male experience and its challenge to traditional masculinities; rather, they aggressively limit themselves to perpetuating a rigid, antihistorical account of male identity.

Realism is the dramatic mode that makes the strongest claim to forging links between a play's theatrical system and its cultural context. The characters in realist drama purport to voice our thoughts; their words are supposed to be our words. But, as recent feminist criticism points out, realist drama's account of reality is thoroughly determined by patriarchal ideology. In particular, the materialist feminist perspective, which, according to Jill Dolan, "deconstructs the mythic subject Woman to look at women as a class oppressed by material conditions and social relations" (10), reveals how realist drama tends to reify "the dominant culture's inscription of traditional power relations" (84). Yet "[r]ather than considering gender polarization as the victimization of only women," Dolan (who acknowledges her indebtedness to Gayle Rubin) argues that "materialist feminism considers it [gender polarization] a social construct oppressive to both women and men," since *both* are "historical subjects whose relation to prevailing social structures is also influenced by race, class, and sexual identification" (10). Inspired by this theoretical position, Jeanie Forte asks "whether or not a realist play could not also be a feminist play" (115), and Elin Diamond wonders if there can be a "feminist mimesis" (69).

Recent explorations into the issue of women's writings, feminism, and realism in literary studies by such critics as Rita Felski, Paulina Palmer, and Anne Cranny-Francis have redeemed the value of a "new realism" in fiction that, as Laura Marcus points out, associates "realism and an identity politics" (24) of diversified female subjects. Felski, in particular, forcefully demonstrates how the "confession [i.e., autobiographical realism] and the novel of self-discovery" by women authors reveal the "search for identity ... as a dominant motif, exemplified in the construction of a model of gendered subjectivity combined with a self-conscious appeal to a notion of oppositional community" (16). In the "search for identity," or as Felski suggests, "the construction of [the] self as a cultural reality" (78), writers of fiction continue to employ realist forms to represent *changing* subjectivities. For this reason, the possibilities of "new realism"—in terms of representation, for instance—stimulate provocative questions if one relates them to issues of gender representation in drama. Can dramatic realism ever be a site for the subversive practice of challenging dominant ideology? Can the "hegemony of realism" be disrupted and dismantled, thereby unmasking what Lynda Hart calls "the *re-creational* power of mimesis" (4)? Can dramatic realism present diverse subjects, women and men, whose individual manifestations of gender are not restrained by conventional social codings? Can drama respond to the notion that "[i]dentity is not a destiny," as Jeffrey Weeks argues, "but a choice. . . . [a] self-creation . . . on ground not freely chosen but laid out by history" (209)?

It would seem that of all realist representations none would be more antithetical to this program than a male-cast play. Surely men among themselves make the best (because most unchallenged) agents of patriarchal mimesis? Yet if one examines the dynamics of male-to-male dialogue, one finds that certain male-cast plays actually do challenge or at least qualify the realist model of rigid gender polarization. Not all such plays automatically and wholly reinscribe dominant ideology, not, that is, if we identify that ideology as the semiotic of maleness produced by the male-cast canon as a whole.

Although realism has traditionally reflected patriarchal ideology and presumed (white) male spectatorship, perhaps more glaringly in male-cast drama than in other plays, several contemporary American playwrights are confronting the assumptions that underlie the representation of male subjectivity. They are embracing the notion that the asymmetries of gender affect the construction of male subjectivity, resulting in a varied range of male identities when dramatizing men alone together. In doing so, they are also acknowledging the presence of a diverse male *and* female spectatorship. The playwrights' pioneering efforts indicate a possible shift—albeit a slight one—in attitudes toward male representation. This shift, in turn, enjoins a new critical commitment to specificity when discussing the limitations and possibilities of realist representation. Critical awareness of exactly *how* cultural codes are materialized in dramatic dialogue allows recognition of those slight, but significant, movements toward dialogue that resists normative gender codings.

During the last decade, the male-cast plays at the forefront in challenging traditional models usually share two characteristics: first, they respond to or are informed by major post–World War II events: the Civil Rights movement, the AIDS crisis, and the ongoing impact of contemporary feminism on American life; and second, they feature persons of color or gays or both. In regard to the latter characteristic and contrary to popular assumptions, minority male-cast drama, historically, has not challenged the patriarchal norm. Rather, its characters have been presented as objects within the dominant culture who become subjects only after they claim their status as gendered subjects—that is, as men, culturally defined. As exemplified by some of the recent plays that focus on minority characters, however, the representation of gender in realist drama, and in male-cast plays in particular, need not be hopelessly static and therefore need not be summarily dismissed, as it has been. While all men "share in the privilege of the phallus" (Schor 264), not all men experience phallic power in the same way. This difference is critical to this project. Diverse manifestations of self-

3

identified power, which exist as counterpoints to culturally coded power, are beginning to be written into male-cast dramas.

Conventional male-male representations adhere to the restraints of a rigid, binary system of gender coding. For the most part, they effectively erase differences among men based upon race, class, and sexual orientation, as they foreground their characters' identification—their subjectivity—according to polarized codings. "The formation of gender identity," argues Rubin, "is an example of production in the realm of the sexual system" (167); the gender system "fashion[s] maleness and femaleness into the cultural categories of masculinity and femininity" (Dolan 6). Up to the last decade, the most prominent feature distinguishing men among themselves in drama was the degree to which a man embodied "masculine" or "feminine" characteristics. The more individualized option that all men are "differently masculine" from one another,[1] for instance, was not a choice in terms of dramatic representation. Quite simply, a man rarely articulates his divergences from traditional gender codings. He does not acknowledge his "personalist terrain," which Una Chaudhuri identifies as one's "difference *within*" (199).[2]

Nowhere is the limiting of the characters in male-cast drama more vivid than in the dynamic of their dialogue. What men on stage say or do not say to each other when women are absent is nothing short of a full-fledged semiotic, one that includes strict rules about the settings of plays, the behaviors of characters, and the topics of conversation. This semiotic appears with surprisingly little variation in a surprisingly large number of plays. The full impact of a male-cast play's deviation from conventional dramaturgical strategies cannot be appreciated without identifying the distinguishing settings, behaviors, and topics of this imposing and hitherto unexamined body of literature. Only then can one recognize the force of the communicative dynamic so long authorized by the male-cast canon.

Where the Boys Are

The American male-cast canon is immense. Over one thousand plays have been produced;[3] of these, over five hundred realist plays have been published. Many of America's noted playwrights have written at least one male-cast play, including Eugene O'Neill, Arthur Miller, Tennessee Williams, Edward Albee, George Kaufman,

William Inge, Paul Green, Lanford Wilson, Charles Fuller, Amiri Baraka, Ed Bullins, Arthur Kopit, David Rabe, Israel Horovitz, Miguel Piñero, Thomas Babe, James Purdy, Ronald Ribman, David Henry Hwang, Philip Kan Gotanda, Harvey Fierstein, Terrence McNally, and Robert Schenkkan. Two of our most celebrated playwrights, David Mamet and Sam Shepard, have, along with Robert Patrick, devoted the vast majority of their dramatic output to the male-cast play. With very few exceptions, male-cast plays are written by men; among well-known women playwrights who have used the form are Maria Irene Fornes, Megan Terry, and Lavonne Mueller.[4] In general, white male authorship far outnumbers all others. White gay and African American playwrights are the most frequently published minorities.

As for the ethnicity of the characters in published plays, the vast majority are, again, white. Fewer than one hundred published plays feature African American characters, considerably fewer still, Latinos and Asians. None, to my knowledge, feature Native Americans. Approximately half of the published plays include one or more minority characters, either men of color or gay men or (very rarely) bisexual men. In short, the heterosexual white male is noticeably the most frequently dramatized figure in male-cast plays; the white gay, followed by the black male, is the most frequently represented minority character.

Where male-cast drama parts company most decisively with other American drama is in its choice of setting. In general, male-cast plays do not bear out what we assume to be American playwrights' preference for domestic settings. Few occur solely in the private sphere of a home, especially if they are cast predominantly with heterosexuals. However, male-cast plays that feature mainly gays are frequently set in homes.[5]

Public spaces—either in institutions of confinement or places of work—are the most frequent locale in male-cast plays. This feature provides a significant but complex link between these plays and an aspect of modern drama that has been theorized, most convincingly by Carol Rosen, under the figure of impasse. According to Rosen, "total institutions"—hospitals, insane asylums, prison, or military training camps—"at once naturalistically and symbolically" express how "different journeys of the human spirit" toward "self-fulfillment [are] thwarted by a relentless Structure" (12, 20, 22).[6] Although American male-cast plays are often set in total institutions (with the noticeable exception of asylums),[7] they nevertheless yield a quite different reading of the theme of confinement. Far from thwarting men's aspirations, institutional settings afford the characters a kind of freedom usually denied to them elsewhere. The kind of freedom I mean is quite precise—it is *self-expression*. Traditionally, writers have found in institutional environments dramatic situations that yield engaging dialogue and action. These confined settings function in male-cast drama as "an apparatus for transforming individuals," Michel Foucault's description of the actual prison system (1979, 233). The infrequency of alternative settings is noticeable and disturbing, for it implies the crippling notion that men cannot talk personally to each other until they find themselves menaced by coercive and confining institutions. Yet, personal engagement is precisely the vital component of American realist dramaturgy.

The other favored site of male-cast plays is the workplace. Here too "action . . . is rigidly controlled" (Rosen 260): workplaces involve congregation at a centralized location and the performance of repetitive tasks. Most importantly, they also have a predetermined hierarchy of authority. This hierarchy directly influences the shape of the plays' dialogue; the "laws of the space [they] inhabit" often determine when characters converse and what they talk about. The most popular setting in what Mel Gussow calls "occupational dramas" (qtd. in Rosen 265) is a professional environment, usually an office; nonprofessional working environments are rarer.[8] This preference reflects the concerns of a middle-class American drama that is invested in perpetuating patriarchal images of cultural power and success. The appeal of these images rests in their ability to capture the society's almost fetishistic devotion to hierarchical structures, as well as to embody the spectator's often private desires for social recognition and influence. Situated far from working-class environments and representing men's interaction in a hierarchical context, these plays help systematize male dominance over subordinate individuals. Occupational dramas confirm the culture's investment in the idea of authority. And within those dramas, "the judges of normality are present everywhere. . . . the teacher-judge, the doctor-judge, the 'social worker'–judge; it is on them that the universal reign of the normative is based" (Foucault 1979, 304).

Boys Will Be Boys

It is precisely when American men are in institutional settings of confinement, and to a lesser extent in workplaces, that the likelihood of their self-expression—or their self-disclosure—increases. By self-disclosure I mean something almost wholly contained within the realm of language: an individualization that overcomes the restrictions of cultural coding, in particular the powerful masculine ethos, but an individualization wholly manifested in the characters' articulation of personal truths. Besides these settings, however, there are several other devices that playwrights employ to prompt self-disclosures: alcohol, drugs, and violence.

Speaking in a voice that recalls many characters who extol the virtues of drugs, Jay, the flamboyant, marijuana-smoking author in Robert Patrick's *The Haunted Host,* remarks that drugs "tend to make one talk rather loosely and honestly" (312). Jay's altered state, like that shared by the men in Mart Crowley's *The Boys in the Band,* allows him to release any self-conscious inhibitions in favor of raw, revealing comments. Just as drugs release candid talk in characters, so does alcohol. As the Coach warns his soused, middle-aged former teammates in Jason Miller's *That Championship Season,* confessional talk, an unmanly behavior, comes from men who "drink like women" (31).

Throughout twentieth-century American drama, men together, regardless of their profile, drink too much or take drugs and then talk self-disclosingly.[9] "Sobriety diminishes, discriminates, and says no," William James submits, while "drunkenness expands, unites, and says yes" (377). Noting the importance in drama of drunken truth telling, Thomas Disch asks, "Are English-speaking peoples such inveterate sots that all their important emotional transactions must be conducted under the influence? Or is it rather that playwrights cannot resist the dramatic convenience of the Gospel according to Dionysus: *In vino veritas*" (661). In respect to the dramaturgy of the male-cast play, this is indeed part of a coded system in which drink and drugs facilitate personal talk among men.

While use of alcohol and drugs generally precedes men's self-disclosing dialogue, it can also lead men into violent abuse, whether verbal or physical, of one another. But male-male violence in drama does not depend exclusively upon this device: in fact, most verbal and physical abuse occurs when the characters are sober. Violent interaction, like alcohol and drug consumption, is coded in male-cast plays as a feature that precedes men's self-disclosing dialogue. Very simply: male characters often fight with words or fists before they talk personally. This feature holds throughout the canon, with one significant exception. Gays among themselves are much more likely to speak personally without first resorting to violence.[10] Interestingly enough, they do make use of the other technique of male intimacy, drink and drugs.

"Booze and women. I tried to protect you from it," the Coach reminds his "boys" in *That Championship Season* (J. Miller 26). Implicit in the Coach's remarks is the belief that both alcohol and women are agents of confessional talk. Or, put differently, a drunk man has the potential to talk openly, like a (sober) woman, who is presumed to speak personally. This comparison raises a critical issue about realist dialogue: what does it mean to have a man speak like a woman? From yet another perspective, what is the function of women characters in dramatic talk? A look at mixed-cast plays reveals the centrality of the women's verbal contributions to the progression of dialogue toward characters' self-disclosures. If, for instance, one examines the scenes between Linda Loman and her sons in Arthur Miller's *Death of a Salesman* as conversation, Linda emerges as an active participant in the talk: she eagerly responds to her sons' comments, asks them pressing questions (especially about their relationship to their father, Willy), and steadfastly refuses to settle for easy, impersonal responses. Linda's contributions substantially influence the play's developing action; they are central to the structure of the play's dialogue as well as to the development of its major themes.

I deliberately focus on Linda Loman since she has come to represent, for many, a quintessential male-constructed object—a female Other—who embodies a damaging stereotype of woman, wife, and mother. Understanding Linda's role as a participant in the play's conversations does not deny her culturally defined positions as woman, wife, and mother within the play's heavily coded language system. Many critics have convincingly addressed the latter, most recently Gayle Austin (1, 46–51). But while Linda may not "act on her own behalf" (Austin 48), she nonetheless actively contributes to conversations at which she is present; she is not a passive, silent presence. Her voiced contributions, like those of most women characters in realist drama, have direct impact on ensuing verbal exchanges *and* dramatic actions—despite, or perhaps because of, her sex and gender.

Precisely because women's words strongly influence these developments—one can argue, after all, that Linda's direct plea that "attention must be paid" stimulates her sons' subsequent actions and talk—the issue becomes immediately sex and gender centered: What happens to dramatic dialogue when women are absent, leaving men alone together? How do men talk among themselves when no woman is present?

On the most obvious dramaturgical level, one can observe the extent to which playwrights initiate men's self-disclosing dialogue via the technical substitutes—alcohol and drug use and violence—for the verbal contributions of women characters. More profound in its implications for dramatic theory and realism, however, is the question of whether men, in the absence of women, replicate a gendered language system, one in which the voices of male and female, masculine and feminine, self and other remain, albeit coming exclusively from the mouths of men. If such a system exists, what are its features, and what can interrupt its otherwise characteristic dialogue and representations? And finally, to what extent is American male-cast drama responsive to the diversities of male experience and changing gender codes in its representation of men?

Gender, Dialogue, and Semiotic Apparatus

While Simone de Beauvoir's model of gender as sociocultural "universals" has been extensively revised by later, multidisciplinary theory,[11] it remains relevant to the study of male-cast drama, in which gender is represented as socially constructed universals.

In her revolutionary book *The Second Sex,* Beauvoir presented, according to Peggy Reeves Sanday, "three basic propositions which articulated the view that sociocultural universals are at the heart of universal sexual asymmetry": (1) "the symbolic structures defining masculine and feminine conform to an essentially static, dialectical pattern of binary oppositions in all societies"; (2) "this dialectic follows a universal pattern: the masculine is associated with culture and the feminine is associated with nature"; and (3) "the nature of the dialectic places males in a position of dominating and exploiting women as culture exploits nature." From these propositions, Beauvoir "saw gender in terms of a semiotic apparatus that followed a universal pattern" (Sanday 1990, 2, 3).[12] This pattern establishes that humanity

> is male and man defines woman not in herself but as relative to him; she is not regarded as an autonomous being. . . . She is defined and differentiated with reference to man and not he with reference to her; she is the incidental, the inessential as opposed to the essential. He is Subject, he is the Absolute—she is the Other. . . . Otherness is a fundamental category of human

thought. Thus it is that no group ever sets itself up as the one without at once setting up the Other over against itself. (Beauvoir xvi–xvii)

Identifying specific, historically constituted social formations of gender, Beauvoir represents gender universals through the opposition between men and women as gendered beings: Man, as male, is subject and Self; Woman, as female, is object and Other; Woman, from her own (ego's) perspective, however, can also be, unto herself, subject and Self.[13] This position on gender construction is the foundation of materialist feminist thinking (Moi).

As Beauvoir points out, "The drama of woman lies in this conflict between the fundamental aspirations of every subject (ego)—who always regards the self as the essential—and the compulsions of a *situation* in which she is the inessential" (xxix; emphasis added). The "situation" in a male-cast play is determined by and limited to the interaction of men among themselves. Hence, one would expect such a play to be filled with male subjects. However, when one examines the semiotics of the realist play, this does not prove to be the case. The semiotic system of the male-cast play relies upon subject-object structures, and the dramatic situation and the men's talk are heavily coded according to the social construction of gender as identified in Beauvoir's model. Some men in a group are essential subjects, and they identify as such only because they refer to absent women or objectify any remaining men as Other.

Beauvoir's definition of *subject* as one who "can be posed only in being opposed—he sets himself up as the essential, as opposed to the other, the inessential, the object" (xvii)—is, thus, an apt account of the distinction between subject and object that determines linguistic and social dynamics among men in drama. In male-cast drama, a man's objectification of another man—or *the male subject's construction of a male object*—is most often located in the latter's difference from the former, which is usually determined by his race, ethnicity, class, religion, sexual orientation, or simply by his inadequate mirroring, or embodiment, of the gender codes of the (white) masculine ethos. (The male as "inessential," to use Beauvoir's term, or the male as object, is more commonly represented in male-cast drama than is the "essentially" diversified, or the differently masculine, male as subject.)

Beauvoir's assertion that gender is a semiotic system of sociocultural codes is further illuminated by revisionist theories of a "sex-gender system," as set forth by such feminist social scientists as Rubin and argued, more recently, by Teresa de Lauretis. A sex-gender system, according to de Lauretis, "is both a sociocultural construct and a semiotic apparatus, a system of representation that assigns meaning (identity, value, prestige, location in kinship, status in the social hierarchy, etc.) to individuals within the society.... The construction of gender is both the product and the process of its representation" (5). A differentiated sex-gender system continues to operate, therefore, in the same-sex gender system of the male-cast play. Here, the "product" and "process" are a representation of masculinity in which the Beauvoirian gender differentiation between subjects (male) and objects (female) is mapped onto and divided among individuals in the all-male group. This representation is most strikingly forged in what Keir Elam calls the play's "discourse coherence" (182–84).

In his influential *The Semiotics of Theatre and Drama,* Elam urges, with certain important qualifications, the extension of theories of speech events in real life, such as John Searle's speech act theories or H. P. Grice's philosophy of language, to dialogue in dramatic texts.[14] Elam's interest in Grice's identification of the "Cooperative Principle" in actual talk exchanges, in particular, is useful in understanding Elam's theory of dramatic dialogue. The Cooperative Principle states, "Make your conversational contribution such as is required, *at the stage at which it occurs,* by the accepted purpose or direction of the talk exchange in which you are engaged" (Grice 45; emphasis added).[15] Elam suggests that a cooperative principle exists in the construction of dialogue, whereby "dramatic speakers... produce utterances which are informative... 'true' with respect to the dramatic world (unless strategically insincere), comprehensible and relevant to the occasion" (173).

While actual talk and dramatic dialogue may share a pragmatic participatory dynamics, the equation between the two kinds of talk "cannot be taken very far" (Elam 178).[16] According to Elam, the systematic difference between dialogue and real-life conversation is "the degree of textual control to which dramatic discourse is subject" (182).[17] In other words, a conversation has fewer textual constraints governing its progress than does dramatic dialogue. Elam identifies six "levels of textual coherence" that usually constrain dramatic dialogue (182–84);[18] the third level is "discourse coherence":

Each exchange or monologue within the drama, according to the "followability" requirement, will be geared towards a clear "topic" of discourse (or overall "theme"), changes in which will be plainly signalled. Similarly, the individual "objects" of discourse (referred to in the course of the exchange or monologue) will be introduced in a strategic order, rather than at random (as is often the case in ordinary conversation). (183)

The literary critic interested in analyzing drama as a semiotic system finds him- or herself most at home at this level of coherence because of its attention to content—specifically topic selection and order of discussion. Since each talk exchange within drama, according to Elam, is "geared towards a clear 'topic' of discourse (or overall 'theme')," I highlight the general topic selections in male characters' cooperative and uncooperative communications (the latter recalls Grice's "conversationally unsuitable" discourse [45]). Less concerned with how the dialogue functions as a comprehensive linguistic interaction (which includes extralinguistic actions), therefore, I analyze what the dialogue reveals at the level of discourse coherence.[19] This emphasis on substance or theme reveals a culturally determined grouping of topics as a consistent feature of men's dramatic dialogue. Furthermore, the male characters engage these topics in a specific order.

Whereas Elam suggests that unique "strategic orders" exist in single written texts, one can argue that an order also characterizes an entire canon. In the male-cast canon, this strategic order is directly aligned with the degree of the characters' participation in cooperative or uncooperative talk exchanges. In order to demonstrate this concurrence I analyze the discourse coherence of thirteen published plays that are paradigms of the canon in respect to this specific focus. The majority of these plays come close to sustaining a *fully realized dramatization of a specific dynamic of communication.* (The only exceptions are the realist plays in which self-disclosing dialogue predictably occurs between men because it is generated within confining institutions [chap. 3] and a nonrealist play that rejects the neoclassic unities [chap. 4].) The majority of plays adhere, in general, to the neoclassic unities (especially as they relate to the structure of discrete acts): these plays represent, in effect, sustained conversations between characters simply because the speakers and listeners are not interrupted or inexplicably transformed because of abrupt changes in time, place, or action. Finally, all thirteen plays represent distinct levels of how American male characters talk among themselves in various contexts; each also illustrates the range of features indigenous to a specific level of the dramatic dialogue's coherence. These features reflect both the linguistic-literary and the cultural codes operating within the dramatic system. These codes, in turn, indicate the power of the semiotic of maleness to determine through characters' dialogue the sociolinguistic dramatic system.[20]

A significant difference between Beauvoir's model of gender universals (which is based in lived experience) and that which operates in nearly all male-cast drama is that Beauvoir's model is flexible in its responsiveness to historical influence and cultural change. The model depicted in male-cast drama is intractable by comparison, unresponsive to such influence and change. But, as Linda Bamber rightly points out, everything *has* changed within the culture since Beauvoir's writing: "the culture changes in response to the claims of individual women and women in turn respond to the changing culture" (10). Asking if this means that women "will cease to be the Other in fiction by men," Bamber concludes, "I presume not"—as do I in respect to male-cast drama. Despite cultural changes, woman does not cease to be Other in the fiction of nearly all (male-authored) male-cast drama. Although male-cast plays reflect Beauvoir's and materialist feminism's perception of the construction of gender in society, most conclude with a contrasting perspective: gender exists independently from and *outside* any evolving cultural history.

This double perspective is possible because the plays' representations of gender operate from two distinct, yet interrelated positions: social constructionism of gender and determinism of gender. A feminist and semiotic perspective on male-cast plays seeks to track the precise mechanisms of this *system* of social constructionism and determinism. Whereas their dynamic relationship is rarely acknowledged, particularly in the formation of the dramatic text, the realist male-cast canon affords the most intense illustration of their dramatic alliance—especially the depth to which determinist gender construction functions.

Although speaking about the semiotic constitution of the performance text and feminist poetics, Sue-Ellen Case indirectly addresses the problematic relationship between social constructionism of gender and realist drama:

Cultural encoding is the imprint of ideology upon the sign—the set of values, beliefs and ways of seeing that control the conno-

13

tations of the sign in the culture at large. . . . For a feminist, this means that the dominant notions of gender, class and race compose the meaning of the text of a play, the stage pictures of its production and the audience reception of its meaning. (1988, 116–17)

From within the interpersonal dynamics represented in the male-cast play itself, characters appear to comprehend and to experience gender as a social construction. That is, they appear to act according to a social prescription that identifies ways men are supposed to be. Thus, the cultural construction of gender informs, if not outright determines, a play's discourse coherence: male characters' dialogue replicates the socially constructed binary of male/female, masculine/feminine, and Self/Other.

It is exactly the schematic predictability of the discourse coherence in the conventional male-cast play, however, that reinforces for the spectator a kind of determinist perspective on gender; that is, the discernible mapping of the language of male representation encourages a "well, that's just the way men are" reading of the characters' lives. The schematic progression in the discourse coherence originates from the tension between the (apparent) desire to particularize dramatic content (through the individualization of character that is otherwise overdetermined by social codings) and to adhere to the (apparently) inflexible demands of realist structure. A reading of the plays' discourse coherence reveals this canon's rigid perspective on gender as monolithic and unchanging.

On the other hand, if one pinpoints through the same semiotic analysis how authors actually attempt to write characters out of a monolithic structure in order to individualize them, one reveals a deeper "language" structure that also shapes male-cast plays and male representation. This structure moves beyond the notion that gender exists independently from and outside of any evolving history and, instead, responds to the notion that gender is socially constructed and thereby changeable. A deeper text and its meaning are generally submerged and overwhelmed by the overdetermination (via conventional, static gender codings expressed in dialogue) of male representation. A dramaturgical tension remains not unlike the theoretical tension that exists in feminism, according to Naomi Schor, between "the interplay of social constructionism and essentialism." This "interplay," according to Schor, remains an "unresolved (and perhaps unresolvable) debate within feminism" (267), a position most recently documented by Donna Landry and Gerald MacLean.

The recurrent dramatization of gender binaries in male-cast plays is a far cry from Judith Butler's vision of gender "as a corporeal field of cultural play" (1988, 531). Rather than being presented as Butler's "basically innovative affair," gender is repeatedly played out as a binary system when men are among themselves in drama. And while Butler's philosophical, phenomenological notion that gender "is not passively scripted on the body, and neither is it determined by nature, language, the symbolic, or the overwhelming history of patriarchy" in lived experience, male interaction in realism continually represents gender as determined by and through language. Gender-based (and, therefore, gender-biased) dialogue in male-cast drama is presented, to turn Butler's use of the phrase, as a "linguistic given." Whereas Butler explores what possibilities "exist for the cultural transformation of gender through [specific corporeal] acts" (1988, 521) in lived experience, I examine here what possibilities exist for the dramatic transformation of gender through "realist" dialogue.

Man to Man

Whether brought together out of choice, necessity, force, or familial bonding, characters in the American male-cast play initially engage one another cooperatively in what I call "social dialogue," which is determined by the American masculine ethos and expressed through familiar male mythologies. These masculine myths, Anthony Easthope suggests, inform and often dictate the way in which a man lives privately and publicly: "within, femininity and male homosexual desire must be denied; without, women and the feminine must be subordinated and held in place" (166). An American male is socialized to embrace the ethos that such myths set forth in order to embody what Peter Schwenger calls a "state of male wholeness" (632). The cultural coding of the ethos—based in the rigid system of the Beauvoirian Self/Other dichotomy—privileges heterosexual white males among all men while marginalizing gays and heterosexuals of color. It materializes itself as the constant social pressure on a man to confirm his masculinity via its *difference* from femininity, thereby denying male diversity. Deeply rooted as it is in American culture and language, this ethos consistently informs the dramatic system of the male-cast play.

Most characters in male-cast plays begin by engaging in social dialogue. They do so in an effort to situate themselves within the hegemonic patriarchy, which they presume to be supported by all the other participants in the talk exchanges. The characters use social dialogue because they want to confirm their common ground with each other. Moreover, social dialogue is safe; it guarantees cooperative communication. What we see and hear at this stage of the plays is an articulated *awareness* of their individual and collective power—political, economic, domestic, and sexual—as men within American culture. The male characters are fully aligned with the patriarchal ethos that creates this power, conscious of its rules and of its role in constructing their public image. Inevitably and pointedly, their power at this level is over women, the Other. Finally, this ethos is not amorphous; it is a rigidly ordered discourse, that is, a structured thematic consisting of certain specific topics. During the social dialogue that begins most male-cast plays, and with virtually no exceptions, the characters engage these topics explicitly. The topics are employment, consumerism, families, women, and their own active identification with the cultural ideal of male virility.

Throughout the twentieth century, the vast majority of characters within the male-cast canon have encouraged social dialogue in order to exercise the culturally coded powers prescribed by male privilege. Only recently have some playwrights begun to present male characters whose desire to transcend the limitations of a culturally coded identity leads them to depart from conventional behavior and social dialogue. These characters move into what I call "personal dialogue," a dynamic of communication in which self-disclosure and individualization are central to the expression of one's identity and desires. Personal dialogue reveals a character's wish to know and to activate his "difference within," which is associated with personal rather than culturally coded terms.[21] Recurrent topics that surface during men's personal dialogue include one's wish to reconnect with a deeper sense of family and home; a desire for relationships and intimacy but a fear of responsibility that inhibits the pursuit of that desire; a yearning to release the "infantile self" without fear of rejection or abandonment; and finally, one's conscious struggle with the "other," generally gender coded as the "feminine" within himself. This latter topic appears quite dramatically, however, as a man's more profound, less conscious struggle with the Other, which Jacqueline Rose, reading Jacques Lacan, identifies as that which "stands against the phallus."

16

In being positioned so against the Other, the phallus, according to Rose, "seeks authority and is refused" (51). The tension created by the paradox of man's dependence upon, rejection of, desire for, and desire to be an "other" provokes some of the most startling, though infrequently articulated, personal dialogue in male-cast plays. It is also intrinsically linked to a man's urge to understand and to accept himself as differently masculine, and thereby to understand and to accept difference in others.

Lest it be presumed that American playwrights are now dashing off dozens of plays about males who are challenging the cultural privileges afforded their gender, let me hasten to say: they are not. It is still the rare male-cast play, whether realist or not, that takes the leap to dramatize American male characters who speak personally and openly in the company of other men. That leap is a political one and a dangerous one, for in breaking with convention the playwright risks provoking an audience's incomprehension.

Chapter 1 discusses three plays that are constructed, first and foremost, to sustain social dialogue. In the first of these, I show how the discourse coherence of David Mamet's *Glengarry Glen Ross* (1983)[22] depends upon topics related to the theme of the masculine ethos and male mythologies. This Pulitzer Prize–winning play can be read as full-scale dramatization of the initial level of male social dialogue. Despite any passing personalized comments that challenge the status quo, the play's traditional white heroes remain committed to the cultural codings of maleness. These codings include one's belief in male myths, which, according to Beauvoir, "imply a subject who projects his hopes and his fears toward a sky of transcendence. Women do not set themselves up as Subjects and hence have erected no virile myth in which their projects are reflected" (142). Mamet's play—with its erection of virile myths—is the paradigmatic American work dramatizing this particular dynamic of male characters' talk exchanges. There are no published male-cast plays that are cast with nonwhite or gay characters that wholly mirror this level of discourse coherence. Therefore, it is a level that, if sustained, appears to capture a dramatic talk that only white, straight subjects authentically pursue and perpetuate. This dramaturgical detail is no doubt due to the fact that such men are culturally privileged by the social codings of the masculine ethos, sanctioned to embody and represent the ideal American man.

The remaining plays in chapter 1 derive their discourse coherence from a specific topic within the thematic of the American masculine ethos: the absent woman. The topic of women is the only one that is sustained, for a play's duration, as the articulated object in male subjects' dialogue. In Alice Gerstenberg's *At the Club* (1930) and Sidney Morris's *If This Isn't Love!* (1982), the male characters talk about specific offstage, or absent, women for the plays' duration. In each play, women are defined by specific socio-sexual roles that are determined from the male characters' perspectives. These female referents, or what Elam calls "objects" of discourse, are cast in what Case has identified as classical roles in the Western tradition of drama: "misogynistic roles," woman as "the Bitch, the Witch, the Vamp and the Virgin/Goddess," or, less frequently, "positive roles," woman as "independent, intelligent and even heroic" (1988, 6). By sustaining their focus on the topic of absent women, male characters perpetuate social dialogue that is, while cooperative, nonetheless restrictive in its representation of women. Women, after all, are not present in male-cast drama; they are not their own subjects. Women remain heavily coded, gendered bodies that are subjected to the power of male authority and privilege.[23]

This level of male interaction clearly reveals men's preference for discussing the Other, rather than their own complicated, conflicted selves, as a topic of conversation. As Beauvoir recognizes, "[W]oman is the Other in whom the subject transcends himself without being limited, who opposes him without denying him; she is the Other who lets herself be taken without ceasing to be the Other, and therein she is so necessary to man's happiness and to his triumph that it can be said that if she did not exist, men would have invented her" (186). The absent woman is the most engaged and thoroughly explored topic in male-cast dramas; in talking about woman, or in "exchanging" her as a topic among themselves (which recalls Rubin's theory of men's "traffic in women" as property), male characters communicate their deepest feelings to each other.

The first chapter, then, illustrates those fundamental features of male discourse that produce cooperative communication. Chapter 2, "Silence, Violence, and the Drama of Abuse," discusses three dramaturgically significant male-cast plays that derive their unconventional structures and content by isolating the dynamic of uncooperative communication: Eugene O'Neill's *Hughie* (1959), Amiri Baraka's (formerly LeRoi Jones) *The Toilet* (1963), and Edward Albee's *The Zoo Story* (1960). For the characters in these three works (and in most male-cast plays as well), uncooperative communication occurs primarily when speakers and listeners are unwilling or unable to create a shared text by engaging either social or personal dialogue. Such a dramatic occurrence could be viewed, for instance, as analogous to an outright failure of the cooperative principle.[24]

Uncooperative communication within a dramatic text is manifested in three general ways: sustained silence, verbal abuse, or physical violence. First, the least frequent sign of communicative failure among characters is sustained silence. This can occur either when participants literally say nothing to one another, or when a speaker engages in monologues because his listener is uncooperative or nonreciprocal in providing verbal responses. In both instances, silence becomes "abusive," or offensive, in its violation of interpersonal communication; silence in and of itself, however, is not automatically an uncooperative feature in talk exchanges. When silence does violate the dynamics of interpersonal communication in drama, it is most often the outcome of characters who either deliberately resist taking any responsibility to share in the creation of a text or oppose revealing why they prefer to remain silent. O'Neill's *Hughie* is historically important in its depiction of this level of interaction. The play is the first critically acknowledged male-cast play that utilizes the dynamic of uncooperative communication as its essential source of dramatic form and content. It is the first play to dramatize in an everyday setting men struggling to engage topics that differ from those within the thematic of the American masculine ethos. The characters strain to communicate, particularly on a personal level, resorting to an interplay of monologues and sustained silence as a way to fill time and space.

Prolonged verbal abuse, through the use of loathsome sexual or racial epithets, for instance, distinguishes the second type of uncooperative communication. When verbal abuse erupts, it effectively diminishes, if not eliminates, any talk exchange among participants. Thus, it can be an outstanding feature of less than cooperative communication (i.e., talk is still occurring, but uncooperatively), or a signal precipitating the talk exchange's demise into uncooperative communication, and possible termination of the exchange altogether.

Finally, the third and by far most common sign of uncooperative communication is physical violence. Physical assault is a frequent response of male characters and indicates their unwillingness or fear to assume any responsibility for creating or furthering a communicative act among other men. At this level of antisocial interaction, men fail altogether to use words in order to connect with other men. Rather, they initiate physical violence. *The Toilet* and *The Zoo Story* rely upon both verbal and physical abuse as primary structural devices. Unlike O'Neill's characters, who eventually relinquish their silence in order to engage in social dialogue, Baraka's and Albee's men move through silence into verbal and physical abuse in their struggle to identify the base of power among themselves.

Chapters 3 and 4 consider seven plays, each characterized by its construction of sustained personal dialogue. It is not insignificant or coincidental that gays or heterosexuals of color appear in seven of these plays. In a striking departure from white heterosexual characters' often deliberate commitment to the preservation of social dialogue, underrepresented male characters—African American, Latino, Asian American, bisexual, and gay—readily initiate and engage in personal dialogue when they are in the company of white heterosexual men. This is not the case, however, when minority men are among themselves (for example when African Americans are alone together or when gay men are alone together); a range of features, therefore, distinguish individuals who participate in personal dialogue. The fact that characters share racial sameness with one another or share the same sexual orientation, for instance, does not, in and of itself, guarantee that characters will engage in self-disclosing dialogue. In many groups of men, notes Lynne Segal, "Open discussion can arouse fear and anxiety, because it is regarded as essentially 'feminine' behaviour" (165).

Often, a minority male disrupts the traditional males' social dialogue. It is significant that a minority male character's relationship to personal dialogue when among white heterosexual male characters heightens the complications inherent in the naming of difference—in the identification of the complex intersection of gender, race, ethnicity, and sexual orientation. In this regard, the discourse coherence of the talk exchanges between marginalized men are reminiscent of the conventional portrayal of women characters in American dramatic texts. As with many women characters, men who are nonwhite, gay, or both are often presented as viewing their relative powerlessness in the white heterosexual patriarchy as a catalyst to be more self-disclosing, or at least to minimize their appropriation of social dialogue and its concern for the (white) American masculine ethos. When representing their marginalized status as Other (or as object) within a play's cast of characters, therefore, these men activate a traditionally female or feminine function within the drama as facilitators of personal dialogue. Yet, from another perspective, they become "othered" subjects in the process—men who are differently masculine from those assuming cultural power. In this way, marginalized men are usually heavily coded to serve deliberate functions within drama's semiotic of maleness.

The white heterosexual male character rarely makes a conscious effort to be self-disclosing in conversation. Unlike most women characters in all-female or mixed-cast plays, he is not represented as easily initiating or engaging in personal dialogue, particularly when in the company of other men like himself. He appears unwilling or unable to create an individual identity through self-disclosure that would distinguish him from those with whom he shares cultural power; to do so would jeopardize his access to that power and its attendant cultural privileges. This anti-individualistic position is a stark reversal of the long-standing American ideology of individualism as set forth by Emerson and his followers; or, perhaps, access to privilege actually reveals an anti-individualistic underside to the American ethos of individualism. Consequently, such men seldom assume any responsibility to understand, or even to acknowledge, their own or another's individuality when it is revealed in personal interaction. White heterosexual characters rarely deviate from the culturally coded themes of the American masculine ethos.

If and when a more personal text is created, however, it usually surfaces as they get drunk or drugged, or find their lives imminently threatened. This latter condition recalls Carol Rosen's definition of American plays of impasse set in confining institutions. My third chapter, "Liberation in Confinement," focuses on the discourse coherence established in the predominantly straight world of David Rabe's military play, *Streamers* (1977) and Miguel Piñero's prison play, *Short Eyes* (1975), as well as the gay milieu of Robin Swados's AIDS hospice play, *A Quiet End* (1991). It qualifies Rosen's argument by illustrating that men among themselves in institutional settings, regardless of their sexual orientation, usually move toward a kind of self-fulfillment as they engage more readily in personal dialogue than men located in noninstitutional settings (Rosen 22).

Chapter 4, "Realizing Freedom: Risk, Responsibility, and Individualization," highlights four noninstitutional dramas—one nonrealist and three realist—that derive their discourse coherence from

21

topics that are essentially identified by the theme of individualization: Philip Kan Gotanda's Japanese American *Yankee Dawg You Die* (1991); Dick Goldberg's Jewish, domestic *Family Business* (1979); David Mamet's Anglo American working-class *American Buffalo* (1977); and Alonzo D. Lamont, Jr.'s African American *That Serious He-Man Ball* (1989). While these authors employ the convention of framing male characters' talk within social and abusive dialogues, they eventually subvert this tendency in favor of sustained personal dialogue, albeit with varying degrees of success, insight, and articulation. Each play locates sites of intervention in characters' language usage by confronting and defying conventional gender representation. Their characters conceive of self-knowledge and personal survival in ways that finally challenge their identities as gender-coded men. Rather, the majority of characters favor self-identifications based upon racial, ethnic, and sexual differences which in turn lead them to claim the specificity of their experiences amid a shared humanity with other men—a humanity that transcends gender codings and biases, thereby making harmony among people a possibility. This sense of a shared humanity, I must sadly note, does not appear in the noticeably few published all-male plays with a cast of multicultural principals.

The epilogue returns to the topic of the "othered" presence in male-cast drama. This disruptive figure, I suggest, becomes the foundation of an alternative theory of American realist dramatic construction—one determined less by the tension between *sexual* subjects and objects than by the power dynamic between *gendered* subjects and objects. At the heart of this postulation is the transformation, via revisioned gender codings, of the male object into a differently masculine male subject—one whose identity centers on his difference within. Having shown that a male object—a male Other, who is traditionally associated with Woman and femaleness—usually exists in male-cast plays, I connect this character's varied manifestations to the deeper constructions that inform the dramaturgy of all American realist drama. American dramatic realism is finally a more gender-coded frame than it is a sexual, racial, or class-coded one. Even though sexual, racial, and class codings may be the originating point from which the conflict begins, gender codings finally subsume them; representations of the sexes, the races, and the classes within American realism are repeatedly dichotomized because they are overdetermined by dualist gender codings. For this reason, the realist male-cast dramatic canon appears as a considerable semiotic system, one so rigidly coded as to restrict severely the range of representations available to the dramatic imagination. Once the mechanics of this system are revealed, however, the playwright has the option—through a radical reworking of the codes of male dialogue—to articulate and to stage new types of male subjectivity, new masculinities.

One

The American Masculine Ethos, Male Mythologies, and Absent Women

Glengarry Glen Ross, David Mamet

Near the conclusion of David Mamet's *Glengarry Glen Ross,* Richard Roma, a sleazy, cutthroat salesman, stands amid his employer's burgled real estate office. The surrounding destruction heightens Roma's lament that "it's not a world of men... it's not a world of men" (1984, 105).[1] Just a day earlier, Roma mesmerized a lead, a potential buyer named James Lingk, with the fantasy that in his desired world of men, a (white) man embodies his own absolute morality: he not only trusts himself, which enables him to overcome any fear of loss, but he also knows that he can "act each day without fear" (49). This, for Roma, is the way of the world, the way the world is intended to be. But Roma's fantasy of man's moral rightness—man's fearlessness—is nearly dashed when he considers his own position within the destroyed office: it is a scene of chaotic disruption that suggests, paradoxically, an imminent dismantling of the myth-driven world that "naturally" empowers (all) men within American patriarchy. It is a scene whose real and symbolic meanings even Roma cannot ignore.

In a bold stroke of self-confidence, however, Roma reasserts his own "difference" from other men as the key to his personal survival (50). He distinguishes his subject position from all Others (who, to him, are women, unmasculine men, and men of color). Like the phoenix, Roma is determined to rise from the rubble that signals the demise of other less shrewd businessmen. He, after all, never loses faith in his ability—in his power—to exploit anyone at any time. This is his right, he assumes, within the capitalist system his actions help to perpetuate. This is his right, Roma demonstrates, as a *male* in American culture. Roma's lust for material success is matched by his belief in the rewards extended to a male for having done well at his job—a success that is determined by the American masculine ethos and perpetuated through familiar male mythologies. Such a belief feeds Roma's ambitious behavior, which is at once touching in its apparent concern for his fellow man's losses while deceptive in its underlying selfish greed.

I have intentionally stressed Roma's maleness to foreground the issue of gender in *Glengarry Glen Ross*. With the exception of Hersh Zeifman's and Carla McDonough's recent, perceptive analyses, and David Radavich's general overview, critics ignore the central, explicit role of gender (as distinguished from sexuality) not only in this play, but in Mamet's work before *Oleanna* (1992).[2] Frank Rich (1984) and Christopher Bigsby (1985), for instance, collapse the characters' gender-coded identities into representations of a non-gender-specific human condition, for the sake of more sociophilosophical, non-gender-related readings. I would argue, however, that it is misleading to universalize the characters' experiences in *Glengarry*. Mamet himself acknowledges the importance of distinguishing the basis upon which his characters' position arises in male-centered plays like *Glengarry* (or *American Buffalo* and *Edmond*): their anguish is a result of the failure of the American dream, Mamet concludes, for "the people it has sustained—the white males—are going nuts" (qtd. in Leahey). And it is the *male* protagonists' "condition rather than a dramatic action," Mamet adds, that serves as *Glengarry's* distinguishing dramaturgical feature (qtd. in Savran 1992, 135).

Mamet consciously favors the world of men when he writes for the theater. When his men are in women's company, an infrequent occurrence, they nonetheless remain acutely aware of their dominance over the Other. At all times, Mamet's male characters see the world through men's eyes, with a vision that assures them that they exist in a culture that promotes the values of the masculine ethos as well as privileges them over women by virtue of their masculine gender. It is a vision that finds its expression in social dialogue. Particular to Mamet's language choices when capturing this vision, according to Ross Wetzsteon, is a

> heady combination of euphemism, approximations, ellipses; omissions of linking words and phrases in some sentences, and additions of unnecessary words and phrases in others; the startling juxtaposition of the stilted and the profane; the "high" and "low" levels of language; the feel for dynamics of spoken

rhythm; and at times the "utter clarity of total grammatical chaos."

And, as unlikely as it may seem, Mamet's characters still appear to adhere to a cooperative principle when speaking to one another. "Within the level of the text itself," claims Ryan Bishop, although "the characters . . . are trying to manipulate one another . . . the text remains cooperative at that level" (264).

Mamet's language is also the language of men who prolong cooperative communication *without* self-disclosure, without overstepping the cultural codings that dictate acceptable male interaction. These cultural codings (as determined within the scope of this study) affect the discourse coherence of the male characters' dialogue that, in turn, reflects both the linguistic-literary codes and the cultural codes operating within the dramatic system, including whiteness and the American masculine ethos. Most realist male-cast plays rely upon this cooperative level of social dialogue for their initial dramatic structure, but very few preserve it for the duration of their characters' interaction. From this critical perspective, *Glengarry* is the quintessential male-cast play.[3]

Mamet's characters consciously choose to remain on the level of social dialogue. "Their language, gestures, desires, and values are social products," Jeanette Malkin suggests, "not expressions of individual will" (160). They prefer foremost to sustain cooperative communication without becoming emotionally or psychologically vulnerable to the other men. Unlike the dialogue in most office plays, where the hierarchy of authority often promotes characters' self-disclosures, Mamet's dialogue resists any such private access to the individual. What results in *Glengarry* is a cryptic, inarticulate coding system that deliberately fluctuates between clarity of meaning and ambiguity while it propels the men's conversation forward. This social dialogue is narrowly confined to the topic of the men's employment. As Julius Novick remarks, Mamet's play depends solely upon the "imperatives of business." It "derives a special purity, a special power, from the fact that it is about nothing but the necessity to sell—which means, in this play, to bend other people to your will and take what you want, or need, from them." In general, the characters forgo an involved discussion on any additional topics that usually surface during social dialogue: women, families, and the men's own active identification with the cultural ideal of virile maleness. Rather, Mamet's men promote a coded language of business, of capitalism, that is defined semiotically—as a system related to other systems, including extratheatrical, cultural systems.

The structure of *Glengarry* is shaped according to two dominant features: a coded language of business, with a hierarchical relationship firmly established between speaker and listener; and a dominant, though diversely realized, thematic of business. This latter feature refers to the various meanings of *business:* from the business of one's public employment to one's personal business (that is, the details of one's private life). The coded language of business *and* the thematic of business are technically linked to one another via the characters' dialogue, an association realized in the practical sales maxim that serves as the play's opening epigram: "Always be closing" (13).[4]

In Mamet's hands, the social dialogue in *Glengarry* is dramatic talk that is "always closing," as it were, not only because of its limited selection of topics (its nearly exclusive, closed focus on one's job) but in its conversational dynamic between participants as well. Mamet restricts the social dialogue in order to illustrate the linguistic constraints that influence *how* a men's closed conversational relationship is constructed, and how that relationship easily becomes the power struggle between speaker and listener as each attempts to secure the position of authority. Because of their topic selections, Mamet's male characters are locked into culturally coded roles as speaker and listener—that is, the men activate a socially sanctioned, predetermined relationship to one another simply because they are discussing, in a nonpersonal manner, a topic determined in accord with the masculine ethos. The balance of power resides with the participant who most adamantly adheres to the principles of the ethos.

In each of the three short scenes that comprise the first act of *Glengarry* the men's professional roles influence the dynamics in their dyadic conversations: Levene, a salesman, speaks with his boss, Williamson, in scene 1; two salesmen, Moss and Aaronow, speak together in the second scene; and Roma speaks with a potential customer, Lingk, in the act's final scene. Only Moss and Aaronow are one another's professional peers; the other participants speak from different ranks within a hierarchy of male authority. However, in each of these scenes, the answer to the question, "Who really holds the power?"—the speaker or the listener—is determined by the individual who adheres unwaveringly to the restrictions advocated by the masculine ethos. "These duologues in fact dramatize primal duels for domination, power and survival"

(Frank Rich 1984). Those who wield the conversational power in act 1 are Williamson, who is predominantly the listener in the first scene (much of his interaction with Levene is metalinguistic, as the two talk about talk in their efforts to understand one another), and the verbose, goal-oriented Moss and Roma. Each of these three men is staunchly committed to dialogue that reinforces the masculine ethos and its attendant mythologies. Consequently, they bulldoze their conversational partners into submission, through calculated silences or evasive remarks, as in Williamson's case, or energetic talk, as in Moss's and Roma's cases, completely denying the value of a topic other than that which is employment related. While the men adhere to a kind of dramatic cooperative principle in their talk, Williamson, Moss, and Roma discourage their respective conversational partners from engaging self-disclosing, personal dialogue. Whether as listener or speaker, each maintains a closed conversational relationship with the other man as he backs up the authority of his own restricted position with the culture's coded authority of appropriate masculine behavior and verbal interaction. As William Demastes remarks, "These men are trapped in their worlds, and their words are trapped in their culture" (91).

In its most obvious, privileged manifestation, male access to cultural power marginalizes woman, the Other. In play after male-cast play, the power of the male subject over the female object is asserted or assumed by most men, regardless of their race, ethnicity, class, or sexual orientation.[5] Thus, cultural factors of *gender* distinction, which rely upon a coded system of subject/object, Self/Other dichotomies, primarily determine men's social interaction, which in turn constructs their dialogue with one another.

The cultural power afforded the male gender also serves to separate "the men from the boys." This division among males, in effect, marginalizes some men as Other, so much so that they assume the dramaturgical position of object within the all-male context. These Other men are those who fail to embody, and thereby represent, the desired masculine ethos. Besides the social expectation of his heterosexuality, a man is subject to tremendous scrutiny and pressure when it comes to securing a respectable economic status. In *Glengarry,* Mamet's men embrace business as their arena for achieving such status, exploiting the primary tenets of the masculine ethos in an effort to advance their careers. Their business world is a gender-coded environment in which man most conspicuously manipulates and displays the extent of his socioeconomic power. Business, according to Dennis Carroll, is a "driving force in a pattern of interaction in which men are involved in competitiveness and shifting power allegiances, embroiled in oscillating admiration and envy; collusion and opposition; active support and aggressive enmity." "All of this," Carroll concludes, "subverts the social ideal of interconnectedness between men" (33). Furthermore, "If a job is what defines a man," proposes McDonough, "then failure in business is what defines the non-man, the woman" (202).

Speaking of the capitalist (male) environment within *Glengarry,* and implicitly of the "pattern of interaction" and disconnectedness that it fosters, Mamet concludes, "To me the play is about a society based on business. . . . a society with only one bottom line: 'How much money do you make'" (qtd. in Gussow 1984). Here, Mamet equates the ethos of the male world of *Glengarry* with the ethos of American patriarchy. His fictional world mirrors the power dynamic that men exploit within American culture, a dynamic that resists connections between men. Carroll identifies Mamet's mirroring technique initially in the playwright's dialogue, which he notes is constructed "on the rhythms of spoken language as used in 'reality'" (150). But Mamet qualifies this view when he suggests that "the language we use, its rhythm, actually determines the way we behave rather than the other way around" (qtd. in Lewis and Browne 65). Finally, in his handling of the thematic of business, in its various manifestations, Mamet highlights not only the fictions that his characters (and ostensibly his fellow American males) create in order to survive but also the corrupted ethical foundations upon which American culture privileges the male ethos and its accompanying mythologies.

In numerous interviews, Mamet harshly criticizes American capitalism and, presumably, the state of men's lives: "The American Dream has gone bad. . . . This capitalistic dream of wealth turns people against each other. . . . The dream has nowhere to go so it has to start turning in on itself" (qtd. in Leahey). White men, according to Mamet, are coming to realize that the cultural mythologies that traditionally have sustained them are, in fact, in jeopardy. Why? Because, "the white race . . . [has] no tragedy." For Mamet, the white man's condition is that he has no "spirit"—no identity outside his culturally coded power of domination. Herein lies the desperate state of Mamet's males in *Glengarry,* despite the author's recent insistence that the play is a "gang comedy."[6]

In Mamet's matrix, white (straight) men usually reject any options (and their attending responsibilities) that might conflict with the masculine ethos. Nonetheless, they inhabit a realist dramatic world shaped not by fate, but by free choice. For this reason, "the only redemption for the individual is not to change with the institution," Mamet states, for him "not to become part of the institution" (qtd. in Freedman). Whether on- or offstage, however, Mamet rarely comments on social movements, including feminism, as having the power to affect men's lives in a constructive way, creating a more balanced cultural power between the sexes. Despite his awareness of its severe limitations in terms of the quality of human interaction, Mamet is still obsessed with the power, the camaraderie, the potential strength in the exclusivity of male bonding (1989a). Prior to *Oleanna,* women's issues are not a central social reality in any of Mamet's plays; his characters and their worlds exist independent from any larger cultural context in which gender roles are challenged and changed. Yet, as Novick points out in respect to *Glengarry,* "Has any professed feminist ever given us so unsparing a picture of the masculine ethos at its most barren, destructive, anguished, futile?"

Glengarry Glen Ross, asserts Demastes, "very clearly focuses on the business ethic, but it is a much broader topic that Mamet is addressing—the decaying of America as a result of this ethic, not just in business, but throughout" (87). The ethics of Mamet's business world, and its intended metaphoric and actual associations to American patriarchy, are directly linked to the culture's masculine ethos. As dramatized by Mamet, this gendered ethos appears unethical: it promotes corruption, exploitation, prejudice, and violence. One could say that Mamet's men communicate through a coded language whose end is also unethical, not only in its subordination of the Other, but in its calculated resistance to personal, frank communication among men. Mamet's men "no longer have access to words," surmises Bigsby, "that will articulate their feelings" (1985, 123). In the mouths of Mamet's characters, this unethical (use of) language is committed to the business of deliberate obscuring of the truth; it encourages illusion, not the actual, as it fosters frustrated isolation rather than meaningful connections among those who speak it. In *Glengarry,* therefore, "It is less the plot development than Mamet's language," as Demastes concludes, "that succeeds in capturing the essence of his themes" (91). It is the pervasive, unrelenting power of the American masculine ethos and male mythologies manifest in Mamet's language that reveal the play's cultural and dramaturgical dynamism.

The plot of Mamet's play is relatively inconsequential compared to the dynamics of the characters' verbal interaction, most strikingly captured in their social dialogue. In brief, act 1 focuses on three different gatherings in a Chicago Chinese restaurant, each involving middle-class real estate agents who work for the same company. In the first scene, Shelly "the Machine" Levene tries to bribe his boss, Williamson, to give him the top prospects for future sales. Levene, a salesman of the old school currently down in his luck, is desperate to make a lucrative deal, especially since management has pitted him against his coworkers in an all-or-nothing sales contest. He who fails to win is out of a job. Levene succeeds only in demonstrating his hopelessness before his boss, who is open to bribery yet refuses his employee's attempt as insubstantial.

During the second scene, Moss and Aaronow anxiously discuss the pressure that has been generated by the sales contest. Moss turns his own bitter anger into a revenge fantasy, suggesting that "someone should stand up and strike *back*" at management: "someone should rob the office" of all its prime leads and sell them to a local competitor for a tidy profit (37, 38). Aaronow, although reluctant to voice his approval of such a plan, is implicated in its possible execution simply because, as Moss tells him, "you listened" (46).

Act 1 ends with slick, affable Roma speaking nearly nonstop to passive, available Lingk. Weaving a bit of down-home philosophy with fraternal gestures, Roma effectively courts his unsuspecting listener to hear his sales line for Florida property, Glengarry Highlands. It is the start of what becomes an apparently successful sales pitch.

Less than twenty-four hours pass between the events dramatized in acts 1 and 2, but within that time span, violence occurs: the real estate office Williamson manages is vandalized. Throughout act 2, Williamson and a detective, Baylen, interrogate each salesman offstage after he comes to work for the day: Moss, Aaronow, Roma, and finally Levene. Outside Williamson's closed door, the remaining salesmen concern themselves with some aspect of the sales contest; business is business, after all, and it—or at least the talk about it—must go on as usual. But business this day is not usual. Lingk, who is following his wife's orders, returns to the office to terminate his previous deal with Roma. And Levene, who is the unsuspecting victim of Moss's plan, is identified by Williamson as the man who robbed the office. The play ends with it being revealed to the staff that Levene, one of the salesmen's own, had turned against them in his desire to win the contest and guarantee the survival of his own job.

The men's involvement with one another reveals what each man thinks of himself, as he talks about or relates to business. In Mamet's male world, one's identity is determined by his success or failure at his job (as in the case of the real estate personnel and the detective), or by the way he engages business (as in Lingk's circumstance). A man measures his self-worth (and has it measured by others) against the cultural standards associated with economic power. In such a system, it is not uncommon for a man to experience the roles of both victim and victimizer.

This cultural context for self-definition is actually a system of set codes, one spelled out in the opening speech of *Glengarry,* when Levene tells Williamson, "I don't want to tell you your *job.* All that I'm saying, things get *set,* I know they do, you get a certain *mind-set*" (15). Levene's language (and eventually every other characters' language) reveals paradigmatic codes that characterize the men's social dialogue: "job," "set," and "mind-set" anticipate other codes to follow—"board," "policy," and "lead." Such codes are "known to both transmitter and destination—which assigns a certain content (or meaning) to a certain signal. In linguistic communication the code allows speaker and addressee to form and recognize syntactically correct sequences of phonemes and to assign a semantic content to them" (Elam 35). What is crucial to note in Mamet's dialogue is that the characters rely upon these codes, which are both dramatic and cultural (Elam 52), as each resonates with meanings that are gender based and gender biased. Mamet's characters are represented as having freely chosen to maintain this level of interaction (distinguishing these men from those in *American Buffalo,* where Don and Teach consciously transcend the conversational limits imposed by social dialogue). In the closed patriarchal microcosm of *Glengarry,* therefore, the coherence in the men's dialogue is firmly entrenched, reflective of a mind-set that is set on adhering to the principles of the masculine ethos and its attendant mythologies. Although the men communicate cooperatively, they remain inflexible in their efforts to restrict the discourse coherence, and consequently the thematics, of their talk.

Introducing initial codes in the first scene that will characterize the men's dialogue for two acts, Levene and Williamson establish another critical feature of Mamet's social dialogue: metalinguistics. They, like Moss and Aaronow in the scene to follow, talk a great deal about their talk. Explicitly, they indicate the discourse coherence of their conversation through their topic selection; implicitly, they struggle to establish the power relationship between speaker and listener, identifying who occupies the position of authority. Levene and Williamson's moment-to-moment metalinguistic dialogue reinforces the play's construction as a closed language system, one in which specific meanings are obscured in favor of ambiguous, nonspecific references. This does not stop the talk, however. With Samuel Beckett's *Waiting for Godot* as an intertext in Mamet's play, Levene and Williamson's speeches recall the conversational dynamic between Didi and Gogo. The men's apparent desire to create (i.e., to release) meaning—or paradoxically in the case of Mamet's men, their calculated skill in avoiding meaning—propels their communicative interaction forward. Just as Levene backhandedly compliments one of his colleagues—"He *talks*, he talks a good game" (17)—so Mamet's men revere a social dialogue that perpetuates the game of business, of male mythology, of power. And the stakes of their particular game intensify when the men talk about talk.

A few extended samples from Levene and Williamson's interchange illustrate not only their metalinguistic patterns, but those of the other characters as well throughout *Glengarry Glen Ross*.

Williamson: [Y]ou didn't close...

Levene: ...I, if you'd *listen* to me. Please. I *closed* the cocksucker.... That's all I want to say.

(16)

Levene: [T]hen what is this "you *say*" shit, what is that? [*Pause.*] What is that...?

Williamson: All that I'm saying...

Levene: What is this "you *say*"?... [T]alk, talk to Murray. Talk to Mitch.... You talk to him.... You want to throw [my skill] away?

Williamson: It isn't me....

Levene: ...it isn't you.... Who *is* it? Who is this I'm talking to?

(17–18)

Levene: *Fuck* marshaling the leads. What the fuck talk is that? What the fuck talk is that? Where did you learn that? In school? [*Pause.*] That's "talk," my

34

friend, that's "talk." . . . You're giving [garbage] to
me, and what I'm saying is it's *fucked*.

Williamson: You're saying that I'm fucked.

Levene: Yes. [*Pause.*] I am. I'm sorry to antagonize you.

Williamson: Let me . . . are you listening to me . . . ?

(19)

And a few minutes later, the two men begin to conclude their
conversation:

Levene: A month or two we'll talk. A month from now.
              Next month. . . . We'll talk.

Williamson: What are we going to say?

Levene: No. You're right. That's for later. We'll talk in a
              month.

(24)

Williamson: Is that what you're saying?

Levene: That's what I'm saying.

(27)

Levene and Williamson's social dialogue is constantly in flux as it
slips in and out of potential meanings. No one is ever certain that
"what [he's] saying" is being heard or understood in the way in
which he intends it. This talk about talk—and its concomitant relationship to the process of receiving and comprehending information—does not, however, diffuse the power of codes in the men's
dialogue. In fact, the linguistic-cultural codes in the men's social
dialogue, those that are informed by the masculine ethos, provide
the only *irrefutable* foundation for communication between the
men. The codes essentially ground the men in their interaction
with one another. When Williamson asserts that he's "given a *policy. My* job is to *do that.* What I'm *told*" (19), Levene knows with
certainty that the policy about which his boss speaks is the same
one that structures their professional *and* personal relationships to
one another. On the level of narrative development, Levene realizes
that policy is not carved in stone, despite Williamson's assertion.
Williamson can indeed be bribed, but only for a very handsome
price. But Levene also learns that in his attempt to break an ethical
code of respectable business, he also sacrifices personal integrity.
To rob from others is also to rob from oneself. Levene's personal
needs are rendered and understood in terms of commerce: one

35

must give an item in order to receive another item in return. As American men, Levene and Williamson recognize that the way "to do business" (26) with one another requires the repression of one's personal self. For this reason, they favor familiar and predictable, socially engendered roles that feed off cultural clichés and stereotypes of maleness. From this more comprehensive perspective, therefore, one can identify the social construct of the Beauvoirian Self/Other, the "policy" of gender, that polices the men's dramatic language (of subject/object) and behavior in Mamet's America.

Metalinguistic dialogue is a structural link between the dramatic forms of act 1, scenes 1 and 2. Moss and Aaronow, like their colleagues in the previous scene, generate much dialogue between them that challenges the meaning of what is being spoken. Following Levene's failure to persuade Williamson to sell him the leads, or prime real estate customers, Moss presents an idea to Aaronow on how the two might steal those same leads and sell them to Jerry Graff, a competitor (who, in turn, may reward the men with jobs). The two men do not directly discuss a specific plan; rather, they allude to the idea of a robbery, then question through metalinguistic exchanges their potential relationship to its possible execution. For example, after being asked by Aaronow if he has discussed this possible robbery with Graff, Moss replies:

Moss: No. What do you mean? Have I talked to him about *this*? [*Pause.*]
Aaronow: Yes. I mean are you actually *talking* about this, or are we just . . .
Moss: No, we're just . . .
Aaronow: We're just "*talking*" about it.
Moss: We're just *speaking* about it. [*Pause.*] As an *idea*. . . .
Aaronow: So all this, um, you didn't, actually, you didn't actually go talk to Graff.
Moss: Not actually, no. [*Pause.*]
Aaronow: You didn't?
Moss: No. Not actually.
Aaronow: Did you?
Moss: What did I say?
Aaronow: What did you say?
Moss: Yes. [*Pause.*] I said, "Not actually." The fuck *you* care, George? We're just *talking* . . .

(39–40)

The talk between Moss and Aaronow is dotted throughout with these metalinguistic interactions. In the previous exchange, the men are unable (or unwilling) to use language to convey specific meanings. They choose to maintain a social dialogue that is vague and ambiguous, or as Moss might estimate, a language that is pleasingly "simple" (35). To "keep it simple" (46) is also for Moss and Aaronow to keep their sights on a basic cultural power that they can (re)gain, if only for a while, if a robbery is successful: economic potency. Their fantasy to possess this power—and thereby to experience the anticipated ancillary patriarchal powers that come from a psychological boost of having achieved a cultural goal—is strong enough to push aside any individual realities that might challenge its realization. In keeping their own interaction simple (that is, intentionally ambiguous), the men deny the complexities that can arise between social and personal endeavors, the public and private self. Moss and Aaronow lust after the cultural powers that define the masculine ethos so much that they are energized simply by their fantasy of securing power.

The language and thematic of business continue to dominate the characters' dialogue and determine its discourse coherence throughout act 1, scene 2. All subjects within Moss and Aaronow's conversation fall under the general topic of their business—their lives as salesmen: they are desperate to "get on the board" (29), to make a sale; they acknowledge that they "fuckin' work too hard" (30), as they hate to work for other men; they envy individuals who own their own businesses, those men who truly have access to the more mythological patriarchal powers; they resent having to prove their worth to male bosses by participating in a contest with other male employees; and finally, they relish the thought of being disloyal to their current employers in hopes of securing jobs with their competitor.

It is this last consideration of business that sparks Moss's thought that someone should "hurt" their bosses (37). This evocation of the power of violence to effect change—and its attraction as an actual undertaking—is a typical position men assume among themselves after they discuss their perceived lack of power. From Martin Flavin's *Amaco* to Edward Albee's *The Zoo Story*, Charles Fuller's *A Soldier's Play*, and OyamO's *Let Me Live*, male characters repeatedly resort to violence as a final solution to their immediate professional or private conflicts. Moss's suggestion that Aaronow and he should rob their employer's office, therefore, lines up behind a long-standing tradition in American male-cast drama in its appeal to men to engage the power of violence in order to get the job done. And, of course, that violence does occur in the dramatic time that separates acts 1 and 2 in Mamet's play; it also occurs outside the spectator's vision, outside his or her immediate experience of the drama. By presenting the effects of the violence rather than staging the violence itself, however, *Glengarry* further distinguishes itself from most male-cast plays in which violence is a prominent, enacted feature.

Throughout Moss's rigorous defense of the plan to rob the real estate office, Aaronow remains an ambivalent, inconsistent listener. From moment to moment the idea either appeals to him or seems the illegal act that it is. Tempted by avarice, this decentered man becomes a postmodern everyman in Mamet's contemporary morality play; he appears to be the central, pivotal character around whom the play's construction and (cultural) ideology develop. As the everyman figure, Aaronow initially wields a great deal of power—especially in the spectator's identification with him—in terms of the significance of the choices he makes. He is free in Mamet's democratic dramatic world to choose whatever he wants: he can either agree or disagree with Moss, the vocal defender of a kind of male power that is essentially based on economic reward through violence. Accordingly, in Moss and Aaronow's interaction, Mamet returns to the critical consideration that surfaces in nearly all male-cast plays—that is, who really holds the power. And what is sacrificed, if anything, when one participant dominates the other(s) through restricted, ambiguous talk?

Unlike the conversational dynamic in scene 1, in which the hierarchy of professional authority grants more power to Williamson (who, in their interaction, is primarily a respondent) than to Levene (the dominant speaker), Moss and Aaronow engage one another as peers. Moss controls the progression of his conversation with Aaronow, however, as he establishes Aaronow, his listener, as a respondent to his (Moss's) speeches. Moss sets out to convince the somewhat uncertain Aaronow that he, too, must fight (at least, through language) to secure individual and collective powers that are "rightfully" his as a man in America. He must either be "in or out" of the plan to rob the office (46). This challenge, in fact, asks Aaronow to declare whether he is "in or out" of the drive to embody more wholly the principles of the masculine ethos. Is Aaronow an "in" male—one who exists inside the power of male mythologies—or is he an "out" male—one who exists outside the male ethos and is therefore inferior to the desired, ideal man. Is Aaronow a Man or is he one of those "Other" men?

Aaronow's predicament links two complementary strands that are characteristic of the male-cast canon. The first strand identifies several terms by which a given male in a talk exchange becomes the more dominant participant, privileging that which he says (or, as the case may be, that which he refuses to say). The second strand focuses on the dramaturgical significance of male characters who willfully create and sustain fictions when speaking among men as a means of (personal) survival.

When a speaker and listener (or respondent) focus on the thematic of the masculine ethos during their mutually agreed upon social dialogue, the speaker establishes a closed dynamic with his listener that effectively secures the listener's compliance with that thematic. In this regard, a listener *chooses* during social dialogue to agree (or appear to agree) with the principles advanced within the thematic of the masculine ethos. In act 1, scene 2, Aaronow eventually chooses to entertain Moss's conversational position; Moss does not force him to do so. Their dynamic illustrates the extent to which social dialogue initially creates, in their words, "abstract" images between speaker and listener that are then realized, or made "concrete," simply through the articulation of their properties, or codings (46).

On the level of plot development, for example, Moss cites Aaronow as an accomplice to the robbery simply because Aaronow hears the plan; the abstract scheme is, according to Moss, concrete once it is articulated. Even though he challenges Moss's logic, Aaronow is unable to convincingly deny or refute it. One could say that between speaker and listener a kind of "truth" is voiced when the abstract is materialized in the language of social dialogue. And the listener is either "in or out" (46) of agreement with that truth. In this instance, Aaronow listens "in" agreement with the position Moss advocates.

Mamet utilizes this same solipsistic logic in establishing a dramatic logic that operates on the construction of his social dialogue. The power of language, as used by Mamet's men, creates the thematic of the masculine ethos that is so crucial to the characters' collective male identity, but it also has the capacity to make one's self-image "concrete" (46) in its compliance with that ethos. Yet, each man is "free," so to speak, to choose his relationship to the construction of that identity, which, as rendered in Mamet's dialogue, is most readily determined by the character's choice of dialogue: social or personal.

The second strand that surfaces in Aaronow's situation is the relationship between the play's closed speech dynamic and the conversational participants' tendency to create fictions as a method of survival. What links this strand with the previous one is its relationship to the creation of "truth." Certainly, Moss weaves a seductive fiction when he suggests that both Aaronow and he will somehow benefit if their attempted robbery is successful. What Moss overlooks and Aaronow fails to challenge, however, is the penalty that each will pay if caught for committing this crime. Both men construct a fiction that they will acquire lasting economic power, a wish that will be immediately gratified when they are hired for more lucrative positions by their current competitors. Yet, Moss and Aaronow manufacture the illusion of truth out of lies. Their social dialogue fosters this indulgence as their language moves in and out of the unlimited possibilities that surface in a closed speech that accommodates illusion over truth, fiction over reality. Simply because he listened to Moss's fiction—and finally succumbed to its allure as truth through its representation in language—Aaronow fails to self-identify.[7] Rather, like Roma in scene 3, he embraces the fantasy of male cultural power as his means of survival. But unlike his assertive coworker, Aaronow is incapable of creating fictions on his own. He is a decentered, postmodern everyman who only responds to that which is thrust in front of him; he, himself, exerts no convincing effort to initiate alternative action or ideas. Aaronow's survival, therefore, is sorely dependent upon piecing together others' lies. He relies upon coded cultural fictions not only for their indication of the choices he is to consider, but for the establishment of his own sense of meaning as well—his own sense of himself. That self is finally, tragically false; Aaronow appears painfully conscious of the absence of personal depth in his life.

In act 1, scene 3, Roma demonstrates the skill, the "act" as Moss calls it (35), of the successful, persevering salesman—the one who, unlike Aaronow, is determined to survive according to the terms of the masculine ethos. Whereas Aaronow is everyman, Roma could be considered the representative, classical (white) everyman who appears in most American male-cast plays. He epitomizes the male characters (regardless of their race) who remain staunchly committed to the values advanced by the masculine ethos. Like the Coach in Jason Miller's *That Championship*

Season, Alan in Mart Crowley's *The Boys in the Band,* Ora in Amiri Baraka's *The Toilet,* and Waters in Fuller's *A Soldier's Play,* Roma unhesitatingly upholds the virtues of masculinist ideology, most readily recognizable in his buddy-buddy, cutthroat approach to business. As speaker, he also depends upon the power of language to create fictions that in turn create the illusion of empowering the listener. These efforts establish the fantasy of interpersonal connections between men that are vital to the continuance of patriarchal authority, to the culturally coded gender system of Self/ Other.

Expressing what at first appears as a stream-of-consciousness monologue, Roma seduces the unsuspecting, but emotionally and psychologically vulnerable, Lingk with what in fact is a strategically calculated speech and performance. (This mode of communication is not unlike the dramatic technique, as we shall see in chapter 2, that Jerry uses on Peter in *The Zoo Story,* as the former desperately wants the latter to understand why he has engaged him in conversation as well as to understand the significance of that about which he is speaking.) In effect, Roma delivers a highly manipulative sales talk (which Deborah Geis rightly sees as the essence of "monologue" [1992, 60])[8] that is initially masked in pseudophilosophical musings intended to lure Lingk into the web of what could be called "Roma Reasoning." One comes to understand Roma's reasoning on the meaning of life through a series of rapid questions and answers (48), each designed to refocus the emphasis from the anonymous human condition to the more crucial status of the little guy, Lingk, who exists amid an overwhelming, faceless condition. Roma's speech is intended to empower Lingk; it is about conventional patriarchal dynamics of action, control, and power. He argues the position that any man can feel powerful simply by *acting* without fear. And this power of direct action is extended to Lingk by virtue of his gender privilege, a privilege about which Roma intends to remind his attentive customer. Furthermore, Roma implicitly reminds Lingk that a commitment to action is a demonstration of support for masculine ideals.

The logic in Roma's monologue moves from the universal to the specific, always with the clear objective to convince Lingk to buy land from him. Roma offers this reasoning as the key to Lingk's empowerment: man is afraid of "loss" and has traditionally turned to "greed" as a false sense of security; unwilling to believe himself to be "powerless," man must "trust" his own power to "do those things which seem correct to [him] *today*"; as a result of his independent thinking, therefore, man can experience himself as secure, "*acting each day* without fear" (48–49). Once Roma suggests the importance of *action* as an expression of one's personal power, he then focuses his attention on motivating Lingk to take personal action on an "opportunity": "stocks, bonds, objects of art, real estate" (49)—each of which, according to Roma, can mean "what [Lingk] *want*[s] it to mean" (50).

Real estate, in particular, Roma suggests, might "mean *nothing*" to Lingk, or "it might not" (50). Roma skillfully maneuvers the power to define the meaning of things into the rhetorical control of his nearly silent listener. And how Lingk names things, Roma implies, is direct evidence of Lingk's relationship (or lack thereof) not only to the culture's expectations of gendered power, but to his sense of himself as a Man. "[T]o talk is to *act,* talk is power," writes Malkin, and "*men* know how to talk" (156). Although men are "all different" from one another, according to Roma (50), each, as a man, has access to the power to define. Man, not God, has the power in Mamet's world to name things, to give definition. He indeed has free choice. Yet free choice is an illusion for many Mamet characters based on a certain notion of identity quite specific to American patriarchy. What passes as free choice is ideologically shaped. The dictates of the impersonal masculine ethos and its social conventions are repeatedly embraced by Mamet's men. Despite voicing his freedom from social constraint, therefore, a Mamet character often contradicts that freedom by reengaging stereotypical action: while he may say one (potentially liberating) remark, he will usually do what he has always done. In this way, Roma represents himself as one who is authorized to name things anew. However, he does nothing of the kind.[9]

Certainly the gender privilege of naming is not lost on Mamet's salesman. Each man, Roma implies, has power over the Other to name the value of life's experiences and expenditures. In fact, it is a man's duty, Roma intimates, to take it upon himself to exercise that power. At no point does the salesman underestimate the importance of inflating his lead's ego with the rhetoric of masculine privilege. He speaks soulfully and hyperbolically to his listener. The irony is, however, that upon his reconnection with Lingk in act 2, Roma realizes that he must rescue his fellow man from the real influence of the Other: he must do battle with Lingk's wife, one of *Glengarry's* absent women, in order to win back his weakening, vacillating customer.

Pontificating before Lingk, Roma animates a voice that recalls other memorable salesmen's voices found in such dramatic landmarks as Arthur Miller's *Death of a Salesman,* Tennessee Williams's *A Streetcar Named Desire,* and Eugene O'Neill's *The Iceman Cometh* (Bigsby 1985, 113), along with Clifford Odets's *Awake and Sing* and Mamet's *American Buffalo.* Roma, like his fellow real estate men in *Glengarry,* "is the creator of myth whose stories must be compelling if he is to survive," according to Bigsby (1985, 113). "So long as he keeps talking, his hopes are alive and, to a degree, so are those of his listeners." Bigsby's observation applies not only to the communicative dynamic among American salesmen but to the interactive dynamic among nearly all men who aggressively engage social dialogue. Nonetheless, the content of Roma's talk, the substance of his social dialogue as well as that of the other brokers, is more complicated in its cultural politics than most critics acknowledge.

Mamet's fictions cannot simply be romanticized for "containing the essence of a possible transcendence" without one's acknowledging more forthrightly the disturbing complexities that constitute the pervasive "corrupted and corrupting" foundation of his fiction (Bigsby 1985, 113). In Mamet's male America, after all, such fictions reinforce repressive cultural ideology in general, and the gender-privileged masculine ethos in particular. In turn, each stimulates restrictive social constructions of gender and identity. Bigsby's suggestion that a belief in these fictions is "potentially redemptive" for Mamet's men seems to move beyond what the dialogue and discourse coherence of the play finally indicate. What is the possible object of the salesmen's redemption? Based upon what the men say to one another in acts 1 and 2, they perceive redemption as individual success in achieving their immediate economic wishes, success that, as dramatically rendered in the play, perpetuates the gender-restrictive principles of the masculine ethos. This gendered ethos, as I suggested earlier, manifests itself in dangerously unethical ways. Mamet's men appear unwilling to abandon or to transcend the privileges extended to them as men in American culture. While some may have fleeting moments in act 2 when they "recognize the moral culpability of what they are doing and know that their 'business' masks are sometimes at odds with their inner aspirations and inclinations" (Carroll 48), each man freely chooses to remain in alliance with the masculine ethos. Each chooses the face, not the mask, of male privilege—each seeks out opportunities with the knowledge that he has the power to name their meanings. "As a result of their readiness to believe in the viability of myth," Geis proposes, "the characters are caught in a matrix of self-perpetuating deceptions" (1992, 62–63). What Bigsby pointedly concludes about Roma's verbal seduction of Lingk is, in fact, an accurate description of all Mamet's salesmen—as well as most American male characters—who sustain social dialogue: "What masquerades as intimacy is in fact the betrayal of intimacy, confidence, trust, the shared experience implied by language" (1985, 119).

Act 2 is set in Williamson's ransacked real estate office. Despite its burgled setting, this act—which essentially is an office play— nonetheless manifests a common characteristic of many all-male institutional plays: a hierarchy of professional authority exists at any one time in the dramatic space. As in other office plays,[10] bosses interact with employees, seasoned employees counsel younger employees, and employees court clients. Added to the setting, however, is Baylen, a police detective, whose appearance overrides the authority of both boss and workers. Baylen thrusts patriarchal law into the office space as his invested legal authority informs both the boundaries (i.e., the constraints) and the freedoms that operate on the characters' immediate interaction. His physical presence or absence from a conversation profoundly influences what other men do and do not say to one another.

Amid this hierarchy of male authority, Mamet's men nonetheless exercise a range of verbal gymnastics within the dynamic of social dialogue. Act 2 is characterized by sustained reliance upon social dialogue, with two unique features of that dialogue— metatheatrical and metalinguistic—occurring midact. The characters' persistent engagement of social dialogue is an unusual quality in an office play, since most men in such settings eventually embrace personal dialogue as a response to the hierarchy of authority. What distinguishes *Glengarry* from most office plays, however, is the fact that the authority figures of Williamson and Baylen are mainly in an unseen room that adjoins the dramatic space in which the play's action develops.

From the act's opening, each broker enters the space commenting on the impact of the robbery on his professional standing. Each is obsessed with his current status on the contest board; each man's job is riding on his success in the sales competition. Roma, Aaronow, and Williamson select topics, therefore, that range from business in general, to the contest, to the value of private property, and eventually to the robbery and its destruction. Only Baylen's infrequent interruptions to interview another employee shift focus momentarily from the men's discussion of business. The men's commitment to this level of social dialogue, however, is more calculated than is initially evident. Each is in fact purposely hiding information from the other, a detail that is not evident, at least to the spectator, until the end of the play.

When Moss leaves Baylen's interrogation room to join his colleagues in the main office space, the men's communication is anxious and resistant to personal interaction. Not one wants to speak truthfully. Each valiantly strives to protect himself from exposure, as each has something to hide from at least one of the remaining fellows: Levene knows he robbed the office; Moss knows he masterminded the robbery and secured Levene's help; Roma knows he wants a percentage of Levene's commissions; and Williamson knows that he left Lingk's contract on his desk. Confident in his private knowledge when among his coworkers, each man feels extremely *powerful*—particularly as he anticipates his ability to survive the immediate crisis in a personally satisfying manner. Both Levene and Moss believe that their robbery is a success; Roma trusts that he can bribe his boss when need be; and Williamson recognizes that by lying he can generally get what information he needs from the others to guarantee his own authority. Each man presumes that he can exercise a power play over the other, that he can secure his domination over all others *if* his secrets remain private. Very simply, each strives to keep the dialogue social and not personal.

Just as someone stole the leads from the office in order to become more powerful, so every character tries to "steal," to acquire, information from the other men. Characters aim to rob otherwise guarded knowledge from their coworkers, not only to secure more power over their colleagues, but to reorder the chaos represented by the ransacked office. Language is the men's weapon of choice; social dialogue, their ammunition. Yet Mamet's men fail to recognize fully the pervasive impact of the most influential component of their social dialogue: the power of a masculine ethos that insists on the presence of hierarchical authority. All men cannot be all-powerful in a male-male context. In the absence of women, therefore, some men among men necessarily become "other," while some do not. Men who experience the loss of power automatically become objects. Here, within the realm of social dialogue, a man's identification as "other," as one who is differently masculine, occurs because he appears vulnerable, insubstantial, and ineffectual: in effect, he is relatively powerless in a world where male power is all.

One way in which "the Machine" Levene distinguishes himself from "other" men (and thereby hopes to secure power over them) is through metatheatrics.[11] In a mock performative voice, Levene plays out before some of his office mates the conversation of his property sale to Bruce and Harriet Nyborg. Through his performance he illustrates the good "*old* ways" of selling real estate (72). He demonstrates the language skills and techniques that his protégé, Roma, undoubtedly called upon during his hard sell to Lingk in act 1. Levene's business talk, his social dialogue, materializes through language, and not just action, the philosophy of "always be closing." Through aggressive association between the values of the masculine ethos and the Nyborgs' presumed desire for ownership, Levene uses language to manipulate his leads. "Believe in your*self*" (67), Levene tells Bruce and Harriet, as he encourages them to grab his real estate offer as a real opportunity for personal empowerment. According to Levene, there is no reason for any Nyborg who lives in a prosperous land driven by traditional male values to believe that "this one has so-and-so, and I have nothing" (68). "What we have to do is *admit* to ourself that we see that opportunity," Levene coaxes, "and *take* it" (72).

Cocky and persistent, Levene recreates the talk between the Nyborgs and himself, acting out his own role in the conversation. The couple's purchase, he presumes, is his claim to victory in the sales contest and therefore worthy of this public replay. Yet, Levene's impersonation, which is based essentially in social dialogue, occurs simultaneously with Moss's hard-nosed social dialogue about the realities of business—the loss of jobs for those who fail to top Levene's apparent success. Mamet creates dramatic tension between the two speakers' distinct uses of this level of interaction: Levene's self-centered metatheatricality (which calls for roleplaying) and Moss's attempts at a regular conversation that reject Levene's "fucking war stories" (67). On the narrative level, tension surfaces between Levene's mock-heroic story of successful selling and Moss's woes of failure at selling. On the level of conversational dynamics, Levene relies upon a variation of a stream-of-consciousness monologue and playacting, while Moss encourages realized, interactive conversation (albeit prompted by his display of anger and anxiety).

It is ironic, however, that just as Levene assumes a character in his imaginary scenario with the Nyborgs, so Moss is possibly also role-playing in the "real" interaction with his colleagues. One cannot trust that Moss's angry words are truthful; he is revealed later on, after all, to be the instigator of the robbery. Whether engaged in metatheatrical or actual social dialogue, therefore, Mamet's men play at talking. The only persistent connection among the men is their perpetual language usage—the fact that they continue to activate social dialogue with one another while in the same space. They move from coded languages decipherable to those within the (business) community (act 1) to self-absorbed diatribes constructed to obscure the truth (act 2).

The same dream of power shared by the businessmen draws the Nyborgs to Levene's fantasy of fulfilled patriarchal capitalism: "This is that *thing* that you've been dreaming of," he tells the ready couple (72). Mamet's men are desperate not to be the "other" men among men: those men without real cultural power. They strive to possess that which they dream of, to acquire the power that they believe to be their *right* within the patriarchy. The tragic irony of Levene's fervent sales pitch, however, and its metaphoric relation to the values inherent in the cultural myths that spring from the masculine ethos (i.e., the American dream), is its inability finally to create lasting meaning for those who respond to it. "I'm selling something they don't even *want*," Levene proudly boasts (77). So it is with American culture, which continues to buy the bill of goods labeled gender privilege. While social privilege may certainly give immediate gratification to men as it marginalizes women and "other" males, it is, in fact, a cultural system that thrives on the bankruptcy of men's self-identification. Men may initially exercise patriarchal privileges, but many eventually realize that they sacrifice self-knowledge. This knowledge, which many often come to see as their desired goal, is tragically lost in time to the culture's coded gender system.

Levene's inflated ego is deflated by Williamson's observation that a sale to the Nyborgs, who turn out to be perennial customers, may not materialize. Williamson's remark challenges Levene's skill and judgment as a salesman, as well as questions his capabilities, his credibility as a Man. But the Machine will not be derailed, as he equates his rejuvenated success with his male prowess: "A man's his job," he tells his younger boss, "and you're *fucked* at yours. . . . you don't have the *balls*" (75–76). Levene relies upon his track record as a salesman as the primary indicator of his manhood. He reminds Williamson that one's history changes one's fortunes

47

of the future. To Levene, his identity, which was shaped by the "old ways" (72), the tried-and-true principles of the masculine ethos, has never really lost its potency, its ability to resurrect. "[T]hings can *change,*" he tells his boss, "This is where you fuck *up* because this is something you don't *know.* You can't look down the *road.* And see what's *coming....* It might be someone *new.... And you can't look *back.* 'Cause you don't know *history*" (76). Levene's notion of change focuses only on the shift that can impact on a man's success at business—a shift that reveals the amount of power a man wields. It has nothing to do with a transformation in an individual's attitude or behavior toward self-improvement. What Levene does not know is that Williamson represents a new generation of men not so unlike his own. While they may refuse to link success and survival with any historical, "factual" personal achievements, they rely upon the power of stable gender codings, the culture's historically grounded positioning of their social privileges as males. Williamson, like many men before him, believes that he has the right to activate any powers to which he has access. He considers this act his privilege as a man within American society. Such efforts of his do not require the achievement of any desired end; rather, the end and the means are one in the same: his goal is the sheer execution of male power.

The key scene in act 2 occurs after Williamson leaves the conversation with his employees to return to the interrogation room. Alone in the outer office, Levene and Roma are interrupted unexpectedly by Lingk. Anticipating that any conversation with Lingk may spell trouble for the closure of their real estate deal, Roma instantly creates another metatheatrical scenario to divert attention. The speed and precision with which Roma directs his partner Levene into action clearly indicates that these guys are old pros at playacting their way out of personal confrontations: "You're a client. I just sold you five waterfront Glengarry Farms," Roma hastily instructs Levene. "I rub my head, throw me the cue 'Kenilworth'" (78). Roma and Levene know only too well how to read the signs of potential conflict within their business; Lingk, indeed, has come to talk to Roma about his backing out of the sale.

The social dialogue in this scene is complex. The three men converse on topics supported by the thematic of the masculine ethos and myths, while assuming a variety of speaking positions not necessarily representative of their own voices. Each man takes on a voice that is, in effect, outside of himself. In so doing, each assumes that he can get what he wants only by using a voice other than his own, one not inside himself. Roma and Levene speak from their metatheatrical positions as, respectively, wheeling-and-dealing salesman and wealthy, satisfied customer (the latter being *the* senior vice president American Express" [82]). Lingk, on the other hand, sporadically interrupts them through metalinguistic intrusions: "I've got to talk with you" (78, 81). Once the very nervous, self-conscious Lingk does talk, he only reports on his wife's legal efforts to back out of the deal. Much is then made between Lingk and Roma about when they will talk about her actions. Eventually, Lingk can only assert his presence before the domineering Roma by adopting his wife's voice, the authority of the absent woman. "It's not me, it's my wife," Lingk claims. "She wants her money back. . . . She told me 'right now.' . . . She told me I *have* to. . . . I can't negotiate" (89–91). The male-cast play often dramatizes the absent woman's power by presenting her transformation into, or her "becoming" the voice of a present male who struggles to assert his own personal voice.[12] This is certainly one way in which "the gender confusion" of Mamet's men, "while not complicated by the physical presence of women," as McDonough points out, "is constantly evoked in language" (204).

The presence of Jinny's voice in Lingk's dialogue disrupts the fictional dialogue of the other men. It is the only authentic voice to be heard; the men, including Lingk (if using his own voice), wish only to obscure the truth. The absent woman's words, however, penetrate the social dialogue and, in effect, demand to be heard, redirecting the conversation away from Roma and Levene's fantastic performance. Yet while Jinny's opinions are spoken by her husband, another new, dynamic topic is added to the men's discourse coherence: the absent woman, herself. She inserts her presence into the men's dialogue, therefore, not only through a character's reiteration of her words but through the characters' discussion of her role. In *Glengarry,* the topic of the absent woman diminishes the metatheatrical and metalinguistic dimension of the men's social dialogue. Roma knows that he must defeat the power of the absent woman if he is to win over Lingk. As Zeifman observes, Jinny is the "'missing link' whose values could destroy Roma's very existence" (132). So, manly Roma instructs the now wavering Lingk: "That's just something she 'said.' We don't have to do that" (90). "Jim, anything you *want,* you *want* it, you *have* it. You understand? This is *me*," the role-playing Roma confides, as he positions himself as someone from the "*outside*" who, through "talk" (91), can put Lingk in touch with the powers of the masculine ethos—those collective, mythic powers that can finally subordinate the power of the internalized absent woman.

Another provocative and complicated level of social dialogue also disrupts the communication when Aaronow returns to the main office after being interrogated by Baylen.[13] "No one should talk to a man that way. How are you *talking* to me" (87), the anxious, paranoid salesman pleads after his session with the police. With no knowledge of the situation he is walking into, Aaronow tries to establish actual conversation. He is desperate to create a dialogue that respects how he imagines men are supposed to talk, a dialogue in which each man, because he is a man, has access to power, to some integrity and courtesy through talk. Aaronow's efforts, however, serve only to comment on the failures of the metatheatrical dialogue between Roma and Lingk, which Williamson loosely calls "*business*" (88). Aaronow unknowingly mimics Lingk in the Roma-Levene-Lingk interaction as he inquires, "Is anybody listening to me...?" (87). Aaronow, like Lingk, struggles to be heard among men as well as to be respected as a man among men. But he fails to engage the other men in either social dialogue or, what he most desires, personal dialogue. The salesman departs for the restaurant, frustrated and humiliated.

Aaronow, using his own voice, fails to capture the attention of his colleagues, and Lingk secures their concentration only when he speaks in the voice of the absent woman. In telling Roma that he cannot negotiate any deal, Lingk moves their dialogue back to a metalinguistic level. Lingk's response to the demanding Roma—"I don't have the *power*" (92)—is an astounding admission for a (white) male character to make. He means that he does not have the power to negotiate the real estate deal, but he reveals a more engrossing, powerless state that many characters experience in the male-cast canon but are afraid to articulate. Male characters are repeatedly presented as not trusting one another and therefore refusing to be vulnerable and truthful in one another's company.

Men feel powerless to create such moments of truth because in doing so they lose the power to control the listener's response to their openness. Partially for these reasons, Lingk chooses to hide behind the words of his wife rather than to speak personally to Roma. Lingk consciously resists Roma's efforts to get closer to him through conversation. Although Lingk is clearly drawn to the male bonding that Roma seductively offers him, he is driven by the more familiar demands of the absent woman. But Roma's loyalty to Lingk as a trusted listener is specious at best. "I can't talk to you, *you* met my wife," Lingk asserts (92), as he consciously pits a man's Man, Roma, against the absent woman, Jinny. Lingk essentially steps outside the battle as he lets these two powerful figures battle over the definition of his manhood—as well as over the possession of his money.

True to male characters throughout the canon who want to break down other men's conversational barriers, Roma offers several times to take Lingk out for a drink. Lingk responds, "She told me not to talk to you" (93). Getting nowhere with the customer, who is now the full-blown Jinny surrogate, Roma tries to appeal to Lingk's ego through another self-empowering monologue that recalls his original sales pitch to Lingk in act 1. "Let's talk about *you,*" Roma contends, "Your life is your own. You have a contract with your wife. You have certain things you do jointly... and there are *other* things.... This is your life." Once again, Roma appeals to the powers of the masculine ethos, male privilege, and male bonding and naming as a means by which Lingk can overcome the influence of the Other. Roma believes that by appealing to Lingk's sense of manhood, appearing to bond with him in this battle against the Other, he can sell real estate. In a blatant violation of human intimacy, Roma adopts a pseudotherapeutic voice to exploit Lingk's personal life. His motives for encouraging Lingk's personal dialogue are entirely self-serving. Like Levene, Roma has no scruples when it comes to "selling something they don't even *want*" (77). A salesman, after all, must "always be closing." Roma has almost succeeded in getting Lingk to go for that crucial drink when Williamson remarks that Lingk's check has already been cashed. This admission, to Lingk, means two things: he has failed to meet his wife's demands and Roma has lied to him by saying that Lingk had time to cancel the deal and the check.

Torn between his loyalty to "God the Mother" (his wife) and "God the Father" (Roma), Lingk makes a hasty exit from the real estate office. "Oh, Christ... Oh Christ. I know I've let you down," Lingk tells Roma. "I'm sorry. For... Forgive... for... I don't know anymore. [*Pause.*] Forgive me" (95). Lingk's final words recall the closing moments in Mamet's *Edmond* as well as Albee's *The Zoo Story* in their metaphysical evocations. Unlike Albee's Jerry, who finds some connection with Peter by the end of their tragic interaction, Lingk feels no lasting "link" with Roma. Lingk has no awareness of powers within himself that can give him direction, insight, and a sense of individualization. He repeatedly turns to those outside of himself to define himself, both externally and internally. In confessing to Roma that he has let him down, Lingk reveals his delusion that Roma actually cares personally for him; conversely, it reveals Roma's success at playacting. But Lingk is also admitting that he has failed to live up to the expectations of a "real" man within the male power structure. He has let down the male ethos, neither enacting nor professing his power over the Other. For all intents and purposes, Lingk is emasculated by Jinny, prompting him to seek out Roma's camaraderie. He is a mortal, decentered man, however, who frustrates a god whom he aspires to please and to emulate (Roma) and disappoints a goddess whom he allows to lead him (Jinny). He is the type of male character who appears doomed to be manipulated by most men and women whose own self-identities are confidently determined *and* who exercise their social powers.

In the final scene of act 2, the men return to social dialogue as actual, realistic conversation. The code of their linguistic interaction, determined by the masculine ethos, is rendered in familiar terms and without role-playing. In no uncertain words, Roma and Levene chide Williamson for contradicting Roma's story to Lingk. "Whoever told you you could work with *men*?" (96), Roma bitterly challenges his boss. Williamson is guilty of breaking the vital code of businessmen's ethics—that of which the "old stuff" is made: "a man who's your 'partner' *depends* on you ... you have to go *with* him and *for* him ... or you're a shit, you're *shit,* you can't exist alone" (98). The credo for the white male, according to the salesmen, is to accept that he is in a partnership with other straight white men, a relationship that may require him to lie about, to be silent about, but most certainly to agree about anything that will help maintain their power position in the "business" of living in America. This strategy has nothing to do with the solidification of self-disclosing, personal relationships. It is purely a survival tactic, based upon a bonding of male ideology, which ensures men's economic power.

But it is Roma who is most cruel as he angrily releases a litany of abusive epithets that clearly align Williamson with the "other," those marginalized in American society over whom the white straight male wields cultural power. For breaking the male code, Williamson is a "fucking shit," "asshole," and "idiot"—all of which warrant his being named a "stupid fucking cunt," a "fairy," and a "fucking child" (96, 97). To align him with women, homosexuals, and children is, according to Roma, the worst humiliation for a (white) male. If a man is not working *for* men, then he must necessarily be working *against* them, siding with the Other.[14] Roma reminds Levene that their survival—as businessmen and implicitly as white men—is in jeopardy: "We are members of a dying breed. That's ... that's ... that's why we have to stick together" (105).

In the end, however, the "child" solves the mystery of the office robbery. During his tirade against Williamson, Levene reveals his knowledge of Williamson's trick on Roma (i.e., that Lingk's contract was not submitted). The boss notes that Levene could know this detail only by having been in his office the previous evening. Levene is exposed as the robber; he hangs himself with his own words. In Mamet's world of men, thieves and salesmen are one in the same. They are all perpetrators of the corrupted American frontier ethic of exploitation in the name of economic gain. And right up to the end, Levene hopes to bribe Williamson not to turn him in to the police. As with his previous efforts, Levene knows that he can only succeed with Williamson if the ante is high enough; his only recourse is to draw from his recent sale to the Nyborgs. This time, however, the boss humiliates his employee by pointing out that Levene is still a loser: the Nyborgs are "insane." Since their checks are worthless, "they just like talking to salesmen" (104). Williamson effectively confronts "the Machine" Levene and his delusions of potential personal and professional power. Like the old system of which he use to be an integral part, Levene is broken down, corrupt, obsolete, and pathetic.

Several new faces on the old system, nonetheless, appear to be existing without diminished authority at the conclusion of *Glengarry Glen Ross*. Collectively, they represent the first of two conflicting, though surviving, ideologies in the play—the recast voice of the masculine ethos in "a world of men" (105). This male voice is manifested differently, however, in the dialogue and presence of three characters: Roma, Williamson, and Baylen. Their voices diverge in respect to their position on patriarchal law; they converge in their attitudes toward the masculine ethos.

Embodying a classic (white) everyman, Roma presumes that the patriarchal system should bend to his immediate needs. This, he believes, is his rightful privilege as a male. While he unabashedly lives outside the law (consider his final directive to Williamson that he expects to claim half of Levene's commissions [107]), Roma still commits himself to the masculine ethos and its myths of masculine power. The boss also lives inside masculine privilege but outside legal law. He, too, likes to play with power. But unlike Roma, Williamson has the entitlement of position to protect his authority. Both men survive in Mamet's impersonal world because each is committed to and skilled at manipulating the powers of the masculine ethos. Each knows how to exploit other men in order *not* to become one of the "other" men.

As a police detective, Baylen represents the uncorrupted authority of patriarchal law. Unlike Roma and Williamson, Baylen lives inside the law and inside the masculine ethos. This combination assures him privilege, security, and power, his for keeping in the American system. His presence affirms that a secular order, one defined in patriarchal terms, exists to dispel chaos. Yet, only one other voice in the play completely embraces the legal law that Baylen courts—and it is not another male.

The voice of Jinny Lingk, the absent woman, is the second distinct ideology to survive in *Glengarry*. Although she has a different relationship to patriarchal law than Baylen, she relies upon that law to protect her rights: she contacts the district attorney's office for protection in her case against Roma. In this instance, Jinny lives inside the patriarchal law and it empowers her. However, Jinny obviously lives outside the male ethos. She does not have access to the same cultural privileges that men enjoy in the patriarchy. But this social imbalance of power does not weaken Jinny when confronted with the male ego. Through her husband's mouth, Jinny challenges the wisdom, the integrity, and the actual and the mythic value of the masculine ethos. She insists that her subject position be heard. In denying Roma all that he wants, including conversation with Lingk, Jinny's voice disempowers the classic everyman. She effectively resists the power play of the masculine ethos by turning its own premises and authority against itself. By simply saying no to Roma through Lingk, she gives voice—and power—to all "others" whom Roma and fellow advocates of the masculine ethos have dominated and silenced.

As these two surviving, clashing voices move toward the center of Mamet's text, the spectator's last sight is Aaronow, sitting at his desk, alone in the destroyed real estate office. His final admission is filled with raw truth: "Oh, God, I hate this job" (108). His words signal the death of the salesman, capturing the defeated man's pathetic awareness that things in life should be better than they are. As Jack Barbera notes about Mamet's plays, "notions of the American way—democracy and free enterprise—become corrupted when they enter the look-out-for-number-one rationalizations of crooks and unethical businessmen" (275). Aaronow struggles to understand the all-pervasive corruption in *Glengarry Glen Ross,* a "moral play," according to Benedict Nightingale, "not a moralizing one" (1984, 5). The play "seeks to 'tell the truth' about the usually invisible violence men inflict on themselves and each other as they grab for gold."

In Mamet's dramatic worlds, characters are challenged to take moral responsibility for men's corruption. Aaronow seems to know that someone needs to create order out of the chaos. Matthew Roudané suggests the importance of Aaronow's "semblance of moral seriousness" (1986, 44). Mamet himself comments,

> Aaronow has some degree of conscience, some awareness; he's troubled. Corruption troubles him. The question he's troubled by is whether his inability to succeed in the society in which he's placed is a defect—that is, is he manly or sharp enough?—or if it's, in effect, a positive attribute, which is to say that his conscience prohibits him. So Aaronow is left between these two things and he's incapable of choosing. This dilemma is, I think, what many of us are facing in this country right now. (1986, 75)

Aaronow knows that in a "world of men" it simply is not enough for law enforcement to police the public's actions. Such authority, according to Aaronow, does not always know the proper way "to talk...to a working man" (88). But Aaronow has no idea how to use his gender privilege to his advantage; he has no sense as to how, when, or where to use this culturally coded power to help to understand it any better. On the other hand, he has no idea of the power that he can unleash through his freedom of choice: he can choose to live as a differently masculine man outside the definitions of the masculine ethos. Like Jinny Lingk, Aaronow is aware that life should be better for those who choose not to break the law. But unlike the absent woman, Aaronow cannot envision a new kind of power, which is flourishing within his grasp, if he only explores his profound discontent with the values of the masculine ethos. Such a vision would necessarily signal the dismantlement of the gender-coded system, and Aaronow fails to envision the potential powers of the "other." His lack of imagination appears to "always be closing" his mind and heart. He also has no voice of an absent woman to listen to; he has no idea of the powers of individualization that reside in her voice. As McDonough astutely argues, Mamet's men resist the "discovery of new identities that would release them from a stance which is antagonist to the female without as well as to the feminine within them" (205). Mamet's own experience complements McDonough's vision: "Men *generally* expect more of women than we do of ourselves. We feel, based on constant evidence, that women are better, stronger, more truthful, than men. You can call this sexism, or reverse sexism, or whatever you wish, but it is my experience" (1989b, 24).

Despite his inability to become a different kind of subject, Aaronow resists immersion in the institution, in the corrupted manifestations of the masculine ethos. The hapless salesman signals some hope for personal change simply in his passionate urge to understand what is going on around him and thereby to understand his deeper rage. In *Glengarry,* Mamet dramatizes the institutional oppression generated by social constructions of gender. He masterfully displays through Aaronow an American man's often contradictory struggle to realize and to claim his individuality among men. This struggle exists for all men who, consciously or unconsciously, yearn for the authenticity of self-identity. All male characters confront the overwhelming context of the American masculine ethos and its male mythologies on their journey to individualization and self-identity. Yes, *Glengarry* is an indictment of the horrors of capitalism and corrupt business. But men among themselves sustain these structures. The degree to which men are victims and victimizers, as dramatized by Mamet, is debatable. Less debatable is the poignancy of his morality play about the lives of the many men in whom human feeling is absent.

Throughout twentieth-century American drama, male characters have focused on women as one of their favorite topics of conversation. During social dialogue, men commonly discuss women who are absent from their immediate environment. In fact, there is a subgenre of male-cast dramas, complete acts or entire plays that derive their discourse coherence from men's obsession with absent women: from Eugene O'Neill's *A Wife for a Life* to D. B. Gilles's *Men's Singles* and Terrence McNally's *The Lisbon Traviata.* Men repeatedly reveal the impact that their real or imagined relationships with women have had upon their own sexuality and identity, their own sense of achievement and power. These revelations nearly always illuminate patriarchal positions: man is subject and woman is object. By decoding and deconstructing this phallocentrism in drama, one can expose the "mystery of masculinity" (Segal 82) and thereby unmask man's relationship to authority and privilege over the Other.

There are several dramaturgical explanations for the material absence of the female in the male-cast play. The female is excluded from spaces defined as male domains: sex-specific prisons, certain military surroundings, and male-identified (or male-dominated) job, educational, and religious environments. She is also absent from sex-specific activities such as men's athletics, fraternal or sex-segregated secret organizations, and "men only" social contexts. Sometimes, though rarely, when the play is set in a space to which women have equal access, men discuss a woman who is absent by choice or by coincidence. For example, Peter is alone in *The Zoo Story* simply because his wife never joins him on his Sunday outings in Central Park. Finally, of course, a woman may be absent because she is dead.

When men speak among themselves about women, they do so within a specific thematic determined by the American masculine ethos. Men's social dialogue at this initial level is essentially sexist. From a Lacanian perspective, "The circulation of the phallus as meaning sketches a *structure* for language in which women are clearly outside of discourse. The phallus is exchanged *between men*" (Dolan 12; emphasis added), and women are Other. The "phallic language" of the male-cast play not only situates but relies upon the female to be referred to from within its specific semiotic and cultural dialogue. In their dialogue, male characters primarily position and understand woman through her culturally sanctioned relationship to a man, as his relative (generally his mother or wife) or as the object of his erotic desires (usually his wife, lover, or sexual fantasy). A significant variation in this schema, however, surfaces within gay male enclaves. Many gay characters position the absent woman (including the mother) as a surrogate upon whom they displace their own sexual desires. Since the female is the object of male erotics with the dominant culture, some gay characters, from their marginal perspective, identify with females as the sexual object of the "male gaze" (Mulvey 11). In creating a symbiotic identification with or desire to be the (absent) woman or object (Isay 41–46), some gays transmute their presumed cultural position as male subjects.

Despite these variations, one fact remains: male characters in realist settings excluding women automatically identify, through their use of *language,* the female as Other. Male-cast plays rarely, if ever, dramatize the cultural transformation of gender called for by Judith Butler (1990), Lynne Segal, and Jessica Benjamin: a transformation of gender "principles," and hence gender representation, away from their rigidly coded social construction in favor of "a reconstruction of the vital tension between recognition and assertion, dependency and freedom" (Benjamin 176). Male characters, therefore, repeatedly define their maleness in Beauvoirian terms: their relationship to and power over the Other. What happens, then, when the Other is absent? How do male characters create the presence of the Other, to "symbolically erect the hierarchies of phallocentric culture" (Segal 90)?

When men are alone together, their biological sameness functions as a social bonding agent. This sameness initially erases male differences; it reinforces dominance over the (absent) Other. In the absence of women, therefore, men initially express themselves through aggressive social dialogue that is driven by male mythologies. Nonetheless, the absent woman's gendered identity—and in more recent plays, her absent sexual body—quickly assumes prominence as the characters struggle to affirm their sameness by creating the presence of (her) difference in their talk. Here, one can argue, the "repudiation of femininity" (Benjamin 159–69) and the return of the "repressed" (Chodorow 163–70, 173–90)—both with their nods toward the complexities of the Oedipal riddle—surface in dialogue. In the male-cast play, characters initially identify differences between male and female, masculinity and femininity, through language. Their determination to discuss topics that are stimulated by the masculine ethos, however, actually masks their deeper fear of losing power, of losing their manhood, to the Other. In play after male-cast play, dialogue depends heavily upon reference to the Other, upon sexual identity as delineated in the symbolic order and as manifested in the social codings of gender—all in an effort to confirm male domination.[15] Consequently, coherence within men's social dialogue relies upon creating "difference" in gender codings and anatomy—and thus upon evoking an absent woman.

The absence of women from the stage, however, eventually forces onstage men to redefine the binary gender system upon which they establish their own identity. Men's differences from one another, determined in accord with strict masculine codings, finally replace the female Other in order to reaffirm phallic hierarchy. The most glaring, divisive challenge to male sameness, an identification of male difference or "otherness," is sexual orientation. Heterosexuality, homosexuality, or bisexuality marks a man as either subject or object in an all-male context within the dominant culture. In the twentieth century, the nonheterosexual male has been the most frequently represented male "other" in male-cast plays. He clearly resides outside the dominant culture's notions of the male subject, yet he remains a subject, nonetheless, by virtue of his being a man in a sex-differentiated world. His "otherness" is essential, however, within a same-sex play that maintains the culture's dichotomous gender codings through phallocentric language. While the discourse coherence of published male-cast plays has been influenced by characters' race, ethnicity, class, religion, and age, these features are generally subsumed by the deeper anxiety of gender and sexuality experienced by male characters when they are alone together. It is the rare male-cast play whose language takes us through and beyond the culture's phallocentrism—which is driven by compulsory heterosexuality—to a world that acknowledges the differences, the "otherness," in male subjectivities.

Two representative male-cast plays whose discourse coherence centers on the topic of women are Alice Gerstenberg's *At the Club* and Sidney Morris's *If This Isn't Love!*[16] Each is essentially a realist play that adheres to the unities of time, place, and action, Gerstenberg's a one-act, Morris's a three-act, although each act occurs a decade after the previous one. Each act in these plays, therefore, is a sustained conversation—focused on absent women. Each play also dramatizes the crucial stage of discourse coherence that often is upheld among men before their cooperative communication collapses into uncooperative, frequently violent interaction. Although neither text has been acknowledged as a play of high critical value, each is dramaturgically significant when considered under the rubric of male-cast drama.

At the Club and *If This Isn't Love!* are also historically notable in their clear mapping of the variations (i.e., the evolution of diverse roles) in the representation of woman as Other and object. In this regard, absent women have taken on two general roles, or images, in men's talk exchanges, similar to those that Sue-Ellen Case identifies for women in classical Western drama: "positive roles, which depict women as independent, intelligent and even heroic; and a surplus of misogynistic roles commonly identified as the Bitch, the Witch, the Vamp and the Virgin/Goddess" (1988, 6). I will refer to these various roles throughout the discussion. Since women do not speak for themselves in male-cast plays, they can never occupy the subject position, even when men speak of them "heroically." This, of course, extends to my own voice here as author, as an authorized male voice commenting upon (fictional) men and their references to women. Despite this paradox—at least in terms of dramatic representation—some male characters in Gerstenberg's and Morris's plays speak about women (and thereby situate them) in positive "roles" that, linguistically and metaphorically, approximate subject positions. In contrast, other male characters speak readily about women in misogynistic "roles" that guarantee their object position in men's dialogue.

At the Club, Alice Gerstenberg

Alice Gerstenberg, acknowledged in recent years as a "seminal American theatrical figure" (Hecht 1), was a pioneer in the early-twentieth-century "little theater" movements in New York City and in her hometown, Chicago. An innovative dramatist, she is best known for her all-female play, *Overtones* (premiered in 1915), America's first drama to present dual personality devices (i.e., characters' unconscious lives) on stage. As Marilyn Atlas points out, "O'Neill's experimentation [in the 1920s] with dramatic form and the rich exploration of psychoanalysis and parapsychology in his drama did not originate with him" (59).

At the Club is unique in the male-cast canon for several reasons, not the least of which is the importance of its author in American theater history.[17] First, it is one of the few all-male plays written by a woman. Just as Gerstenberg dramatized original, multidimensional voices for women in *Overtones,* she created another atypical voice in her handling of men's dialogue in *At the Club.* Very few male writers come close to capturing the sustained, generous heterosexual male voice of Gerstenberg's main character, Prentice, in his articulate, insightful, and compassionate evocation of an absent woman. This observation, of course, raises obvious questions: Do women writers hear (or imagine) males' voices differently from male writers? If so, how does gender difference between playwrights affect the dramatic development of their male characters and the ways in which men talk among themselves?

Second, Gerstenberg creates in Prentice one of the first male feminist voices in the male-cast canon. Before inventing Prentice, it should be noted, Gerstenberg had already joined other noted early-twentieth-century American women playwrights, like Susan Glaspell and Rachel Crothers, in contributing to the rise of the female feminist voice in American drama. Similar to such lesser known contemporaries as Alice C. Thompson, Helen Sherman Griffith, Alice Chaplin, and Clara Denton, however, Gerstenberg contributed most dynamically to this movement through her creation of feminist heroines in female-cast dramas and comedies.[18] Gerstenberg's heroines break out of culturally defined, gender-restricted roles when speaking of women's lives; they are subjects who individualize their own stories. As subject, Prentice still speaks of women as objects; his female authorship does not automatically liberate his vision, which confines women to misogynistic or positive roles.

Third, Gerstenberg alters the customary social dynamics of male characters' interaction by creating a feminist-inspired male speaker. To the degree that Prentice aggressively articulates and defends the concerns of Hyacinth, the absent woman, he assumes the position usually filled by the Other in the talk exchange; he is decidedly marked as a male "other" to the four men with whom he converses. Prentice exists outside the boundaries of proper allegiances that define the men's club, even though he, like the other men, is white and heterosexual.

Set in the lounge of an exclusive men's club on a hot summer evening, At the Club is infused with the patriarchal values of privileged white males. These men—Prentice, Sherman, Boyd, and Whitmarsh—enjoy their leisure, assume the loyalty of their male comrades, and are obsessed with discussing the impact that females have on shaping their lives. Gerstenberg has structured her play in two alternating movements: from one character who is alone in the club room, to two, then three and four characters interacting, followed by the diminishment of these numbers until one person again remains alone at the play's conclusion. Punctuating these movements are four occasions when the telephone is in use. Each of these interruptions inserts an absent woman into the play: Prentice calls Hyacinth two times, Whitmarsh phones a male friend about his wife's house party, and Hyacinth calls Prentice at the play's closing.[19]

At the core of each movement is Prentice, a bachelor lawyer, who never leaves the room. Prentice is unlike Sherman and Whitmarsh, the married men at the club, and unlike Boyd, a fellow bachelor. Prentice speaks about Hyacinth as Virgin/Goddess as well as a heroic, independent person; Sherman's and Boyd's female referents, on the other hand, are Bitches and Vamps. Whitmarsh, a manufacturer by profession, does not distinguish among absent women since, as he says, "a man with a wife and three daughters hasn't any time to *think* about his condition. It's all he can do to manage to keep it" (Gerstenberg 1930a, 164).

At the play's opening, Prentice engages the Club's old servant,

Gittens, in social dialogue. The men discuss their jobs, food, and Gittens's deceased wife. Gittens breaks with the tenor of their congenial conversation, however, by remarking that the gossip that has come his way during his forty years at the Club has taught him that "the secrets of men's souls wouldn't seem so bad if one knew all the reasons" (150). This philosophical assertion is an unusual interjection into social dialogue, in that it invites each man to particularize for the other his own secrets. It suggests that the play's discourse coherence may shift to include more intimate topics. In response to Gittens's statement, however, the men return to the topic of absent women to speak in code about their own lives. This unspecific, theoretical dialogue then leads toward another possible moment of personalization that is abruptly (but predictably) interrupted—by a telephone buzzer:

> Gittens: [M]arried men . . . do what their wives want.
> Prentice: Not *all* wives are like that. One or two of them are suffering from husbands—unworthy of them.
> Gittens: Maybe. You can't tell where the blame belongs. Every time a Club member dies and they take his strong box out of the files to destroy his letters, with no living man's eyes allowed to read them, I always feel they're destroying what was the real heart of him.
> Prentice: Maybe so. Maybe not—some men have secrets that are only—silly. [*A buzzer rings at the telephone near them.*]
>
> (151)

Taking the phone call, Prentice is left alone in the room to speak privately to his lover, Hyacinth. Prentice's relationship with Hyacinth is not public knowledge. Thus, the secrets of his life are bound up in facts of his life that he has disclosed to no man in either social or personal dialogue. Just as the "real hearts" of the men to whom Gittens refers (that is, their personal, truthful, self-disclosing parts) are bound up in inanimate letters, so Prentice's real heart is voiced privately in conversation with Hyacinth, the absent woman. Only Hyacinth and the audience hear his words. Throughout her play, Gerstenberg foregrounds the thematic of the "secrets of men's souls," and what men do or do not do with those secrets when among other men.

Prentice's phone conversation with Hyacinth reveals that their relationship is in fact part of a triangle. Another "he" is involved, one whose presence necessitates that the couple meet clandestinely. Hyacinth hastily cuts short their conversation, leaving Prentice in the company of newly arrived Whitmarsh. Whitmarsh promptly speaks of other absent women—his wife and his daughters—and an upcoming party. Whitmarsh proceeds to the telephone and calls an eligible bachelor about attending the party, only to find that his listener is getting married on the same day. In these back-to-back phone calls, Gerstenberg's men give textual presence to an array of absent women, all connected to the men through marital bonds or sexual objectification: wives, daughters, fiancées, and lovers.

Once Whitmarsh is off the phone and moves toward leaving the room, the conversation turns to alcohol. Glenn Sherman, a real estate agent, arrives to talk to Prentice. Drunk, dissipated, and angry, Sherman has come to talk to his former college buddy about a woman. Since he has been drinking heavily, Sherman dismisses social dialogue in order to speak directly, and therefore more personally, with Prentice. As he says of his need to speak the truth, "These thoughts! They're driving me mad!" (155). Prentice encourages the still drinking Sherman to contain his rage toward the absent woman, a combination Bitch-Vamp whom Sherman identifies as his wife, Hyacinth, and her lover—who Sherman has yet to know is Prentice. Prentice, in his soon-to-be-revealed association with Hyacinth, will also be encoded as a male Vamp, a traitor to his own sex, at the Club—but this identity will be bestowed upon him only from the men's perspective, not from Gerstenberg's perspective.[20]

Sherman confesses to Prentice that he knows about his wife's lover from an anonymous letter he just received. Prentice dismisses this notion, suggesting that the message may well be the handiwork of one of Sherman's "enemies," some absent woman, one of his "discarded mistresses" who seeks revenge (156). Sherman's response: "That's too straight talk!" Sherman's strategy to deal with his marital problems is not to speak straight talk. Because his drunken feelings are unguarded, however, Sherman forgoes social dialogue and continues to speak directly. But he will not wholly embrace personal dialogue. He is still far too resistant to speaking the truth. To do so would undercut his gender-coded power and make him vulnerable to the absent woman. Nor, finally, does Sherman care to foster an un-self-conscious personal dialogue with his best friend; after all, Prentice is clearly a man who is unlike

Sherman. Since Prentice "take[s] a situation and examine[s] it from all angles" (156), he can understand why Hyacinth would reject Sherman's double standard of male behavior as grossly inequitable for women. Sherman prefers "wild emotional orgies of sentimentality [and] outraged egotism," allowing the male to indulge his every complaint and desire. Sherman can see himself only as pure subject; he refuses to consider that different sides exist to any story, that "other" subjectivities coexist with his own. As Prentice reminds Sherman, "Judging [Hyacinth] from *your* standards, a little adventure on her part wouldn't much matter."

Sherman, however, judges Prentice as a limited observer, a prisoner of his own powers of analysis and an unqualified commentator: "*You* aren't even capable of a *real* emotion" (157). Here, Sherman suggests that the lawyer's support for Hyacinth—a support that is feminist in its origin and execution—is simply void of any emotion, as it fails to reflect any real understanding of the complexities within the married couple's relationship. Anyone who supports the Bitch-Vamp, Sherman implies, is obviously incapable of "understanding" the need to protect the male's cultural position of authority. A man must be married, Sherman also presumes, if he is to understand how heterosexual men are victimized by their mates.

In a detailed, energetic exchange, the two men talk about Sherman's behavior upon his receiving the anonymous letter in Hyacinth's presence. Sherman responded to the news of being cuckolded, he tells Prentice, by choking his wife. Breaking away from her husband's grasp (after he broke her pearl necklace), Hyacinth, according to Sherman, then humiliated him: "She said she was laughing because she didn't have any more *tears*. She said her tears had frozen into pearls" (158). Upon repeating the absent woman's words—here in the form of figurative language—Sherman illustrates a dramaturgical convention in male-cast plays: one's remembrance of women's words are more likely to express emotional concerns and the "reality" of situations than are men's words, since men are too busy trying to cover up such feelings. In response to his wife's remarks, Sherman, who is prone to violent outbursts, confesses: "I—wanted to beat her but I crushed her into my arms instead." Woman, to Sherman, is an object toward whom to direct both physical violence and sexual aggression.

Just as the discourse coherence of the male-cast play moves from social dialogue about the absent woman to men's expressions of violence, so Sherman's personal narration moves: he first talks about the absent woman, then he graphically describes his violent assault of her, followed by his expressed desire for further violent revenge—"She has a lover and I've got to kill him" (158). Sherman's own progression from social dialogue to violence encapsulates the linguistic dynamics of male interaction that characterize the overall structure of most male-cast plays. Furthermore, and entirely predictably for men among themselves, Sherman's personal tirade is curtailed as Whitmarsh and Gittens reenter the room, bearing more liquor. At this point, Sherman and Prentice suspend discussion of their personal crisis. They choose, instead, to remain in the room and thereby to reengage the most conventional of social dialogues with the newly arrived men.

The two dramatic episodes that follow confirm the structural convention that three or more men are most likely to engage in social dialogue if the majority of men are *not* drinking or taking drugs. When Gittens leaves the room, Prentice remains in the company of two married men, Sherman and Whitmarsh. Even though each has a drink poured, only Sherman is identified in the stage directions as taking a drink. Whitmarsh initiates the dialogue immediately by discussing the weather as well as his own job; he does so in an attempt "to give Sherman a chance to help the conversation" (159). When these topics fail to stimulate interaction, he switches focus to Sherman's job. In capturing Sherman's reaction to the suggestion that he discuss his real estate business, Gerstenberg perfectly capsulizes the appeal of familiar, predictable social dialogue to a man whose previous efforts at personal dialogue have stopped: Sherman responds, not unlike the men in Mamet's *Glengarry Glen Ross,* "automatically speeding his reply like a lesson well memorized, but his heart is not in it" (159–60).

One might say that social dialogue throughout the male-cast canon is relatively "heartless," as the verbal sparring of *Glengarry Glen Ross* illustrated earlier. Social dialogue occurs without emotional, psychological, or physical commitment from the characters. Consequently, it does not require its participants to reveal personal intimacies or, for that matter, to personalize the conversation at all. By the very nature of the ethos that frames its topics, social dialogue is language used to pass time in as unfeeling a way as possible.

The entrance of Adin Boyd, a wealthy, bachelor playboy, initiates the second major episode in *At the Club* that also relies upon social dialogue in its most conventional form. Joining the other three men, Boyd is the peer foil to Prentice; his beliefs are also antithetical to Prentice's "feminist" leanings. Unlike Prentice, who promotes a more personal dialogue, Boyd, just returning from vacation, cares only to discuss his association to the challenging and manly activities of fishing, shooting, riding, motoring, tennis, and golf. In the course of his remarks, Boyd, one "to walk along with the crowd" (162), is revealed to be a racist and a sexist. He is demanding, demeaning, impersonal, arrogant, and elitist, and these qualities inform his spiteful references to absent women.

Even though Gerstenberg intends Boyd to provide comic relief from the personal tensions created between Prentice and Sherman, he also illustrates the power of a bigoted, opinionated male to dominate a conversation.[21] He impedes the progression of the play's discourse coherence through his insistent manner and disruptions; his contributions to the conversation focus only on the absent woman, as he claims that he has been "looking for a wife but ha[sn't] found a girl yet with the qualifications" (162).

Boyd's wishes for marriage partially match a clichéd white American dream of the early twentieth century: a "large estate and half a dozen children" (164). But threatening Boyd's dream are a couple of powerful, evil forces: the "dark races" and diseased females. The material reality of these forces demands, according to Boyd, an urgent response. Shamelessly, Boyd articulates the racist beliefs at the bottom of his idyllic vision: "I think we ought to do our patriotic share in saving the future from the dark races.... If something isn't done this overwhelming dark horde will vanquish our early American stock." Patriotism, here, is linked to procreation and the preservation of white culture, generally, and white male authority, specifically.

Raging on with his audacious, and now sexist, remarks, Boyd also expresses his concern for a "question of disease" (165) that threatens to keep him from his dream: associations with absent women who may pollute his otherwise pure, privileged person. For the men in the group who appear unconcerned, Boyd recalls an "early lesson which taught [him] caution" about females and disease. In a brief, expository speech he recounts his relationship with a girl whom he nearly married, until a former lover of hers told Boyd of her history (of course, from his male perspective). Without hearing details about this absent woman's history, Prentice, the supporter of women, confronts Boyd: "Did you ask her? Did she defend herself?"—in other words, did Boyd give the woman an opportunity to speak for herself, to be the subject of her own story, rather than the object of a man's discourse? Boyd responds that he did not talk to the woman about this matter, that he in fact left the relationship without any discussion whatsoever—all because he "wasn't going to take any chances and be haunted by doubt the rest of [his] life." The woman, from Boyd's perspective, is guilty in her silence and unworthy to be the object of his attention. She is rejected and scorned, her alleged past clearly marking her as Bitch-Vamp. Male accusations that discredit the integrity of the absent woman do not, in this case, warrant challenge. Her silence itself—enforced by a man, and not by any actual admissions—condemns her.

In respect to the absent woman's life, he alone, Boyd asserts, knows the truth—a truth that has been constructed by the two men about the absent woman. Prentice rejects Boyd's arrogant, presumptive power play over silenced women: "she might have been deeply wounded by [Boyd's] lack of faith" (165), in her self-worth, her integrity, and in their shared intimacy. Boyd repudiates Prentice's empathetic observation; a man should expect a Bitch-Vamp, who has the "sweet, warm, power of drawing [a man]" (166) to her, to deceive and abuse him without remorse, as a cat does a mouse.

Not missing a melodramatic opportunity to build up an even more formidable composite of this absent woman, Gerstenberg has Boyd name Hyacinth as his former lover, the individual who links females to disease. Without acknowledging their relationships to Hyacinth, Sherman and Prentice pump Boyd for more information, seizing an opportunity to hear another man's detailed account of their previous topic of conversation. Repeatedly, Hyacinth is characterized as the Bitch-Vamp by the two men who fail to secure her as their own. She's "cool and remote—didn't go after men," claims Boyd (166); Sherman condemns her "maddening reserve, fake purity, false to the core!" As Bitch-Vamp, Hyacinth fails to become the desired Virgin/Goddess in Boyd's and Sherman's fantasies. She fails to embody "a woman's most important qualification...her virtue" (167). Yet either image traps Hyacinth in misogynistic roles.

In his response to these attempts at character assassination, Prentice defends Hyacinth by acknowledging that her apparent power over men resides in her cultivation of a more "heroic" identity, one that justifies her unwillingness to play gender-coded games with men: "Sherman and you [Boyd] expect all women to measure into your preconceived ideas. You cannot stretch your minds *to understand* a *type* like Hyacinth...and women like Hyacinth are so *conscious* of your minds which cannot understand, that they consider it too much trouble to enlighten you. They withdraw behind a mask and let you think what you please" (167; emphasis added).

The lucidity with which Prentice justifies Hyacinth's actions—and those of all women of Hyacinth's positive type—illustrates the extent to which he understands and even identifies with her choices. Such choices place her and him on the margins of patriarchal discourse. In *At the Club,* however, the female playwright has positioned this otherwise marginal voice at the center of her play. Through Prentice, Gerstenberg gives voice to those absent women's lives that, certainly in the first half of the century, were otherwise doomed to remain stereotypical, cliché-ridden objects in men's dialogue.

In his unrelenting defense of the absent woman, moreover, Prentice is like no other male character in the male-cast canon. It can be argued that Gerstenberg's handling of Prentice's dialogue is heavy-handed in its polemical, analytical quality. But Gerstenberg is aware of this possible criticism of Prentice's "unreal" manner of speaking. When Sherman asks him to stop his "court haranguing," Prentice puts him in his place with, "You don't think. You don't really *think*!" (167). Prentice effectively subverts Sherman's criticism by legitimizing his own authority and his manner of speaking. He is, after all, an articulate, coherent speaker—an otherwise atypical character for an American male-cast play. Prentice's unconventional male voice is unfamiliar to most spectators and therefore subject to being labeled unreal. We simply are not used to this representation of American male characters who, in the presence of other men, remain individuals who are self-reflective (and at relative ease) with language. Gerstenberg is aware of gender differences manifested in the traditional handling of dramatic speakers, yet she is mining new conversational territory. She has her eye on a political agenda that represents the absent woman's voice within the structuring of a straight white male's voice. In doing so, she offers an alternative realist vision of talk among men. She presents an American male talking differently among men.

Prentice challenges his rejected club mates to see the unfairness of their demand that females "be beyond reproach" (167). "What have both of you done to raise yourselves to so lofty a pedestal in your demands [of Hyacinth]. Are you both beyond reproach?" "You don't understand a word I am saying," Prentice accuses Sherman and Boyd, "because you are still slumbering in your senses. Hyacinth is spiritually so far advanced that for either

68

of you to question her motives or her actions is an impertinence!" (168). While Hyacinth remains the Goddess in Prentice's eyes, she is the secularized Bitch-Vamp in Sherman's and Boyd's eyes—not because of the men's "belief in her faithlessness but the fear of an outrage to [their] vanity" for her desiring anyone other than themselves. Hyacinth's actions strike at the heart of the men's sexual anxiety. At such a moment of debilitating identity crisis, Gerstenberg seems to say, men rely upon the power of their egos to position women as objects, power that stands between their efforts to understand women and women's subjectivity and their wish to perpetuate lies about them.

Clearly, Prentice's defense of Hyacinth in front of other men is shaped by his acknowledgment of her as an independent agent, but he is also acutely aware of his private desire for her as the object of his own fantasies. And it is to this perspective of Hyacinth as sexual object that the dialogue returns when Boyd rejects Prentice's spiritual evocations of Hyacinth. After all, Boyd says, Hyacinth's other jilted lover told Boyd that she was, essentially, a slut. To this statement, yet still without identifying himself as Hyacinth's husband, the drunk Sherman calls Boyd a liar, as he seizes Boyd's hunting revolver and holds it up to Boyd's throat. Sherman pulls the trigger, but the magazine is empty. From frustrated, though revealing, social dialogue about the absent woman, Gerstenberg's dramaturgy now moves to more conventional interaction of violence. In the context of male interaction, it is irrelevant whether the statement about Hyacinth is true. What is pivotal is that Sherman responds brutally on "impulse" (169), as most American male characters do, because he forgoes any investment in language as a way to deal with his feelings. His ego has been undermined by a remark that may very well be true. Unwilling to know the facts, Sherman wants to eliminate anything or anyone that might try to represent the truth. Once this sudden outburst of violence has passed, however, Whitmarsh helps an understandably shaken Boyd from the room, leaving the two buddies alone once again.

Rather than ending the men's interaction violently, Gerstenberg uses Sherman's murderous threat as the source for jolting Prentice into self-disclosing dialogue. Following the pattern of most male-cast drama, Prentice's remarks progress from the absent woman to frank, personal dialogue only after some kind of violence intervenes. Once again rejecting Sherman's efforts to deny Hyacinth the double standard that he has enjoyed during their marriage, Prentice now identifies himself as Hyacinth's current lover. Unlike

Sherman, who has been intimate with lovers outside of his marriage, Prentice and Hyacinth have remained "technically true" to Sherman, although "mentally" they have been "traitors" (170). While a traitor to Sherman, Hyacinth remains the ideal object to Prentice: a Goddess in spirit and a Virgin in body. "What Hyacinth is today is the sum of what Hyacinth has been all her life, and I ask for no-one more perfect.... I only treasure what you took no trouble to keep" (170–71), Prentice concludes about his "perfect" absent woman, as a determined, angry Sherman is ushered out of the room by Gittens.

Confident that his truthfulness with Sherman has "ploughed through to a new clear road" with Hyacinth (171), Prentice, alone once again in the room, calls the woman of his dreams to warn her that her violent husband is on his way home. He gets her to agree to leave immediately for a hotel, but not until he has taken the chance to tell her that Sherman knows about their relationship. The men's interaction has moved through social dialogue determined by absent women, to violence, to a momentary level of personal dialogue within which a man reveals his deeper feelings—albeit through his relationship to an absent woman. By calling Hyacinth on the telephone to tell her of his accomplishment, Prentice not only secures her approval of his actions, but he links his perception of his own identity to the degree to which he is connected— through language—to the absent woman.

Upon Gittens's brief return to the club room, Prentice draws strength from Hyacinth's and his personal victory in order to reintroduce the topic of men's secrets. Unlike their conversation at the beginning of the play, when Prentice spoke theoretically and impersonally about man's relationship to secrets, Prentice and Gittens now reengage one another more as wise, thoughtful peers. Prentice has matured through his interaction with the men at the Club, and he appears ready to begin to speak more directly about himself instead of through the code of the absent woman. Yet Prentice still moves away from complete self-disclosure in favor of waxing philosophical: "[W]hen I'm dead and they open my file box to burn the letters I have there—there will be faint perfume with the smoke. What a pity that letters like that can escape into the light only as essence. And yet—the secrets—are more precious because unshared by a glaring world!" (172).

In this ironic twist, Prentice romanticizes and heightens the essential value of secrets—as written in letters—over spoken truths and fantasies that are known by a "glaring world." While placing value solely on the "essence" of secrets, Prentice undercuts, I think, the deeper insights and connections that he has come to experience through his verbal action. Prentice and Hyacinth's potential happiness actually has two sources: the intimate truths revealed in the absent woman's secret letters, referred to by her lover; and in the lover's articulation of *his* desires (as informed by the absent woman's secrets) to the "glaring world" (which includes her husband). Together, then, written secrets and verbal declaration (or at least the articulation of the effect of those secrets on and by the recipient) prompt the merging of fantasy and reality (albeit in a "precious" way). This merging makes dramatic sense if a character appeals to the glaring world for its understanding of his or her experiences. In fact, this is Prentice's final plea upon receiving Hyacinth's call at play's end.

Hyacinth phones to say that she got out of the house before Sherman arrived and that she is safe at a hotel. "It is the beginning of our happiness," Prentice joyfully exclaims over the phone, alone again in the room (172). Upon merging private secrets (i.e., Hyacinth's letters as well as their telephone calls) and public confessions (i.e., Prentice's disclosures to Sherman), the couple anticipate their release to experience greater freedoms and deeper intimacies with one another. They can now choose which aspects of their relationship are to be private and which public; openly acknowledging the truth of their connection has set them both free to do so.

But the power of the absent woman to influence a man's thoughts and actions remains central to this couple's evolving private and public identity. Dramaturgically, this power motivates narrative desire in the plot. Characterologically, however, it serves to underline an essential paradox in the male character's psychology. On the one hand, the power of the absent woman depends on woman's erasure, since she is not a "real" body in the play; she is, to some extent, a fantasy of male need. On the other hand, the absent woman *is* "embodied" through her dramatically present, "real" offstage voice and its actual influence on the "real" onstage male voice; Hyacinth is reembodied onstage through Prentice's voice—through him, her absence is made present and "real."

Right up to the final line of dialogue, Hyacinth's voice (unheard, of course, by the spectator) elicits a response from Prentice that capsulizes a profound thematic pervasive not only in Gerstenberg's play, but in the male cast canon: "[W]hat dear? Are you *crying*?—Oh, my dear, I'm glad you're crying—Yes dear, some day the world will understand" (172). By repeating the line he just heard from Hyacinth, Prentice not only acknowledges the desires and insights he shares with the absent woman, but he also reiterates *her* actual plea for a culture's "understanding" of that which is coded as unconventional, as Other within the patriarchy. In having a heterosexual male character express his agreement with an absent woman's utmost desire—for the world to understand *her* position, *her* subjectivity—Gerstenberg concludes her male-cast play with a radical choice, both dramaturgically and politically. In Prentice, Gerstenberg created a male character whose personal life is informed by an emerging feminist consciousness. He is capable of speaking about absent women not only as objects, but for them as subjects. This emerging feminist male voice—a substitute for the absent woman's voice—is unique in the history of American drama.

During the nearly fifty years following Gerstenberg's play, male-cast plays perpetuated the misogynistic roles of women. These included the absent woman's representation as articulated object in the non-realist, experimental plays of the 1960s and 1970s, such as in Megan Terry's *Keep Tightly Closed in a Cool Dry Place,* Arthur Kopit's *The Day the Whores Came Out to Play Tennis,* and Sam Shepard's *Geography of a Horse Dreamer.* Some realist male-cast plays of the same period derive their discourse coherence from men who focus on the topic of women as objects, among them Lee Falk's *Eris* and William Inge's *The Call* (the latter foreshadows the trend toward woman as spoken-of subject).

It is not until the late 1970s that male characters begin to evoke the absent woman more frequently as an individual, as anticipated in *At the Club,* rather than in strict adherence to gender codes. While they continue to position her in misogynistic roles, playwrights also begin to introduce male characters who speak convincingly of the absent woman in positive roles: through men's words, she is depicted in a way that corresponds to Case's description of this type of woman character—"independent, intelligent and even heroic" (1988, 6).

If This Isn't Love! Sidney Morris

Sidney Morris's *If This Isn't Love!* is a striking example of the more recent representation of women in male-male dialogue, one that approximates a female subject position, albeit constructed from men's talk. Furthermore, its three-act structure maps out this transformational representation of women as each act occurs not only in a different setting (where the neoclassic unities of time, place, and action are maintained) but also in a different decade: "The Fearful Fifties," "The Seeking Sixties," and "The Succulent Seventies" (Morris 1982, 9, 43, 73).[22] Hence, the movement from the first to the last act depicts the change in men's images of women: from misogynistic roles to positive roles. By discarding absolute adherence to the unities, Morris structures a play that allows male characters to develop over time and thereby to alter the ways in which they speak about women—often, to reflect the shifting societal views toward women's lives within the culture at large.

Sidney Morris has been writing plays since the 1960s, at the beginning of the Off-Off-Broadway movement. Although his works are not widely known, Morris remains a popular, respected writer within the gay community. He is a "generational" playwright, so to speak, as revealed through his passionate emphasis on the links between gay history, gay liberation, and gay pride. *If This Isn't Love!* in particular has enjoyed success countrywide on the gay theater circuit, perhaps for the audiences' shared concern with the playwright's passions. A pre-AIDS play, *If This Isn't Love!* is the romantic story of a gay couple's relationship over three decades: from their first private meeting, in which they "come out" to one another, to a celebration on Gay Pride Day of their twenty-year commitment. Adam and Eric's relationship is profoundly shaped by the degree of female presence in their lives. The key women for the men are Adam's Jewish mother and his alleged girlfriends; Eric's Irish Catholic mother; his sister, Ana; and his "girlfriend" Catherine. In the spirit of Gerstenberg's Prentice, each of Morris's men embodies a "female" presence as a counterposition to the other man's "male" authority (this occurs less, however, as the play progresses, which is to say, as the men mature). Often, this embodiment acknowledges the depth of psychological, societal impact that a particular absent woman has had on the life of one of the men. Unlike Gerstenberg's Prentice, however, Morris's men initially appropriate the voice of the Other, of the absent woman, as a way to come to accept their own "other" voices. This occurs not as an effort to unite with her or to complement her, but rather as a device by which they can learn from her as well as separate from her. Eric, in particular, becomes like the absent woman (or, rather, he mimics his fantasy of her), acknowledging her impact on his development and bestowing upon her, paradoxically, more power to be herself through his eventual separation from her. Hence, otherness exists in various forms in the play: the Other (coded as female) is "present" through Eric's expressed wish to *be* the Other; and the "other" (coded as unmasculine) is present through the gay men, Eric and Adam.

The unusual historical sweep of *If This Isn't Love!* (unique in the male-cast canon)[23] captures two critical phenomena: first, a vision of woman as subject, a direct response to contemporary feminism; and second, a more complete depiction of the evolution of the absent woman from Virgin/Goddess, Bitch, and Vamp, to Hero. Although act 1 takes place in the 1950s, the men speak about women in each of these roles. For this reason the discourse coherence of act 1 is, in fact, a microcosm of the entire play's depiction of the absent woman. An examination of the first act, therefore, establishes the pattern Morris relies upon in constructing dialogue in the play's remaining acts.

In act 1, Morris captures the dynamics of a coded, social dialogue in which some gay men might engage as they seek out the company of other gays. Morris identifies this language as part of a pre-Stonewall, pre-gay-liberation social milieu—one that sounds sweetly innocent, yet slightly desperate. It is certainly not, in its tentativeness and evasiveness, the language of youth who are coming of age during the 1990s in the radical gay movements of ACT-UP and Queer Nation. In Morris's text, eighteen-year-old Adam invites his classmate, Eric, over to his Lower East Side apartment in Manhattan to tutor him in their night high school English course. The boys plan to study vocabulary lists for school. The boys are also together to struggle to identify a common vocabulary—a language—that will allow them to speak truthfully to one another, to name their sexual identities through words.

Adam's immediate reason for inviting Eric to study is to tell the young man of his infatuation with him—after he has confirmed that Eric is indeed gay. Eric, unbeknown to Adam, has the same intention. Thus, act 1 is filled with layers of innuendoes that take on, in language, an attack and retreat quality as the traditional notions of masculinity are played out or talked out, even though they are undermined by the boys' erotic desires. For this reason, there is a slight shift in the conventional definition of social dialogue as these men engage each other; each one is conscious of his desire to speak personally as he perpetuates the social dialogue.

Since this is the first play in this study to feature minority characters, a few observations are immediately relevant. It is critical to acknowledge that, in general, the semiotic priorities that hold true for white straight characters also hold true for dialogue between gays or straight men of color. The specificity of diverse features that define individual characters (such as sexual orientation, race, or religion) does not immediately alter the dynamics of men's talk; nor does the context within which they converse, unless they are in an institutional setting. Regardless of the extent of their desire for self-disclosing dialogue, male characters still adhere to a general pattern of topic selection, whereby they first engage social and then personal dialogue; usually some form of verbal or physical violence separates the two dialogues. Within this semiotic and thematic schema, gay men among themselves, African American men among themselves, or straight white men among themselves, for example, are not automatically dissimilar groups—all are men united, initially, in a presumably undifferentiated subjectivity. All are subject to the semiotic of maleness.

Consider, for example, Adam's topical tactics during social dialogue with Eric. Early on in their conversation, Adam alludes to homosexual lore and icons (such as Tchaikovsky, Walt Whitman, Tennessee Williams, and Milton Berle) and exaggerates (that is, "camps up") his behavior as a way to elicit a possible telling response from Eric. Eric, on the other hand, evades reactions that would reveal a gay identity, let alone gay sensibility. Each is uncertain of the other's sexual identity. Between men, such lack of knowledge heightens tension since neither can guarantee his role as subject and its accompanying conversational boundaries. Social dialogue, therefore, initially preserves their status as subjects. For each to perceive (possibly) the other as object is to create a strikingly different dynamic between males—one that obliterates the gender-coded criteria for the boundaries of proper male interaction that dominate the American masculine ethos.

As their dialogue continues, Adam remains aggressive, alert, self-assured, and on the prowl; Eric is passive, sensitive, a bit fearful, and uncertain of Adam's motivations in pursuing him so aggressively. After this pattern is established, a shift begins in their otherwise subject-to-subject relationship. Their identities become more encoded: Adam becomes a promiscuous male "butch" (a role he belies with his initially campy interaction), while Eric, the Eve of Adam's story, becomes a shy, virginal "femme" (not unlike the Virgin in Case's identification of women's roles). Their social dialogue evolves into a masculine/feminine model of behavior, one that assumes the existence of an embodied, "encoded" female presence within the male-male interaction. Such a model is distinct from the conventional same-sex model of male-cast plays, which assumes the absence of the female.[24]

However, absent mothers—and particularly Eric's—initially motivate the men in their cat-and-mouse encounter of act 1. The authority of the absent woman is most obvious in Eric's dialogue, as he perceives that his role is to be like his own mother. In act 2, however, Eric will actually express his awareness of his "Mom-like" behavioral pattern. Once he names it, he consciously works toward breaking it.

To emphasize the ongoing presence of Eric's mother in her son's life, act 1 begins and ends with a phone call to his mother. The act is framed by the intrusion of the absent woman; like Hyacinth in Gerstenberg's *At the Club,* she affects the immediate action through her telephone presence. Eric initially calls to tell his mother that he will be home late from Adam's apartment. He later retracts that message, announcing to her that he will not be home that evening. Between these two phone calls Adam pursues cautious Eric, breaking down his tie to his mother.[25] That tie is clearly represented in Eric's verbal exchange with Adam. Eric answers Adam as he anticipates his mother would answer, since she is the object model by which he understands male subjectivity. Eric sees himself not as subject in his interaction with Adam, but as object. He wants to be the object of Adam's sexual desire and to be pursued as such. What better way, therefore, for this boy of the 1950s to understand his attraction to men than to subvert his own identity as a male subject (a not unfamiliar device in gay drama) in order to assume a "female" presence. This posturing is informed by his perceptions of the absent woman's (heterosexual) identity, one who is sanctioned by society as the sole object of men's desire. From his youthful, dualist perspective, becoming more "womanly" is the way to connect sexually with another man—the way to be homosexual. This appears also to be Morris's vision of how many gays in the pre-Stonewall "Fearful Fifties" came to understand their sexuality.

In the course of their social dialogue in act 1, Adam and Eric discuss their current jobs (Western Union messenger and secretary, respectively) and their dream jobs (wealthy actor and teacher). Eric refers to his mother with reverence, as Goddesslike; she stays at home and takes care of her developmentally disabled daughter, Ana. Eric works to support the home he shares with them; he takes on the role of the breadwinning father. Yet, as the impressionable child that he is, Eric adopts his mother's values with Adam. He goes so far as to refuse to borrow Adam's copy of *Cat on a Hot Tin Roof* because, as he unhesitatingly remarks, "It's not the kind of book I'd want my mother to see" (20).

Adam, on the other hand, adamantly refuses to talk about his mother, a Bitch-Witch. Instead, he brings up the topic of homosexuality, keeping his remarks impersonal: so-and-so famous person is gay; McCarthy is after Jews, blacks, and gays; gay men often marry to avoid coming out of the closet. Eric feigns ignorance of these issues yet lets slip one coded exception: "Maybe those [gay] guys get married because they think there are no other men in the world like them" (20).

Noticing that Eric is more revealing when he speaks of absent women—a pattern in the play's discourse coherence—Adam asks his new friend to talk more about Ana. Of course, Adam has a hidden agenda; all his replies lead back to gay life. He moves from Ana's condition, for example, to doctors' opinions about homosexuals. After each of Adam's "gay" digressions, Eric resolutely returns the subject back to his sister. Determined, however, to leave no stone unturned in his quest to identify Eric's sexuality, Adam announces that he does not want children. In a fleeting moment of self-disclosure, Adam openly rejects a major tenet of the masculine ethos; explicitly he will not procreate, implicitly not marry. His candidness remains a ruse, nonetheless, by which he hopes to force Eric to reveal his own relationship to conventional male codings. Still evasive, Eric "thinks" he would like kids, but he is not sure. "I hate sounding mysterious" (25), Eric concedes, his first hint that he may have some personal secret.

A common sign, in male-cast drama, of a character's (alleged) homosexuality is his hesitation to discuss a common topic of the social dialogue: the institution of heterosexual marriage and its attendant assumptions about child-rearing. The characters' dancing around this issue—essentially the naming of one's sexuality—becomes the main dramatic tension in many straight and gay male-cast plays. However, when Adam hears hesitation in Eric's talk about parenting, he responds boldly and provocatively, introducing the personal subject of their bodies. A straight character rarely speaks of, or deliberately exhibits, his body, because to do so is to risk homoerotic desire. Such a risk pushes the discourse from the social to the personal level of communication.

After each complements the other on his "beautiful" and "handsome" body, Adam decides to "get into something comfortable" (25–26). Because Eric is nervous and intimidated by the ease with which Adam exhibits his body, and because his motivations for doing so still confuse Eric, Eric is anxious to perpetuate social dialogue. Adam, on the other hand, who has pursued personal interaction with moderate success, momentarily dispenses with words in favor of seductive body language. He allows his body to do his flirtatious talking for him as he "strips down to his shorts, revealing a compact body" (27). Then, in a gesture inspired by teasing cross-dressing, Adam puts on a "lovely, short, short robe," discarding his work uniform (a sign not only of his class, but of his passable heterosexual identity in the dominant culture) in favor of a sign of his "other" self. This ceremonial redressing prompts Adam to associate a cultural stereotype that he hopes will signal more boldly his own gayness: "You ever hear—*Milton Berle* is gay?... I never saw an actor put on so much drag."

Eric: Drag?
Adam: Putting on women's clothes.
Eric: Drag! Sounds like a dirty word. Why use such a dirty word to talk about women?
Adam: I have good legs! [*Shows off his legs.*]
Eric: [*Hushed.*] Yes—

(27)

Adam relies upon layered meanings of social dialogue to be distinguished by his listener; each layer is coded with patriarchal meanings that are to be subverted, recoded with personal, homoerotic, antipatriarchal significance. To decode the meaning, one must be aware not only of the social position of the female, but of the antipatriarchal significance of the subject's appropriation of the woman's position. This performative inversion of subject/object positioning allows the male to embody—behaviorally as well as metaphorically—the Other. By commenting upon and invoking the spirit and aesthetic of drag by "putting on" his revealing, feminine robe, Adam transgresses the boundaries of culturally acceptable male behavior. He displaces the function of the absent woman by redefining subject-object relations: Adam appropriates the absent woman's sociosexual role as object of male desire to claim his otherness yet he remains a subject by virtue of being a male first, and gay second. He will always be likened to the female as Other in his nontraditional male or gay otherness, but he will never *be* female because he is still a male subject. This is a transgressive act that Adam implicitly invites Eric to share. Eric still does not understand how to decode Adam's efforts, but Adam escalates the sexual tension between the two men, a tension that Eric and Adam have yet to decode together and to face honestly in their dialogue.

The conversational topic and the exhibition of the male body are catalysts for what now occurs. These stimuli provoke two cycles of interaction, each with the following pattern: first the men evoke absent women in social dialogue, then a "violent" dynamic erupts in their talk, stimulating a metalinguistic exchange, which ends by a reference to an absent woman. The cycle stops only when a character breaks through *two* codes: the code of socially acceptable (i.e., heterosexual) male behavior; and its antecedent, a kind of anticode that supports gay behavior and choice but obscures self-disclosure. Such a breakthrough occurs only if a character takes the risk to utter personal truths, truths he knows may be rejected by a (potentially homophobic) listener.

Dressed in his revealing robe, Adam volunteers to take Eric to Greenwich Village some Saturday night where he can see "*all* the gay guys" (28). Personalizing his remarks by suggesting that Eric may harbor unspoken desires—the "I" will guide "you" offer—Adam sets off the first cycle of evasive communication: Eric retreats from the offer by bringing up another absent woman, his girlfriend Catherine. Adam responds in kind, referring to all the girls in the theater whom he dates. Frustrated by the introduction of these new absent women and the assumption that each man has been intimate with them, both start to yell at one another. Escaping into his anticode, Adam explodes: "You won't drop one lousy hairpin. Damn it! Maybe you don't have any hairpins to drop." Eric angrily responds that he will leave if Adam continues "to talk in code" (30).

In many straight plays, this might well have been the moment when fists start swinging. But, like some of Mamet's men, Morris's characters respond to potential violence by discussing their need to talk and their impression of the act of talking. They slip momentarily into a metalinguistic exchange. Unlike Mamet's characters, however, Morris's men eventually break through that impasse to engage personal dialogue:

Adam: All words have two meanings for me.
Eric: How do you ever believe what anyone ever tells you?
Adam: Tell me something upfront—about you, about me, and see if I believe you! . . .
Eric: *I don't know what you want from me!* . . . All night

you've been asking funny questions—putting down—
hinting at—

(31)

The initial conversational cycle ends as the boys complete their
talk about talk only to return to the familiar but now problematic
topic of the absent woman. Their metalinguistic interaction, nonetheless, is primed to repeat itself.

Anxious to break this cycle, Adam reintroduces a general but
personal topic, one less confrontational than his invitation to take
Eric on a tour of gay New York: "You don't understand from love,
and you don't understand from hate. What about sex?" (33). Eric
still hears Adam's "funny questions" as a threatening affront (31).
Recalling Eric's ease when discussing absent women, Adam spurs
Eric on to talk about his sexual activity with Catherine. Eric does
so, braggingly, but his remarks regress into hostility. He shouts at
Adam to confess his own relations with absent women: "What girl
did you screw last? How many times did you shoot? . . . Did it make
you feel like a real man?" (34). This fleeting verbal assault, followed
by Adam's grabbing Eric to keep him from leaving, combine as the
"violent" instant that gives way to this second cycle's metalinguistic moment. "Talk to me!" Adam demands. "Don't go away mad!"
(35). The cycle ends as Eric takes the risk to respond frankly to
Adam's call for personal dialogue. He relinquishes control to his
listener, control over their verbal interaction: Adam is now in the
position to accept or reject Eric's personal dialogue; his response
will either initiate further personal dialogue or insist upon a return
to social dialogue.

Eric refuses to speak in or tolerate code, and his subsequent
personal speech is pivotal in act 1 for both structure and content.
Structurally, it signals the swiftly approaching conclusion to the
men's conversation, because such self-disclosure was the driving
force behind the men's immediate interaction. The men break
through the barrier of absent women as topic to engage another
level of discourse coherence. In respect to the content, Eric now
articulates directly his "otherness," that which he was reluctant to
do from the moment the men began to interact. "You questioned—
if I was a man!" Eric asserts, "You wanted to know if I was a
homosexual! . . . (Shouting.) Well, I don't give a fuck if you do
know! So there!" (35). Here, Eric names himself a gay man, the
embodiment of the antithesis of the masculine ethos. Eric does not
register, however, Adam's now direct response, "I'm on your side!"

(36). Instead, Eric opens a floodgate of private confessions about his virginal life as a gay male. He is hypersensitive to others' knowledge of his sexuality because he anticipates persecution from a homophobic culture. He is never more vulnerable to that rejection than when he blurts out to Adam, "I love you. . . . [But you're] someone who can't love me back!" (38). It is an astoundingly direct admission even for a naive and, yes, repressed young man. Eric has been so misled by Adam's anticode that he heard not a disguised invitation to solidarity and community with another gay male, but debasement and gay-baiting. Coded language has kept Adam from personal disclosure.

Eric's admission prompts Adam to abandon language to convey his feelings. He does not want any additional misinterpretation of his intentions. Consequently, the two men immediately embrace and kiss passionately. They dispense with verbal language in favor of body talk. Once *nonviolent* contact between bodies occurs, the dynamics of the men's interaction alters drastically. Often, men can trust their relationship with other men only after they are convinced of the boundaries of their relationship, specifically, whether they are defined homosocially or homoerotically.[26] When the societal barriers imposed upon the male body are transgressed and the boundaries of the body redefined and particularized (that is, when a man clearly acknowledges his body's relationship to its own erotic desires), male characters, regardless of their sexual orientation, usually ease into personal dialogue.

For Adam and Eric, the erotic connection of their bodies initiates their deeply desired trust in one another. This trust persuades them to reengage language, now as an extension of their intimacy rather than as a weapon of their denial. Their personal dialogue, therefore, is filled with swift confessions about their past histories. Each man is eager to share confidential details about himself, details he has desperately wanted to release from the beginning of their conversation. This outpouring of pressing demons serves to get the facts about one's self out as quickly as possible, so that each enters the relationship with fuller knowledge of the other person. Love, for Morris's characters, is based upon individuals' trust in and regard for the truthfulness of mutual self-disclosures.

Amid the joy of the men's amorous bonding, act 1 concludes with a dramatic return to the broadening influence of the absent woman. In relationship to one another, each man takes on the role of the "other," a kind of metaphoric, drag rendition of the roles assigned to the absent woman. Eric is the male Virgin/Goddess, an eager object at this point, ready to embrace a misogynistic role available to him within the alternative ethos of his marginal culture. Adam is the renegade, the male Vamp who not only sleeps around, but who also is on probation for his disregard of patriarchal law (it turns out that he is the victim of police entrapment for sodomy).[27] Despite his "anger and humiliation" at this affront to his personal identity (40), Adam remains not only the subject of his own actions, but the object of desire for other gay men.

Eric and Adam are unconscious of the extent to which they embody roles *in relation to one another* that are similar to the roles they accord absent women. Eric, a Virgin/Goddess, thinks of his mother as a Goddess; Adam, a "traitor" Vamp, sees his mother as a Bitch, the one who does not adhere to the strictures of passive motherhood within patriarchal culture—after all, he claims, he is free to be himself only because she "kicked [him] out of her house" because she "couldn't stand" having a gay son (42). More than a hint of misogyny underlies Adam's remarks; he also links himself to *her* outsider status as Other. Each man initially meets the other in a manner informed by his identification with his mother. Act 1 dramatizes the profound influence of this symbiotic connection between a man and an absent woman, here between some gay sons and their mothers. It also highlights the ways in which a man begins to differentiate his own identity from that of the absent woman, and to reassess her influence on his self-development.

Act 1 ends with Eric taking the first crucial step to separate from the absent woman. He calls to tell his mother that he will not be returning to her house that night, but instead will stay at Adam's home. Like Gerstenberg's Prentice, he is willing to risk becoming a traitor to his Goddess mother and to patriarchal culture (as Adam reminds the young man, "What we do here—you can go to jail for it" [42]). Eric's final words of the act—"I won't be coming home tonight!"—signal not only the initial differentiation between the absent woman and her son, but also the possibility for other homes—homes created between men—as alternatives to homes in accord with the masculine ethos.

While the construction of home is a principal theme in the personal dialogue of men throughout the male-cast canon, it becomes a particularly vivid, engrossing focus when it surfaces in the personal dialogue of gay characters who are a "family." Acts 2 and 3 of *If This Isn't Love!* dramatize the conflicts that arise as two men establish their home together—but two men whose sense of relating to one another is still deeply influenced by the heterosexual Adam-and-Eve model. Adam is the husband and Eric his wife (51, 60). Their standard of conversation remains personal dialogue as "[t]hey chatter away at one another—a typical long-married couple" (43).[28] Imagined by the men in positive roles, absent women nonetheless continue to inform the topics of the lovers' conversations and the dynamics of their intimacies. Since the conversations in the remaining acts are no longer restricted, it is unnecessary to analyze their dialogue for shifting semiotic dynamics of discourse coherence. However, it is useful to note how the image of the absent woman shifts from misogynistic roles to positive ones.

In act 2, which occurs during the 1960s, Eric has transformed from a man who used to "identify with a certain kind of a woman" (the Virgin/Goddess type) to a man who emulates the liberated woman—like his mother and Betty Friedan—who rejects the "playing out of stupid roles" (66). As in act 1, Eric models his behavior toward another man after absent women, whom he now images as independent persons who resist gender codings. Adam, on the other hand, "never identified with women," which explains his adherence to rigid gender-coded roles that have come to characterize his relationship with Eric. The men's relationship is tense and uncomfortable at the end of act 2, as each now operates under a different code in his gendered identity.

Morris frames act 3 with the "presence" of the men's absent mothers. It is Gay Pride Day in the 1970s: Adam is a successful, closeted actor; Eric, a gay and feminist advocate who, nonetheless, is still closeted at the school where he teaches. The men's unresolved relationships with their mothers are the final factor keeping them from fully accepting their identities as gay men. For Adam, all women still embody misogynistic roles and are homophobic; this is how he judges his deceased mother, the "Bitch" Bessie. Therefore, Adam persistently identifies his idea of manhood from a gender-coded, misogynist's position. Underlying his stringent perspective is, of course, his own homophobia. Eric remains proud of his mother's achievements, but he still is unable to accept that her confident openness in her self-identity is a true model for the liberation and declaration of his own identity.

The act begins with Adam reading a letter from Bessie, her ethical will; it was written a year earlier, and she has since died. The sheer power of the dead woman's words compel Adam to transform his image of her. Her words also force Adam to confront his own buried truths: "I wasn't a good mother," she writes, "but *you* were not a good son. . . . I mean the lie you told yourself. . . . I kicked you out of the house. . . . All I said was try to change from loving boys. I never said I didn't want you any more if you didn't change" (85). Bessie reconstructs herself through language into a positive role—as a loving, independent thinking and feeling person. Her language frees Adam to accept his own truths. Admitting her complexities and willing to accept herself and Adam as they are, Bessie invites her son to do the same. At the close of act 3, Adam rises to the challenge so boldly written by the absent woman.

The play ends with a surprise that Eric has for Adam. As the two men watch the Gay Pride parade from their balcony, Eric points out his mother, who is marching behind the "Parents of Gays" banner. As the two men shout out their names to her on the streets below, they proclaim publicly their own identities. Encouraged by her model, the men, too, find the strength to claim their own names—to claim their independence. It is pivotal that the woman's offstage, political "presence"—and the men's desire to connect with her—validate the lives of the onstage male characters. Through their evocation of the independent, heroic woman and her public actions, the men hint at their own increasingly heroic stature. They come to understand, through the absent woman, the urgency of their own personal drive toward self-acceptance and self-definition. In doing so, they also solidify their relationship as family for one another: a family defined in unconventional terms, but a paradigm nonetheless.

It is striking that within this specialized subgenre of male-cast plays, twentieth-century playwrights have increasingly created male characters who represent offstage women's lives as dynamic, changing entities. This is true of plays written both before and after the emergence of contemporary feminism. Yet male characters, in general, have become increasingly static in their behavior, perceptions, and activity—particularly in their (in)ability to respond to female dynamism. Eric and Adam are exceptions to this trend, as was Gerstenberg's Prentice nearly sixty years earlier. Male characters, in other words, have become increasingly dependent upon their response to (and representation of) the more organically conceived female identity as they engage the task of shaping their own male identities—their own subjectivities and masculinities. This dramaturgical feature is certainly linked to the material absence of women from the all-male setting: in plays written after the rise of contemporary feminism, men usually make woman less of a stereotype (an Other) and more of a symbol of change, a subject. In her place, male characters increasingly position "other" men as objects in their talk exchanges.

Two

Silence, Violence, and the Drama of Abuse

Male characters among themselves initially speak about the self through topics outside the self. From premodern to contemporary and postmodern playwriting, from Gerstenberg's *At the Club* to Mamet's *Glengarry Glen Ross,* American realist male-cast plays foreground topics defined by American male mythologies and absent women. As chapter 1 illustrates, male characters communicate successfully on these topics; that is, they connect to each other through cooperative talk exchanges. As culturally coded American men, they relate information about themselves through relatively impersonal means, by speaking about their "masculine" activities and about their relationships with offstage women. This strategy bonds the men socially but keeps them personally apart in their gender-role placement, coded expectations, and accomplishments. Such placement within our patriarchal society serves to distinguish men's from women's lives. Such expectations pressure men to succeed within a competitive, goal-oriented culture. And finally, such accomplishments indicate men's need to maintain a socially acceptable context within which to identify themselves, even if it misrepresents or opposes their actual achievements and desires.

In pointed contrast to the plays analyzed in the previous chapter, this section focuses on male-cast plays in which characters either have difficulty connecting and creating a text or have come to rely upon verbal or physical abuse as their text. Either way, these plays, to varying degrees, present male characters whose communication is essentially imbalanced, disconnected, uncooperative. Their dialogue is disordered, as abusive talk or disruptive behavior interfers with their exchange.

I will be focusing on three plays as paradigmatic of this communicative breakdown: Eugene O'Neill's *Hughie,* Amiri Baraka's (formerly LeRoi Jones) *The Toilet,* and Edward Albee's *The Zoo Story.*[1] It is significant that all three dramatize instances of male-male interaction that dismiss masculine mythologies and women as suitable themes for sustained conversation. However, no other agreeable themes surface to be shared, a fact reflected in the plays' discourse coherence. Either the discourse coherence advances within monologues (rather than in talk exchanges) or it is altogether absent, replaced by a pseudotext of verbal or physical violence or both. The structures of the plays realize distinct manifestations of uncooperative communication among men. Furthermore, these texts are striking examples of a phenomenon that haunts the canon: male violence.

Exemplified by *Hughie* and *The Zoo Story,* the naturalist play that dramatizes men's uncooperative communication is typically cast with two characters who are strangers to one another.[2] The greater the number of men (strangers or not) who are present on stage, the more likely it is that they will communicate cooperatively. They will do so, however, by limiting their interaction to impersonal dialogue. Conversely, when two men are alone with one another, their interaction seldom remains on the level of social dialogue. Perhaps the immediacy and potential intimacy of onstage one-to-one confrontations heightens, challenges, and exposes the limitations of a character's allegiance to the masculine ethos. Often the artificial, impersonal patter that characterizes social dialogue becomes more conspicuous in two-character interaction. Characters sense their vulnerability to its posturing and usually become self-conscious of their behavior. As a result, two men who are engaged in sustained talk often progress through social dialogue to other levels of interaction, generally characterized at first by the tensions of uncooperative communication.

Most of the plays that are paradigms of males' uncooperative communication are one-acts: the brief, unepisodic time frame lends itself especially well to capsulizing such stasis. These specialized one-act male-cast plays follow a similar progression in charting the dynamic of men's uncooperative communication on verbal and nonverbal levels, as I will briefly summarize.

Initially, a speaker offers his past, present, or future associations to the male ethos as topics of conversation. These topics share the central themes of the American masculine mythologies and absent women. The men's social dialogue, however, cannot sustain a series of shared messages. Their talk exchange is limited to a question and answer or observation and comment format that does not develop into an agreeable topic. Eventually, the central speaker makes his intentions more obvious (e.g., to give or to get information, to entertain, to gesture socially, to solve problems, or to relate feelings); his possible intentions become clearer at least to the spectator, if not immediately to the listener or to the speaker himself. This clarity occurs as the speaker selects more self-disclosing topics, thereby indicating his willingness to assume personal responsibility for their communicative interaction. Regardless of the listener's response, the speaker usually undermines the context (i.e., the circumstances under which the men are conversing and their relationship to one another) and the accuracy of any of his presuppositions. Determined to maintain at least the illusion of shared personal dialogue, the speaker then often engages in extended monologues.

During this process, the listener is not affected by the intentions behind the speaker's self-disclosures, since they are either impolite, are of no interest, or remain unclear. As the speaker's personal dialogue increases, the listener becomes more silent. Usually, the listener does not want to share in the speaker's topic, yet he is subjected to it simply by remaining in the speaker's presence. It can be argued that, more often than not, the listener's *sustained* silence in a male-cast play is *intended* as an abusive, even somewhat "violent" response to the other man's personal dialogue. Such a listener relinquishes any responsibility to share in the creation of a culturally or personally defined text. His lack of cooperation is an aggressive response against interpersonal communication. This dynamic can be overcome only through the listener's reengagement of dialogue with the speaker or by a participant's departure from their shared space.

In effect, the speaker and listener resolve their communication imbalance through the creation or obliteration of a text. If the men create a text, one of the characters reintroduces a previously discussed theme (i.e., masculine mythologies or absent women) within which agreeable topics surface. Resuming social dialogue, the characters assume a kind of responsibility for one another as they connect as Men. By dramatizing this level of communicative dynamics as its resolution, *Hughie* concludes similarly to *Glengarry Glen Ross*.

On the other hand, men create an alternative context if one or more of the males terminates, or perhaps sustains, their noncommunicative state through abusive, violent verbal behavior that overwhelms any possibility of regularity, reciprocity, and cooperation

in creating a text. As in *The Toilet,* some men choose an uncooperative dialogue that is intended to be violent and noncommunicative.

If the men fail to create a text, some form of violent, nonverbal
physical behavior is expressed by the speaker or listener or both.
This action effectively precludes any possible verbal communication between them. Consequently, the men fail to accept either
social or personal responsibility for one another since their circumstances make it impossible for them to create a shared text. This
process is manifested in *The Zoo Story* and *The Toilet.*

Hughie, Eugene O'Neill

Written in 1940, *Hughie* is the first critically acclaimed American
male-cast play that utilizes uncooperative communication as its
source of dramatic form and content. Ruby Cohn claims that
Hughie is also the only unqualified masterpiece among O'Neill's
forty-six published plays (67). In its pervasive use of silence,
Hughie is atypical for a male-cast play in American drama. Very
few such plays represent, let alone sustain, silence.[3] Silence creates
too threatening a dramatic space for American males to negotiate;
they would rather talk or fight among themselves than experience
silence.

From the spectator's perspective, *Hughie* is a classic example
of American realism. Set in the lobby of a third-class, New York
hotel in 1928, *Hughie* is faithful to the neoclassical unities of time,
place, and action. Erie Smith, a hotel resident, is a small-fry gambler and horse player. He has now sobered up after a several days'
drunk following the burial of his friend and the hotel's former desk
clerk, Hughie. It's 3:00 A.M. as Erie comes upon Charlie Hughes, the
new night clerk.

The tension between the two men is obvious: Erie tries desperately to engage Charlie in conversation while the desk clerk wants
only to "sit down and listen to the noises in the street and think
about nothing" (O'Neill 1967, 267),[4] not an unreasonable wish,
considering the late hour. Nonetheless, one man wants to talk, to
be heard, to connect; the other wants to be isolated with his
thoughts.

In structure, *Hughie* is two distinct plays, one the verbal, external, realist text, the other the nonverbal, interior monologue. The
realist play is manifest in the speakers' onstage dialogue; the interior monologue—a "psychological" text—surfaces in O'Neill's rich,

descriptive stage directions, which reveal the characters' thoughts.[5] As the roles of speaker and listener become defined and consistent in the audible script, the texts of the two plays take on distinct characteristics.

In the realist text, Erie, "a teller of tales" (261), tries to engage Charlie in topics related to the masculine ethos. Failing to do so, he eventually monopolizes the stage through stream-of-consciousness monologues. The discourse coherence of these monologues mirrors the progression of topics typical of male-cast plays. Charlie, a passive listener in the realist play, experiences himself as the active speaker in a stream-of-consciousness interior monologue. To the spectator, the realist play exists because he or she can hear Erie's words; Charlie's psychological drama is much less evident. Without consulting a script, few would be aware of the extent to which O'Neill provides an onstage inner life for Charlie, including actual (or "mental") dialogue that is never spoken. Because of their intricate relationship to one another, each text must be analyzed in conjunction with the other, as well as independently, if the dynamics of communication are to be revealed fully. Each text simultaneously affects the form as well as the content, or discourse coherence, of the other.

Erie's conversational hook is man-to-man talk on topics selected from the American masculine ethos: jobs (gambling, horse racing, clerking), women or "dolls," marriage, and children. Refusing to pick up on these topics, Charlie eventually punctuates Erie's "expectant silence[s]" (270) with a token "yes" or "no." When he gives an answer at greater length, he "wonders sadly why he took the trouble to make it" (268). Charlie has "[l]ong experience with guests who stop at his desk in the small hours to talk about themselves [which] has given him a foolproof technique of self-defense. He appears to listen with agreeable submissiveness and be impressed, but his mind is blank and he doesn't hear unless a direct question is put to him, and sometimes not even then" (266). Charlie "wishes [Erie] would stop talking" (267), since he knows that social dialogue leads into the dreaded verbal onslaught, "The Guest's Story of His Life" (269). Charlie retreats further into the noncommunicative privacy of his interior monologue as Erie attempts to advance their dialogue in the realist text.

Charlie's silence is the most influential element of structure in *Hughie*. Leslie Kane suggests that "[s]ilence, like speech, is interrelational and manipulative. Nonparticipation in the speech act does not constitute nonparticipation in the social act" (20). Yet, in its

intentions and effect, Charlie's unwillingness to communicate is
also an obstruction to interaction, a rejection of one-to-one verbal
involvement and its responsibilities. The clerk, nevertheless, still
exercises a range of powers. By denying Erie the power to stimulate
conversation, Charlie frees himself to interact with a third presence—the offstage sounds of night. Stimulated by realistic clang-
ings, roarings, and wailings, Charlie imagines that he is banging
garbage cans, riding in ambulances and fire engines, questioning
doctors and firemen. Perceiving interaction with Erie as limited,
Charlie prefers the options available in his mind. Like Erie, Charlie
wants some type of power, but he chooses not to discover it
through immediate one-to-one dialogue.

As the fleeting moments of cooperative communication between the two men diminish, Erie becomes more aggrieved at their
inability to sustain social dialogue. Time and again, Erie waits to
no avail for the Night Clerk's approval after his stories of women
or race horses. As both men become more certain of the limits of
their interaction, they also become more engulfed in isolated roles
within the realist text. Each also becomes firmer in his intentions,
dooming their communicative relationship.

O'Neill relies upon physical movement in the realist play to
foreshadow shifts in the dialogue's topics. Resigned to the limitations of their social dialogue, Erie turns to leave the lobby to go to
his room. But knowing that he will "just lie there worrying" in bed
about his string of bad luck (272), he returns to the clerk's desk.
Trying a different approach with Charlie and being more responsive to his own lingering grief over the death of Hughie, Erie now
introduces a more "confidential" topic—the private life of the absent Hughie. Throughout the play, Erie responds to his own movement back toward the desk as an impetus to advance the discourse
coherence away from the social to the more personal. He initiates
this progression despite Charlie's increasing lack of interest.

Back at the lobby desk, Erie speaks of his dead friend, Hughie.
Erie's progression toward self-disclosure at this point is in line with
the discourse coherence in other male-cast plays. "I'm still carrying
the torch for Hughie," he admits, "I guess I'd got to like him a lot"
(273). Erie intends to speak about him whether Charlie listens or
not. He is direct and only a bit selfish in insisting that tales from
Hughie's social and personal life be his sole conversational topic.
As his monologues lengthen, however, Erie loses his commitment
to cooperative interchange. Unwilling to further pursue shared dialogue with the unresponsive Charlie, Erie becomes as disconnected

from his listener as the listener has been from him. Charlie's silences, which stifle communicative interaction, liberate Erie's personal monologues. One man feels freer to speak intimately knowing that the other man is not listening.

Just as the men in *Glengarry Glen Ross, At the Club,* and *If This Isn't Love!* reveal much about themselves through their comments on absent women, so Erie discloses private sides of himself through his tales of the absent Hughie. Erie's recollections reveal foremost the contrasting roles the two men assumed in one another's company. Since Hughie was a "sucker" who "didn't run in [Erie's] class," Erie wants no "misunderstanding" about the nature of their relationship (273). For instance, upon realizing that quiet, unassuming Hughie would believe anything, Erie manipulated him by adopting the metatheatrics of patriarchal authority figures: Erie was the father to Hughie's son, a "Wise Guy" to his "dumb, simple guy" (276), an aficionado to his novice, an Uncle Ben to his Willy Loman. Assuming the role of the worldly man, Erie gladly initiated Hughie through masculine rites of cheap women, gambling, and the excitement of the racetrack. Such rituals served to validate Erie's own existence as well as to demonstrate his power to affect another man's life, to "restructure Hughie" as "each man modified the other's identity" (S. Smith 176). In the tone of his recollections, Erie conveys a still fresh sense of the usefulness, confidence, adoration, and virility he felt in Hughie's company. As Erie says to Charlie, "Hughie was as big a dope as you until I give him some interest in life" (280). But Charlie chooses not to make such connections. He is not listening to Erie.

Although he fails to involve Charlie with tales of his influence over Hughie, Erie is "well wound up now and goes on without noticing that the Night Clerk's mind has left the premises in his sole custody" (277). Forfeiting any social responsibility to create a text with Charlie, Erie has commited to a monologue whose discourse coherence fixes on the subject of Hughie. As Erie's monologues begin to dominate the stage's verbal action in parallel to Charlie's interior monologues, Erie's narrative becomes more intimate. He is now at liberty to say anything he wants without fear of being judged. What becomes clearer to the spectator, however, is that Erie casts Hughie and himself in the roles of quasi lovers.

While nothing in the text indicates that Hughie and Erie were sexually attracted to one another, there is evidence that the two men courted one another's friendship in a manner associated with romance. Referring to their initial encounters, Erie notes that

Hughie "wouldn't open up...like he couldn't think of nothin' about himself worth saying" (278). Yet, relentlessly pursuing him with his nightly visits and stories, Erie succeeded in breaking down the clerk's defenses. As Erie remarks, the clerk "got friendly and talked" about his childhood, hometown, jobs, marriage, wife, children, and "Old Man Success." Infatuated with Erie and his unbridled machismo, Hughie invited Erie home for dinner, as if on a first date, to meet the family. But the gambler failed to win over Hughie's strict, narrow-minded wife, Irma, who "tagged [him] for a bum" and a "bad influence." "I coulda liked her—a little," Erie says, "if she'd give me a chance" (279, 280).

As outcasts from Hughie's home, the two men created an alternative sanctuary around the lobby desk—away from the absent woman and outside of, or rather "within the structural context of triangular, heterosexual desire" (Sedgwick 1985, 16). Erie offered an appealingly vital, male companionship to Hughie that was distinct from his resigned relationship with Irma. From Erie's perspective, the two men were satisfied to bond, often clandestinely, without female approval. For Erie, the hotel lobby and Hughie's presence behind the desk constituted home, despite any women's efforts to discredit it. In essence, the gambler's sadness is over the death of his beloved friend-companion-family *and* the loss of their home.

Just as Erie perceived Irma's disapproval of a "home" existing between Hughie and himself, so Erie anticipates Charlie's resistance to forming a comparable arrangement between themselves. He becomes insecure, hurt, and depressed. His fond memories of home are wasted on Charlie. The hotel lobby becomes "a dead dump [and] about as homey as the Morgue" (282); Charlie is no substitute for Hughie.

In terms of the play's discourse coherence, a speaker's willingness to be self-disclosing is connected to his perception of his own powerlessness as well as to the impact of a kind of "violence"—here in terms of a listener's unrelenting silence—upon his consciousness. Erie acknowledges his powerlessness to shape a shared text when confronted with Charlie's noncommunicative presence. He knows that his words fail to manipulate any change in the men's relationship. He has been talking to himself. Only when Erie accepts that Charlie is not listening to him—that his words have no apparent power over this spectator—does he address himself more honestly.

Male characters who engage personal dialogue are conscious

that, in doing so, they risk losing power. Ceasing to censor himself, Erie experiences a powerlessness that is a prelude to the most self-revealing moments in the realist text; he risks vulnerability only when he openly engages the traditionally unmasculine position. In Erie's case, his powerlessness and, therefore, openness to self-disclosure, is rendered not by alcohol, drugs, or threats of death, but rather by the passive "violence" of Charlie's deliberately unrelenting silence. Erie is unaware that Charlie's silence is not as inactive or lifeless as it appears.

O'Neill has structured Erie's final monologue in the realist text so that its climax coincides with a distinct, though parallel, climax in Charlie's interior monologue. It is striking and ironic that these two moments cohere after a dramatization of the abuse inherent in men's uncooperative communication. Paradoxically, in response to the climax in his respective text, each character momentarily embraces in his text's denouement the structure of the other man's text, as we shall shortly see. In this effective twist of intertextuality, Erie hopelessly retreats into a quasi soliloquy (i.e., Erie assumes no one is listening as he verbalizes his "thoughts," or an interior monologue), while Charlie eagerly pursues a verbal, realist text.

Lonely Erie forgoes any storytelling in his final realist monologue. Acknowledging why he tells tales and how he has avoided loneliness in the past, Erie sees himself as a "dream guy," a "romantic" figure whose presence allowed the married clerk to experience vicariously the excitement he associated with unrestrained virile masculinity. Exercising his power to create a hero for Hughie, Erie "gave him anything he cried for": "The bigger I made myself, the more [Hughie] lapped it up" (283). As such, Erie constructed a heroic life for himself based on words alone. These words are the stuff not of "illusion" but of "fiction," which is "born in the real," and therefore possible (McKelly 18). Nonetheless, they are still words.

Less self-defensive in the realist play, Erie is now vulnerable in the face of certain personal truths. He admits that his words are often "lies" and that his heroic deeds of late are limited to "running errands" for the "Big Shots" (283–84). He is, as O'Neill describes him, "living hand to mouth on the fringe of the rackets" (264). Yet, through self-disclosure, Erie confesses that all his heroic, illusionary tales "done [him] good, too, in a way": "Sure. I'd get to seein' myself like he seen me. . . . But what the hell, Hughie loved it, and it didn't cost nobody nothin', and if every guy along Broadway who kids himself was to drop dead there wouldn't be nobody left. Ain't it the truth, Charlie?" (284). Truth has been the power of language to create illusion, to kid oneself and others. Yet, Erie, like the Wizard of Oz, also has the curtain pulled back to reveal the source of his magic: he is an illusionist existing on words alone. Hoping that his confession will stimulate Charlie's and his mutual survival through shared dialogue, Erie awaits some recognition of his candidness. He knows from experience that without a shared text the power of language to create illusion *or* truth is strained, if not impossible. As one who thrives on communication, Erie cannot survive through sustained silence.[6] He is now more vulnerable to Charlie than at any other point in their encounter.

Simultaneously with Erie's personal confessions, the night sounds peak in Charlie's interior monologue. Charlie's mind hops and rushes as the sounds outside the hotel multiply and spark a series of dramatic images (282). Such preoccupation is not disturbed by Erie's plaintiveness. As a power play, Charlie ignores Erie in the realist text—and this indifference is what the spectator sees and hears throughout *Hughie*. While Charlie hears none of Erie's confessions, his mind is saturated with sound and dialogue. The pervasive silence that Erie and the spectator witness in Charlie is not really one of stasis, numbness, or vacuousness: it is filled with vital dramatic and theatrical elements. The dynamics evident between Erie and Charlie during this heightened moment in the realist text—Erie's obsessive, personal disclosures amid Charlie's impenetrable, but internally alive, silence—epitomize the "violence" against interpersonal communications that can occur between individuals who fail to communicate cooperatively. Each man becomes so absorbed in his own text that he erases—he kills, if you will—the other.

Erie's final question ("Ain't it the truth, Charlie?" [284]) initiates a series of climaxes and denouements. The first is an unexpected, yet dramatically convenient, climax in Charlie's interior monologue. Just as Erie builds to his question of truth, Charlie is unable to fasten his mind to a noise in the night because "a rare and threatening pause of silence has fallen on the city" (284). This interruption thrusts him, bewildered, into a new role in the realist text. He realizes that Erie "won't go to bed, he's still talking, and there is no escape" (285). Faced with an abnormal absence of night sounds, Charlie can no longer escape involvement in real time and space with Erie. Fearing that "the night vaguely reminds him of death," Charlie turns desperately to Erie's life-embodying physical presence as he thinks to himself: "I should use him to help me live through the night. What's he been talking about? I must have caught some of it without meaning to."

It is ironic that Charlie now suffers from the silence to which he has subjected Erie. He is, however, oblivious to the demoralizing effect his silence has had upon Erie. Charlie's tragedy is that he never connects his pain from silence with his "violent" silence toward Erie. This fact undercuts his climactic, "deferential" reply to Erie's question: "Truth? I'm afraid I didn't get—what's the truth?" (285). The only truth apparent to Charlie is his need to use Erie to survive, a tact he repeatedly and consciously denies the other man until he, himself, is desperate.

Charlie fools no one with his abrupt regard for the gambler's thoughts. Having endured enough inattention, Erie stops this exhausting travesty. Erie's private, realist text climaxes with his quiet response to Charlie that the truth is "Nothing, Pal. Not a thing" (285). Erie knows that Charlie has heard nothing and that nothing remains to be said if Charlie rejects not only Erie's dialogues, but also his axiom, which could be proclaimed, "Illusion is Truth." In resignation, Erie abandons his realist text and retreats, momentarily, into a "semi-soliloquy," a term Cohn uses to describe *Hughie* in general (60), although it more closely describes this section in the play: when "Erie begins talking again ... it is obviously aloud to himself, without hope of a listener" (285).

Through this unusual reversal, the denouements of Erie's realist text and Charlie's interior monologue occur in a dramatic structure that is nonexistent for its characters prior to each text's climax: the characters function briefly within the frame that the other man originally engages. O'Neill structures these denouements as isolated, momentary metaplays that independently rise in action and climax and resolve at the curtain.

Erie completes his personal scenario by recalling Hughie's funeral and the horseshoe of roses that he bought him. Erie is now absorbed in the noncommunicative realm previously occupied by Charlie. When Charlie blurts out comments, hoping to lure Erie into his realist text, "it is Erie who doesn't hear him" (287). Oblivious to Charlie's presence, the bitterly resigned Erie longs for Hughie to be alive; through their grand tales the two friends survived "the whole goddamned racket [of] life" (288). Sparing no personal feelings, the customarily spirited, life-oriented Erie admits that "Hughie's better off, at that, being dead. He's got all the luck. He needn't do no worryin' now. He's out of the racket." Isolated, lonely, disconnected, and without anyone to share in the creation of a text, Erie finds himself homeless and struggling to survive. His metaplay ends amid silence.

On the other hand, Charlie, who urgently needs company, realizes that there is only one escape from the "spell of abnormal quiet . . . to fasten onto something" Erie has said (286). Desperate though he may be, Charlie makes no attempt to integrate Erie's current talk, which he can hear, into the creation of his own realist metaplay. The fact that Erie continues to discuss personal topics out loud is not assimilated by Charlie as a possible subject for their dialogue; Charlie neither listens to Erie nor considers what communication the grieving man might desire. For Charlie, sound and sound only needs to fill the air. Consequently, the clerk fastens onto a topic that originally surfaced during the men's attempts at social dialogue: gambling, and specifically the "ideal of fame and glory," Arnold Rothstein. Focusing on Rothstein, Charlie momentarily retreats back to his former internal state, where he "dreams a rapt hero worship" (287). With his "mind now suddenly impervious to the threat of Night and Silence," Charlie is satisfied because the mere sound of Erie's voice fills the air as, essentially, background noise.

Within moments, however, Charlie is jolted into his realist text by the silence that completes Erie's semi-soliloquy. When no audible sound is apparent in the room, the clerk responds with talk to dispel any "suffocating" silence (286). But Charlie's response is so uncustomarily verbose that it grabs Erie's attention and draws the gambler back into the realist action. In turn, Erie's directness toward the increasingly receptive Charlie is sufficient to secure the clerk's attention. Each man's metaplay climaxes as the overall realist text moves toward its resolution: the two men finally communicate with one another within the same dramatic frame. Although the discourse coherence of their shared text is initially unresolved, Erie and Charlie—only moments from *Hughie*'s ending—are on the brink of initiating their most cooperative communication since meeting one another. Both men become what Kane identifies as "active listener[s] and active speakers" participating in the "interrelational language game by forcing the speaker to redefine and refocus his speech" (18).

Although irritated by Charlie's uncharacteristic interruption, Erie is "comforted at having made some sort of contact" with the clerk (288). But the gambler is also aware of the limitations of that contact. Unless Charlie gets involved in Erie's personal "gabbin'," Charlie "can't do [Erie] no good" (290). At this stage of their interaction, Erie is not interested in returning to a dialogue focused on masculine mythologies. In their first power play with one another over the control of their dialogue's topics, Erie lost confidence when Charlie failed to share in the creation of gender-inscribed illusions. In response, Erie abandoned social dialogue in order to comfort himself through the pursuit of self-disclosing topics. Erie relies upon the sound of his own voice as a way to get through his long night's journey into day. By taking the risk to name his feelings and to articulate self-criticisms, the gambler hopes to validate, if only to himself, his existence and right to be heard.

Intent upon mourning Hughie's death, Erie abandons all immediate responsibility to reengage social dialogue with Charlie; he also comes to recognize the pointlessness of his presence in the hotel lobby. As the gambler moves in silence toward the elevator, however, Charlie verbally insists upon Rothstein, whom he cunningly identifies as Erie's old friend, as the topic of conversation. The clerk strikes at the core of Erie's faltering self-identity with this association. By linking Erie to the mythic Rothstein, Charlie grants Erie a sorely needed illusory, reconstructed identity as well as momentary salvation.

Encouraged by the clerk to assume a fantasy role, the gambler confidently anticipates the clerk's desire to create illusion through social dialogue. They accomplish this by developing a text that focuses on the theme of the American masculine ethos. As *Hughie* concludes, Erie shoots dice with Charlie to show how easy success is "when you got my luck—and know how" (292–93). The two men gamble, satisfied with their momentary resolutions: Erie embodies a mythic role and Charlie defeats silence. Peter Egri reads the men's gambling as an "illusory substitute for [their] former failure to bring about meaningful communication" (135). Cohn, on the other hand, positions the men's final interaction within the absurdist traditions of Sartre, Camus, Beckett, Ionesco, and Genet, as she suggests that Erie and Charlie are an "eternal couple threatened by the night, [who] learn to kill the time of their lives by gambling together, and their game is a parable of humanity seeking the courage to live through reality" (63). As do most critics of *Hughie,* Egri and Cohn elevate this gambling moment to one of "human solidarity and personal warmth" that occurs during the men's "game of chance" (Egri 135). Such readings, however, tend to reduce *Hughie* to a parable. They underestimate the multilayered system of signs in the text—evident in its structure, discourse coherence, and the dynamics of the two men's interaction—that suggests that the play's resolution is more calculated and impersonal than is often recognized.

By creating the illusion for Erie that the gambler has power over him, Charlie, like Hughie before him, demonstrates his ultimate power over Erie. Having flattered Erie's ego by offering him an illusory role to play in their relationship, Charlie not only secures Erie's attention but guarantees that elements of his own dream will remain the focus of their dialogue as the curtain falls (288). From the beginning, Charlie has controlled the dynamics of the men's communication. Whether through his sustained silence or his lone attempt at social dialogue, Charlie's actions or inactions have dictated the progression of the discourse coherence. Contrary to the position that "[n]o one really has the upper hand" in *Hughie* (S. Smith 177), the clerk is shown to be in the position of power for much of the men's interaction. Erie's revelation that Charlie, too, needs illusions in order to survive is subtly undercut by the clerk's persistent manipulations, which prompt that revelation. In this light, romantic readings like Fredric Carpenter's are misleading: "By the power of his imagination, [Erie] had compelled the new Hughie to listen and to share" (166). This often repeated response to the text fails to acknowledge the dynamics of O'Neill's dialogue. Charlie neither listens to nor shares spontaneously with Erie; rather, the clerk creates his own topic for conversation and willfully calculates the kind of sharing to occur with the gambler. In the end, Charlie is not quite the "Sucker" (291) that Erie takes him to be.

Although certainly to some extent Erie is aware of Charlie's manipulative techniques, the gambler does not seem bothered by the impersonality of the clerk's overtures. This response may well be an accepted dynamic of social dialogue based in male mythologies; after all, "[A]lienation...can be ameliorated if not overcome by altering perception, by myth-making" (S. Smith 177). Charlie Hughes is not completely convincing as another Hughie, whose company Erie wants passionately to duplicate. Right up to the play's end, Charlie cares more for the ideal, "the friend of Arnold Rothstein" (291) than he does for the man, Erie Smith. As revealed in his interior monologue, Charlie's selfishness contrasts with Erie's portraits of Hughie's generosity. Each clerk's power over Erie appears to have manifested itself differently. Yet it is Charlie's deliberate power plays, his urgency to "use" Erie (285), that undercut the supposed solidarity and warmth so eagerly urged by the play's critics. Ironically, solidarity and warmth are inherent in Erie's attempts at personal discourse with Charlie, efforts that are aggressively rejected. In the end, the characters' return to social dialogue, and specifically to the creation of illusions, is disconcerting in its implications of men's inability to be personally engaged with one another. Even more unsettling, it demonstrates, as in *Glengarry Glen Ross,* the willingness of the traditional hero—the white heterosexual male—to empower himself through mythmaking and impersonality, and thereby to embrace these agents as the essential components of a man's survival.

For all these reasons, then, Egri's conclusion that in *Hughie* there is "only one solution for alienation: a lying pipedream" (133) does not sufficiently address the text's thematic and structural complexity; Susan Harris Smith, on the other hand, astutely opens up such readings, as she problematizes not only the men's final actions but the entire play within a postmodern aesthetic.[7] Although O'Neill's critics uniformly mark the "lying pipedream" as a major theme and praise it for its commitment to human survival (Bogard; Floyd; Gelb and Gelb; Hewes; Quintero; Raleigh; J. Rich; Scheibler; Sheaffer), they do so, I argue, by ignoring the conversational dynamics of the play's dialogue, which actually reveal a striking alternative theme. Erie does engage in personal dialogue, and he does offer it as a viable option to what Egri calls the "evil duality of facing emptiness or escaping into make-believe" (135). However, the men finally choose not to ask any more of one another than to embrace a pipe dream. "*Hughie* begins in silence," notes Christopher Bigsby, yet "it ends in a tumble of language that is no more than another version of that silence" (1992, 31). The men consciously elect this option amid other choices. The offering and elimination of personal dialogue as a solution for alienation is disturbing, particularly in light of the vulnerability and frankness that Erie reveals in the realist text as well as the personal reflectiveness inherent in Charlie's interior monologues. O'Neill dramatized disconnected moments in two men's lives—lives that are filled with personal, intimate inclinations.

The men's rejection of personal dialogue in favor of lying pipe dreams in *Hughie* is poignant, particularly after the former surfaces within the text's discourse coherence. Yes, the men finally communicate, an improvement upon their initial interaction. And yes, they appear content with their connection in the final moments of the play. But attention must also be paid to the quality of the men's final, social dialogue, which denies that any depth of character has been revealed previously. From this perspective, Erie's self-disclosing dialogue serves two basic functions: it provides a cathartic moment within which the gambler can grieve alone for his dead friend; and it allows the spectator to learn personal information about Erie. It has no impact, however, on the relationship between Erie and Charlie. For Charlie, Erie's personal dialogue never exists.

O'Neill masterfully captures this absence of intimacy that the male-cast canon continually uncovers in male communication. But it cannot be overlooked that *Hughie*'s finale—the "ah, but at least the men are *talking* to one another" phenomenon (regardless of the talk's content)—is the typical playwright's choice to resolve dramatic conflict in the canon. Time and again, American playwrights presume that spectators are satisfied (or at least expect) to see and hear male characters cooperatively connect with one another, regardless of how banal or impersonal their communication. Not surprisingly, therefore, *Hughie*'s resolution is somewhat predictable when assessed in conjunction with other male-cast plays; that which finally occurs in O'Neill's hotel lobby is quite familiar to the American spectator. O'Neill opts not for enlightened male interaction, but for clichéd behavior. *Hughie* differs from most male-cast texts by dramatizing man's desire for self-disclosure as well as his frustration upon failing to realize personal intimacy between men. Men's capacity for each interaction, however, remains deeply buried underneath the shared social dialogue of O'Neill's men.

The Toilet, Amiri Baraka

Whereas *Hughie* is characterized by its sustained dramatization of uncooperative communication, *The Toilet* portrays males who uphold a cooperative, ongoing social dialogue, but it is a dialogue punctuated, and finally overwhelmed, by physical violence. The accumulation of the text's violent, physical actions as well as its social dialogue and static discourse coherence represents a dimension of uncooperative communication that is distinct from O'Neill's world of monologues, silence, and nonphysical interaction.

The eleven youths in *The Toilet,* all of whom know one another, are engaged in an immediate, volatile situation: a boy is to be punished for violating the cultural code of acceptable masculine behavior. Jimmy Karolis, a white boy and the object of his classmates' aggression, is accused of sending a love note to another student, Ray—better known as Foots, the leader of a black male group. *The Toilet* begins around 3:00 P.M. in the school latrine as the boys gather to witness Foots's punishment of Karolis. The impersonal appearance and putrid smells of the toilet suggest "the ugliness and filth that Baraka attributes to his characters' social and moral milieu" (L. Brown 142). Dialogue is dominated by the boys' obsession with the moment-to-moment status of their victim. Several, including Ora, who vies with Foots over the group's leadership, anticipate their pleasure in this assault. Through Karolis's injury and humiliation the boys expect to defend and reaffirm the honor of their culturally coded masculine images. "This blunt and brutal tale is one of Baraka's most chilling examinations of split identity, crushed sensitivity, and victimization," according to Kimberly Benston. "The whole tone of the play is consistently violent" (189).

Mainstream critics responded with mixed reviews to the 1964 premiere production of *The Toilet,* a play that Stanley Crouch identifies as "extremely influential on black theatre for the next decade" (1980). Having been praised only nine months earlier for *Dutchman,* a penetrating allegory of race relations in America, Baraka was chastised for "endless, repetitious, senseless, mindless and unrestrained obscenity" (Bolton). Some were eager to close down the show on charges of obscenity.[8] Critical of *The Toilet*'s dramatic strategies, Howard Taubman concluded that Baraka could not "resist the urge to shock by invoking violence and all the obscenities he can think of. There are times when these shock tactics perform no useful dramatic function, when they clarify no meaning, when they merely set up needless resistance to what the play is saying."

While generally unified in their criticism of the play's foul language and excessive violence, the critics disagree on the play's meaning.[9] Its issues of gender—let alone of sexuality—are usually ignored, minimized, or appropriated within more conventional interpretations based upon issues of race and class. Upon considering the gender codings that construct the male characters' lives, as well as position the text's discourse coherence within the canon of male-cast drama, it becomes clear that Baraka, too, complies with traditions of male representation. The play is not only a dramatization of "the ideological drift from the sense of what is a boy to the sense of what is a man" (Tener 207); it is also a kind of experiential case study of males' confrontation with the "other," the differently male, who is coded here as "feminine."

An analysis of *The Toilet* based upon gender representation complements and broadens the play's racial issues (L. Brown 142–43; Lacey 30, 34–39; Sollors 106–7). Owen Brady believes, for instance, that Foots's split identity is a metaphor for the corruption of African American traditions within the white American experience. Framing his provocative analysis with W. E. B. DuBois's position on the Negro's "double consciousness," or his "archetypal position in America" (69), Brady also points unintentionally to the appropriateness of examining the text from the perspective of gender codings. While explicitly critiquing *The Toilet* as Foots's story, Brady implicitly identifies it as Ora's and Karolis's stories as well— stories whose conflicts also arise out of issues of gender and sexual identifications.

Quoting DuBois, Brady writes that the African American "ever feels his twoness—an American, a Negro; two souls, two thoughts, two unreconciled strivings, two warring ideals in one dark body ... with ... the longing to attain self-conscious manhood, to merge his double self into a better and truer self ... to make it possible to be both a Negro and an American, without being cursed and spit upon by his fellows" (69). The African American male, DuBois suggests, desires to unite under one consciousness—that of "manhood." He desires, from an ideological as well as sociopolitical perspective, to become a Man in America. Cultural codes, therefore, that stringently differentiate between man and woman, masculine and feminine, self and other as *gendered* categories coexist in tension with racial codings. Gender, however, initially privileges some bodies over others in their quest for patriarchal power. All men, according to a Beauvoirian premise, have access, albeit to varying degrees, to the experience of "ideal" manhood in America. And all men are also subject to the expectations of the dominant culture, those perpetuated by its male mythologies.

Baraka's play, therefore, participates in a tradition that is not solely determined by racial codings; rather, it dramatizes the DuBoisian double bind, which incorporates implicitly Beauvoirian binarisms. This tradition thrives on the degree of success with which a male—any male—embodies the mythic image of manhood in America. While race is certainly part of the originating source from which the conflict begins in this male-cast play, gender codings subsume ones of racial difference. *The Toilet* is about what it means to be a Man in America. It is clearly "American" in the discourse coherence of its dramatic representation of men, while still "distinctly black" in its "atmosphere and feeling" (O. Brady 73). If the text operates metaphorically in its contrasting values of African community and white American perversity (O. Brady 71; Haskins 146; Tener 210), it should also be taken literally, as a dramatization of a type of communicative interaction among American men. In this light, Baraka's reliance upon vile language and brutal violence serves less to create shock value or racial tension than to elaborate upon the dynamics of uncooperative communication that can occur among American males when they reject personal dialogue. "The subject of [The Toilet] is communication," writes Michael Smith. "Its desperately inarticulate characters are able to communicate only within a formula so strict that almost all feeling is excluded. The characters who break through this formula and become individuals are punished."[10]

The number of males conversing with one another increases steadily throughout The Toilet. While the males initially talk cooperatively among themselves, their text is dominated by a discourse coherence that rarely progresses beyond topics determined by the masculine ethos and male mythologies. At first, two black males, "Big Shot" Ora and Willie Love, engage briefly in dialogue in the latrine. They are joined immediately by Hines and Holmes, soon to be followed by Perry, George, and Farrell. Later, Knowles and Skippy enter bearing an already beaten Karolis, who besides Farrell is the only white boy in the room; and finally Foots arrives, the "weakest physically and smallest of the bunch, but he is undoubtedly their leader" (Baraka 1966a, 51). Baraka sets up three groups of three men apiece who interact with Ora. This strategy distinguishes the inflammatory, violent power that males like Ora hold over Foots's reserved, rational power. Ora's brutal actions are gender-coded responses that arise from both his racial community and the broader American semiotic of maleness.

Ora and Love's initial social dialogue, as well as Hines and Holmes's contribution, indicates the specific topics that the others in the group will pursue: females, sex, the penis, and the current status of their prey, Karolis. "Since it is believed that the spoken word has power" in the African American tradition, writes Geneva Smitherman, "it is only logical to employ it with what many regard as men's most formidable obstacle—women" (83). Immediately within their interaction, the boys jive one another about absent women. Their mothers, girlfriends, or teachers become easy targets for their degradations: females keep smelly houses, abandon their children, masturbate penises, and "beat" delinquent males' heads. The boys take turns urinating in the commodes while bad-mouthing females, or "playing the dozens," which Roger Abrahams describes as a "folkloristic phenomena found among...lower class Negro adolescent[s]" (1962, 209).[11]

Unlike most characters in the male-cast canon, these adolescents promptly become physical with one another. Hines and Holmes begin to push and to spar with Love. They intersperse their jabs with remarks about females and Karolis—who, as the suspected gay, embodies the feminine and, soon, the position of the absent woman. The three menacingly shift their loyalties, so that at any moment a boy may find himself no longer the attacker, but the object of aggression. Their dialogue, which aligns them with the virility of a boxer's "professional demeanor" (41), relates their various fighting maneuvers. As close friends Hines and Love grab Holmes in order to "put the little bastard's head in the goddamn urinal" (40), Ora, who had momentarily left the room, rushes in to participate. This "crude, loud" boy also wants to punch the "prick" Holmes (35, 41). With his reentry, however, Ora and his torn shirt become the focus as the first round of the boys' physical interaction ends.

There are five discrete, physical altercations in Baraka's text. The boys' violence is curtailed only when another male steps forward as a kind of referee to break up the fighters or when a new character enters the latrine, deflecting attention from the fighters' abusive intentions. Describing his efforts to help Knowles and Skippy drag Karolis, the "paddy bastid," down to the latrine, Ora reports that the "cocksucker" ripped his shirt and scratched his hand (41). "I punched the bastid right in his lip," claims Ora, before hiding the screaming Karolis in a broom closet. Now keeping watch at the door for their victim's delivery, Ora controls the conversation by reasserting the singularity of the boys' mission to harm Karolis.

Anxious to channel their energies without delay, the trio of Love, Hines, and Holmes bursts forth with a second round of physical activity—this time, they play an imaginary basketball game. A boy's success in sport is a sign of his virility, strength, skill, endurance, and desire to be a winner. It is also a sign of his ability to bond in an activity shared with other men. As the males activate this imaginary sport, each constructs his own successful image; each becomes, in front of his peers, the hero he aspires to be.[12] As Ora peeks out the door, Love, Hines, and Holmes dribble, lunge, sweep, spin, scoop, whirl, and leap around one another. Feeling powerful through their demonstrated ability to "score," the boys engage Ora, in between their shots, as to how Karolis is to be punished. Despite their ongoing feats of prowess, however, Hines and Holmes displace onto Love their response to Ora's challenge to "kick that little frail bastid's ass" (43). To this, Love, the most independent thinker of the four males, responds, "Karolis never bothered me." Zeroing in on Love's resistance to fight Karolis and his vulnerability in being honest, Ora takes revenge by positioning Love as an exemplary victim. He does so to humiliate Love into participation and to establish his resistance as unmasculine behavior. Ora's logic: in the absence of the real thing (Karolis), create a scapegoat. Ora anticipates that if he succeeds in embarrassing Love into action, the others will join in, hoping to avoid the same personal challenge to their manhood. Consequently, Ora returns to the topic of an absent woman to disgrace Love.

Ora associates Love's mother with the accused degenerate, Karolis: "Karolis is always telling everybody how he bangs the hell out of Caroline, every chance he gets" (43). Holmes, Hines, and Love, in ever-shifting loyalties, react to Ora's power plays: Holmes sides with Ora, Hines sets up Holmes to be criticized, and Love punches Holmes. Ora is left unscathed, freely reasserting that no one "fucks" with him. He alone has free reign to say or do anything he chooses; he is the Man among men who maintains power through exaggerated, threatening, authoritarian presence and voice. Owen Brady marks Ora's actions as specific to a leader of his community, "a ghetto-cult devoted to ultramasculinity and toughness, one with its own language" (71)—a language unabashedly misogynistic and homophobic. "Verbal facility becomes proof of one's conventional masculinity," comments Phillip Brian Harper about African American men's speech patterns (124). Ora readily establishes the dialogue's topic, then lets the other boys fight among themselves over their positions on that topic. Their dissension is diverted, however, as Perry, George, and Farrell enter the latrine.

The discourse coherence of the seven boys' talk remains on the level of social dialogue, though the topic changes to newcomer Donald Farrell. In one of the few explicit references to the racial, and not just homophobic, tensions that underlie Karolis and Foots's anticipated confrontation, Ora, a "symbol of blackness" to the boys (O. Brady 70), immediately challenges the "blond, awkward, soft" (35) boy's presence. Farrell "threatens the homogeneity and security of the black community as well as the secrecy of their plan to beat Karolis" (O. Brady 73). (This critical position based solely on race is countered by other critics who consider Ora to be a "latent homosexual" whose "tremendous desire to express love" must be "invert[ed]" since "his world does not allow this expression" [Lacey 35–36].) Ora's accusation is met head-on by Perry, who voices the first real threat to Ora's authority over the other boys.

Defending Farrell's place in the latrine, Perry tells Ora to "sit [his] ass down for awhile and shut the hell up" (45), an order he threatens to enforce if need be. This thrown gauntlet signals the next round of battle, which focuses on group leadership. Moving to the center of the space, Ora dares the "black sonofabitch" Perry to fight him (46). This confrontation is sidetracked as George, who is responsible for bringing Farrell along, intervenes.

Deprived of "speaking" with his fists, Ora warns the group that Farrell "ain't gonna do a damn thing but stand around and look" (46). It quickly becomes apparent to the boys that Ora is correct: Farrell knows neither that Karolis is to be "gang[ed]" in the latrine nor why (47). When Farrell learns of the plan, his astonishment at and questioning of this intended violence only fuels Ora's efforts to control the interaction in the room. Once again effective in silencing his detractors, Ora, who is "always going for bad" (48), or for the most overtly macho actions, moves freely in the space to accost Farrell physically. Accusing Farrell of wanting to defend Karolis if he stays in the room, Big Shot punches Farrell in the stomach, sending him crumbling to the floor. This brutality ignites yet another verbal clash between Perry and Ora, as Ora again challenges Perry to fight. Ora reduces every encounter to a physical confrontation when his efforts to control the dialogue and action are threatened. Perry remains the only one in the group to challenge Ora's authority and racist behavior, yet George repeats his role as referee as he steps in between the two men before they start throwing punches. This third physical clash among the boys halts as Knowles and Skippy enter the latrine holding their crying, bloodied victim, Karolis.

The embodied object of much of the boys' previous dialogue, Karolis remains the topic of conversation as Knowles drags him to a corner of the latrine amid the newcomers' proud claims of inflicting Karolis's injuries. Ora's continuing power reaffirms itself. Even though Perry and Love talk critically of his behavior, Ora still speaks and acts as he wants to: no one stops him from shouting down opponents or from sadistically taunting Karolis. His brutish masculinity dictates the room's dynamics.

Ora's direct addresses and violent innuendoes to Karolis are what Walter Kerr once called "bear baiting" (1964), now referred to as queer baiting or gay bashing. Nudging the slumped youth with his foot, Ora baits "baby" to perform fellatio on his "nice fat sausage" (50). Only Love draws attention to Ora's request as a sign of Big Shot's "kicks ... [to] rub up against half-dead white boys." Ora undercuts any homoerotic suggestion by mentioning his desire to "rub up against [Love's] momma" (51). Here, the gay male and the absent woman are linked as sexual objects for (ab)use by the (allegedly) straight male. Throughout the male-cast canon, women and gays are associated with one another as the coded "other" in the dominant culture, as the nonmasculine, as the feminine, though "[h]atred of homosexuals appears to be secondary in our society to the fear and hatred of what is perceived as being 'feminine' in other men and in oneself" (Isay 78).[13] In Baraka's text, the link between homosexuality and femininity, I suggest, is represented dramatically as a more powerful agent of division among "masculine" men than are men's racial differences. Ora and the black gang are threatened more by Karolis's homosexuality and its anticipated, attendant femininity, than by his whiteness.[14] Within the semiotic of maleness operating on the play, not race but rather homophobia—and implicitly, misogyny—resides at the heart of the text, propelling the characters into a whirlwind of verbal and physical violence.

These two factors—accusations of homosexuality and a mounting aggression to punish unmasculine behavior violently—shape the remaining discourse coherence and physical action in *The Toilet*. This occurs despite the fact that Foots enters the toilet hoping to avoid any revenge fight with Karolis. Foots is conscious of having to play a role of unbridled masculinity to maintain his power position over his peers and influence their actions—to get them to leave the latrine without harming Karolis. Unbeknownst to the other males, Foots masks his true desires and identity by rationally manipulating his authoritative powers as a leader of dependent men, men who are desperate to maintain a culturally coded image of "authentic" manliness.

Horrified and disgusted upon seeing the badly injured Karolis, Foots keeps any emotional response under control. His immediate priority is to maintain the appearance of being a "real" man among men. He focuses on the still silent object, Karolis: How was he injured? Who hit him? Why continue to hurt him? In Foots's judgment there is no "reason to keep all this shit up. Just pour water on the cat and let's get outta here" (53). Ora's response is a direct challenge to Foots's authority and its indirect suspicion of the leader's self-identity: "You mean *you made us* go through all this *bullshit for nothing*" (emphasis added). The emphasized phrases reveal Ora's assumptions, and presumably the other boys'. First, Ora grants that Foots is leader, the one who can make other males respond to his wishes. Second, Ora indicates that all of the boys' preceding efforts are worthless if nothing happens. And, of course, the only thing that can satisfy Ora is a fight between Foots and Karolis. Anything less would signal that Ora and the other boys were fools to participate in Foots's "bullshit." Anything less would also make Foots less of a man before this group of males. For Foots to step out of a role rigidly defined as proper male behavior is to risk rejection by his peers as an unacceptable male. He is, after all, what Baraka calls the "possessor of a threatened empire" (35). Foots is required by the dictates of the code to violate and injure Karolis further. The choice remains, nonetheless, within Foots's personal power, as he concludes, "I can't fight the guy like he is" (54). Foots is surprised, however, to hear his position supported by Farrell; he was unaware that Farrell was in the latrine with his black buddies.

Baraka has structured the text's discourse coherence so that the two white boys introduce the last general topics of dialogue. In the first exchange—among Farrell, Foots, and Ora—Farrell's comments invite possible tensions surrounding racial allegiances, but they quickly dissolve into homophobic responses; the males' dialogue terminates with physical violence. In the second exchange—among Karolis, Foots, and a seemingly collective voice comprised of the remaining hostile youths—issues of the male ethos, homosexuality, and self-hatred fuel the clash between the black males' social dialogue and the white boy's rejected efforts at personal dialogue. This interaction also ends in physical violence.

In the first exchange, Farrell pursues an explanation as to why Foots wants to beat up Karolis. Unable to secure specific detail through personal dialogue, Farrell claims that he will leave the latrine with the other white boy, who is so badly beaten that he "can't do anything" (55). Both Ora and Foots threaten Farrell with physical harm if he does not leave immediately, since an explanation is none of his "goddamn business" (54). Ora steps back from the white boy's resistance to let Foots and Farrell verbally battle over the latter's access to information. Ora's manner of dealing with conflict is to fight, not talk. In front of his peers, Foots is now under pressure to exert his power and influence over Farrell. If successful, he demonstrates that he warrants their confidence in his leadership; if his words fail, he risks being judged ineffectual, particularly if he continues to resist using his fists. He also risks being seen in alliance with a white outsider. Foots's efforts to withhold information from Farrell are dashed, however, when Perry speaks of Karolis's love letter to him.

At this point the tensions among characters move swiftly from any potential conflict based solely upon racial pride or authority to a more complicated intersection of volatile issues: interracial desire and homosexuality. Foots does not want this topic to be addressed in front of Farrell. To do so will only heighten his and the group's awareness of his split identity in relation to his ties with the black and white communities, to violence and nonviolence, to diverse sexualities. He simply does not want dialogue to focus on personally challenging issues. From the beginning of their interaction, nevertheless, Farrell has indicated a certain familiarity with the individual side of Foots, whom he—like Karolis—calls Ray. In pleading for Karolis's release, Farrell appeals to that intelligent, personal self and not the group leader. Upon hearing of the letter, Farrell turns to question Foots. He is stopped, however, by Ora's punches, the fourth physically violent clash.

As evidenced throughout the male-cast canon, one's efforts to pursue the topic of homosexuality within a group of predominantly straight males (whether male youths or adults) are most often met with verbal abuse or physical violence.[15] Generally, this violent reaction effectively curtails the men's dialogue. In *The Toilet,* Ora exercises the authority of fists over words in order to halt Farrell's efforts to address the issue of homosexuality through personal dialogue. His violence is less a result of racial tension than it is a response to this conversational topic. Foots fails in his attempt to keep Ora from further injuring Farrell, as Big Shot pushes him into the latrine door.

The battle lines are now clearly drawn as the two black men's methods clash over how to deal with this crisis that threatens their manhood—which threatens to unravel their sense of (African American, heterosexual) community. Nonetheless, Farrell still has his last words heard before he is shoved into the school's hallway: "Oh, Ray, come on. Why don't you come off it" (56). Farrell challenges Ray to stop his charade as a macho, revengeful hero, to stop being someone he essentially dislikes for the sake of the group's approval. Implicitly, Farrell asks Foots to be himself; he asks him not to define his identity and actions according to cultural and gender expectations. In the semiotic of maleness, Farrell can access this voice because he, too, is "other" in *this* space: whether through his (seemingly) gay-affirmative public persona or his minority status as a white (he is not a colonizing authoritative power as manifested in the [white] master/[black] slave paradigm).

In a striking dramaturgical choice, Baraka heightens this tension between one's gender-defined, social persona and one's personal identity—he gives voice to the differently masculine Karolis, the text's openly "other" male, who now rises like the phoenix from the latrine's distant corner.

Insisting that all the boys remain in the room to bear witness, Karolis engages the discourse of violence. Weak and battered, he gets to his feet to face his enemies. "I want to fight you," the very skinny boy says to Foots. "I want to kill you" (57, 58). Karolis constructs himself as the subject, not object, of his dialogue and thereby forces the others to deal with him as he is self-identified. No longer willing to remain their sole victim, he comments upon the nature of violence by appearing to be a willing participant. Through this choice, Karolis exerts a kind of power over Foots, a power centered in the articulation of personal truths. He sets up Foots to make his own choice: to embrace the truth by naming it and thereby claiming his self-identity; or, to deny the truth, to fight it and beat it away, through physical violence. Each choice offers a distinct type of power to Foots: the cultural power of the social self or the personal power of the self-identified. In Baraka's text, the only real choice that men must make—one that will reveal who they are to themselves and to others—is between self-disclosing dialogue and physical violence. The former releases personal truths, while the latter represses those truths.

Foots becomes an "angry snarling figure" (58), choosing to repress the truth by capitulating to the demands of being a macho hero among his black peers. The leader becomes like Ora, the one who would "stomp anybody in any damn condition" (54). Foots's anger sets in motion the rest of the room as the other boys "become animated, clapping their hands, shouting, whistling, and moving around as if they were also fighting" (58). The vicarious rush of pleasure that the group acts out takes on ritualistic significance, as the boys collectively convey their animalistic lust for a victim, a victor, and violence. Amid their aggressive, hostile dialogue and activity, however, "sissy-punk" Karolis persists undauntingly in the naming of that which Foots refuses to hear in front of other men: "You have to fight me. I sent you a note, remember. That note saying I loved you. The note saying you were beautiful. . . . The one that said I wanted to take you into my mouth. . . . Did I call you Ray in that letter . . . or Foots? Foots! I'm going to break your fucking neck. That's right. That's who I want to kill. Foots!" (58–59).[16] Foots lunges after Karolis, trying to silence him. Karolis's expression of his desires elicits powerful reactions from Foots and the group; it is as though in naming them, he materializes them. As Karolis articulates his various crimes against the social order through his personal dialogue, however, he still refuses to raise his fists. Even though Karolis speaks of physical action, he does so without actually engaging it—that is, until Ora pushes him into Foots. This move activates the fifth and final round of physical violence in *The Toilet*.

Baraka's stage directions reveal the most common manifestations of verbal and nonverbal behavior for men who are in crisis over speaking self-disclosingly: confrontational, personal dialogue versus physically violent (re)actions. After being hit by Karolis's pushed body, Foots slaps the white boy. This contact is their first physical interaction in the text. "Are you Ray or Foots, huh?" Karolis responds, "backing up . . . *wanting to talk*" (59; emphasis added). Foots strikes out in violent denial that there is anything (or anyone) to be named—especially as it relates to his sexual identity—in front of this male group; Karolis, on the other hand, insists on personalizing his relationship with Foots through direct address. Karolis essentially asks his attacker the play's pivotal, self-disclosing question: Who are you *really*? To respond, Foots must choose between an identity based upon self-knowledge and one shaped by social expectations. In Baraka's democratic context, exemplified by Karolis's talk and actions, each man has within himself the power to name and claim his identity as differently masculine.

Meanwhile, Karolis's is the lone voice in the room committed to the power of personal dialogue and its truth: he reveals that Foots and he had physical contact with one another prior to the love letter. This damaging remark, indicating Ray's acquiescence, threatens to destroy the boys' image of their leader: "Ray, you said your name was. You said Ray. Right here in this filthy toilet. You put your hand on me and said Ray!" (60). The conflicting naming of one's self in private and public contexts takes on grave proportions here as Karolis confronts Foots to distinguish between his own truths and lies. Karolis's earlier charge to Foots—"You have to fight me" (58)—takes on deeper resonance as Foots's name is challenged. By fighting Karolis, Foots is also fighting Ray, or the Karolis side of himself. He is fighting that which he both denies and desires—a part that Karolis represents and embodies and yearns for in Ray. While Ray is a black man in white America (O.

Brady; Haskins; Sollors; Tener), his conflict is eventually determined by his relationship to society's construction of masculinity and sexuality for black and white alike. The boy's conflict is less with whiteness than with gender and sexual identity.

Like lions circling their prey, the crowd moves in, forcing "the two fighters [to] have to make contact" (59)—which, again, Foots and Karolis can choose to make either violent or nonviolent. Demonstrating behavior that is not stereotypical, presumably, for a "dick licker" (57) in male-cast plays, Karolis rejects personal dialogue; he, retreats into uncooperative communication, lunging at Foots and locking him into a choke hold. In a highly dramatic moment, Ray is actually being choked by the truth teller, Karolis. And, paradoxically, he is unable to defend himself from the truth, despite Karolis's battered condition. Physical violence, nonetheless, wins the round and the contest over personal dialogue.

Always primed for action, Ora smells blood. Jumping on Karolis's back to rescue their fallen leader, he pulls Karolis off Foots, who slumps to the floor. Ora is determined to defend Foots's race and sexuality—the black heterosexual's manhood. Literally and metaphorically disconnected from Foots, Karolis is once again vulnerable prey for the hungry male pack. His final plea before being beaten mercilessly: "No, no, his name is Ray, not Foots. You stupid bastards. I love somebody you don't even know" (60). To know Karolis's Ray would be to know a male who exists outside the boundaries of culturally acceptable male behavior—since both his racially specific community and the dominant culture are homophobic. This recognition simply cannot occur, no matter how ambiguous or contradictory the possibilities for Foots's life may appear to these macho fanatics.

The boys' final choice of action is fueled by their defense of a culturally engendered, patriarchal image of manhood. It is not enough to explain the youths' attack as their "will to preserve their [African American] comrade against the attack of a [white] outsider" (O. Brady 76). Unlike Billy in David Rabe's *Streamers,* who is haunted by the sexualities of his hero, Frankie, and their implications for his own sexual identity, the boys in *The Toilet* collectively reinforce heterosexuality by repressing any invasion of the "other" within their ranks. Their violent behavior erases the challenge within the syllogism to which their activity has brought them: Ray is our leader, Ray flirts with queers, therefore, are we ... or what does it say about us to have chosen a leader like Ray?[17] "The fierce, irrational passion of homophobia in many men," writes Lynn Segal, "can only be understood in terms of men's fear of what they see as the 'feminine' in themselves—the enemy within" (158). Therefore, the outsider, Karolis, must be crushed along with any ambiguities that threaten the patriarchy's constructed image of Man.

For this reason, Baraka constructs a dialogue, argues Kerr, that "refus[es] to use language as an imaginative tool ... [whereby] illumination [could keep] pace with the turn of our stomachs" (1964). I suggest that Baraka refuses to use language imaginatively, in Kerr's sense of the word, simply because to do so would be to represent an atypical dramatic vision of American men among themselves—imaginative language usage among any men would necessitate their cooperatively communicating with one another through personal dialogue. The playwright uses the racial topoi that are also present in the scenario (and certainly operative in the spectators) to grid or to bolster this larger feature of men's communication within patriarchy. Baraka's conscious dramatic intent, finally, is to present men among men as he perceives them, not as he envisions them, at the complicated, volatile intersection of race and sexuality. Consequently, the males' violence escalates uncontrollably as chaos overwhelms *The Toilet.* Baraka, like Piñero in his interracial *Short Eyes,* materializes male gang savagery before the spectator: "[T]he whole crowd surges into the center punching the fallen Karolis in the face....He is dragged to the floor. The crowd is kicking and cursing him. Ora in the center punching the fallen Karolis in the face....Karolis is spread in the center of the floor and is unmoving" (60–61).

The abusers quickly leave the scene of their "mock battle of honor" (Tener 214), taking their limp leader with them, bonded in their victory against the enemy. Ora, however, has the last words of the text, as he joyously brings to the group's attention that the "fuckin' paddy boy almost kilt" Foots (61). Pleased that violent action has defeated anything attempted through language and dialogue, Ora in his final gesture signals his disrespect for Foots and his increasingly nonviolent behavior. Ora tosses toilet water on Foots's face, water from the commode into which the boys have been urinating all afternoon. The fallen hero's humiliation as "one of the boys," so to speak, is complete.[18]

In a remarkably moving tableau, Baraka structures a concluding instance in which Karolis, gradually gaining consciousness, painstakingly crawls to a toilet. At the moment he collapses in front of it, Foots reenters the space. "Look[ing] quickly over his shoulder" to make sure that no one sees him, Foots "runs and kneels before the body, weeping and cradling [Karolis's] head in his arms" (62). No longer forcing themselves to be Men among Men, the two battered boys come home to (and through) one another, to their shared knowledge of "difference within," away from those who seek to deny them their otherness. Amid their tears, they do not speak. The play ends in silence, rich with meaning.

If Foots's reentry into the latrine is read within the political agenda of Baraka's dramatic writing in the 1960s, then the youth's action is not merely a renewal of his "attachment to the white society" (O. Brady 76). If race were Baraka's sole agenda—if his goal were to speak for the "brutal social order" of young black males—then, as Werner Sollors suggests, "homosexuality now becomes a metaphor for acceptance in the white world. . . . the gesture of individual assimilation, of trying to rise above the peer group" (107). To overcome such individualism—that is, for gay Ray to accept himself as black Foots—a "painful exorcism of interracial and homosexual love" would have to transpire. *The Toilet* would then reveal why and how one's racial and ethnic reality must necessarily erase the reality of one's sexual identity.

On the other hand, if one reads the play within the semiotic of maleness—a system with its own power relations and "politics" of racial, class, and sexual difference—then Ray Foots returns to embrace and care for, both literally and metaphorically, the only male with whom he has come in contact to embody a more integrated individualization. This image does come from within the text, as Benston argues: it is "an accurately conceived image of a natural desire undermined and destroyed by a world that condemns such desire" (192). In his action, Ray Foots acknowledges not only his "mature victory over hyper-masculinity" (Witherington 162), but more importantly the power of self-knowledge to heal oneself. This awareness is not bounded exclusively by one's racial or sexual identities, but rather by the limits of one's passion to strive for a self-identity that is less encumbered by social codings. As Robert Tener notes, "At that moment with another human being, Ray expresses a mature tenderness and love which his mythic destiny had denied him with his gang" (214); he is not just "pathetic, at best," as Lloyd Brown suggests, "in his belated, and secret, demonstration of love" (143). But the toilet setting of the final moment does "confirm the continuation of these prevailing social codes which encourage a guilty secrecy about sex and emotional experience." "Baraka has severely taxed the tools of naturalism in his effort to give expression to the black leader's conflict between inner and outer world," Benston concludes, "between the possibility of tenderness and the reality established by the harsh necessities of the social world" (193).

Nonetheless, this illuminating active moment is primarily Karolis's victory (which is not to say it is a "white" victory). The gay male has not compromised his dignity despite his assailants' terrorist tactics. "The real man," according to Henry Lacey, "is the individual with the strength to divorce himself from the inhibiting influence of the majority. In [The Toilet] that individual is the homosexual" (37). Karolis's characterization hardly reinforces, as Tener claims, "the demoralization and confusion of standards for behavior within the white system" (210). Rather, as viewed within the semiotic of maleness, Baraka dramatizes a future that belongs to both Ray Foots and Karolis. Each male, and not just Foots, as Tener argues, represents a "different kind of model" of human being (214). Both are new models for men among themselves. "It's a struggle all the time," surmises Issac Julien, "negotiating and renegotiating, asserting oneself" (hooks and Julien 1991, 184); Foots and Karolis hint at the possibilities inherent in such a struggle.[19] It is as if the play's final image answers the questions raised by Baraka in his 1961 poem, "Look for You Yesterday, Here You Come Today." Depending upon one's dating of the play, The Toilet is either based upon this verse (Hudson 160) or the play inspired the verse (Lacey 33–34):

Was James Karolis a great sage??
Why did I let Ora Matthews beat him up
in the bathroom? Haven't I learned my lesson.
(Baraka 1961, 15)

The historical and contemporary fact is that American dramaturgy repeatedly represents men among themselves who are unable or unwilling to engage in personal dialogue, the primary means by which most realist drama reveals its themes. In realist male-cast plays these "points" are often made implicitly, as shock tactics such as verbal and physical violence eventually dominate the discourse coherence and action. For this reason, Taubman correctly notes that underneath The Toilet's coarseness, there "runs a strong sense of the needless debasement of human beings." Yet his assertion that Baraka "could have made his points without the shock tactic" overlooks an established pattern throughout American theater history. Often, what the male-cast text "means," to use

Taubman's term, is not found in the characters' dialogue, but rather in that which is absent, and therefore implied by their dialogue. In this way, *The Toilet* both literally and metaphorically represents the dramatic dynamics of American men among men who do not transcend the limitations of uncooperative communication.

Nonetheless, in the play's final nonverbal stage action, Baraka presents a radically dramatic *image* that is markedly distinct from his previous shock tactics. Ironically, it is equally shocking in its impact: the recognition of human truth as represented in the compassionate (physical) interaction of male characters. In realizing this moment, Baraka contributes to the sorely needed revolution of the male-cast play's dramaturgy, initially called for in 1959 by Edward Albee. *The Toilet* is the first significant American male-cast play to explore the artistic and cultural challenge set forth in Albee's landmark male-cast drama, *The Zoo Story*. Albee's challenge to American playwrights was to dramatize a communicative dynamic that transcended what had come to be accepted as man's inevitable union with violence. By keeping the curtain up in *The Toilet* for the dignified final image between Karolis and Foots, Baraka dramatizes ever so tentatively the existence of a power greater than violence—love, a love of *inclusiveness:* powerful enough to bond men in their humanity, yet able to acknowledge the specificity of men's differences based upon race, ethnicity, class, and sexual orientation.

This was not to be the case for Albee's male characters in *The Zoo Story,* where the power of violence defeats all understanding and compassion.

The Zoo Story, Edward Albee

Edward Albee has remarked that "communication is the only thing that is really viable to write about. That's the only thing you can write about" in the theater (qtd. in Wolf 117). As in *Hughie, The Zoo Story* involves a spontaneous meeting between two strangers whose relationship is determined by the dynamics of their talk: one is eager to converse, the other is not. During a summer afternoon in Central Park, Peter, an undistinguished, middle-aged textbook publishing executive, is reading a book. Peter's solitude is disrupted by Jerry's entrance. Jerry, a carelessly dressed, "permanent transient" in his late thirties, approaches Peter with his thrice repeated proclamation, "I've been to the zoo" (Albee 37, 12).[20] This announcement introduces what will become the pivotal conversational topic by the conclusion of the men's dialogue. Although Albee identifies this topic now and it is frequently referred to by Peter as a topic to engage, Jerry's "zoo story" is not spoken until the men are on the verge of unadulterated uncooperative communication. Albee positions the zoo story at the point where cooperative communication between the men ceases. It acts as a kind of summary of the failings of men's shared social dialogue; Jerry's telling of it only makes sense as a prelude, a foreshadowing, of the violence that is about to explode.

Upon seeing Peter, Jerry immediately imposes upon him: "Do you mind if we talk" (14). From this moment on, Albee's play is a verbal rush orchestrated by a single voice. With the enthusiasm, self-interest, and directness of O'Neill's Erie, Jerry inflicts upon Peter a "need to talk"; Jerry, like Erie, initially does not want "a friend but a sympathetic listener" (Rutenberg 21). Not unlike Erie's listener, Charlie, whose silence masks an active interior text, Peter patronizes Jerry with guarded exchanges. Attacking these calculated communication barriers, Jerry types Peter as a successful product of the American masculine ethos; Jerry has not experienced a comparable level of cultural success in his life. Because of his apparent achievements and ordered life within the patriarchy, Peter is the unsuspecting target of Jerry's manipulative questioning. As Michael Rutenberg notes, Jerry is an "alienated failure bent on making contact," at all costs, with the "establishment" (4).

Jerry and Peter's initial talk is based upon topics within standard social dialogue. While cooperative, their exchange is seldom mutual, as there is little sharing of one-to-one information. Jerry, who likes "to talk ... really *talk*" (17), fires question after question at his new acquaintance. Establishing a rhythm to this inquisition and accenting it with frequent non sequiturs, Jerry frequently catches Peter off guard, eliciting spontaneous, revealing responses. Conversely, Peter simply does not have the chance, nor does he particularly care, to ask his own questions; he admits to not talking to many people.

Albee structures the dialogue according to Jerry's interrogation. This enables the character to fulfill his desire "to get to know somebody, know all about him" (17). For this reason, Jerry first focuses the dialogue on the women in Peter's life: his wife and two daughters. Once satisfied that he has a working knowledge of these absent women, Jerry accumulates details of Peter's public life: his Madison Avenue job, good salary, fashionable private address, and favorite authors. This litany of credentials reveals Peter to be a "modern

version, in middle-class stereotype, of Everyman" (Zimbardo 46).
He has been relatively successful in achieving the mythic "American Way of Life," which Brian Way associates with the "structure
of images . . . [the] pattern to which many Americans tend to conform" (26–27). Peter's affluent, white collar embodiment of the all-
American success image outdistances the achievements of most
males. But Peter is separated, as Rose Zimbardo remarks, "from his
own nature and from other people [by] material goods and the
prefabricated ideas with which he surrounds himself. He has himself carefully constructed his isolation" (46).

Peter is uncomfortable discussing the facts of his social self
with Jerry. "Bewildered by the seeming lack of communication"
(15) in their social discourse, Peter tells Jerry: "You don't really
carry on a conversation; you just ask questions. And I'm . . . I'm
normally . . . uh . . . reticent" (19). Peter interacts with Jerry out of
politeness; cultural conditioning has led him to expect such gestures from himself and others. Yet, as will be revealed, Peter also
shares with Jerry a kind of isolation; their solitary existences initially draw them together (Bigsby 1992, 131). As a gender-coded
American male, however, Peter assiduously avoids "talking about
any subject that has real relevance, anything that has roots penetrating the carefully prepared mask which he presents to the world,
and even to himself" (Zimbardo 46). Such topics, according to
Peter, are "none of [Jerry's] business" (16). They also challenge the
foundations of Peter's perceptions, informed by his white
heterosexuality, of the American masculine ethos and how he has
come to construct his "prepared mask." Is he the man among men
who he aspires to be: dominant over women and without a trace
of femininity within himself? Unknown to Peter, however, is Jerry's
motivation for talking to him. Jerry needs "to view his life with
some semblance of true perspective" (Rutenberg 23), here measured
by his approximation to Peter, the traditional male. Peter, on the
other hand, is oblivious to any role he is to play in helping Jerry
gain that perspective.

Jerry's curiosity about Peter's life proves to be short-lived. His
wish is to talk, to have Peter eventually understand that their interaction has something to do with "go[ing] a very long distance . . . to
come back a short distance correctly" (21). Throughout their social
dialogue, Jerry tosses out arcane notions of this type to Peter without explaining what they mean. These thoughts do cohere, however, in the personal dialogue at the end of their afternoon's inter-

action. Until that point, such comments demarcate a shift in focus from Peter's to Jerry's social self.

Out of both envy and contempt, Jerry pigeonholes himself as a social outcast in contrast to the successful Peter. To "make sense" of his life, to "[b]ring order" to it for Peter's benefit (22), Jerry distinguishes himself from Peter through social dialogue. In the first of several lengthy monologues, Jerry hopes to allure Peter through their shared interest in descriptive language, as he dives into the unlocked "strongbox" of his life (23). He details those who live in his run-down boardinghouse and itemizes what he owns. He then personalizes his remarks by discussing his dead parents and sex: his mother was a whore, his father was a drunk; he neither sees women nor makes love with anyone more than once; he had an adolescent homosexual liaison with a Greek boy; and he has had to ward off the lusty, sweaty advances of his grotesque landlady.[21] Jerry is "incapable of the relaxed, spontaneous flow associated with friendly conversation" (Rutenberg 19). Rather, Jerry "unburden[s] his mind of his private miseries and resentments in a flow of wild, scabrous, psychotic detail" (Atkinson). This detail is broken only by Peter's slight, impersonal reactions. When asked about his own sex life and fantasies, Peter responds evasively: "I'd rather not talk about these things" (26). Embodying a "truly enviable innocence" (23), Peter does not believe that "others," like Jerry, "really are" (28). He is shocked, embarrassed, disgusted, and irritated by Jerry's candor. For himself, "fact is better left to fiction" (29).

Peter is fascinated *and* repulsed by Jerry's life. "Peter has been conditioned enough not to be too demanding or original," as Rutenberg remarks. "He is not used to voicing his own opinion, taking the initiative, or exerting pressure on those around him. It is not difficult, therefore, for Jerry to keep him listening" (22). Whereas Jerry (the talker) reminds Peter (the listener), "Nobody is holding you here; remember that" (29), it is Charlie (the listener) who indicates similar sentiments toward Erie (the talker) via his prolonged silences in *Hughie*. In a reversal of dramaturgical strategies, O'Neill keeps the monologuist Erie glued to the desk of the silent, inactive clerk, whereas Albee keeps the active, (relatively) silent listener Peter glued to the park bench hanging on to Jerry's every word.

Jerry's persuasive, abrasive linguistic style effectively channels Peter's willingness to be his audience. He convinces Peter that his telling of the zoo story is yet to come. Whereas O'Neill actually uses the through line of Hughie's life as the narrative core for Erie's monologues, Albee only implies the zoo story as the anticipated end of Jerry's narrative. While Erie speaks nonstop about Hughie, Jerry speaks about everything but the zoo. Rhetorically, Jerry displays his mastery of the "promise without delivery" technique, one used by skillful jokers, for instance, who hold an audience's attention while delaying the punch line to a merciless extent. Unlike Erie's single verbal strategy, Jerry successfully manipulates various theatrically oriented techniques to achieve his goal.

For example, from the moment he encounters Peter, Jerry creates a metatheatrical event, handling himself as a performer in front of a spectator. First, he establishes a social rapport with Peter, the warm-up technique of audience participation. Responding to an improvisational impulse, performer Jerry then reshapes his spectator's input into a quasi-social–quasi-personal dialogue. This dialogue extends into monologues as Jerry begins to establish his "character" for the approaching "performance" of what may be the telling of the zoo story. Meanwhile, conscious of his motivations and the artifice within which he performs, Jerry indicates the performance's stage directions for the spectator's benefit. Jerry tells Peter during the participatory section, for instance, that he (Jerry) will soon walk around and eventually sit down (19). To his unsuspecting spectator, Jerry indicates exactly what he will do once his performance begins. All of this dramatic preparation builds to the staged event of the afternoon: "THE STORY OF JERRY AND THE DOG!" after which the master actor-director promises to tell "what happened at the zoo" (29). Finally alone in the spotlight, Jerry tells his lengthy tale. At this point, his communication with Peter is at its least cooperative in terms of creating a shared text. This piece of metatheater is not unlike O'Neill's in *Hughie*: both use this technique to dramatize sustained periods of men's unsuccessful communication. Jerry's sole wish is that Peter will be able to connect with the text upon its completion. Intent upon storytelling, Jerry hopes that he will survive his crisis initially through hearing the sound of his own voice. Meanwhile, Peter sits back in silence and listens. Jerry is in complete command of the dialogue's discourse coherence.

Jerry also takes command of the space, moving "with a great deal of action" as he tells his tale (29). The story begins with Jerry's relationship to an absent woman, his drunken landlady. As the "object of her sweaty lust," Jerry fools her daily into "believ[ing] and reliv[ing] what never happened" between them (28). Satisfied, she leaves Jerry alone, yet her dog continues to torment the young man. "Animals are indifferent to me...like people," says Jerry, "but this dog wasn't indifferent" (30). As such, these two males— Jerry and the dog, "malevolence with an erection" (32)—engage in a vicious battle over the dynamics of power within their relationship. According to the facts in Jerry's story, whenever he entered his building, the landlady's dog attacked him; he had clear passage whenever he left. Determined to connect with the dog and thereby come into his home without violence, Jerry tried to win the dog over with "kindness" (31)—bags of hamburger meat. Although the dog devoured the meat, he still attacked him. "Less offended than disgusted" (32), Jerry decided that the dog had an antipathy toward him and that only through a comparable act of "cruelty" might he connect with the animal (35). Thus, the young man fed poisoned meat to the beast. But Jerry did not want the dog to die. Rather, he saw truth embedded in their struggle, and, as he remarks, "I wanted the dog to live so that I could see what our new relationship might come to" (33).

Prior to his speaking of the dog's survival, Jerry implores Peter to "please understand...we have to know the effect of our actions" (33). Although the facts of the dog story are true, they are not really the narrative point: what Jerry intends is for Peter to understand how their own present struggle to connect is comparable to Jerry's relationship with the animal. Jerry implies that both men need to be responsible for their communicative interaction with one another. After all, the effect of their actions directly reflects their ability to deal with the truth. By hinting at these connections, Jerry assumes he is communicating successfully with Peter; that is, that Peter understands what he is being told. His assumption, however, is premature. If anything, Jerry has had a hypnotic effect on his seated listener (34). Peter's silence is neither a sign of comprehension nor connection.

With increasing rhetorical and physical tension, Jerry builds to the climax of his allegory, the reunion with his "friend," the surviving animal: "I looked at him; he looked at me. I think...I think we stayed a long time that way...still, stone-statue...just looking at one another.... But during that twenty seconds or two hours that we looked into each other's face, we made contact. Now, here is what I wanted to happen: I loved the dog now, and I wanted him to love me....I hoped that the dog would understand" (34). Jerry wanted the dog, as well as Peter, to understand that without contact—without communication—there can be no possibility of love. Therefore, for a person to have "some way of dealing with

SOMETHING" (34), one must forgo indifference; and to deal is to make contact, to communicate, to unmask life of its illusions. Just as Jerry tried "to communicate one single, simple-minded idea" to the dog (35), so he hopes that Peter grasps the implications of his story about the power of communication. Jerry anticipates that his personal dialogue can be the "beginning of an understanding" between the two men. Any denial of that understanding will make them more vulnerable to the dynamic of violence within uncooperative communication.

In a disturbing denouement to this metatheater, Albee resolves Jerry's relationship with the dog, in turn illuminating the dynamics of the two men's interaction. Albee succinctly characterizes the limitations of male characters' discourse as dramatized throughout the twentieth-century male-cast canon:

> Whenever the dog and I see each other we both stop where we are. We regard each other with a mixture of sadness and suspicion, and then we feign indifference. We walk past each other safely; we have an understanding. It's very sad, but you'll have to admit that it is an understanding. We have made many attempts at contact, and we have failed. . . . We neither love nor hurt because we do not try to reach each other. (35–36)

The indifference is similar to the indifference Jerry experiences when he attempts to communicate with people. Most characters in the male-cast canon are represented as accepting a comparable indifference when they engage other men in dialogue. This linguistic and behavioral phenomenon is presented as a socialized and, at times, instinctual trait of the male "beast."

Although Jerry understands the existence of indifference in human interaction, he resents the limitations it imposes upon interpersonal communication. Having shared earlier with Peter the conventional levels of male dialogue, Jerry intuits their social dialogue as "indifferent" involvement. Essentially, Jerry represents those male characters who cannot connect through a text that fails to require from its speaker and listener either compassion or pain. His efforts dramatize a recurring representation of men's talk: connections facilitated through social dialogue are generally superficial, evasive, and impersonal in their rigid cultural codings. Upon engaging topics within the theme of the American masculine ethos and male mythologies, men gain an unthreatening "free passage" of communication among themselves (35). By maintaining a text whose discourse coherence remains within the topics of social dialogue, men "walk past each other safely." They have an understanding to "not try to reach each other" in a personal, self-disclosing manner, since such behavior in American culture is heavily coded as feminine (Segal 165).

Given the patterned discourse coherence of the male-cast canon, it is not surprising that Peter exclaims at the conclusion of Jerry's tale, "I DON'T UNDERSTAND!...I DON'T WANT TO HEAR ANYMORE. I don't understand you, or your landlady, or her dog" (36–37). Peter essentially tells Jerry that he chooses not to engage in a communicative interaction based upon self-disclosing subject matter. As Albee has said of his characters: "all of my people are terribly articulate, they could communicate if they chose to. But they don't choose to" (qtd. in Wallach 1988, 132). As with most representations of American male characters, Peter "flees from the responsibility that understanding would demand" (Zimbardo 51). Like Charlie in *Hughie,* Peter's "nonparticipation in the speech act symbolizes" what Kane calls a "withdrawal from temporal, spatial, or social reality" (19). Sitting on the bench for the first time in the play, Jerry wearily acknowledges his own otherness as the source of Peter's misunderstanding. The younger man's personal dialogue and his "performance" initiate neither an agreeable text nor an emotional sharing between the two men. Consequently, the characters are vulnerable to other dynamics of uncooperative communication as long as they remain in each other's company.

Committed to monopolizing Peter's attention, to making contact with him and gaining some truth about human communication, Jerry is driven "to go a very long distance" in order "to come back a short distance correctly" (21). He recalls: "I have learned that neither kindness not cruelty by themselves, independent of each other, creates any effect beyond themselves; and I have learned that the two combined, together, at the same time, are the teaching emotion. And what is gained is loss" (35–36). Theoretically, Jerry adheres to the power of the "teaching emotion." In actuality, he offers his story, his personal dialogue, to Peter as an act of "kindness." But Peter rejects that kindness. Knowing that he must continue to "go a very long distance," Jerry then consciously activates the "cruelty" within himself in an effort "to come back a short distance" to the purity of his teaching emotion. This activation prefigures the play's climax. Jerry's cruelty is initially manifested through physical action, as the determined young man tickles Peter into delirium. This action is curiously appropriate. On the one hand it allows Jerry to penetrate the ordered barriers of Peter's social self, as the tickling unleashes Peter's more spontaneous instincts in a chaotic surge of energy. But it also introduces the play's most absurd elements in respect to male interaction. Hence, the initial joviality and childishness surrounding the tickling is unusual adult male behavior. It breaks with the decorum of anticipated masculine interaction.[22] "I wouldn't have expected it," responds Jerry to Peter's "mad whimsy" (39). Nevertheless, their playfulness quickly metamorphoses into behavior that is likened to Jerry's "cruel" behavior toward the dog, a development not wholly unlike men's violent interaction throughout the canon when communication becomes progressively less cooperative.

Having secured Peter's attention, Jerry begins his zoo story. Wanting to infuse it with an allegorical significance comparable to the dog story, Jerry prefaces the tale by voicing his desire to understand "more about the way people exist with animals... [since] everyone [is] separated by bars from everyone else" (40). However, the spectator can safely assume along with Jerry that Peter still will not make any connection between Jerry's stories and their immediate interaction. This unawareness remains at the core of the men's communicative imbalance. But Jerry knows better than to repeat techniques that have already proven themselves ineffective. Language and dialogue fail in *The Zoo Story*. Without any warning, Jerry abandons his previous kindness and storytelling in favor of physical and verbal cruelty. He masterfully manipulates his next performance back to an improvisational theater of abuse. He encourages chaos, not order, as the text of their interaction.

Hoping to jolt Peter out of his gender-coded identity into a kind of primal confrontation, Jerry appeals to the male "animal" within Peter (49). In a final effort to connect, Jerry assumes that Peter's "other" side will respond to the alluring power plays of violence. Jerry's tickles quickly escalate into pokes, punches, and pushes that, as in *The Toilet,* reflect the breakdown of order between the men. Unlike the earlier dog story, Peter suddenly finds himself an active participant in Jerry's living theater piece, his zoo story. Peter and his secluded bench are no longer safely disconnected from other men.

Desperate to realize his teaching emotion, Jerry abandons his story to focus on a concrete goal that will activate that emotion: the sole occupancy of the public park bench. By physically attacking Peter, Jerry hopes to intimidate him into taking an action—into fleeing the bench. With the prowess of an animal determined to be king of the forest, Jerry couples his physical jabs with humiliating insults at the sacred foundation of Peter's masculine identity. The now antagonistic young male devalues Peter's home, wife, and children—the actual embodiments of the executive's cultural success. Stalking his victim, Jerry probes Peter's sense of the American masculine ethos: "You have everything, and now you want this bench. Are these the things men fight for? . . . [I]s this your honor? . . . Can you think of anything more absurd?" (44). Here, Albee intentionally questions not only Peter's values, but those of the capitalistic patriarchy—as Mamet will do twenty-five years later in *Glengarry Glen Ross*—into which American men are socialized. Typical of the dynamics within male-cast plays, the characters' relationship as represented within their dialogue is ultimately reduced to a power struggle. For Albee, it is frighteningly real that the only genuine contact Peter and Jerry seem capable of creating is a violent power play over the ownership of a material possession. As Bigsby notes, the play "seems to stand as an indictment of materialism" (1992, 129). Any O'Neillian contact achieved between men through illusions and pipe dreams is no resolution for the men in Albee's zoo.

Through his cruelty, Jerry succeeds in shaking Peter's walls of reserve and rationality. He also succeeds in establishing a text between them, as Peter responds, "I want this bench to myself . . . GET AWAY FROM MY BENCH!" (44). However, in challenging Peter's honor, Jerry slices directly through the once confident, powerful heart of Peter's white heterosexual male identity. In response, Peter exclaims, "I'm not going to talk to you about honor, or even try to explain it to you. . . . You wouldn't understand." Reminiscent of another tragic American voice, Tennessee Williams's Blanche DuBois, Jerry contemptuously replies: "You don't even know what you're saying, do you? . . . Don't you have any idea, not even the slightest, what other people *need*?" (45). Ironically, Peter has no conception that Jerry, of all people, just might understand—and if Jerry did not, he might at least try. Jerry recognizes that men can be like animals; men often persist in being "separated by bars" (40) of racial, ethnic, class, religious, and sexual identities amid their refusal to individualize, to humanize the other through self-disclosing dialogue. Jerry also intuits that men need to try to understand one another, no matter how complicated the process. Again, Albee brilliantly encapsulates the fear and denial that male characters experience as they attempt to connect more personally with one another.

Since Jerry's cruelty creates no effect beyond itself, Peter cannot identify the young man's needs. When Peter refuses to try to explain his ideas because he assumes that Jerry will not understand, Jerry turns to all-out violence. This action necessarily contributes to the evolution of his teaching emotion. For Jerry, there is no better time nor space than here in the park "to communicate one single, simple-minded idea" to Peter (35): that humans, unlike other animals, must take responsibility to understand one another if they are ever to overcome hatred or indifference to know love. Furthermore, the young man is determined to convince Peter that there is no honor in an isolated life that values a bench more than human contact.

In a climax that some critics see as melodramatic and sentimental (Atkinson; Esslin 267; Way 40), Jerry taunts Peter to defend "his" bench with a knife that he tosses at his feet. He is to defend the masculine ethos: to "fight for [his] self-respect ... two daughters ... wife ... and manhood" (46–47). This overture to violence is a paradigmatic example of the action men initiate when they utterly fail to understand their diverse needs—but still find themselves forced to deal with one another. However, the men's violence is not a contrived technical device or a "catastrophe" that Albee inserts in order to precipitate "a resolution of the situation" (Way 40). Throughout the male-cast canon, when men fail to progress beyond social dialogue yet remain in the same time and space with one another, they create a violent dynamic. Since Peter chooses not to flee Jerry's company, he leaves himself really only one viable alternative under the circumstances: to "fight like a man" in self-defense (45). Such are the codings in the semiotic of maleness, which define any man's vulnerability as a feminine, emasculating weakness. Jerry's drilling slaps and spits into Peter's face are the final blows, therefore, as an enraged and now equally irrational Peter holds the knife out in order to defend himself. Peter, the embodiment of the American masculine ethos, is reduced to Jerry's kind of animalistic behavior. With his survival at stake, Peter finally frees himself to take some action in order to understand the dynamics of his present interaction. Ironically, a man's needs for survival have been the focus of Jerry's dialogue from the start. But like most male characters, Peter does not acknowledge any relationship between his own needs and those of others until his personal survival is challenged. Then, and only then, does the "other" man truly exist. Peter's final wish, however, is to remain isolated, to be left "alone" (47).

Jerry comes to accept his success in reaching Peter. He sees in

Peter's actions the other man's need to survive and his ability to act upon that need. The truth that Jerry sets out to demonstrate prevails: for better or worse, all men are essentially the same. Working through kindness and then cruelty, therefore, Jerry must now unite the two if he hopes to create a vital and profound effect. The power of the teaching emotion is only realized through a stark combination of kindness and cruelty. Men must be made to witness the dictum, "what is gained is loss" (36). Numbed by indifference, a state he now shares with the dog, Jerry refuses to let indifference determine his contact with Peter. He is determined to intimidate Peter "into a real confrontation with the isolation and despair of the human condition" (Way 38). Through that confrontation he hopes to "bring out the feelings in Peter that might have made [their] sharing possible" (Swan); "a life lived without pain is a life without consciousness" (Bigsby 1992, 132). Thus, just prior to the curtain, Jerry charges Peter and impales himself on the knife. The silence that follows immortalizes the moment, the message, and the contact between the two men (47). Their connection is violently completed. Peter flees the death scene a different man—one who, Albee concludes, "is not going to be able to be the same person again" (qtd. in Sullivan 187).

Unlike O'Neill's characters, Albee's men finally communicate more intimately through their silence than through their words. Even Jerry's curtain speech is somewhat redundant in light of the resolution inherent in both men's screams, which eventually pierce their devastating silence.[23] The men's connection to one another is complete, if only momentarily. Five years later, Baraka captures a similar connection in Foots and Karolis's curtain tableau. Yet, few male characters throughout the canon experience these onstage moments of personal connection—that is, a connection infused with the quality of insight, emotion, and comprehension inherent in Jerry's teaching emotion. While not condoning violence, this position contextualizes it and dramatizes its relationship to the dynamic of men's personal communication.

It is horrifying, of course, that the only real contact in *The Zoo Story* is realized at the end of a knife. How tragic and ironic that the price the characters pay for their understanding is death. But as Albee himself points out, Jerry is "oversane. Though he dies, he passes on an awareness of life" to Peter (qtd. in Gelb). Hence *The Zoo Story* and *The Toilet* dramatize men who do personally connect, achieving—however briefly—a dynamic often unrealized in male-cast plays. Like Karolis's and Foots's lives, Jerry's and Peter's lives are profoundly changed by interacting with each other. Unlike most male characters upon the conclusion of their interaction, neither Albee's (Way 38; Zimbardo 49) nor Baraka's couples remain as they once were. Both sets of men are given the chance "to advance as human being[s]," as Katharine Worth observes about Albee's play; theirs "is a moment of evolutionary choice" (42). Can they return to the familiar, standard pipe dreams of O'Neill's Erie and Charlie? Whereas José Quintero maintains that "fantasies . . . are necessary [and] life-giving" for O'Neill's men, one can argue that such illusions violate human reality and dignity in Albee's and Baraka's texts. Both writers insist that their characters grapple with the limitations inherent in the American masculine ethos and male mythologies. In doing so, they represent characters who have an opportunity to connect with one another as individuals rather than as gender-coded, social constructs. "Because humans create their fictions, they can both control and change them. . . . hold[ing] forth the possibility . . . that the disintegration of an old identity . . . may be the means for a new, more consciously formed personality" (Anderson 106). At the end of their interaction, which is paradoxically and ironically at the "beginning of [their] understanding" (Albee 35), Albee's and Baraka's men recognize their otherness, their difference within. If only for their representation of this dynamic within and between men, *The Zoo Story* and *The Toilet* remain revolutionary male-cast plays.

Unfortunately, the canon repeatedly offers its characters only O'Neill's illusions or Baraka's and Albee's violence as viable choices for overcoming their uncooperative communication. A third option, particularly involving self-disclosing dialogue, remains a rare choice. The dramatic representation of American men among men is, in many ways, still stuck in Albee's zoo.

Granted, *The Zoo Story* and *The Toilet* are extreme theatrical representations of men. However, each play implicitly challenges us to imagine other levels of character interaction in other dramatic contexts. They ask us to consider those male behaviors that deviate from the expectations and role models established within the dominant culture—especially as men encounter the potential destructiveness in communicating uncooperatively among themselves. Each play raises questions regarding the universality or pervasiveness in the male-cast canon of this central issue: is "the problem" for male characters, as Jane Brody concludes about *The Zoo Story,* "not within a relationship, but in forming a relationship"?

Charged with the psychological and emotional complexities of what it means to be a man or Man in America, Albee's and Baraka's characters engage in violent power plays over their rights to self-identification, as well as to their connections with other men. This struggle continues to rage within the American male's (un)conscious, as represented in American drama.[24] Speaking of Albee's play, Walter Kerr asks, "Does modern man have to murder someone before he can establish an emotional relationship with him?" (1960). As an absurdist writer, Albee horrifies us with his image of men's soullessness and isolation. As a realist, Albee—like Baraka—dares American playwrights to invalidate his perceptions of male communication. Aspiring to create in *The Zoo Story* a shared male dialogue that liberates one's self-identity, Albee pursues a very real struggle that O'Neill conveniently bypasses in *Hughie* through theatrical conventions and stereotypes. Out of necessity, Albee penetrates O'Neill's silence, exposes its vulnerability, and pursues its alternatives. Only within the last ten to fifteen years have American playwrights created alternatives to Albee's violent representation of male interaction. Nearly all male-cast plays written since 1959 have contended with, if not responded directly to, the challenge of Albee's vision in *The Zoo Story*. His text points to the hitherto "un-American," uncharted dramaturgical territory yet to be traversed by our native playwrights: to present American men among themselves who not only engage in self-disclosing dialogue but are also nonviolent individuals.

Three

Liberation in Confinement

Albee's *The Zoo Story* and Baraka's *The Toilet* dramatize the extent to which a male will engage in violent power plays in an effort to forge an identity and to pursue a connection with other men. Jerry's and Karolis's struggles are all too familiar in the male-cast canon. Time and again, male characters face the failure of their social dialogue. Unlike those few men—O'Neill's Charlie in *Hughie,* for instance—who retreat into silence when communication breaks down, most male characters at some point during their interaction resort to verbal abuse or physical violence or both of the kind that Albee's and Baraka's males exhibit. Frequently, men reengage cooperative communication only after such violence has occurred. And if their talk resumes, it generally moves from social to personal dialogue. There is, therefore, more often than not, a direct link—a cause and effect relationship—between the experience of violence among male characters and their subsequent engagement of personal dialogue.

The next two chapters focus on plays that derive their discourse coherence from characters' insistence upon and realization of personal dialogue. The first of these plays, Miguel Piñero's *Short Eyes,* David Rabe's *Streamers,* and Robin Swados's *A Quiet End* are set in confining institutional environments: a prison, a military barracks, and a hospice, respectively. In this book's introduction I argue the position (one that qualifies Carol Rosen's view on the limitations of such settings [22]) that institutional settings afford the characters of male-cast plays a freedom of self-expression, or individualization. If they are not drunk or drugged, most American male dramatic characters speak freely, that is, personally, with one another *only* if they are "literally . . . condemned to be free" (Rosen 24). Hence, the paradoxical title of this chapter. As a critical complement to this discussion, chapter 4 focuses on those plays in which men who are *not* confined to institutional settings desire to speak personally with one another.

Short Eyes, Miguel Piñero

Rosen's observation that Kenneth Brown (*The Brig*), Brendan Behan (*The Hostage*), and Jean Genet (*Deathwatch*) "all had first-hand experience of the ordeal of the prisoner, and . . . bring the impact of that experience to bear on their approaches to drama" (148) also applies to Puerto Rican American playwright Miguel Piñero. Piñero wrote his award-winning *Short Eyes* while he was a prisoner at Sing Sing, serving a five-year sentence for armed robbery. Upon his release in 1973, Piñero joined The Family, a unique theater group composed primarily of male former prison inmates. The group was founded by Marvin Felix Camillo, its director, in 1972. The Family's production of *Short Eyes,* after its successful run at the New York Shakespeare Festival in 1974, was named the year's Best American Play by the New York Drama Critics Circle and the recipient of an Obie Award as Best New American Play. Upon the occasion of Piñero's untimely death at the age of forty-one, Joseph Papp, the producer of *Short Eyes,* praised Piñero as "the first Puerto Rican to really break through and be accepted as a major writer for the stage" (qtd. in Bennetts).[1]

Short Eyes mimics the realistic detail of daily prison life. A two-act play with an epilogue, Piñero's work basically adheres to the neoclassic unities, following the inmates from morning to evening in a single locale. Each of the three sections of the play occurs at a discrete period of the day. From their moment-to-moment coded conversations (Piñero even provides a glossary of the prisoners' slang at the end of his text for his reader's reference) to their innocuous, regimented chores, the incarcerated men participate, according to Piñero, in "a society within a society." Prison is "a reflection of life in the streets," says the playwright; "the jargon may be different, but we think and feel the same as on the streets and we recreate that in prison." "There's tension in the streets, but there's concentrated tension in prison and not the same outlets. You release it by masturbation, fighting, all sports. You know, you build your own *routines*" (qtd. in Wahls; emphasis added).

The range of these routines—sports, fighting, sex talk—is familiar to us. They are coded as masculine within the prison as well as within the society that contains the prison. They also extend to the ordinariness of the discourse coherence in the men's initial talk. Yet unlike many playwrights' renderings of the linear progression of men's realist dialogue (that is, from social dialogue to violence to personal dialogue), Piñero constructs a stage talk in act 1 that moves from conventional social dialogue to physical violence to social dialogue and back to violence. This cycle is eventually broken when two men are left alone together to engage in personal dialogue. Their interaction changes, however, upon the reentry of the other inmates, which reactivates verbal and physical violence at the end of the act.

Gathering in the dayroom of their "House of Detention" at the opening of act 1 (Piñero 1975, 5),[2] seven inmates immediately establish the coded duality of their gendered roles to one another. Through their social dialogue, the racially mixed group of men address Julio "Cupcakes" Mercado—the young, beautiful Latino— as the object of their desire, as the object of their verbal masturbation. Despite his resistance to their naming of him, Cupcakes is marked by the men as the sexual "other." "In the penal institution, totally run and inhabited by men, where the male is the absolute master," Carla McDonough proposes, "femininity must be constructed out of masculinity" (199). Here, Cupcakes's (male) adolescent prettiness codes him feminine. His presence makes visible the coded cultural politics of Beauvoir's Self/Other model and the otherwise absent woman.[3] Cupcakes "enjoys all the attention that he receives from the other love-starved prisoners," remarks Camillo; he is the prisoners' "youth, hope, and [is] very vulnerable because of his own fears" (xiii).

The sexual uneasiness created by these introductory speeches in the play serves, in fact, as a useful frame within which to consider the men's communicative interaction throughout *Short Eyes*. Within the play's semiotic of maleness, sexual anxiety subsumes the racial, class, ethnic, and religious tensions also evident in the dialogue. Although these latter tensions surface in the men's talk— and any one may well be a point from which a conflict begins— they are displaced by the perceived or desired transgressions of one's sexual identity. The men's discourse of sex also graphically thrusts man's *body* into the dramatic arena of reference, play, and appropriation. For this reason, the male body becomes a possible object for other men's erotic desires. Up to this point in the analysis of male-cast plays, only gay drama (as discussed in chapter 1) has deliberately positioned the male body as a sexual object. Men in confined, institutional settings, like the characters in *Short Eyes*, bring their bodies into the (performance) space of (the) play.[4] In the texts analyzed here and in chapter 4, the male body is present, active, and demanding to be dealt with when *any* men are among themselves.

After the identification of Cupcakes as "other," the politics of the men's "home" splits again, this time along black and white lines. William "El Raheem" Johnson, an outspoken Black Muslim committed to "teaching *his* truth about the original black man" (Camillo xiii), clashes with Charlie "Longshoe" Murphy, a wise-cracking, rough Irishman. Longshoe is sick of hearing El Raheem's spiritual ranting; El Raheem is undeterred by this "Yacoub," or white devil. The relationship between these two men encapsulates the racial tension in this roomful of prisoners. They verbally and physically abuse one another throughout their morning activities. Yet, even these supposed staunch enemies later unite in violence to punish a prisoner who is perceived to be a sexual deviant.

The sexual and racial tensions in the dayroom—all part of the daily routine that Piñero speaks of—are contained by the generally invisible presence of the prison guard, Mr. Nett. Once visible in the room, however, Nett relies upon social dialogue to reassert the power of the system over each prisoner. In an exchange with Omar, for instance, Nett reminds the virile, black amateur boxer that he may not be able to secure him a prison job if Omar cannot guarantee that he will break his routine of fighting with other men. Omar's response: "I can't give you my word on something like that.... My word is my bond. Man in prison ain't got nothing but his word, and he's got to be careful who and how and for what he give it for" (13). One's naming of a personal truth—a man's word is his bond— is taken seriously in this room.

Nett, the white authority figure, along with the other prison guards, embodies Foucault's "privileged locus of realization" (1979, 249). With his seemingly "permanent gaze" (Foucault 1979, 250), Nett controls his prisoners regardless of his presence or absence. The authority that Nett represents ultimately contains the prisoners' actions. He punishes, denies, permits, or encourages behaviors that mirror the patriarchal mechanism of subject-object authority outside the prison. From Nett's subject position of power, each prisoner remains necessarily "other." Nett's absence from the dayroom, however, prompts two contrasting hierarchies of authority to surface among the men in the room. In this shift of power positions, the prisoners create two determinants of "otherness" among themselves. The first, and most obvious, is racial identity. The predominantly African American and Puerto Rican American group of inmates codes Longshoe, the only white in the dayroom, as the "other." But the alternative identification of the "other" as sexual object—that is, the remaining men's relegation of a male to a female position—crosses over racial boundaries. In Piñero's play, as well as in most realist interracial male-cast dramas, the naming of the "other" as sex object is color-blind. Its definition is determined by who pursues the object for sexual pleasure: either as a compromised substitute for the Other, an absent woman (the case for heterosexual men) or as an intended partner (the case for homosexual or bisexual inmates). When Netts departs the dayroom, black and white alike unite to participate in a discourse of sexual desire, as most of them pursue and harass the unyielding "parfait," Cupcakes (125).

In making known their lust, Paco, Omar, and Juan tease and bluntly confront Cupcakes. "Why not let me fuck you?" challenges the older Juan, as Cupcakes affirms, "That's definitely out" (18). El Raheem speaks only after Omar, his black brother, joins in the inmates' queer talk. Such speech, El Raheem argues, is not "black original man talk"; homoerotic speech reflects the "thinking [of] the white devils, Yacoub," who "infects the mind of [El Raheem's] people like a fever."[5] Reading El Raheem's comment for its ironic logic, we see that both black and white are guilty of racism (white devils infect blacks, and El Raheem hates whites), but only the "real" black man is homophobic and, therefore, the exemplary, original man. A true man, by El Raheem's definition, is necessarily homophobic.

The African American's interruption of the multiracial group's sex talk predictably redirects the social dialogue. Piñero has already established that El Raheem and Longshoe will bypass the sexual innuendos of the others to clash over issues of racial purity and superiority. After briefly tolerating El Raheem's word game, which is intended to frustrate him (in its overall cleverness and speed, it is akin to the dozens played in The Toilet), Longshoe speaks the unforgivable: he insults Allah. El Raheem responds with physical violence to Longshoe's verbal offense. Social dialogue gives way to the uncooperative communication of physical abuse. Nett reappears on the scene, but, with an ironic twist, the patriarchal authority figure whose job it is to control the inmates lets the men's uncooperative communication be resolved in combat. His actual control is never threatened; Nett chooses to remain in the room to witness and to officiate over the contest. Adhering to the powers of the masculine ethos, which value a man's virile defense of his beliefs, Nett sanctions an all-out fight.

As embodied in Nett, the patriarchal system in effect condones violence as a way for men to deal with their differences. Violence is coded in the play's semiotic of maleness; it is not just, as Ariel Ruiz suggests, "a response to the monotony and alienation characteristic of the prison" (96). Nett knows that as prisoners, no inmates are "really gonna end up the winner[s]" (21). Nett lets the men box and wrestle one another, calling a halt only when the black man appears to be the likely winner. Nett uses his power as white authority figure to privilege Longshoe over El Raheem. Here, race distinguishes men among themselves, as the power outside the room, now inside the room, determines the outcome of the confrontation. This battle between races encourages each man to locate with his own racial group at the fight's closure: Puerto Rican Americans "go to their table," (22), African Americans to theirs, and white to his. This altercation, however, is the last instance in which race is presented overtly as the primary division between the inmates. Sexual "otherness" will once again replace racial difference as the great divide among men in this "school of self awareness" (22). For this reason, Steven Hart's claim that "the most important theme in *Short Eyes* is the relationship between individual responsibility and the issue of racism" (436) slights the play's thematic density.

To break the stressful postfight atmosphere in the dayroom, Cupcakes takes it upon himself to entertain the inmates with a fictional dimension of social dialogue, not unlike Roma and Levene's metatheatrics in Mamet's *Glengarry Glen Ross:* first, Cupcakes performs as an MC while the other Puerto Rican Americans bang out rhythms on their table; and second, he offers a raplike prison toast, a "long epic poem created and recited by prisoners for diversion" (126). Cupcakes must be coaxed to perform the toast, however, after his initial role-playing. Paco pinches Cupcakes's buttocks in between "acts," causing the young man to withdraw from his playfulness. Cupcakes is the only male in the room with the physical beauty (coded by the majority of men in the room as feminine beauty) and behavioral abandon (which the men interpret as flirtatious and available conduct, again aligned with femaleness) to transport the others into a realm of sexual fantasy and pleasure. His actions, which step out of the traditional masculine mode, are viewed by most of the inmates as a signal to liberate their own libidos. Communal sexual spontaneity, animated at the end of Cupcakes's performance, incites the other inmates to chase him, with all his virginal appeal, around the room. This seemingly innocent homosocial, erotic foreplay stands in stark contrast to the complexities of sexual identity and sexual otherness that disrupt it when Clark Davis, a new white prisoner, enters the penal "home."

The subjects of the social dialogue in the introductory scene between Clark and the veteran inmates—sex, race, sex—mirror the overall structure of the play's discourse coherence. Youthful, handsome Clark is immediately pegged as a potential sexual object for the men; Paco slips into Spanish to remark that Clark "esta' bueno" (25). Longshoe, a "homey" to the white man (26), does not deny the newcomer's appeal, but he does insinuate that Clark is not like Cupcakes. It is not surprising that Longshoe, obligated by the code that operates on the multiracial group's coherent identity as well as driven by his own obsession with race relations, shifts the dialogue's topic from sex to race. The Irishman maps out for Clark the room's terrain, pointing out the racially segregated areas along with the dos and donts of interracial mingling. Longshoe's instructions warn Clark about the violence that he could encounter if he acts improperly; the constant threat is coded into the men's talk and actions with one another. He is especially concerned that Clark know that whites are "the minority here, so be cool" (27). "Niggers and the spics don't give us honkies much trouble," the older white adds, but Clark is still never to get too close to anyone.

Longshoe saves the most grave demand for last: "You're a good-looking kid.... You ain't stuff [i.e., gay] and you don't want to be stuff. Stay away from the bandidos [i.e., those who chase attractive young prisoners for sexual purposes]" (28). Once again, the homosexual/heterosexual dichotomy presents itself as a source of disconnection between men more volatile than racial difference. Identification with maleness remains one's chief bond with other men. In a realist nongay play, therefore, the issue of sexual orientations will determine, textually or subtextually (that is, consciously or unconsciously), the progression of interactive and communicative dynamics.

Returning to homosexuality as his final topic, Longshoe reaffirms the heterosexual masculine ethos for all the men. Even within the all-male context of the prison, this ethos identifies sex objects for the racially and sexually unspecific subject's pleasure and domination. While Paco is identified by Longshoe as a bandido, for instance, he is not stuff. Juan, Ice, and Omar are also ready bandidos. Within the prison, homosexuality is tolerated if it substitutes for (the allegedly preferred) heterosexuality, yielding a hybrid bisexuality. The man placed in the object position assumes the role that otherwise would be thrust upon a woman. Accordingly, the male aggressor retains his privileged masculine position as subject in the matrix. The male relegated to an archetypal homosexual object position is decidedly "other." He substitutes for the absent woman and he takes on, as it were, all her marginalized social, political, and sexual identities.[6]

The social dialogue between Longshoe and Clark is short-lived, as Nett reappears to disrupt it with an unexpected, violent monologue. Within moments of having warned his "homey" against men's sexual advances, Longshoe listens to Nett name Clark a "short eyes"— a child molester (29). Without hesitation, Longshoe transforms his position to one of absolute rejection, since Clark, in his eyes, is a sexual pervert. Homosexuality is repulsive to Longshoe, as well as to the other inmates, yet no crime is as vile as child molestation.

Nett threatens "the sick fucking degenerate" that he can "break [Clark's] face so bad [his] own mother won't know [him]," that he will "take a night stick and ram it clean up [Clark's] asshole" (29, 30). Nett reveals that his eight-year-old daughter was assaulted by one of Clark's kind. Letting himself be known via this intimate detail regarding an absent female, Nett ushers in a structural shift in the talk, anticipating the elimination of social dialogue. From this point on, the discourse coherence will be marked by a tension between the uncooperative communication of violence and the intensity of self-disclosure in personal dialogue. This shift is signaled by Longshoe's spitting in Clark's face. It is a gesture in which nothing is left to be said, and yet everything remains to be said. Longshoe forgoes any racial solidarity with his white brother or solidarity on the grounds of their heterosexuality. He declares unequivocally his own sexual normalcy and bonds with the remaining inmates, who are also, presumably, straight. In this regard, gender identity and sexual orientation take precedence over the "programs" of conduct based upon racial and ethnic differences.[7] The "law of survival" (75) demands that any prisoner must first establish his manhood, usually accomplished by his willingness to fight to defend it. If a man fails, he is labeled a "creep" (44, 124), a sexual deviant, the target for all other prisoners' abuse.

The discourse coherence for the remainder of the act moves from lengthy personal dialogue (of a confessional mode similar to Erie's musings in *Hughie* or Jerry's monologue in *The Zoo Story*) back to swift, spontaneous violence (of the type in *The Toilet*). Left alone in the dayroom after most of the inmates leave to do their daily chores, Clark and Juan have a prolonged discussion, during which Juan asks probing personal questions about Clark's crime. Clark is unabashedly candid in his detailed responses. This communicative dynamic is notably different from that in many noninstitutional plays. Juan and Clark engage forthrightly in personal exchange. Most importantly, Juan acknowledges in his responses that he hears everything the new inmate says. This does not imply that Juan accepts or "understands" everything (39); rather, it highlights the fact that Juan never denies that Clark speaks self-disclosingly and that he, Juan, at least hears the other man's words.

At this point, it is important to recall a primary interest of this study: to reveal *how* the discourse coherence in a male-cast play arrives finally at sustained personal dialogue. In doing so, one can acknowledge how the realist play "works" by focusing on how the talk works between the characters. Prior to Clark and Juan's private conversation, the discourse coherence in Piñero's play is strikingly similar to that represented in the six plays previously analyzed. That is, the men's talk initially rises out of a commitment to the masculine ethos (which includes a possible focus on absent women). If the talk progresses beyond this dynamic of social dialogue, it becomes violence driven. However, as Clark and Juan sustain their personal dialogue, *Short Eyes* takes on a crucial feature of most institutional plays: many men who are captive in confining institutions eventually respond to their circumstance by being verbally intimate. This same intimacy is evident in many noninstitutional plays where characters drink or take drugs. (The noninstitutional plays that I discuss in chapter 4 are among the rare exceptions to this latter observation.) It is fair to say, therefore, that Clark's expression of personal detail to another man is not unlike the discourse coherence of the drunk and drugged men in Jason Miller's *That Championship Season,* Mart Crowley's *The Boys in the Band,* and a great many other noninstitutional male-cast plays.

Self-disclosure, therefore, turns out to be a fairly common, albeit *conditional,* feature of male-cast plays. Most, after all, involve characters who drink, take drugs, or are restricted to a confining institution. Yet, what is the content, the detail of that private talk? At this more confidential level of cooperative communication, males assert their right to individualization. Whereas men differentiate only slightly from one another when they engage the discourse of the masculine ethos, they become self-identified beings during personal dialogue.

A revealing feature of men's often hard-earned personal dia-logue, however, is a paradoxical sameness in their immediate fanta-sies and fears. In the deeper structure of their dialogue, male char-acters express individual concerns about many of the same topics: home, survival, a desire to be understood, and an awareness of the difference within. In his revealing monologues to Juan, Clark oddly enough reconnects with and identifies himself as another kind of archetypal American Male character, one who frees his inner strug-gles by truthfully telling his story. Less important, then, than the specific details of Clark's personal story, or those of any character's to be discussed in the remainder of this book, is the interactive dynamic between speaker and listener that, in enabling men to sustain personal dialogue, sheds light on the question of male rep-resentation.

Regarding Clark's individualization, first Juan directly asks Clark for the truth about his crime: "did you really do it?" (31). In his struggle to answer Juan's question, Clark traces his history as a child rapist through a series of monologues. (One can hardly avoid mention that much of the focus is on an "absent woman." He re-lates "little picture incidents" about the little girls whom he abused [34], citing with a seemingly unconscious, racist overtone his pref-erence for third world children.) Pivotal in distinguishing the pro-gression of discourse coherence in *Short Eyes* from that of the pre-viously analyzed plays is that Clark not only volunteers innermost details from his life but also responds honestly to Juan's inquiries about his feelings surrounding these facts. Juan's willingness to listen to and to respond to that which he hears is a relatively com-mon occurrence in plays set in confining institutions—decidedly *not* the case for noninstitutional plays. These two settings, after all, are coded differently within the semiotic of maleness as repre-sented in male-cast plays. When Juan permits Clark to tell his pri-vate story, to "run it," agreeing to participate in a talk exchange, their shared dynamic is a far cry from the basically uncooperative communication that can characterize male strangers in noninstitu-tional settings, such as those in *Hughie* and *The Zoo Story*.

During his graphic narrative and reflective commentary, Clark admits that the boundaries between his "conscious [and] subcon-scious" are blurred (37). This state of mind relaxes self-censoring during his confessions to Juan, as his fantasies and fears rush to the foreground. Clark divulges that "something drove" him to his crimes: "I wanted to stop, really I did...I just didn't know how....I know what's right and I know what I'm doing is wrong, yet I can't stop myself" (39). And in an appeal that recalls Jerry's plea to Peter in Albee's play, Clark finally implores, "Juan, try to understand me."

There is a noteworthy difference, however, in Peter's and Juan's responses. Peter replies to Jerry: "Why did you tell me all of this?...I DON'T UNDERSTAND!...I DON'T WANT TO HEAR ANY MORE. I don't understand you" (Albee 36–37). Juan, on the other hand, replies to Clark, "Motherfucker, try to understand you...if I wasn't trying to, I would have killed you" (Piñero 1975, 39). Juan's response is extraordinary for male dramatic talk. Piñero's choice creates a striking dramatic option for male characters' interaction. Again, this observation is remarkable not because a character understands a specific detail about another character, but rather because a male listener acknowledges that a male speaker who is clearly "other" still deserves to be heard. In and of itself, it is a sign of neither the listener's agreement with nor condemnation of the talk's content. Rather, it is a sign of mutual participation in a process that values an ongoing exchange between or among individuals. Such listening is part of not only Clark and Juan's cooperative communication, but of any successful communicative process between or among men who engage personal dialogue.

Juan is not without conflict in listening to Clark. "Shit, why the fuck did you have to tell me all of it," Juan asks. "Why the hell did you have to make me your father confessor? Why? Why didn't you stop, why?" (40). Clark's response accurately substantiates the conversational dynamic the two men mutually established: "Cause you asked....I needed to tell it all...to someone...Juan, you were willing to listen." Unlike Moss in *Glengarry Glen Ross,* who implicates Aaronow in his robbery plans simply because his apprehensive colleague listens to those plans (Mamet 1984, 46), Clark acknowledges Juan's willful participation in their conversation. Juan not only asks questions of Clark, he also reacts to Clark's narrative. Yet, Juan, "the listener...the compassionate" one (37), makes it clear that only he is trying to understand Clark. Juan knows that he does not speak for the men who are about to reenter the dayroom. "If you remain on this floor you're asking to die," Juan warns Clark. "You'll be committing involuntary suicide" (39). Juan recognizes the aggressive, judgmental power of this group's authority over the "other." The exercise of that real power, after all, is part of the male's prerogative in his prison routine. This foreshadowing of violence manifests itself repeatedly through the remainder of the play. Framing its actual physical manifestations is a "rhetoric of violence" (de Lauretis 32). This rhetoric alternates with personal dialogue to characterize the remaining discourse coherence in act 2 and the epilogue.

Act 1 ends violently. The remaining prisoners interrupt Clark and Juan when they return to the dayroom. From the moment Clark is identified as short eyes, he is marked by his fellow prisoners as the "lowest, most despicable" "other" in this male ordering (126) and by his sheer presence becomes the focus of the conversation. Here, the embodiment of the "other" amid a male group restricts the characters' interaction to violent behavior or personal dialogue. Clark's presence guarantees that a cycle of violence and personal dialogue will denote the interaction. Clark and all that he represents interrupt the room's order and, paradoxically, reaffirm that order.

Soon after their reentry to the dayroom, the convicts gang up on Clark in a chorus of metalinguistic taunts: "Did you say something," "You got something you wanna say," "Don't talk to yourself too loud," and "Talk to the shitbowl" (44–45). One of the African Americans, Ice, also calls Clark a "faggot" (44), a slur that will become more meaningful to the dynamics later in the day. For now, however, it is revealing that Juan distinguishes himself from the vicious perpetrators simply by asking them to "drop it . . . cut it loose" because "the dude is a sicky" (45). The other men respond to Juan's request as indefensible. Ice warns Juan, "[D]on't know why you wanna put front for that freak. . . . don't go against your own people." Ice acknowledges that Clark brings both racial and sexual issues to bear. Yet he challenges Juan to deny that he is "out of order" in his effort to protect Clark (46). Ice essentially demands that each man in the room identify his allegiance to order—the codes of male identity and power. Hesitant to do so, Juan (already out of order, so to speak, as one of the "other" men who engages personal dialogue) leaves the dayroom with Cupcakes (also "other" in the men's group). Clark now has no ally in the room. He is at the mercy of the remaining men, who insist that the power of masculine sameness—established in terms of heterosexual/ homosexual opposition—bonds them together as "real," "straight" Men. This confirms what is in fact true for most male characters. Despite their racial (or class, or religious) identities and allegiances, men diminish the significance of such codings in favor of culturally sanctioned, homosocial bonding (Sedgwick 1985, 1–11).

Within moments of Juan and Cupcakes's departure, Clark is harassed, mocked, and terrorized by the lingering convicts. His

immediate threat is Longshoe, who assumes that his shared whiteness with Clark justifies his right to assault him. Once Longshoe
strikes Clark, he is open to the others' attack. The prisoners alter
their program to allow interracial assault on short eyes. In a scene
reminiscent of *The Toilet,* the hostile, united convicts—Anglo
American, African American, and Puerto Rican American alike—
push, hit, and kick Clark before picking up their screaming victim
and plunging him headfirst into a urine-filled toilet bowl. Even the
authority figure, Nett, reappears momentarily in the dayroom, only
to turn his back on, and thereby sanction, this brutality and humiliation. In Piñero's prison, the punishment of the deviant, the "faggot," rests inside the law. Clark's bashing is perfectly acceptable
within the order of this room, which condones the exercise of
"real" men's power over the "other."

At the beginning of act 2, a half hour after Clark's dunking in
the toilet, the convicts (sans Clark) are still passing time in the
dayroom. Juan, the "Poet," leaves the space to receive a visitor (60).
Despite Longshoe's efforts to talk Juan into refusing this company,
Juan affirms that "visits and mail . . . that's my ounce of freedom
and I ain't gonna give it up for nobody" (64). Juan's freedom is his
connection with those who are outside the confined institution. All
his actions (including his efforts at good behavior) reflect his desire
to exist again outside the prison. Choking on his own anger, his
own resistance, and his inability to connect with anyone, Longshoe
gets ill from drugs he has taken. The lingering convicts help him
out of the dayroom, leaving Cupcakes, who is taking a shower,
alone with Paco.

The remaining movements in act 2 are pivotal ones, in which
the male characters struggle to connect personally with someone
or something. They hope to feel less alone, to demonstrate that they
belong to a (male) community, to get approval for who they are.
The three scenes that conclude act 2—the first two with their personal dialogue, the last with its return to violence—reflect the paradox of man's need for connection to someone outside of himself,
yet his abhorrence at association with the male "other." The first
scene is personal dialogue between Paco and Cupcakes; the second
is Ice's personal monologue to his fellow inmates; and the third,
which grotesquely illustrates the thematic of a man's wish to bond
with other men, is the group's final violent attack on Clark. It is
striking and disturbing that all three interactions center on (intima-
tions of or actual) physical violence, two of which are rape, and
one murder.

Alone in the shower with Cupcakes, Paco embraces and kisses the young man on the neck. "I don't play . . . that faggot shit," Cupcakes proclaims, to which Paco replies, "Man, cause I kiss you doesn't mean you're a faggot" (65). Cupcakes asks Paco to stop his advances. Paco slips into their native Spanish in order to speak intimately of his love and lust for Cupcakes. Cupcakes accuses Paco of being "sick" as well as afraid to "hit on" Clark (the real degenerate) because he is white (68). Since Paco transgresses the sexual boundary between (allegedly) straight male subjects—and thereby violates, from Paco's perspective, the code of acceptable male behavior—heavily coded levels of meaning surface, focusing on each man's sexual, racial, and gender identities. And the only way that Cupcakes is able to keep Paco from raping him on the spot (since he outrightly exercises his right to name himself as subject in order to reject Paco's earlier assumptions and efforts to position him as object) is to challenge Paco to first prove his racial *and* gendered manhood by abusing Clark.

"Racial retaliation," then, temporarily displaces sexual gratification and violation (Ruiz 96). The former becomes the means by which the latter, presumably, can be consummated. And so Cupcakes's appeal to Paco's manhood via the power of the masculine ethos (and its accompanying penchant for violence) momentarily, at least, takes priority over the threatened sexual violation. But Paco's undeniable rape mentality is only temporarily assuaged: "I'm going to have you . . . if I want you," Paco threatens. "I'm gonna show you I ain't scared of nobody," Paco warns Cupcakes. "I'm gonna take that honky and you're gonna help" (69).[8] Racial retaliation is the agent by which sex, finally, can be claimed and maimed. In Piñero's play, as well as in many male-cast plays, a male defends his manhood by visibly demonstrating his virility. A "real" man must be willing to fight, to be physically violent, if he is to ever be considered as a man among men. In Piñero's world, the man who will not fight is automatically coded Other.

Paco and Cupcakes's personal dialogue in the shower is interrupted as the inmates gradually return to the dayroom. This confined space is now charged with sexual energy derived from a tension between subject/object, Self/Other, man/absent woman. From the moment the play started, however, sex was in the room to stay. But now, this roomful of "stiff dick[s] knows no conscience" (72). To add to this atmosphere, most of the returning men express their own sexual desires, which, it should be noted, involve diverse manifestations of the absent woman, in some cases

146

via homoerotic displacement: Omar tells Cupcakes, the male object, that he wants to seduce him; Omar and Ice graphically taunt two drag queens who are new prisoners on their floor; Juan talks about the masturbatory fantasies that his girlfriend evokes; and finally, while the other inmates look at pornography, Ice recounts in effusive, vulgar detail his private, masturbatory fantasy of raping Jane Fonda.[9]

Before falling victim once again to the inmates' persecution, Clark is momentarily left alone with Juan. Repeating his plea for understanding, Clark engages personal dialogue with "the only human being [he's] met" (87), hoping to convince Juan that he "told [him] the truth before" (84) about his confusing sex crimes. For Clark, his blunt admissions are signs of his repentance. He pleads with Juan for protection from the other men. Qualifying Clark's accusation that he hates him, Juan replies: "I don't hate you. I hate what you've done. What you are capable of doing. What you might do again" (85). Not only is Juan's generosity of spirit—his willingness to engage Clark in personal dialogue—an unusual gesture within male conversation, but his articulation of an understanding of Clark's personal torment is rare outside of plays set in confining institutions. But Juan also expresses *why* men confess to one another in such restrictive situations: "What you told about yourself was done because of the pressure. People say and do weird things under pressure." According to Juan, men speak truthfully, or at least more personally, if they are under pressure. The pressure on Clark? To stay alive in this institutional cage of entrapped men.

Returning from sick call, the six convicts rejoin Juan and Clark in the dayroom. They have decided that a "council" decision regarding Clark is necessary; the men need to name Clark as stuff, which grants them, via their prison's program, the right to punish him accordingly. Speaking for the group, Paco claims that "[a]nybody that has to rape little girls is a faggot" (88), a reasoning Paco relies upon to distinguish himself from Clark in Cupcakes's eyes. To Paco, and apparently to the other five men, a child molester and a gay man are the same degenerate. In making this link, the convicts return to familiar, ordered territory that establishes the context within which "real" men rightfully assume the power over "other" men to punish them violently for not adhering to the strictures of the masculine ethos. Juan points out to his fellow inmates that the council was set up "to help, not to destroy" (89), which Paco interprets as Juan's efforts to protect the two men he fears that Juan is seducing: Cupcakes and Clark. In his crazed state to win Cupcakes's affection, Paco taps into the collective homoerotic desires and raging homophobia of all the inmates. He does so in order to win their support for violence against Clark. After all, in Piñero's world, real men demonstrate and claim their manhood only by engaging in violence. "I hit the truth," claims Paco, as he boldly announces before the group that "everyone wants you, Cupcakes." Men among men respond to the *naming* of homoerotic tension in the room with fear; male characters deny its articulation (and thereby its range of possible meanings) through an immediate, stark homophobic response—one that is repeatedly violent and rarely accompanied by discussion of the controversial topic. This raw moment of articulation and response in *Short Eyes* crystallizes what is often the pivotal, unspoken tension toward which most male-cast plays dramatically move, regardless of their settings.[10]

And so, Clark's fate is cast without real discussion. Despite several inmates' hesitation, it is a foregone conclusion that Clark is to be punished savagely for his crime—which by now has been transformed from child molestation to homosexuality. The inmates symbolically deny their own homoerotic feelings, or at least think of them as something other than gay, by displacing their fear onto an act of homosocial aggression. In punishing Clark, they avoid and repress their own (anticipated) punishment. During this momentary challenge to their collective identity as men, they value only their realignment as Men among themselves. Clark's final "haughty racist contempt" (S. Hart 437) may be the linchpin that releases the men's violent behavior, but one must not overlook Paco's construction of this confrontation as a means to prove his manhood to Cupcakes. While Clark's taunt may be intentionally racist ("you filthy bastards" [93]), it is also a clear challenge to *all* the prisoners' identities as Men. Piñero's final "irony" is not that Clark is white and middle-class and therefore must suffer (Platinsky), but rather that he suffers because he does not fit into the masculinist hegemony of the penal and cultural system. This system and its codings dominate the power plays in *Short Eyes*: a homophobic group insists upon the elimination of the "other" to keep its own identity intact.

Only Juan speaks unwaveringly on Clark's behalf. "You want to be an animal, too," Juan says to Cupcakes (91). "This place makes animals out of us," Ice concludes. A knife appears and changes hands several times among Piñero's "animals." From Puerto Rican American to African American hands, the knife finally falls into the white hands; Longshoe unhesitatingly slits

Clark's throat—all before the watchful eye of the figure of order, Nett. The murder, then, occurs precisely in order to facilitate homoerotic desires: the ironic paradox of homosocial bonding (Sedgwick 1985, 1–5). The only order to be restored is that of realigning men under the banner of the masculine ethos, the banner of sameness.

But chaos remains in the prison after the killing. White prisoner now turns on African American, as the violence initially fostered by sexual anxiety and fear transforms into what appears to be gay *and* racial hatred (the men slur each other with taunts of "faggot," "cocksucker," "nigger," and "honky"). Act 2 ends with Longshoe and Ice poised on the edge of violent battle with one another, as Cupcakes screams, "Stop it, goddamn it. Stop it. . . . Oh, my God . . . is this really us" (99). As in the finale to *The Zoo Story,* the male "animal" appears destined to (re)construct the Other in order to survive, in order to know himself. But he also appears, at least in Albee's, Piñero's, and, to be shown later, Rabe's plays, destined to confront that relationship violently. "Is this really us": the dynamic progression of *Short Eyes*'s discourse coherence indicates that this is precisely who the playwright thinks men really are.

Piñero offers a fully developed, verbally intimate epilogue after Clark's brutal killing, a rare dramatization of male interaction after violence (here, later in the evening on the day of Clark's death). It may well be that the perpetuity of confinement enforces, as it were, more "sentences." Nothing is over, finished.[11]

The epilogue is structured as two distinct movements. The first recalls the situation in act 2 of *Glengarry Glen Ross:* a crime has taken place and an investigating officer is on the scene to ask questions of those who may be involved. Unlike Mamet, however, who leaves the officer's inquiry undocumented and unheard, Piñero focuses on the immediacy of the investigation, highlighting Captain Allard's social, and finally personal, dialogue in meetings with various inmates. When speaking with Cupcakes, for instance, Allard broaches the subjects of homoeroticism, homosexuality, and Cupcakes's vulnerability to rape in the prison. When attempting to break down Longshoe, Allard appeals unsuccessfully to the convict's known racist attitudes. But the inmates remain unyielding in their commitment to resist authorized inquiry. As Cupcakes remarks when asked if he would confide in the officer: "I'm no rat, I'm a man" (107). Indeed, Cupcakes *is* a man, now; in fact, all of them are Men, with the possible exception of Juan, the sole independent voice in the room.

Captain Allard concludes that the inmates, and his supposed ally Nett, are lying and that they will continue to lie. He nonetheless announces to the men on the floor that he is ruling the white man's death a suicide. His reason: it is "for the Department" (115). Order in the male house of detention must be maintained at all costs, or so Allard's decision indicates. But he also leaves the inmates with the news that Clark had been mistakenly identified as a child molester. Clark, at least in this current arrest, appears to have been an "innocent victim of circumstances" (117). Upon hearing this latest detail, Cupcakes, once the "hope" of the other prisoners (xiii), wants to know the extent to which he is implicated in the crime. Cupcakes's definition of manhood, however, still refuses to incorporate one's taking responsibility for his actions, an understanding that would move him toward truthful self-engagement.

Responding to Cupcakes's plea, "What have we done?" (117), the convicts, in a rare exchange of personal dialogue, articulate their role in this heinous crime. "We [all] did the killing" (118), El Raheem tells Cupcakes. Yet, since he refused to slit Clark's throat, El Raheem "loses face for exhibiting a degree of humanity that is outside the inmate code" (S. Hart 437). "No, I didn't swing the knife," says Ice, "and neither did you, but we're guilty by not stopping it. . . . We sanctioned it. . . . Only Juan is free" (119). Yet, Juan is free for reasons beyond the inmates' immediate comprehension. Juan speaks truthfully, acts nonviolently, resists being the Man, and encourages personal dialogue with the explicit intention of trying to understand the "other." He is the moral center of the play, an exemplary position for a Latino character, since he all too often is only the (token) "other" who is victimized by racist ideology and privilege. Juan rises above the constraints of the system while remaining a prisoner in the system. All this he achieves without having to terrorize or kill his fellow man. He is neither consumed with hatred for the person (but rather for the crime) nor homophobic toward Clark (or any other men for whom homosexuality is presented as a possibility). He works toward understanding the male "other," embodied in Clark, as well as the difference within his fellow inmates. After all, he accepts the other within himself, essentially freeing himself to recognize the value of the other within all men. Very simply, Juan is not afraid of the Other, nor of the "other" in man. For this, he wins the respect and often the admiration of his fellow prisoners. The crucial significance of Juan's presence to the play's overall meaning—a meaning that incorporates but is not strictly confined to issues of race—is repeatedly underplayed by the critics (Camillo; S. Hart; Ruiz).

In his self-identification, a singularity that is liberated repeatedly during his confinement, Juan has the wisdom to tell Cupcakes the error of his ways. "[Y]ou placed yourself above understanding" (120), the older man tells his favorite disciple, and for that, the prison "stole your spirit" (121). Whether in or out of confinement, Juan seems to suggest, a man among men who seeks release from social constraint can do so through communion with his spirit, with his soul. In Piñero's world, man's access to a spirit distinguishes him from the animal. However, the human spirit is dangerously close to extinction, as David Mamet has noted (qtd. in Leahey), if the state of male characters' interaction is any indication of the human condition. From a Piñerian viewpoint, *The Zoo Story,* therefore, is finally a "spiritless" world. And because of his spirit—which, again, is a commitment to (try to) understand that which is different from one's own identity—Piñero's hero offers an alternative to Albee's vision. He has the potential to understand the "other," to reject violence, *and* to rise above the system's efforts to rob him of his individualization. Yet, for a male character to have such insight into the power of the spirit, into the power of individualization, is rarely dramatized in male-cast plays that occur outside of confining institutions.

Streamers, David Rabe

Despite much criticism to the contrary, David Rabe's war play, *Streamers,* is a strangely hopeful piece about man's potential to connect with other men—if the play is read within the semiotic of maleness and if attention is paid to its discourse coherence. Most critics read the play as a drama about man's chaotic, random existence, from which few or no redemptive qualities can be gleaned (Demastes 36; Kerr 1976a; Rosen 257; Watt; Zinman 15–16). Yet, the power of individualization, of truth telling—of not putting oneself outside of understanding—builds steadily through *Streamers,* I suggest, coming with bittersweet dignity to the foreground at the play's conclusion.

The winner of the 1976 New York Drama Critics Best American Play Award, *Streamers,* according to Toby Silverman Zinman, is the "best play of the [Vietnam War dramatic] canon" (16). For N. Bradley Christie, Rabe's play "achieves a dramatic intensity and power unmatched . . . perhaps in the whole of contemporary American theatre" (107). I would supplement this sweeping praise by emphasizing the need to focus on *Streamers'* remarkable dramaturgical and cultural contribution to the canon of realist male-cast plays, a focus that yields as yet unacknowledged achievements in the area of gender representation in American drama. I would agree with Bonnie Marranca that Rabe is "the voice of the American conscience" (92), although my reasons for thinking of him thus are different.

Streamers is the third play, along with *The Basic Training of Pavlo Hummel* and *Sticks and Bones,* to comprise what has come to be known as Rabe's Vietnam trilogy. "The problem of language lies at the center of all three plays," according to Craig Werner, and in *Streamers,* Rabe "show[s] the nearly insurmountable barriers to human communication" (518). *Streamers* is set in 1965 in an army barracks outside Washington, D.C. It focuses on the conversational dynamics among the men who find themselves in the one-room "home" of army enlistees Billy Wilson, Roger Moore, and Richie Douglas (Rabe 1977, 49).[12] These bachelor roommates, according to William Demastes, are "representative of American culture" (43), which I would particularize as "male" American culture: Billy is a white, alleged heterosexual from Wisconsin; Roger is a straight African American from an unnamed urban center; and Richie is a white, affluent homosexual from New York City. Although presented somewhat stereotypically, "the three men are living in harmony despite their culturally and geographically varied backgrounds," remarks Demastes; "though not a complete cross-sample of American society, they do illustrate the fact that in America different lifestyles and backgrounds co-exist and must somehow comprise a single culture" (43). Moreover, as military personnel, they are encouraged to live harmoniously in their enforced situation. And overshadowing their daily lives is the Vietnam War, raging thousands of miles from their barracks. "The war—the threat of it—is the one thing [the men] share" (30), Rabe observes.

For all intents and purposes, the discourse coherence throughout *Streamers* is comparable to that in *Short Eyes* after Clark enters the prison's dayroom. In both institutional settings, the male characters engage a cycle of dialogues that progresses alternatingly between the cooperative communication of personal dialogue and the uncooperative communication of violence. Carol Rosen rightfully emphasizes the importance of the fact that "the action of the play proper . . . begins with an image of blood, of violence prefigured" (254). Yet, from the start of *Streamers,* violence and personal dialogue exist in a symbiotic relationship. Once again, interaction at this level of communication illustrates that violence and self-disclosure are dynamically connected in male-cast drama.

Streamers opens at dusk in the cadre room. Richie is comforting another recruit, Martin, who has just unsuccessfully attempted suicide by slitting his wrist. The two army friends are frank, emotional, and self-disclosing with one another as Martin contemplates the reasons for his self-mutilation. The characters do not hesitate to express their hatred of the military, their fear of their unknown futures, and, as Martin says, their disappointment that the army is not "different from the way it is" (5). Their interaction is not "failed communication" (Werner 525), nor, for that matter, is Martin merely a "device" (Christie 107). In its outspokenness about the injustices and frights of military life, the men's conversation is not unlike the personally revealing moments shared by soldiers in other realist military plays.[13] Within the confining institution of the military, Martin and Richie liberate the self through their personal dialogue. They frankly speak their feelings and, in doing so, resist the authority that not only contains them but also threatens to deprive them of their individual voices.

Unlike *The Zoo Story,* which ends in bloodshed, as does act 2 of *Short Eyes, Streamers* opens with the stark reality of a man who is wounded and bleeding. In this respect, it is possible to argue that Rabe intentionally presents bloodshed as a feature in male interaction. Rabe imagines, as we shall see, an ongoing cycle between violence and personal dialogue when men are together. Martin brings his wound into the bachelors' home. In doing so, his action foreshadows not only future incidents of physical violence that ignite among the men, but also the painful opening up of other soldiers' repressed, personal wounds that have scarred them psychologically and emotionally. The characters' disclosures exist, however, within the dynamics of their shared, interpersonal conversations.

At this stage in my argument, it does not seem imperative to continue to demonstrate the pattern that repeats itself throughout the discourse coherence of male-cast plays. I hope that the preceding seven play analyses have effectively illustrated that such a linguistic, conversational pattern is a distinguishing feature of realist male-cast plays. To repeat at this point a moment-to-moment conversational analysis of another play jeopardizes the exploration of an equally vital layer to the structuring of male-cast plays—a layer that is distinct and pervasive during men's personal dialogue. Since the previous analysis of *Short Eyes* demonstrates in detail how the discourse coherence in a drama set in a confining institution is structured according to a tension created between the uncooperative communication of violence and the cooperative communication of personal dialogue, it stands as an illustration of the general structuring device that Rabe also uses in the institutional milieu of *Streamers*. It is more useful now to explore in greater depth than provided in the Piñero analysis the thematics that surface in institutional plays, using Rabe's and Robin Swados's dramas as examples. My immediate focus on specific conversations that occur within the cycle of violence and personal dialogue in *Streamers*, therefore, will identify thematics in personal dialogue that are also dramatized in other male-cast plays set in confining institutions. Are these thematics different from those that characterize social dialogue? And do the thematics in *Streamers*, shared with *Short Eyes* and *A Quiet End*, resurface in the personal dialogue of plays that are not set in confining institutions, the dramas that are the focus of the following chapter?

In their brief opening scene together, Richie and Martin establish a serious level of personal, reflective interaction that is also generally characteristic of other men's conversations throughout *Streamers*. Subsequent personal interaction between any of the characters is broken, and then only occasionally, by the men's challenges to physical exercise or by their avowals to clean up the living space (that is, to execute the daily tasks necessary to maintain proper care of their home and personal belongings). Billy and Roger continually engage one another in these routine activities. Roger, in particular, appears determined to keep his home "straightened up" (24), which he eagerly attempts to do soon after Richie and Martin leave the room.

While performing their evening tasks, Roger and Billy talk about the army and the toll that it is taking on them. Like Martin and Richie before him, Billy is candid in speaking about his fear of death, of his inability to absorb what it means to be a soldier who may go to Vietnam. But he also deliberately tries to be casual about it all. Billy does not want his questions and apprehensions to diminish his hard-won male image, even in front of his friend Roger. Billy's remarks reveal him to be an earnest, thoughtful young man who is genuinely troubled by his situation. His demeanor, while sometimes strained, seems generally sincere. This quality presumably enhances the believability of his personal dialogue. Above all, Billy does not want to let his guard down in front of Richie when Richie returns to the room. Billy, whom David Savran cites as the "play's representative of middle-class, middle-American values" (1993, 194), tries to affect a stalwart male image to deflect attention from his otherwise insecure sense of maleness. He chooses to maintain a more macho attitude around Richie simply because Richie threatens his masculinity and sexuality.[14] Richie, who is more casual and unconventional, is culturally coded as an unmasculine, effeminate male; Billy, on the other hand, is "caught in a self-image that leaves no room for acceptance of the 'other'" (Hurrell 105), embodied by Richie. In their first collective interaction as roommates, however, the three men appear generally to get along well together despite tension that occasionally surfaces between Billy and Richie. In this trio, Roger is typically the peacemaker.

Just as Piñero's inmates are sober while conversing in the prison dayroom, so Rabe's three soldiers remain sober while talking in their barracks. In each play, one character quickly introduces the general topics of sex and (male) gender identification into the conversations. This topic, in turn, soon concentrates on homoeroticism. Richie reenters the barracks in a "playful and teasing" mood (13): he tousles Billy's hair; he invites Billy to go to a movie with him where he might "kiss and hug" him (14); and he even proclaims his "love" to the young midwesterner (15). Regardless of Richie's intentions in making these titillating remarks, in "acting gay with a vengeance" (Clum 1992, 220), Billy hears them as overt, sexual overtures that, coming from Richie, disgust him. His response to Richie is hostile and threatening: "I am gonna have to obliterate you" (13). Richie dismisses Billy's nastiness as he blithely heads off to the showers.

In male-cast plays in which characters are sober, the most threatening topic for men to discuss during personal dialogue is homosexuality.[15] (When male characters are drunk, no specific personal topic they may engage—including homosexuality—is taboo. The alcohol, after all, is perceived to be the agent responsible for loosening the men's tongues; male characters rarely take responsibility for the topics they discuss or the opinions they render during their drunken conversations.) Yet, it is ironic that the topic of homosexuality often surfaces early on in sober men's talk that occurs within confining institutions, particularly if the men have exhausted their erotic remarks about absent women during social dialogue. Issues of gender identification surface frequently amid men's social dialogue as the characters aggressively and confidently align themselves under the varied strictures and codes of the masculine ethos. From the perspective of the semiotic of maleness, however, the early inclusion of (homo)sexuality as topic makes some sense in male-cast plays—like *Streamers* and *Short Eyes*—that aggressively move toward personal dialogue between men: gender and sexuality, homosexuality in particular, are the most controversial, tension-ridden topics for men to engage when conversing among themselves.

In Rabe's interracial company, as in Piñero's interracial group of prisoners, sex and gender issues intersect with, and then finally subsume, race and class differences in the men's talk. This does not mean that the latter do not present conflicts for the characters—they do; but they are not, finally, the most divisive or threatening features. The idea and realization of male bonding are paramount to the soldiers. The criteria upon which they establish this more inclusive bonding is based on the identification of the characters' shared gender and presumed heterosexual orientation, not on their racial or class similarities. Much of this is attributed to the fact that sex and gender issues foreground the physical presence of the male *body* in the confined spaces within which the play's dialogue and action occur. Just as in *Short Eyes*, the presence of the male body in *Streamers*, which is initially thrust into the conversation and action by Richie, derails any character's efforts to maintain either social dialogue or personal dialogue not erotically oriented. Once male characters address sex and gender as topics and code their bodies accordingly, it is difficult for them to discuss anything else. All men, at this point during personal dialogue, are subject to naming their sexuality (regardless if they do or not) as well as confronting the fact that they may well be the object of another's desire. This latter occurrence is seen by some male characters as their becoming substitutes for the absent woman if the traditional heterosexual matrix is mapped onto an all-male context. Nonetheless, during personal dialogue, straight men who are among straight, gay, or bisexual men often refuse any acknowledgment of their bodies, deny any comprehension of the potential range of their (erotic) desires, and disavow any understanding of the power that (conscious) fear might hold over their fantasies of and fascination with the Other. For instance, Billy, who is increasingly paranoid and homophobic in *Streamers*, says to Roger: "These bitches [i.e., gays] ... they're so crazy they think anybody can be had. Because they had been had themselves. So you tell 'em you're straight and they just nod and smile. You ain't real to 'em" (17). On the other hand, gays or bisexuals among themselves who engage in personal dialogue (as will be illustrated in *A Quiet End*) more readily acknowledge their bodies, explore the potential range of their desires, and understand the power that fear holds over their fantasies of and identification with the Other.

Richie's flirtatious remarks about same-sex attraction introduce homosexuality as a topic that remains in the men's dialogue throughout the rest of the play. It exists independently from what Christie calls the characters' only "real fear" (108–9) in the play: Vietnam. Homophobia *coexists*—as does racism (Beidler 1982, 1991)—with fear of war in *Streamers*. Nonetheless, whether presented inside or outside the context of war, male characters among themselves in realist drama perpetuate established patterns of discourse coherence and gender codings. On a profound level of personal interaction, Rabe's characters continually confront homosexuality and struggle to understand it as well as their position in relationship to it. After sharing with him his uncomplimentary view on homosexuals, Billy declares to Roger, "[W]e all got to be honest with each other—you understand me?" (17). This specific issue of one's sexuality permeates the dialogue of the sober characters in *Streamers*. I emphasize this distinguishing feature of the characters' physical state, since several drunk characters eventually visit the men's room. Amid their drunken musings, these men will discuss diverse topics (including, but not limited to, homosexuality) within their personal dialogue as they reveal a range of intimate feelings.

Carlyle, an angry African American bisexual enlistee who feels completely dislocated in the white military machine, is the first drunk in the play to invade the trio's home. But just before he does so, Billy persists in getting Roger to express his attitude toward gays. "[E]ver since we been in this room, [Richie's] been different somehow," Billy remarks (16). Roger responds that Richie is "cool" and not a "swish." "[E]ver talk to . . . queers. . . . [E]ver sit down, just rap with one of 'em?" the midwesterner persists. "Hell, no; what I wanna do that for? Shit, no," Roger replies. On the issue of homosexuality, at least, these two men—when alone with each other—appear to be in agreement. Yet, when the three roommates are together, the balance of their collective dynamic fluctuates. Richie, Billy, and Roger are in an uncommon sleeping arrangement since their room is not a military dormitory. Their living quarters, therefore, do not privilege (based upon the sheer breakdown in the number of occupants) any individual's particular cultural or racial identities, or sexual orientation. Each of the roommates is marginal to the others in this particular living arrangement. Outside of their shared gender identities, each man is in an equal position of power to the others simply because each embodies unique differences, whether they be racial, class, religious, or sexual—that is, until someone from outside their home comes inside: enter drunk Carlyle.

It is sufficient to say that when Roger and Carlyle are alone in the barracks, these two African Americans generally discuss race as it relates to the military.[16] When other characters join them in the room, however, Rabe's two African Americans usually forgo talk about race in favor of that dealing with sexuality and gender. Carlyle, who sees himself as a ghetto outsider "amongst a whole bunch a pale, boring motherfuckers" (19), angrily expresses his hatred of the white-led army and his overwhelming fear of going to Vietnam, which, he tells Roger, "ain't our war, brother" (22). "I ain't gonna be able to endure it," the intoxicated soldier confesses, as he desperately asks Roger to "understand" what he is saying (21). Regardless of what they specifically confess during personal dialogue, male characters in confining institutions, as exemplified by Carlyle in his speeches, repeatedly seek and directly ask for the understanding of their listeners.

Just as Carlyle seeks understanding from Roger before he leaves the room, so Billy, after having appealed earlier to Roger for under-standing, turns for compassion to Richie, the source of his anxiety. Conversational movement of this type—which focuses on the the-matic of one's wish to have his confessions understood by another man—only occurs during personal dialogue. For a man to really understand another man at this dynamic level is for the listener to believe that the speaker articulates the (speaker's) truth. On the other hand, for a man to liberate himself while in confinement is for him to be self-disclosing, and to name his feelings as best he can. He does not have to secure the understanding of the listener, however, in order to achieve self-knowledge. Ironically, Billy asks for a "straight talk" with his gay roommate as he intensely chal-lenges the flippant young man: "Are you gonna listen? You gonna hear what I say, Rich, and not what you think I'm sayin'? . . . No b.s. No tricks. . . . [C]ut the cute shit with me, I'm gonna turn you off. Completely. . . . you understand. . . . And I'm talkin' the simple quiet truth to you, Rich. I swear I am" (27). Rabe's play is unique in the male-cast canon for speeches like this. Sober characters ar-ticulate their commitment not only to the speaker-listener dynam-

ics necessary to carry on a meaningful conversation, but they struggle to name their "quiet truths" in order to overcome the oppressive
demands made upon them by an often confusing and contradictory
configuration of gender codings, sexual desires, and the masculine
ethos. What must also be noted, however, is that at this particular
moment in his interaction with Richie, Billy speaks the "truth" as
he presently knows it, or at least admits to it. Billy's sentiments,
as with those that a character expresses at any given moment in a
conversation, are actually relative to the immediate circumstances
and to the present degree of the speaker's self-knowledge. Therefore, what Billy now thinks is the truth, may not be true for him
later on.

One's right to sexual freedom, including interracial homosexual desire (as will be shown later), is another major thematic central to the discourse coherence in *Streamers*. For this reason, Philip
Biedler's claim that Billy's "terror and incredulity" are "*our own*
because, *like* Billy, we know, deeply, inescapably, that Richie is for
real; that Carlyle is for real" (1991, 133; emphasis added) not only
privileges the white "straight" male gaze, but it insists upon its
exclusivity at the expense of all "other" perspectives. Of course
Richie and Carlyle are real; no more, no less so than Billy is. How
each man *chooses* to behave, however, is not predetermined by his
sexual orientation nor by his race, if, in fact, that is Biedler's impli-
cation. In such a reading, which codes both men only as objects,
as "other" via their gay and black identities, Biedler denies the
liberating power of Rabe's representation of multiple subjectivities.
All men are not "like Billy"; Billy is not the universal subject. Billy,
from "other" perspectives, appears just as terrifying and incredu-
lous as Richie and Carlyle appear to Billy and Biedler. This, I think,
is one of Rabe's major achievements in the play.

Nonetheless, Billy's appeal to Richie is actually one for sexual
freedom. He adamantly claims his right to be a heterosexual, despite Richie's desires and efforts to claim Billy as a gay comrade.
It is ironic, however, that Billy speaks up on behalf of his own
sexual freedom, only to deny that same freedom to Richie later on.
"I don't know how else to be," Richie concedes. "I'm not like you
are." In response, Roger also expresses his difficulty in accepting
Richie's sexuality: "You ain't sayin' you really done that [fag]
stuff," Roger asks. "Do you even know what it means to be a fag?"
(28).

Richie replies without hesitation. His remarks are noteworthy
for their honesty, directness, and cultural (albeit overly simplistic)

associations between minorities. "Roger, of course I know what [being gay] is. I just told you I've done it. I thought you black people were supposed to understand all about suffering and human strangeness. I thought you had depth and vision from all your suffering. . . . I just told you I did it. I know all about it" (28–29). In naming himself, in claiming his sexual identity, Richie moves closer to realizing his own liberation.

In the presence of this naming, however, each of the other men is also challenged to name *himself* as truthfully. The burden of responsibility now rests with Billy and Roger to hear, and hopefully to understand, that which Richie speaks. Any denial of Richie's confession or any efforts to reinterpret it are signs of *their* state of being and not Richie's condition. Richie openly claims as his own his "strangeness" (28), his outsider status as the "other" as subject. In doing so, he permanently reorders the conventional hegemony in the men's room; his self-disclosure, one might project, even threatens to rearrange the hegemonic structure in the military institution as well. Those who exercise the power of (true) individualization (here, exemplified by Richie's claiming of his sexual orientation) appear to be at least "spiritually" free of the engendered constraints that the power of the masculine ethos exerts over others. He who demands of himself the execution of the power of individualization—regardless of the personal identity revealed in that naming—is necessarily empowered by it. It is, after all, self-knowledge.

Richie's declaration releases a flood of disclosures from Roger and Billy. Once homosexuality is engaged as an open topic, no other conversational topics remain taboo (presumably, since nothing else could be more threatening). Each man talks at length as he associates personal experiences evoked by the deeply felt emotions expressed in Richie's stark speech. Such a conversation could only occur during personal dialogue. In his monologue, Roger focuses on harsh, childhood memories from his urban neighborhood. As a "little fella" (30), Roger first comes in touch with his fear of homosexuality, with gay bashing, and with the random violence and killings that threaten all men's lives. Roger's recollections of violence trigger for Billy the anticipated horrors that await them in Vietnam. Despite his apparent support for the war, Billy knows that his "fear is real" (31).

The progression of specific topics—namely, within the frame of sex and violence—that surfaces during personal dialogue after Richie names himself a homosexual is noteworthy: homophobia, urban violence, and the violence of the Vietnam War. After the latter topic, Roger reinstitutes social dialogue as he asks the room-mates to finish their routine room cleaning. In doing so, he appeals to the men to return to some recognizable order. Yet this social dialogue is swiftly overcome as Roger and Richie return again to the subject of male (homosocial) bonding and homosexuality. Richie expresses his envy for Roger and Billy's (straight) friendship (33); Roger hears this sentiment as Richie's lament for his homo-sexuality. "Nobody wants to be a punk," Roger concludes. "Not nobody" (34). But Richie does not capitulate to Roger's attempt to strip him of his identity, even when Roger suggests that Richie enlisted in order to "run with the boys for a little [to] get [him]self straightened around" (35). Once again, the male committed to the strictures of the masculine ethos—regardless of his racial, ethnic, or religious identities—is unable to comprehend men's sexual dif-ferences. He is unable to understand the existence of, or possible choice of, male "otherness." And as Rabe has remarked, *Streamers* contains "the danger that if you don't have uniformity of feeling with someone, then you have no connection with them. That forces people into making dangerous demands" (qtd. in Berkvist).

The remainder of the dialogue and actions in act 1 are essen-tially dictated by drunk men who intrude upon the "home" of the three sober roommates (50). First, Sergeants Rooney and Cokes pay the boys a visit, followed by Carlyle's unexpected return to their room to stay for the evening. Drunk male characters nearly always dominate conversations. Their presence not only draws attention to itself, but, as subjects, they redirect whatever topic is under discussion. Sergeants Rooney and Cokes have this impact on the enlistees' earlier personal talk; they also try to get the boys to drink with them. The officers are out "looking for fun" (35) to avoid the harsher realities that confront them: Rooney is soon to leave for Vietnam while Cokes has recently returned from the war because he may have leukemia. To forget their troubles, the sergeants per-form past military experiences—nearly all filled with violence and destruction—by telling stories, singing songs, and boasting of their macho accomplishments: all directed at objects. Most of their recol-lections center on violence against the "other." Unlike the "other" identified in the boys' previous conversation—the homosexual—the "other" defined here is Asian, the non-American enemy.

Thus, in their consecutive, extended conversations, the aggres-sive, "coupled" speakers (Richie and Roger, followed by Rooney and Cokes, all advocates of the male bonding inherent in the

American masculine ethos) find it necessary to identify an enemy, someone who is set up as a failed manifestation of the ideal Western Man. The talk in the barracks, therefore, moves from homosocial topics to homophobia, racism, and violence. When Carlyle returns to the room, his remarks about the military, home, and friendship stimulate a provocative merger with the previous cluster of topics and signal the origin of a pivotal new dimension to the dynamics of the young soldiers' conversation.

But sandwiched in between the intoxicated officers' departure and drunk Carlyle's entrance is Billy's return to the subject of homosexuality. He is obsessed with confessing that he knows someone who is gay. In doing so, Billy bridges the current conversation with the one that he was sharing with his roommates prior to the arrival of the sergeants. He also reveals "his own fascination with homosexuality" (Werner 526). In a lengthy monologue, Billy details his own gay baiting as a teenager with his good buddy Frankie. Frankie's tale, however, turns out to be a "coming out" story. "He was hooked, man. . . . [O]ne day he woke up and he was on it. . . . He was a faggot, black Roger, and I'm not lyin'" (48–49). Billy speaks of Frankie's homosexuality as though he became addicted to a drug, one from which he could never unhook or recover.[17]

From his bunk in the darkened barracks, Billy addresses only Roger when he speaks about Frankie. Billy, one can presume, believes that Roger is able to hear this story without jumping to any conclusions about Billy's sexuality. This speaker does not want to lose control over his listener because to do so is to risk being vulnerable to the listener's judgment. And Billy is still holding on desperately to the codings of the masculine ethos and his wish to be judged favorably by its standards. Clearly, Frankie's story— which essentially *defines* Frankie's sexuality—terrifies Billy, since Billy's deepest fear is brought about by his frustration in defining, in naming with confidence, his own sexuality; he also fears that this sexuality may be out of his control. Yet, what I initially identified as the thematic of sexual freedom that characterizes the personal dialogue of men's talk must again be qualified to acknowledge many male characters' persistent homophobia at this level of interaction. Despite his efforts to exclude Richie from his storytelling, Billy knows that Richie is actually listening in the dark: gay Richie—who not only names himself in the light but who is here to stay in the barracks. The dramatic tension in the soldiers' room is now clearly marked. How do men live with real differences among themselves? How do they live with "other" men when they are in confining institutions? Enter Carlyle, yet another "other," whose race distinguishes him from Richie and Billy, and whose sexuality distinguishes him from Roger, his African American brother.

"You got a little home here, got friends, people to talk to. I got nothin'," drunk Carlyle confesses to Roger (50). This notion of home will take on added significance throughout *Streamers*. (As we will see, home will eventually constitute a major thematic in men's personal dialogue throughout the canon.) Carlyle is envious of the homosocial bonding—including the roommates' willingness to converse with one another—in the boys' interracial home. Rosen, one of the few critics who treats Carlyle sympathetically, remarks that Carlyle "tries to communicate his pain to the three boys who tell stories and pointed anecdotes while Carlyle just says what he wants, expressing directly what the others will not admit" (254). He sees in their arrangement and interaction the qualities he desires in a home of men who "got it made" if for no other reason than they have one another (50). Since he does not feel a part of anyone's home, Carlyle assumes that he is not safe from harm. He is enraged at the prospect of his being sent to Vietnam and terrified at the thought of dying, feelings that he presumes are only those of one who is homeless. And so Carlyle curls up on the floor of the barracks and falls asleep in someone else's home. He does so under the illusion that in this place he is safe, that in this room he is welcomed as a male intimate. He yearns to be, as it were, part of this (male) family. Carlyle, the doubly marginalized male who is black and bisexual, essentially forces himself on the trio of men and demands that they deal with him. Like Richie, he refuses to go away, to be invisible, despite criticism from the other family members.

Act 2 breaks with the neoclassic unities established in act 1 since it occurs several days later. Most male-cast plays that break with the unity of time initiate each new series of conversations with social dialogue. Rabe's play is unconventional, however, as Billy and Roger immediately reengage personal dialogue at the start of their conversation that opens act 2. It is as though there is no substantial lapse in the characters' train of thought,

There are five distinct conversations during this late afternoon in the cadre room (act 2, scene 1). All are basically personal dialogues; four out of the five are dyadic interactions. Billy and Roger's opening talk is not wholly dissimilar from Richie and Carlyle's conversation, which follows it. Both moments are metalinguistic at their core, as Billy and Carlyle, each to his respective partner, explores the nature of talk and its place in meaningful communication. I highlight these two moments for their dramatization of yet another thematic in male-cast plays: men's desire, their *need*, to connect personally with other men.

"All I do is talk," Billy concludes after asking Roger if he thinks he (Billy) is a "busybody" (58, 56). Billy fears that he does not "know how to behave in a simple way," that he "overcomplicate[s] everything" by "seein' complications that [are] there but nobody else [sees]" (56). Roger, the supportive friend, gives Billy the freedom to chat about these personal concerns, yet he never stops trying to get Billy to leave the room to play basketball (which, in its own covert way, is Roger's attempt to get Billy to stop talking). But Billy wants and needs to secure a sense of Roger's feelings about engaging in male conversation. For Billy, this knowledge is intrinsic to the intimate dynamics of male friendship that he so desperately seeks to retain. He remains uncertain about appropriate male identities and relationships since confronted with Richie's sexual innuendoes and his coming out. But Billy does not ask Roger for this information directly. Rather, he initially displaces this query by expressing his wishes to know a local barroom dancer "to talk to her [and] tell her stuff" (58). Through his reference to the absent woman, Billy expresses his genuine desire to talk with someone—to engage actively in talk that is not misconstrued as busybody interaction. Billy uses the absent woman to introduce the topic of intimate conversation and as a buffer against pressure that Roger might feel regarding Billy's need to talk. Most importantly, Billy does not want Roger to hear his need for personal conversation as a sexual advance; hence, the rhetorical positioning of the absent woman prior to his direct questioning of Roger.

"[Y]ou remember how we met," Billy tells Roger. "You started talkin' to me. You just started talkin' to me and you didn't stop. . . . Did you see somethin' in me made you pick me?" "You was just the first [white person] to talk back friendly," Roger replies (58). Despite this compliment to Billy's personality and his expression of confidence in their friendship, Roger does not encourage Billy to go on talking. He insists that they maintain some order, forgoing personal, verbal play in favor of the impersonal, physical play of basketball. He wants them to return to the social activities aligned with the masculine ethos, activities that ground their identities as Men. Billy picks up on Roger's reluctance to continue personal dialogue. He registers his disappointment, however, by claiming, "I don't know what it is I'm feelin'. Sick like" (59). Soon after, the two boys leave for the gym, making the room available to Richie and Carlyle.

Despite his display of a more erratic, uneven temperament—and the fact that he continues to drink—Carlyle mimics Billy's desire for personal dialogue with another man. Whether drunk or sober, men in Rabe's play crave interpersonal involvement so much that they are willing to *ask* for it. This request is an uncommon dramatic action for men among themselves. Unlike Billy, however, Carlyle uses his body to initiate personal interaction. The black man, according to Carlyle, is "too close...to his body....he BELIEVE in his body" (67), a belief that, in turn, influences his actions. Returning to the only home in the army that he has been able to penetrate, Carlyle is determined to find out "who the real Richie" is (62). The "real Carlyle" is eager and ready to have sex with Richie (Carlyle assumes that the men arranged this home because Richie is sexually servicing Billy and Roger). In a schizophrenic minicycle of personal insights and outbursts of violent behavior (a cycle that mirrors the larger cycle of the play's discourse coherence), Carlyle admits that he is "restless" and does not "even understand it" (63). But he does understand that he wants something from Richie. Yet the expression of his desire refuses to center comfortably on either sexual or conversational signs because he naturally intertwines them.

For Carlyle, personal talk can be the language of seduction, while seduction is personal action. "I want to talk to you," Carlyle submits to Richie, "why don't you want to talk to me?" "We can be friends. Talkin' back and forth, sharin' thoughts and bein' happy" (64). But Richie is understandably hesitant to engage this explosive personality, whose motivations are not clear. Sensing Richie's rejection of him, Carlyle "ignites [in] anger." "DON'T YOU TELL ME I AIN'T TALKIN' WHEN I AM TALKIN'!" Carlyle shouts, only to move immediately into personal dialogue. If Richie will not ask Carlyle about his feelings, then Carlyle will go ahead and tell him anyway: "It like [the army] think I ain't got no notion what a home is....like I ain't never had no home....IT LIKE THEY THINK THERE AIN'T NO PLACE FOR ME IN THIS MOTHER ARMY." Here, two major thematics in male-cast plays converge: a man's desire for a "home" and his desire to connect personally with another man. Frustrated by his failure to achieve either of these wishes, Carlyle, according to traditional representations of male behavior, has two options: either to continue to talk or to become violent. True to his fashion, he chooses both. "How come you talk so much?" Richie asks Carlyle, a paradoxical echo of Billy's concern about his own conversational habits in the previous scene. The big man initially replies, "I don't talk, man, who's gonna talk? YOU?" (65), only to follow up with a violent outburst of repeated, homophobic slurs at Richie: "You goddamn face ugly fuckin' queer punk!" (66). Carlyle has moved, therefore, through a cycle of gay desire, to violence, to gay desire, to violence, to homophobia. His "vicious... spit[ting] out" at Richie ends their conversation, one that is nonetheless characterized by Carlyle's obsession to find, as he concludes, "words to say my feelin'" (67). This commitment to personal language for the sake of naming things and feelings—all in an effort to connect with other human beings—comes from the mouth of one whom the other men label "crazy" (73). Carlyle may well become crazy, as his later actions suggest, but his frustrated efforts to understand his relationship to others and to articulate his needs and wishes are not without meaning in the context of the often-failed interaction of male characters among themselves.

Before leaving the room, Carlyle has a brief, telling moment with Billy. Each man privately confronts his actual and ideological foil, as well as his unconscious. Their point of friction, predictably, involves homosexuality. Carlyle tells Billy that he wants sex from Richie; Billy, when asked by Carlyle to talk about gay sex, resists naming anything about it. In fact, Billy starts to get physically ill, a possibly psychosomatic response. Capitalizing on Billy's weakness, Carlyle warns him: "I can see your heart, Billy boy, but you cannot see mine. I am unknown. You... are known" (69). Carlyle, the bisexual African American, proudly distinguishes himself from the heterosexual white male, the one upon whom the American masculine ethos is constructed. Carlyle values his identity as the doubly marginalized "other" subject despite its codes, which keep him on the outside, because he *knows* his own power to disrupt the order of those inside. And those like Billy, who are privileged within the cultural structure, are repulsed by, dismissive of, threatened by, and utterly fascinated with the power that the male "other" represents in all his various manifestations. Here, the "other" (Carlyle, or for that matter, Richie) "knows" who Billy is and what Billy represents because the "other" must confront, must understand, what he is not in order to survive. All that Billy knows is that he is privileged in the culture, that he expects to establish those privileges in his army home, and that his words are to be the final ones. Billy's battle to know the male other—as well as the difference within—in order to know how to live with the "other" captures yet another primary thematic in the male-cast canon.

Act 2, scene 1 comes to a rapid close after Roger returns to the room and convinces Billy to join Carlyle and him on a boys' night out in the big city. For Roger, Carlyle "brings back home" (72), a home that legitimizes his roots, his race, outside of the white military structure. Talk of absent women dominates, as Roger promises whores galore for each man who comes along. "You always talkin' how you don't do nothin'," Roger accuses Billy. "Let's do it to-night—stop talkin'" (73). Riding the momentum of Roger's energy to act, Billy takes this opportunity to go outside the boundaries of their shared, private space and publicly prove his manhood to everyone at home. He has given up on language as an effective tool for naming himself. So, off he goes into the drunken maelstrom of homosociability, determined to *act* like a man.[18] Ironically, Billy gives himself over to the "other" to guide him on his journey; he makes the male "other" responsible for his education, for the identification and demonstration of his manhood, if you will. "We all goin' to be friends" (75), Carlyle concludes, as the soldiers' departure from and their anticipated return to the room seems to signify for Carlyle his permanent place in this home.

The play's final scene continues the previous scene's cycle of personal dialogue and violence while introducing several new thematics. The drunk men return to the barracks room to join Richie, who is sober since he has not gone out. They all speak openly and self-disclosingly: some do so because they are drunk, Richie, because he likes to talk (often coded as a trait of gay characters). In their opening monologues, Rabe's men trade memories. In the dark of night, the men's interaction takes on the quality of young scouts sharing confidences while sitting around a campfire, bonding with one another through their mutual storytelling. First Richie, then Carlyle, reminisces about his upbringing, each addressing his complicated relationship with his father. Carlyle clearly remains exhilarated by the evening's apparent outcome. "We gonna be one big happy family" (78), the soldier announces to the others, as he feels their sense of community through their interactive personal dialogue.

Believing that he has a new ally in Carlyle, another man who unabashedly identifies himself as "other" in the room, Richie uses his explicit bonding with the bisexual to tease Billy with more sexual overtures. In light of Carlyle's expressed sexual appetites, Richie knows that their home is no longer dominated by straight men. Reacting to Richie's baiting, Billy warns the gay man, "You just keep at it, you're gonna have us all believin' you are just what you say you are." Richie's curt reply: "Which is more than we can say for you" (78). From the start of their interaction, Richie distrusts the persona that Billy exhibits among men. The gay soldier believes that Billy's posturing is just that—a fictional construction aimed at creating a more "pseudo-earthy quality" (79), and therefore a more socially acceptable identity for a man to assume when among men. But "lies and ignorance offend me," Richie claims as he challenges Billy to a counterattack. Richie is determined to force Billy to speak honestly about himself. And the quickest, *nonviolent* way to create the tension among men that may facilitate that disclosure is to foreground the male body—to privilege the physical body, in all the power of its active, silent presence, over words.

Amid a silence that "goes on and on," Richie and Carlyle begin to play erotically with one another, a sight that "fills" Billy "with fear" (80). Going beyond the talk of interracial desire that permeates the dialogue in *The Toilet,* the actual physical display of interracial lust escalates the tensions generated by the racial and sexual codings already at play in the room.[19] Richie eventually asks Roger and Billy to go for a walk in order to leave Carlyle and him in privacy. But "we live here," Roger asserts, to which Richie replies, "It's my house, too, Roger; I live here, too" (81). Richie's claim reminds all of the room's occupants that no one is privileged over the "other" in this space; in this house, all "others" are subjects. Demanding the recognition of his right to be with Carlyle (just as the others exercise their right to go to the whorehouse, for instance), Richie is not, as Marranca asserts, the "real villain" in *Streamers* (87). To judge Richie from the position of his villainy is to privilege Billy, his subjectivity, and all that he represents. Roger, who in his own right has suffered social oppression, cannot deny Richie's claim to rights in their barracks: "He your friend. This your home. So that mean he can stay. It don't mean I gotta leave" (82). Billy, however, takes a different tack, interpreting Richie's actions as a temptation to initiate a "war at home." In each case, "[A] soldier attempt[s] to shield himself from unwanted stimuli in order to protest a familiar sexual orientation: Billy holding back from homosexuality, Richie advancing his claims" (Herman 105).

Gay sex "ain't gonna be done in my house," Billy promises. "I don't have much in this goddamn army, but *here* is mine" (83). As Richie and Carlyle are about to engage in fellatio, Billy retaliates by again moralistically asserting that sex between men "ain't right"

(84). Unable to "let people be" (85), if only for a moment, drunk Billy makes the fatal assumption that his standards determine acceptable male interaction. The strictures of the American masculine ethos dictate that homosexuality is forbidden—and as the straight white male, Billy assumes not only the power to police this family but represents the authorized voice of a homophobic, patriarchal American military and society. It never sinks into Billy's consciousness that not every male emulates him. Very simply, Billy does not know how to live with difference. All he knows is that difference—and especially the difference within—terrifies him. His enemies are men who are differently masculine, men whose ideologies or sexual orientations or both are other than his own. And so, unconscious that his immediate actions anticipate his combat with the Vietnamese, Billy self-righteously practices on the gays at home.

Carlyle's anger steadily rises amid his growing confusion over the authority in this house (84)—and consequently a feeling of uncertainty over his rights in this place. "Don't you got no feelin' for how a man feel? I don't understand you [Billy and Roger].... DON'T YOU HEAR ME!? I DON'T UNDERSTAND THIS SITUATION HERE" (83). Again, note Carlyle's direct, desperate appeal for understanding, which includes the acknowledgment of a man's feelings. Repeatedly, Carlyle—who in his drunken state speaks with a voice of personal appeal—tries to engage the remaining men in a dialogue that explains the situation. Instead, the others elect to speak around Carlyle, each man with his own agenda. Not taking Carlyle seriously and in effect denying his individualization, Billy accuses him of being a "fuckin' animal" if he engages in gay sex (81). Carlyle rejects this slur: "I KNOW I ain't no animal, don't have to prove it" (84). Carlyle, as Janet Hetzbach suggests, "is alienated by his race, his education, and social status" (184); yet, one must also recognize that he is alienated by his sexuality as well.

But when Billy again tries to stop Carlyle from having sex with Richie, Carlyle resorts to physical violence (of the kind that Jerry relates to animal behavior in *The Zoo Story*). First, he slices Billy's hand with a switchblade. In an immediate, passionate plea, Carlyle says, "[I]t don't make me feel good—hurt me—hurt on somebody I thought was my friend. But I ain't supposed to see. One dumb nigger. No mind, [Billy] thinks, no heart, no feelings a gentleness. You see how that ain't true, Richie" (87). Carlyle struggles between the power of dialogue, which may help him to understand the truth of the situation, and the power of violence, which attests that only the "knife [is] true" (86). Carlyle's private battle—his conflict of choice between the powers of personal dialogue and violence—is a classic example of male characters' struggle to identify the means by which to understand the truth of their relationship to other men. In the dramatic and semiotic tradition of the discourse coherence in male-male representation, Carlyle's "explosion" is less "random" (Rosen 250), "unexpected" (Demastes 36), or "manipulat[ive]" (Barnes 1976) than critics generally observe (see also Marranca 87; Kerr 1976b; Gill 1976; Beaufort).[20] Rather, one recalls Jerry's "teaching emotion" in Albee's zoo of male interaction as a possible resolution to this conflict. The knife is "the only connection possible" (Rosen 256). This physical brutality is an expected component of the cycle of personal dialogue and verbal abuse that circulates in *Streamers*. It is actually part of "a design, a shape" of male interaction that Walter Kerr otherwise finds wanting in the play (1976a). Kerr does not recognize this pattern, however, since it is only apparent if one positions the play's discourse coherence within the shaped structure of the male-cast canon.

Ironically, Billy reveals the "difference within" only after Carlyle's violation of his body. Amid an outpouring of racist, homophobic bile—a verbal abuse that, to Demastes, "seems justified" (44)—Billy names himself as a privileged college graduate and not the streetwise persona he has been projecting. Billy finally liberates his identity in this confining institution. But his self-identification is frightening in its deep hatred of the "other." Billy's homophobia and "racism as miscegenation" are undeniable (Herman 106). "I put you down, I put you down—you gay little piece a shit cake—SHIT CAKE," Billy verbally assaults Richie, only to turn next on Carlyle: "AND YOU—you are your own goddamn fault, SAMBO! SAMBO!" (88). Carlyle matches Billy's verbal abuse with a swift knife stab into the white boy's stomach. "Don't nobody talk that weird shit to me, you understand?" Carlyle declares, as Billy dies (89). But Carlyle's bloody actions are not over until he also kills Sergeant Rooney, who returns, unexpectedly, to the enlistees' home.

Rabe's play comes full circle in its return to uncooperative communication and bloody violence; it both begins and nearly ends at a point of male violence that recalls the conclusion of *The Zoo Story*. But the qualifier, "nearly," is significant: the remaining characters do reengage personal dialogue, as Rabe accepts the challenge to present men in the moments after horrendous violence. Unlike Elizabethan male characters, for instance, American male characters are rarely presented amid the immediate aftermath of the inhumanity, injustice, and tragic chaos they create or observe. Rarely are they shown wisely explicating the lesson we expect them to have learned. Consider as exceptional the dramaturgical and thematic value of the epilogue in *Short Eyes*. This is an unusual dramatization of male interaction (although it is also one that is encouraged simply because some characters remain as they must; not all characters are free to leave the room in confining institutions). Rabe's play also departs from the norm—in fact, one step beyond Piñero's conclusion—as he presents men among themselves amid death. Although John Clum asserts that the survivors learn nothing from the violence (1992, 222), the playwright forces some of the characters, as well as the spectator, to go beyond violence, keeping the action moving forward. He introduces new military personnel who arrive to clear the room of the bodies. Other soldiers drag Carlyle, howling a now familiar phrase, from the scene of the crime: "I don't understand you people!" (100). And as Rabe posits, "The play is about people misunderstanding each other. The violence comes out of everybody lying to each other—the games, the lies, the masquerading, the maneuvering, are what make the violence happen" (qtd. in Berkvist). But what happens after the violence?

Richie and Roger remain alone in their home, and *Streamers* dramatizes the awkwardness, the shock, and the personal guilt that the two youths experience. Despite Roger's first impulse to clean the room, to return to order, to dispel chaos from his house, he nonetheless engages in personal dialogue with a sobbing Richie. Their topic is Billy's sexuality, the truth of which only Billy knew. Each survivor is true to his own perception. "I just wanted to hold his hand, Billy's hand, to talk to him," pleads Richie, to which Roger replies, "But he didn't wanna; *he* didn't wanna." "He did," claims Richie. "No, man," retorts Roger. "He did. He did. It's not my fault," urges Richie (102–3). Their exchange is interrupted as Cokes, who is drunk, enters the room to look for Rooney. It is important to note that Cokes has no idea of the murders. Therefore, the depth of insight that he conveys in his remarks to the boys is unprovoked by the preceding actions. Here, one could argue, Cokes speaks frankly either because he is drunk and his resistance is low, or he is pensive due to his fear of failing health. Whatever the case may be, Cokes's comments are poignant. The sergeant clearly has "difficulty maintaining the brand of bravado his macho code demands" (Christie 111). And unlike Erie in *Hughie,* men listen to Cokes's words.

Cokes's insights are also notable since they alter the play's thematic direction. While Cokes never denies the existence of violence (nor his own ability to be violent), he finally refuses to sanctify violence—whether toward himself or "others"—as the sole definition of man's existence. His remarks are inspired, finally, by his awareness of his own mortality, which "gives you a whole funny different waya lookin' at things" (108). Speaking from his experiences, Cokes essentially expresses a hope for man to accept others for who they are ("Don't be yellin' mean" at Richie, Cokes warns Roger, "There's a lotta worse things in this world than bein' a queer" [107]) and a hope for man to learn from his past mistakes in order to value life ("that little gook [in] that spider hole he was in, I was sittin' on it. I'd let him out now, he was in there" [108]). This last reference recalls Cokes's story about his trapping a Korean in a spider hole with an active grenade. "I can feel him in there, though, bangin' and yellin' under me, and his yelling I can hear is begging for me to let him out." Like the vast majority of characters in the canon, Cokes is in conflict not only with the male "other" who exists outside of himself, but with the difference within himself as well. *Streamers* dramatizes this thematic from its opening dialogue. But, significantly, Cokes comes to realize that he would release the "little gook" now, if he had the choice again. Cokes also speaks implicitly for the long-range personal value inherent in the release of the difference within himself—the "otherness" that personalizes his own identity. For a man to release the "other" is to free his identity from the powers of the masculine ethos, male mythologies, and simple inhumanity.

Like Carlyle before him, Cokes remains in the room to sleep for the night. Again recalling sad, desperate Carlyle's wishes, Cokes also wants to be a part of a home and family, to connect meaningfully with other men, to know that he has the right to be himself, and to be able to express his feelings when among men. He also adds a "crucial element" to the play, as Werner rightly suggests: "the recognition of his own share of responsibility for the chaos which surrounds him" (528). But Cokes confesses all these wishes and observations while he is drunk. Although Rabe pushes against the male stereotype by having Cokes (as well as Richie and Carlyle) speak as personally as he does, he has nonetheless settled for clichéd, predictable male behavior when it comes to the men's heavy drinking. Thus, sober Richie's self-disclosing dialogue among an interracial, sexually diverse group of men (albeit within a confining institution) is one of Rabe's most surprising contributions to the dramatic representation of male communication and identity.

In the fading moments of *Streamers,* Cokes sings a "makeshift language imitating Korean, to the tune of 'Beautiful Streamers.'"[21] This music signals both closure and (a need for) a new beginning, as it eventually becomes a "dream, a lullaby, a farewell, a lament" (109). After the silence following his song, Cokes "makes the soft, whispering sound of a child imitating an explosion, and his entwined fingers come apart" (110). This image resonates with meaning for all male characters. To a tragic extent, language fails the men in *Streamers* (or rather, they fail to use language constructively), yet the soldiers still urgently desire to reconnect to something meaningful. As the "lingering light fades" in the room, this vision of men's willful destruction is juxtaposed with the tranquil simplicity of its execution, a simplicity that wells from man's enduring, unbounded imagination. Like a child, a man, too, can mindlessly destroy (his) creations. Man and child alike have the powers to recreate, yet they must do so from the beginning. It is this infantile self—a spirit of imagination, vitality, and promise (a spirit, therefore, which is distinct from Piñero's spirit of understanding)—who intuits and reveals the risks necessary to create anew. This spirit of the infantile self creates beginnings. In this closing gesture, Cokes implicitly accepts men's power to *change.* Armed with the self-knowledge that comes through change, a man can face his fear of powerlessness by exercising his power of individualization, which in turn, recognizes his awareness of the difference within all humanity. Cokes projects this self-knowledge cumulatively: first through his personal, reflective comments to Richie and Roger, and then in his final childlike gesture. *Streamers* ends not in violence, but in a riveting, inarticulate image of a man's expression of truth.

And so, another trio of men now sleeps in this room. Amid their collective losses, they give birth to a different unity. Different men reconnect, if only for a moment. Rabe finds a beginning for new communicative levels, and in particular for male interaction. This optimal dynamic resides in men's willingness to free the difference within themselves. Only by starting here—by releasing the "little gook" in the spider hole—can men gain self-knowledge and, in turn, begin to know "others" more fully. In this vein, the pressing challenge facing today's playwrights is to present male characters who, neither drunk nor facing death, come to express this understanding. For one to dramatize such a character convincingly

and un-self-consciously constitutes a radical act of male representation in American drama.

Human contact in *Streamers* is the sharing of personal words,
fleeting as it may be in this devastating play, which is distinguished
by its glimpses of atypical representations of men among men. Despite much criticism to the contrary, *Streamers* takes a decisive
step to dramatize one direction that may eventually lead male characters out of Albee's zoo.

A Quiet End, Robin Swados

For the men in *Streamers*, Vietnam is a horrific menace that looms
before them—an experience they have yet to face in person, the
fear of which relentlessly informs their entire being. In Robin
Swados's *A Quiet End*, Tony, a Vietnam veteran who survived the
Asian killing fields, returns home to find years later that he must
face yet another life-threatening battle. Thirty-eight years old, the
unemployed gay actor and athlete is living with AIDS. At the opening of *A Quiet End*, set "early last winter" in the 1980s (Swados
1991a, 8),[22] Tony resides in an AIDS hospice in Upper Manhattan
with two other unemployed gay men who are also living with the
disease: Max, a witty and articulate, often cynical Jew in his early
thirties, who has been dismissed from his teaching position for
distributing AIDS information to an inquiring, possibly ill student;
and midwestern Billy, a lapsed Catholic in his late twenties, who
is a struggling pianist-composer.

In its blend of medical care in a domestic environment, the
hospice is a unique setting for the gravely ill. In a rundown apartment converted by an AIDS support organization called the Project,
Swados's three men find themselves living under the same roof
solely because of their health and their need for psychological,
emotional, and economic sustenance from others. Medical personnel are a phone call away, as these men try to live independently
amid some semblance of home—a home that, in the end, they must
create for themselves. They must also take responsibility for the
operations of their hospice-home for as long as they remain in it.
Thus, unlike the more restricted, monitored, dependent life of a
patient in a conventional hospital,[23] the person living with AIDS
in the hospice is part of a community of the ill, a community that
takes responsibility for its own immediate needs.

The discourse coherence in male-cast plays like *A Quiet End*,
Corinne Jacker's *Terminal*, and Tom Cole's *Medal of Honor Rag*,

which are set in hospitals, hospices, or nursing homes, differs markedly from the discourse coherence in plays set in other confining institutions such as prisons or the military. Whereas plays like *Short Eyes* and *Streamers* move in a cycle of personal dialogue and violence, *A Quiet End* adheres to social and personal dialogues, with the latter dominating the men's communication. Unlike *Streamers,* where alcohol readily flows, the characters in Swados's hospice neither drink nor ingest unprescribed drugs. And most noticeably, there is no physical violence or verbal abuse.

Physical contact between Swados's men surfaces, not as a threatening act of aggression, but as a consoling means. Nonerotic physical gestures—a heartfelt hug, a knowing touch, or a firm cradling—spontaneously happen between the characters. One man's efforts to combat another's "rage and hurt" (77) through physical comfort is as common as personal dialogue to untangle a web of angry feelings. This physical interaction, nonsexual yet familiar, extends the dramatic options we have covered so far available to men. Such coded gestures, while infrequently exercised in male-cast plays, remain within the domain of gay and bisexual characters' actions. In this regard, Swados's choices remain part of the traditional pattern in male representation. A heterosexual character rarely initiates physical contact in his efforts to comfort any man, especially if the two males are in a nonfamilial relationship to one another.[24]

There are fourteen discrete conversations in *A Quiet End,* of which twelve are dyadic. This nearly exclusive reliance upon dyadic talks in a play cast with three or more characters distinguishes *A Quiet End* from plays like *The Toilet* and *Short Eyes* whose structure relies upon group conversations. Only one fully realized group talk occurs among the roommates, and that is early on in act 1 (a brief encounter involving all three men, however, ends act 2, scene 1). When the roommates speak collectively, their conversation circulates between social and, predominantly, personal dialogue.

When it maintains a unified realist structure, *A Quiet End* is kin with two-character plays such as *Hughie* and *The Zoo Story.* Unlike the discourse coherence in these plays, however, all twelve dyadic interchanges in *A Quiet End* are personal dialogues. In five of the talks, the only participants are the roommates; in three, either Max or Billy speaks with Jason, who is Max's lover; and in the remaining four, each roommate or Jason speaks privately to a psychiatrist.

I draw attention to the breakdown of characters' conversations in the play for two reasons. The dyadic relationship between men in a confining institutional setting yields personal dialogue, as in *Short Eyes* and *Streamers*. But Swados interrupts "real" dramatic time. A remark made during a conversation between Billy and Max triggers a flashback for Max to his private talk with the Project's psychiatrist. Each man in the play has a comparable flashback to a conversation with the doctor; only Jason's talk with him occurs in present time at the play's conclusion. For all intents and purposes, the otherwise realist structure of the play is interrupted by the characters' interaction with the psychiatrist, who is heard but not seen. As in so many male-cast plays, men are self-disclosing to authority figures whose cultural or professional role is to get information, to get someone else to talk and to reveal more about himself: a therapist, a doctor, a police officer, a judge, a boss, a clergyman.

What is interesting in Swados's play is that the men's conversations with the psychiatrist do not substantially alter the roommates' or the lovers' desire and ability to speak frankly among themselves. From the start, the men appear to be comfortable in interacting personally with each other. Although they are still getting to know one another, linked in time and space through their circumstantial living arrangement and the shared threat of death, the roommates are still presented as receptive, conversant individuals. This quality stems from a sense of each man being content with his self-identity, which, initially, is defined by his sexuality. No man in this play threatens another man's sense of himself. In terms of discourse coherence, therefore, *A Quiet End* is based on personal dialogue. What, then, is the function of the therapist in this play's discourse coherence? While the men may well reveal details to the psychiatrist that they would not otherwise (Swados 1991b), such information primarily adds to the spectator's composite of a particular character. It does not appreciably alter the personal dynamic that each man brings to and demands from his interaction with the others. Let me illustrate this with an example, one that is characteristic of the dynamics among the men outside their brief talks with the psychiatrist.

During the only significant interaction involving all three roommates, each man is an eager participant in the conversation. A fascinating feature in the men's triadic talk is that the topics that surface during their social dialogue—football, for instance—become catalysts for their personal reflections, including their deeper feelings. By being interested listeners and respecting each individual's right to his own history and feelings, Swados's men create a safe space for a speaker's self-disclosures. The quiet end is the result of the characters' commitment to maintain personal communication, a commitment evident in how they talk with one another. If they do not "understand" a comment (19), they ask for an explanation— and get one in return.

When Tony reveals to Max and Billy that he was a high school football player, the two roommates respond differently. Max is repulsed initially because it is such an "animalistic," macho activity (19). Billy, who is a noncompetitive athlete in his own right, is captivated by the thought. What distinguishes the lengthy discussion of football is the immediacy with which the men move from cliché (Max, the college graduate and nonathlete, hates the sport; Billy, the athlete with a high school diploma, admires it) to personal truths about what the subject triggers on a deeper level. Billy admits that he finds football "sexy" and that he "fantasize[s] about football players... [with] [a]ll those clothes to take off" (21). And Max admits to Billy why he hates sports: "I was always the last to be chosen" (24). Moving effortlessly from social to personal, self-examining dialogue, Swados's characters are aware that, literally, "football's got nothing to do" with the intimate feelings they are revealing and accepting (24). They demand complete, honest relationships from one another in their hospice-home, and they caringly, yet aggressively, establish that they will settle for nothing less. This communicative dynamic appears "natural" for these men; it also surfaces in the absence of an authoritative figure.

As an institutional play, *A Quiet End* begins where *Short Eyes* leaves off. Only after witnessing death do Piñero's characters come to realize that they fail as men because they place themselves "above understanding" (Piñero 1975, 120); on the other hand, Swados's roommates, each of whom is acutely aware of his incurable disease and hence his mortality, affirm their commitment to try to understand others while expecting others to work toward understanding them as well. Certainly, it is arguable that the men in the hospice speak truthfully to one another simply because they are facing death. (For example, Cokes, fearful of having leukemia, releases his personal feelings in the monologue that closes *Streamers*.) But there is a less conscious explanation if one connects the speaker's relationship to the "other," to the difference within himself; I will return to this observation a bit later.

For now, however, just as Piñero's Juan demonstrates the

power a listener possesses in any given conversation, so each of Swados's men goes one step further by verbalizing the importance of the listener to a speaker of personal dialogue. Hearing Max's complaint that Tony has no idea of the humiliation Max experienced as a youth, Billy criticizes the former schoolteacher for his failure to negotiate the comprehensive dynamics that are essential to meaningful conversation. Again, those dynamics are propelled by the participants' mutual commitment to work toward an understanding. "You don't listen," Billy accuses Max. "You don't listen to *any*one. Did it ever occur to you what *he* [Tony] might have gone through? You were already out in high school" (25). Aware that he may be callous to another's needs because of his compulsion to articulate everything, to rely upon "words, too many words" (24) and not listen generously, Max comes to understand that he can expect to be heard by others only if he is willing to listen in turn. Embarrassed at his insensitivity, Max follows Billy's advice to "talk to [Tony] and find out" how he is doing (26). Tony needs to hear that Max has come to talk *with,* not to, him—to hear that Max has come to listen.

As demonstrated in previous chapters, metalinguistic interaction characterizes many characters' conversations. *A Quiet End* is no exception (although these characters talk about talk much less than, for example, the men do in *Glengarry Glen Ross* or *American Buffalo*). Along with their expressed desire to have each other listen well, the roommates say what they want from verbal exchange. A quick sampling of the direct appeals for talk: "Will *he* talk to *me*" (30); "Why don't you say something" (31); "It's me you're talking to" (44); "Listen to me" (61); "You're not listening to what I'm saying!" (62); "I'm trying to talk to you" (62); "Talk about the truth?" (67); "Talk to me" (69); "Talk to them" (76); and, "I *wanted* to talk about it" (80). When faced with such appeals, Swados's characters *choose* to engage in conversation. In talking, they refuse to "avoid reality." Only twice do characters appeal for silence. First, after becoming ill at the end of Max's football tirade, Tony asks Max to "shut up ... just shut the fuck up" (23). The second instance captures one's choice to sustain indefinitely the power of silence. After the psychiatrist asks him why he has not come out to his Iowa family, let alone told them that he has AIDS, Billy replies, "Certain things are better left unsaid" (56). But Billy changes his opinion two months later, after Tony's death (act 2, scene 2). Speaking to Max, Billy expresses his need to return to his birth family (that is, to his mother and sister, the only absent women mentioned in the play) to "talk to them ... [to] get to know them" (76), since he has come to value his own identity and to desire to name that self at "home." Not to do so is to "hide" (74). For Billy to feel, perhaps for the first time in his life, the power residing within the liberation of self-knowledge, he must engage speech. Over the course of the two-month period of the play's action, Billy matures significantly. As a gay man living with AIDS, he comes to realize that on every front, including the familial, silence = death.

Billy's finding his own voice, as it were, is part of an ongoing revolution in the representation of gay men's lives in American theater. The early years of the American dramatic representation of gay characters is "distorted" and restricted (Shewey xi). Positive images of gay life, and of most American minorities' lives, were for all intents and purposes absent in the American theater until the 1960s. Caught in stereotyped portraits that presented them as "frivolous fairies, psychotic bulldykes or suicidal queens,"[25] gay people began in the late 1960s to "demand honest portrayals of ourselves onstage; we wanted positive images, role models, alternatives to stereotypes" (Shewey xi)—a movement for community control over the dramatic images of its own lives. In this regard, the positive, realist portrait of gay men in *A Quiet End* is part of a historical, dramatic continuum. Billy, Max, and Tony accept without regret their identities as gay men. While each regrets some of his past choices, not one ever apologizes for being gay.[26] The issue for a character is not that he is a gay man but rather how he chooses to live his life as a man.[27] Each man's challenge is as essential as that facing any character: how to live life honestly.

The lengthy scene that closes act 1 focuses on Max's conversation with his boyfriend, Jason, who arrives at the hospice to visit. Jason and Max have not spoken in two months, each harboring his own reasons. Jason comes to break the silence, to find out how he can help Max, and also to tell him that he had the AIDS test earlier that day. In their interaction, the two men cover a wide range of poignant, unsettling personal issues: the future of Max's pets; their mutual dislike of the other's friends; Max's all-consuming commitment to group "therapy talk" (44); Max's history of sleeping around with lots of men; Jason's AIDS test; and most importantly, their complicated feelings toward one another. Each man is direct in expressing what he knows to be the truth, even if it momentarily hurts his partner. Facing their lives, knowing the fragility of their own mortality keenly, Max and Jason struggle to express that which needs to be said for each to be able to go on living constructively.[28]

After Jason's initial question to Max about his health—"How are you feeling" (35)—the men blurt out, protest, mull over, ignore, and measure their feelings. Confronted with such intimacy, the men are stung, humiliated, angry, defensive, nearly out of control, affectionate, frustrated, anxious, and eventually heartbroken. It is easy to see from this range of emotions that Max and Jason do not desert one another in their verbal exchange. Amid their painful confrontation with one another, the men keep the conversation alive as they talk, listen, analyze, and challenge. They accomplish this *without* the presence of a psychiatrist. It is important to acknowledge the advance in dramatizing male characters engaged in this level of self-disclosure outside of the therapist's office. Max and Jason trust, as best as they know how, that they must continue to talk to one another if each is to know again the integrity and genuine compassion that exists between them, regardless if they are or are not to be lovers. The two men are necessarily beyond silence if they are committed to understanding their future relationship.

Thematics by now familiar for male interaction arise during the personal dialogue here and in act 2. Repeatedly, the characters express a longing for home (both an external and an internal place where one does not feel abandoned, isolated, or alone), a fear of death, and a passionate plea "to be understood" by or "to understand" another person. When Jason confronts Max with "I don't *understand* you!" (48), Max steadily pursues an explanation. Two further thematics undramatized in the male-cast plays previously analyzed (with the exception of *If This Isn't Love!* and Juan's actions in *Short Eyes*) are fully realized in act 2 of *A Quiet End* (thematics that also figure prominently in the personal dialogue of the noninstitutional plays to be discussed in chapter 4): first, man's responsibility, when and wherever possible, to engage actively in efforts to minimize another man's suffering (47); and second, the strength and human dignity to be found in the power of love.

Act 2 is composed of four scenes that break with the neoclassic unities. Scene 1 takes place two months after the conclusion of act 1; it occurs in two locations, the realized hospice and the imaginary psychiatrist's office. At the conclusion of scene 1, Tony dies in his hospice-home, comforted by his family of roommates. After his memorial service, Billy and Max return alone to the hospice in scene 2, and Billy informs Max that he will soon return to his

Al Pacino, as Teach, muses while Clifton James, as Donny, and Thomas Waites, as Bobby, converse in the 1980 Long Wharf Theatre production of *American Buffalo*. (Photo by William B. Carter.)

Jason Robards, Jr., as Erie, and Jack Dodson, as Charlie, reach another impasse in the 1964 Broadway production of *Hughie*. (Photo by Friedman-Abeles. The Billy Rose Theatre Collection. The New York Public Library for the Performing Arts. Astor, Lenox and Tilden Foundations.)

Karolis staggers toward Ray Foots in the 1964 Off-Off-Broadway production of *The Toilet*. Jaime Sanchez and Hampton Clanton. (From *In the Shadow of the Great White Way: Images from Black Theatre*, photographs by Bert Andrews, text by Paul Carter Harrison and Bert Andrews, published by Thunder's Mouth Press. Copyright © 1989 by Bert Andrews and Paul Carter Harrison. Reprinted by permission

Jerry (Mark Richman) harasses Peter (William Daniels) in the 1960 Off-Broadway production of *The Zoo Story*. (Photo courtesy of Photofest.)

"El Raheem" Johnson threatens to kill Clark Davis in the 1974 Off-Broadway production of *Short Eyes*. J. J. Johnson and William Carden. (Photo by Friedman-Abeles. The Billy Rose Theatre Collection. The New York Public Library for the Performing Arts. Astor, Lenox and Tilden Foundations.)

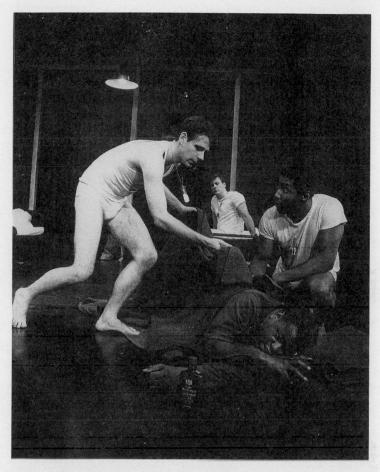

Richie (Peter Evans) cares for Carlyle (Joe Fields) while Billy (John Heard) and Roger (Herbert Jefferson, Jr.) look on, in the 1976 Long Wharf Theatre production of *Streamers*. (Photo by Martha Swope.)

Facing page, top

Max, Billy, and Tony (Lonny Price, Jordan Mott, Philip Coccioletti) share a playful moment in the 1990 Off-Broadway production of *A Quiet End*. (Photo by Martha Swope.)

Facing page, bottom

Vincent and Bradley spoof cultural stereotypes in the 1989 Off-Broadway production of *Yankee Dawg You Die*. Sab Shimono and Stan Egi. (Photo by Gerry Goodstein.)

Bobby (Richard Greene) embraces his brother Jerry (Joel Polis) in the 1978 Off-Broadway production of *Family Business.* (The Billy Rose Theatre Collection. The New York Public Library for the Performing Arts. Astor, Lenox and Tilden Foundations.)

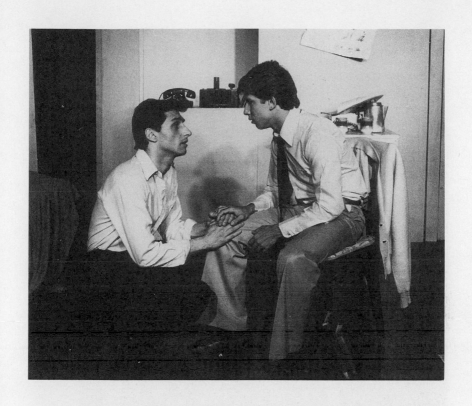

Jello (Tom Wright) referees between Twin (Walter Bennett, Jr.) and Sky (Roger Guenveur Smith) in the 1987 Off-Broadway production of *That Serious He-Man Ball*. (Rehearsal photo by Martha Holmes.)

native home and relatives in Iowa. In scene 3, several days after the memorial service, Jason returns to the hospice to take Max to his (Jason's) house, where they will create a new home together as one another's family. And in the final scene, weeks after Max's funeral, Jason, on the verge of redefining what home and family will now mean to him, speaks with the psychiatrist in his (imaginary) office.

I have focused on the various shifts in time and place that occur in act 2 to illustrate how the act, amid change, is driven forward by the men's steady efforts to confront the relativity of such heavily coded concepts as home and family. The discourse coherence in the act is structured as personal dialogue, and home and family are concepts in process throughout, with no single meaning valued more preciously than another. What the men come to treasure is the knowledge (and experience) that these terms remain in flux: their manifestations reflect the dynamics that are, out of necessity, relative to their immediate situations and needs. Thus in scene 1, Tony dies knowing that he is with men who, despite their individual differences from one another, still connect with him "as is," to borrow the title of William Hoffman's AIDS play. For Tony, the hospice *is* his home and his roommates *are* his family. Most importantly, Tony is not alone when he dies—he is in the presence of, as well as loved by, those with whom he shared a home.

Billy, in particular, actively involves himself in doing what he can to ease Tony's psychological and physical pain. "What do you want me to do?" Billy asks the lonely, hurting man, to which Tony replies, "Listen to me" (61).[29] Through the sustenance of conversation, Tony fully engages the power of personal dialogue to lighten his soul's burden about his unsuccessful career and unsatisfying sex and love life. For Tony, there is long overdue relief in "talk[ing] about the truth" freely in front of another person (67), one who is also suffering.[30] Amid Tony's confessions, however, the horror of living with AIDS is more rawly dramatized than at any other point in the play. Suffering from increasing dementia and paranoia, Tony is seized periodically by multiple spasms of pain. "I just want this to be over," he reveals to Billy (66); "I fucked up....I *want* this pain. I *like* it. I *deserve* it....I hurt so bad" (67–68). Rejecting Billy's efforts to call a doctor, Tony screams out, "I DON'T WANT TO KEEP GOING! Don't you understand?" (68). In desperation, Billy resorts to the only nonmedical relief that he trusts *and* mutually understands with Tony—physical contact and conversation. Cradling the dying man in his arms, Billy encourages him: "Talk to me. . . . C'mon. Say something. Say anything" (69–70). Communication, here, becomes the sign of life. And when the words stop, Billy knows that Tony is dead.

Soon after the opening of scene 2, Max echoes Billy's words to Tony as he tells Billy, his surviving roommate, "Talk to me" (72). Billy proceeds to tell Max that he is leaving the hospice to return to his childhood home; he does not "want to die alone," which, to Billy, means that he wants to renew a relationship with his mother, one of the play's absent women (74). The roommates' conversation is filled with firm, conflicting opinions, but the men insist that some understanding of what is being said occur before the conversation ends. (Thus, the scene goes several rounds beyond the singular "I don't understand, I don't want to understand" closing interaction between the men in *The Zoo Story*.) Unlike the characters in *Short Eyes* and, to a lesser extent, *Streamers* who are confined to their institutional spaces, Billy and Max can leave their space any time they want. They choose, however, to remain until they have communicated with one another as clearly and caringly as is possible—all for the sake of establishing a base of mutual understanding.[31]

Acknowledging to Max what he learns from Tony's life and death, Billy succinctly articulates the components of his model for personal change, a change that will lead to the benefits one can claim from self-identity. In the male-cast canon, such change is nearly always dramatized as beyond the experience or imagination of most characters, since it implicitly connects to the difference within one's self. "Tony wasn't ashamed to cry," Billy recalls. "He wasn't ashamed to tell me he was in pain. He wasn't ashamed to ask me to hold him. He just grabbed me and I knew. He refused to hide from anyone" (74). The role of speech—and particularly the value placed on the honest expression of personal feelings—distinguishes this alternative model of male behavior. In his refusal "to hide from anyone" anymore, Billy no longer hides from himself. Although his immediate act of self-recognition foreshadows his impending coming out to his mother, on a more profound level, Billy accepts that he is going to die soon. He also realizes that he needs the strength of someone who is healthy to help him through that demanding process. And while Max is certainly a friend (74), he is nonetheless a friend who is seriously ill. Billy chooses to hide from these facts no longer. In doing so, Billy frees himself through the truths of self-disclosure and self-identity to the vital energy of self-empowerment that he will draw upon during his remaining lifetime.

In turn, Max overcomes his pride in order to understand that he, too, cannot and does not want to die alone. Through their tireless personal dialogue in scene 2, Billy and Max help one another better to understand, as best as they can, what the next step of their lives is going to be all about. Billy, increasingly more forceful in his convictions, forces Max to be aware of his need to "let [Jason] in" to his life (75). Jason, after all, is the appropriate one to be there for Max during his final days; the two men are "crazy" about each other. Furthermore, Jason wants to *and* is able to help Max "make it through" (78). And so, in scene 3, Jason comes to "take [Max] home" (79), as Max "now manifests a terrible weariness, both from physical illness and psychological fatigue" (78).

Through Jason's act of coming to take Max home in order to care for him, the two previously undramatized thematics converge. Not only does Jason turn his understanding of Max's suffering into a direct action that serves both of their personal needs, but he does so through the unconditional power of love. As Jason admits to Max: I "want to make what's left of your life meaningful. Filling it with some warmth—some kindness. . . . Getting you to believe that you're valuable. To yourself, and to me. I don't think I knew how to let you know before" (80). Jason's self-disclosing admission illustrates the characterological flexibility that a playwright has at his disposal when he chooses not to adhere to the neoclassic unities in his play's structure. (Following this line of thinking, one can deepen one's appreciation for the rare representation of men's personal dialogue that occurs in *Short Eyes'* epilogue and, even more immediately, at *Streamers'* conclusion—two plays that are structured more closely to the neoclassic principles than is *A Quiet End*.) Through the passing of time (apparently over the two months of dramatic time separating acts 1 and 2), Jason "changes" (80), just as Adam and Eric "change" over decades in *If This Isn't Love!* The change in *A Quiet End* encourages Jason to accept some responsibility for the life and death of someone he knows and loves— someone who desperately needs him at this time. Finding strength and dignity in his love for Max, Jason tells him: "Allow me the luxury of making your life something more than this emptiness" (80).[32]

It is irrelevant whether Jason comes to Max as a friend or as a lover; he comes to him as one who loves him. In response, Max acknowledges that Jason is "asking something very major" by inviting the ill man "to open up [his] heart all over again" (81). For Max, life has become only "silence and sickness" (82). Although he can do nothing about Max's illness, Jason knows that he can at least offer words to defeat the ominous silence. As Oswald in Jacker's *Terminal* says of those who are ill, "Nobody's in a mood to chat" (23). It is Max's choice to judge if such an offering will soothe or wound his heart. Nevertheless, Jason admits, "I *wanted* to talk" (82), knowing—as Billy experiences with Tony—that conversation can be part of a lifeline if genuinely engaged. And so Max accepts Jason's lifeline for as long as he is alive. As Jason tells the psychiatrist in the play's closing scene, "[Max] told me, before he died, that he wanted me to read [his journal]. I wouldn't have, when he was alive—I didn't need to. If there was something on his mind, he told me" (84). In reopening his heart to Jason, Max makes the right choice. The men share unconditional love and conversation, not deadening silence, until the end.

In terms of realist drama, Swados's play makes a remarkable contribution to gay theater and to the canon of published American male-cast plays. Male-cast plays that focus on the AIDS crisis are at the forefront of the present movement in drama that is challenging the representation of men among themselves. Most, if not all, such plays have come from within the gay community. While "AIDS is not a gay disease," as Douglas Crimp reminds us, the gay and lesbian communities have responded artistically and politically to the crisis because it has become a pandemic "of stigmatization rooted in homophobia" (250). Crimp also argues the political limitations of dramatic realism to represent effectively this crisis. Criticizing Larry Kramer's mixed-cast play, *The Normal Heart,* Crimp states, "Because the play is written within the most traditional conventions of bourgeois theatre, its politics are the politics of bourgeois individualism" (248). Crimp would likely criticize *A Quiet End* also on the grounds of its being "a purely personal—*not* a political—drama" (248),[33] an end that the playwright actually intended. "*A Quiet End* is not about politics," Swados says. "It's about taking care of others and believing once in a while in this 'me' decade that taking care of others should be more important than taking care of yourself" (qtd. in Fredman). For my immediate purposes, however, and perhaps at odds with both Crimp and Swados in their respective meanings of political theater, I suggest that *A Quiet End* is noteworthy for its unconventional representation of male communicative interaction, an interaction that assumes (as dramatized, intentionally or not, from the characters' perspectives) that the personal can be, and often is, political.

It is necessary first to place Swados's work on the continuum of gay theater. While the discourse coherence in most post-Stonewall, pre-AIDS plays has circulated between social and personal dialogue, it has also generally focused only on a one-dimensional representation of homosexuals, and often only on their sexuality. It has neglected to represent a culture that "isn't just sexual" (Kramer 114). What has been missing in the realist gay male-cast play (to be distinguished from the more recent representations in nonrealist gay male-cast plays such as Harvey Fierstein's *Safe Sex* or Robert Chesley's *Jerker,* or from the representation of gay relationships in mixed-cast plays such as *The Normal Heart,* Lanford Wilson's *Fifth of July,* and Tony Kushner's *Angels in America*) is a dramatized awareness of the deeper pleasures of sex that can accompany homoerotic desire—the sharing of intimacy and vulnerability, the personal risks undertaken, the trust established, the freedom to move safely between fantasy and reality; in short, the world of the emotions, with all its possibilities for growth and knowledge. "If you want somebody to understand who you are," remarks Fierstein, "it's not enough to talk about your sex life, but what your emotional life is as well" (qtd. in P. Miller 22). To this end, Don Shewey notes the caution under which all minority cultures function: "The despairing view is that by making one attribute the basis of our identity—whether it be sexual preference, race, or religion—we give others permission to persecute us on the same basis" (xxvii).

In response to the AIDS crisis, plays focusing on the disease have, appropriately and paradoxically, begun to fill in this character and situational depth.[34] As John Clum concludes, AIDS "challenges gay men more strongly than ever to make their identities known" in drama as well as in the streets (1989, 189). But as Mark Gevisser qualifies, the AIDS epidemic "has served, in many ways, to mainstream gay men: we carry a deadly virus, and whether this elicits sympathy for us or stigmatizes us, it makes us known" (48). For these reasons, dramas dealing with AIDS, or those in which AIDS is at least a present reality in the lives of the plays' characters, seem to accomplish what Shewey cites as a desirable feature of gay theater: to "explore the content of gay lives rather than parading propaganda . . . or melodrama" (xxi).

Few pre-AIDS, realist gay male plays dramatize men capable of sustaining personal discourse, especially without drinking (or,

occasionally, resorting to violence), for the purpose of establishing
something in addition to a relationship based solely upon sex.[35]
Again, this observation is intended only to identify representations
traditionally absent from realist gay male-cast plays; it is not a
judgment on the value, whether cultural or dramaturgical, of gay
plays that do not emphasize personal dialogue. My point, rather,
is that while many of these early plays (and many that continue to
be written) performed an important part in helping to shape a community's identity, in allowing members of the community to see
images of itself that they had otherwise been denied, it is not until
the advent of drama focused on AIDS that gay men see themselves
among themselves three-dimensionally. As Edmund White remarks, "[T]he tragedy of AIDS has made gay men more reflective
on the great questions of love, death, morality, and identity, the
very preoccupations that have always animated serious fiction and
poetry" (24). And for the purposes of this study of the American
male-cast play, that dimension is strikingly evident in the discourse
coherence—in what the men talk about during their personal dialogue—in male-cast dramas that focus on AIDS.

If *A Quiet End* advances the dramaturgy of realist gay male-cast
plays, it simultaneously contributes to the representation of men
among themselves, as captured within the canon of male-cast
drama. While no one should deny the shared features that bring
Swados's men to their hospice room—gay men living with AIDS—
no one should assume that those features guarantee the roommates
will relate personally to one another. Different gay characters in the
same situation might just as easily become one another's enemy or
engage only in social dialogue. It is the semiotic of maleness in
male-cast plays that codes gay characters as active participants in
talk exchanges; such a coding, however, is determinist and unreal-
istic. And one can be gay and homophobic. Homophobia, quite
often the major barrier that men must overcome for themselves,
underlies most straight, and many bisexual and gay characters'
anxieties prior to their engagement of self-disclosing dialogue.[36]
From the beginning of *A Quiet End,* however, Swados's characters
are beyond that barrier; they relate to and understand each other
as self-identified, proud gay men. In respect to the representation
of American men among themselves, this is no small accomplishment.

Viewed strictly from the position of its structure, Swados's
play achieves and maintains a level of discourse coherence that is
uncommon for a male-cast play, regardless of the characters' race,

ethnicity, class, or sexual orientation.[37] While Piñero and Rabe present men who accomplish comparable feats of individualization—occurrences that distinguish their works from most other plays set in confining institutions—neither writer sustains that talk without outbursts of violence to rupture the men's communicative dynamics. *A Quiet End*, therefore, sets a standard for the dramatic representation of men who are committed to self-disclosing, nonviolent interaction. It also establishes a rare visual reinforcement for the normalcy of nonsexual physical comfort between men while still foregrounding the standard dramatic portrait in gay theater of the naturalness of sexual intimacy between gay characters. These qualities, in and of themselves, are both aesthetic *and* political achievements when it comes to representing diverse male subjectivities in American drama. It remains to be seen in chapter 4, however, if this dramaturgical standard is evident in any realist male-cast plays that present men who are neither confined to an institution nor faced with a merciless illness in the mirror.

Four

Realizing Freedom: Risk, Responsibility, and Individualization

Twentieth-century American playwrights have rarely imagined male characters whose dialogue is not overdetermined by the power of the masculine ethos and male mythologies. Likewise, playwrights seldom elect to represent men among themselves without their being at some point drunk or drugged, verbally or physically violent toward one another. But this dramatic picture of men's lives is starting to change as the male-cast play makes its way toward a new century, a time that will undoubtedly be marked by changes already animating American culture: changes in the ways in which men think about, as well as live among, themselves.

It remains the task of American drama to imagine men at such a challenging time in human history. Due in large part to the revolutionary influence of feminism on contemporary thought, ideology, and culture, American men are more conscious than ever of the powers of the masculine ethos, male mythologies, and violence as forces that shape their lives. "[N]ot all men have found it possible, and not all men have found it desirable," according to Lynne Segal, "to participate in the social relations which generate dominance" (130). Consequently, many of these men are aware that other powers—nonviolent, personal means—exist to encourage one toward self-definition. Man has choice whether or not to name and claim his difference within. It is on this level of self-realization that processes of change—personal, cultural, political, and moral— are located.

The four plays in this chapter focus on male characters who experience and realize a kind of personal freedom. They achieve this sense of freedom by breaking through critical cultural barriers of gender codings that otherwise limit, or prohibit, such growth. They move toward a level of self-knowledge that approaches codelessness, as it were, in its adherence to the power of individualization. This codeless, or decoded, sense of male subjectivity, when revealed in the discourse coherence of realist drama, is quite possibly the most challenging—even threatening—male dramatic representation: it is, after all, the most unfamiliar stage image.

It may come as no surprise at this point that only two plays in a chapter that focuses on characters' risk, responsibility, and individualization are cast primarily with heterosexual white males: Dick Goldberg's *Family Business* and David Mamet's *American Buffalo*. Privileged in patriarchal culture, straight white men stand to lose the most if they challenge the structure of their empowerment. Yet the traditional hero, if he engages in personal dialogue for the sake of individualization, necessarily questions such privilege. Hence, it is perhaps an inevitable reflection of social reality that the majority of plays to follow in this discussion include minority characters, those on the margins of the straight white-male power structure: Philip Kan Gotanda's comic drama *Yankee Dawg You Die* centers on two Asian American actors; Alonzo Lamont, Jr.'s drama *That Serious He-Man Ball* concentrates on three African American friends; and even *Family Business* represents degrees of marginalization—this Jewish family includes one gay relative. Gotanda's and Lamont's plays are the first in this study in which the casts are not only exclusively men of color, but men of the same color among themselves.[1]

Yankee Dawg You Die, Philip Kan Gotanda

During the 1980s, Asian American playwrights began to receive long overdue critical attention and popular acceptance in the American theater. Several have written male-cast plays or monodramas or both: David Henry Hwang, Lane Nishikawa, Laurence Yep, James Yoshimura, and Philip Kan Gotanda. As has Hwang, Gotanda has enjoyed numerous productions of his work, most notably, of *Yankee Dawg You Die,* across the country. The structure of *Yankee Dawg* is atypical among the plays I have analyzed: it is a nonrealist play, composed of realist scenes framed with interludes (Gotanda 1991, 4, 6).[2] The majority of these interludes are monologues delivered before a nonrepresented audience.

Utilizing monologues and soliloquies to precede and follow dialogues, Gotanda foregrounds both novelistic and cinematic features. During monologues, each man speaks before imagined individuals or groups; these different listeners elicit personal traits that often differ from those suggested in shared conversations. When soliloquizing, each man expresses inner thoughts, his difference within, that might go unspoken if *Yankee Dawg* were structured as a classical realist play. Freeing characters' lives from the constraints of time, space, and action to create variations in male subjectivity, the playwright of nonrealism deconstructs cultural codings that forge, in drama, one's social identity.[3] And because Gotanda shows us the men's lives outside of their immediate relationships, the spectator has the opportunity to understand what events influence the growth of the men's interaction with one another. Personal changes occur, therefore, both inside and outside the characters' shared realist conversations. In this way, the single-voiced talk in the interludes influences the shared talk in the scenes that in turn influences the talk in the interludes, and so on.

The sixteen scenes in *Yankee Dawg* occur over one year at settings in and around Los Angeles. In the opening interlude, Vincent Chang, a "former hoofer" who is in his late sixties, is seen in one of his 1940s film roles as Sergeant Moto, a prototypical World War II Japanese detention guard (6, 4). Such roles illustrate "the humiliation that Asian American actors have suffered when enslaved by screen stereotyping" (F. Rich 1989). In a monologue delivered in "an exaggerated, stereotypic—almost cartoonish manner" (6), the Japanese American man (who markets himself as a Chinese American) articulates what becomes the play's basic concern with racial and sexual self-identity: "Why can't you hear what I'm saying? Why can't you see me as I really am?" This concern, captured in a voice with multiple layers of diversity and marginalization—that is, in the voice of a minority actor playing a character whose race is different from his own—actually frames the discourse coherence in the play's realist scenes as it develops from social into personal dialogues. This progression into personal dialogue supports Richard Christiansen's contention that "the substance of the play" is "how [the men] come to terms with their work and their personal lives, each man learning from and teaching the other." *Yankee Dawg* is about one's struggle to be heard and seen for who he truly is.

In the play's opening realist scene at a Hollywood Hills party, Vincent meets Bradley Yamashita, an aggressive, ambitious, self-confident, twenty-seven-year-old fellow actor. Engaging in social dialogue, the two men discuss, somewhat defensively, the status of their professional careers. Quickly, Bradley focuses on race and how it shapes a minority actor's career in popular entertainment.

The young man admires the veteran actor because he himself, after some success in New York as a film actor, is now pursuing a career on the West Coast. But Bradley, unlike Vincent, talks about the broad impact of cultural codings on marginalized people: "I think it's important that all of us know each other. Asian American actors. I think the two of us meeting is very important. The young and the old. We can learn from each other" (9). Bradley (like Gotanda) is a sansei—a third-generation Japanese American.[4]

Vincent, on the other hand, epitomizes an older generation of performers who think of themselves as Orientals and not Asian Americans (8). He has a reputable career playing parts that many younger Asian Americans now consider demeaning. In Bradley's opinion, art and politics go hand in hand. Bradley remarks upon the absence of worthy Asian American role models, "We have [a need] for legitimate heroes. And... when you don't have any... you'll go [far] to make them up" (20). Despite Vincent's high profile in the community (8), he embodies the negative stereotypes of and limited roles for Asian Americans that the dominant culture perpetuates both on- and offscreen. More importantly, Vincent is a certified product of the white system. In his compliance with that system, Vincent "injures his own people and their image in society"; this, according to Clive Barnes in his harsh review (1989), is Gotanda's only thematic insight in *Yankee Dawg*. Vincent sees himself through white and not Asian American aesthetics and consciousness, or so Bradley assumes. He knows himself not through self-definition, nor within cultural-specific identification, but rather as the white man's "other." He is object and not subject. Knowing that a coded, generational distance exists between them, the two actors "want to pursue conversation but [are] unsure how to" (16).

Gotanda structures his eight remaining realist scenes as discrete conversations that occur over a twelve-month period. Through the changes of time and space, linked by interludes, each man evolves to a more comfortable position with the other. The progressive dynamics in their shared dialogues (which contain the actors' frequent role-playing) reflect this ease. A closer look at a key sequence, interlude 2, scene 3, and interlude 3 (22–28), reveals Gotanda's technique, which informs the men's talk when they are together and the play's thematics.

Interlude 2 consists of four monologues delivered before different, unseen listeners. Vincent speaks twice: first, he accepts an award from his "fellow Asian American actors" (22), and, second, he is the MC at a Tupperware convention. Bradley speaks to commercial auditioners and later to his Asian actor friends. Each man expresses his perception of truth as he filters it through the codings of his profession. Acting takes on metaphoric meaning in this section, as the men grapple publicly with the ethical issues involved in accepting roles that are racist portrayals of Asian Americans. Each man reveals his relationship to the dominant culture's coding of the "other" and to his own identity as subject.

Vincent expresses, unapologetically, his enslavement to the cultural codings that deny him an individual voice. "I am an actor," he says. "I can only speak the words that are written for me. I am an actor. Not a politician. I cannot change the world. I can only bring life, through truth and craft, to my characterizations" (22). Bradley, on the other hand, perceives truth in art only as it relates to truth in life. When asked to giggle during a commercial audition, for instance, Bradley argues, "I'm sorry but I can't do that. Look, it's not truthful to the character. Japanese men don't giggle." Bradley speaks with a principled, personal voice as he resists the white system's overwhelming power to represent the "other" via its own stereotyping, misunderstanding, and fear. Gotanda's men voice their conflicting notions about the nature of truth—notions that determine their ability to assume professional "roles" that either mirror or distort their sense of themselves as individuals who embody a specific race and gender. At this point, Vincent not only accepts his culturally coded racial otherness (paradoxically through his willingness to ignore racial difference [8]), he deliberately exploits it as a crucial component of the dominant culture's fantasy of the exotic "other." Bradley, on the other hand, resists this coding both professionally and personally.

Scene 3 picks up on the issues of racial pride, self-identity, and truth telling that are introduced in interlude 2. During their third conversation, Vincent and Bradley forgo social dialogue in favor of a more demanding personal interaction. Vincent immediately engages personal dialogue because their previous talk ended when Bradley insulted Vincent by calling him a racist, a "Chinese Steppin Fetchit" (21). Such strong accusations, we have seen throughout this study, often prompt a verbally abusive or physically violent response if the conversation continues. Since scene 2 ends with this insult and time passes before the two men converse together again, Gotanda bypasses the interactive stage of the men's uncooperative communication: the exercise of violence that generally separates social and personal dialogue. Instead, an angry Vincent immediately confronts Bradley with his verbal offense, whereupon he receives an apology from the young man. Their dialogue from this point on is personal, and it generally remains so throughout their remaining conversations. In scene 3, therefore, each man instantly peels away layers of cultural codings in order to reveal more of his self-identity. He does so in an effort to substantiate his beliefs and his truths, both of which are relative to his life experiences.

What has been missing from nearly all of the male-cast plays analyzed and cited in this study is a character's articulated sense of history. By this I mean that a character rarely discusses his current time and place relative to a history of identifications with others of the same race, ethnicity, religion, class, or sexual orientation. Since this is primarily a published canon of white-authored, white-cast plays, the traditional male-cast play assumes an Anglo American historical context with a heterosexual bias. Recent minority writers, however, challenge and reinscribe historical contexts. Without becoming pedantic, Gotanda, Piñero, and Lamont, as well as such white gay authors as Sidney Morris, present men who educate others on the history of the people who inhabit their plays.[5] In this way, the playwrights position characters who confront, through their language, the codings of the dominant culture by reclaiming their rightful positions in a history *they* construct. They essentially deconstruct the white heterosexist mythologies of self and reconstruct the realities of the "other" as self and subject. In doing so, they become the center of their own history rather than existing solely on the margins of the dominant culture's tale.

In scene 3, Vincent and Bradley clearly identify through personal dialogue their positions within the frame of Asian American history. Their racially specific history, in turn, interrelates with (in the form of their victimization) the history of the dominant culture—a reflection of the values of the white masculine ethos disseminated throughout American culture. Believing that he represents the self-identified generation of "Asian American consciousness" (24), Bradley challenges Vincent's willingness to be a victim, on his past efforts to assimilate into the stereotypical expectations of the dominant culture. "All that self hate, *where does it begin*?" the young man demands to know. "You and your Charley Chop Suey roles" (25). Pushed to the limit to defend his personal place in racial history, Vincent replies,

> [Y]ou want to know the truth? . . . I'm glad I did it. . . . And in some small way it is a victory. . . . At least an oriental was on

screen acting, being seen. We existed. . . . I would have killed for a better role where I could have played an honest-to-god human being with real emotions. . . . You seem to assume "Asian Americans" always existed. . . . You, with that holier than thou look, trying to make me feel ashamed. You wouldn't be here if it weren't for all the crap we had to put up with. . . . We built the mountain, as small as it may be, that you stand on so proudly looking down at me. (25–26)

Bradley, however, is not easily won over by Vincent's arguments; rather, he assumes a posture later revealed to be idealized and untested by experience. He replies confidently, "Everytime you do any old stereotypic role just to pay the bills, someone has to pay for it—and it ain't you. . . . You ask to be understood, forgiven, but you refuse to change. You have no sense of social responsibility. . . . [W]hat good is it to lose your dignity" (26). For Bradley, the personal as it relates to racial identity is political—and no one should relinquish his power of self-determination and racial identity to "business" (24–26). To the young man's harsh judgments, however, the older actor replies repeatedly, "You don't know" (26).

Despite their confrontation, the men end their conversation on a hitherto uncharacteristic level of bonding. They do so by referring to an absent woman, a character in one of Vincent's old movies. "I got the woman once," Vincent proudly claims. "And she was *white*" (27). In this moment, the two actors bond as American men who assert their power over the female. Although their race marks them as "other" next to the white male subject, their gender clearly marks them as subject next to the female object, the one who is to be "gotten." These Asian American men privilege gender over race as soon as the female Other enters into their dialogue. Their only apparent power in American culture, based in gender privilege, is over the Other. And, in the play, it is a power that initially appears color-blind.[6]

The end of scene 3 introduces the play's central issues—the impact of racial and gender codings upon the development of the self-identified, marginalized American character. By claiming his individual place outside of or within the history of the Asian American movement, each man eliminates any ambiguities about the realized position of his racial identity. That is, by the conclusion of scene 3, Vincent and Bradley clearly define for one another their racial boundaries. They speak about themselves as Asian Americans and, in doing so, they leave little unspoken regarding

their racial selves. These selves evolve throughout the play, however, as does the men's connection to their community. In fact, the
final scenes of act 1 focus on Vincent and Bradley working together
on a project at the Asian American Theatre. Issues of race, therefore, are outspoken from the start of the men's shared communication.

While the two men focus on the absent woman through the
coded, social dialogue of business, they have yet to discuss in extended personal dialogue either the absent woman or themselves
as gendered beings. A hint that these topics may emerge surfaces
in the brief interlude 3. Two dramatic instances are juxtaposed
within it, one silent, the other verbal. First, Bradley appears "si-
lently practicing tai-chi.... suddenly break[ing] into savage kung-fu
kicks...[then] quietly beginning the graceful tai-chi" (28). As
Bradley's movement fades into darkness, the light comes up on
Vincent, who is heard on the telephone speaking to "Kenneth": "I
can not. You know why. Someone might see us together.... People
talk." Bradley engages in the traditionally masculine-identified martial arts, whose codings signal "real" male behavior. Although
silent, Bradley conveys an image coded as heterosexual male behavior. Gotanda juxtaposes this identity with words that suggest
that Vincent is doubly marginalized—that he is a closeted gay Asian
American who assumes that his "outing" would destroy his commercial acting career. Introducing into his characters' profile the
tension of gender codings and sexuality yet to be addressed in their
dyadic talk, Gotanda takes a bold step to dramatize the impact of
difference between already marginalized men who otherwise see
themselves as similar to men, here, of the same race. Gotanda's
position, as for any writer of color who exercises it, is hardly a
popular one: group and self-critique within one's already marginalized community. Whereas we will see how a playwright dramatizes
the interaction between straight and gay white men in Goldberg's
Family Business, and we have already observed playwrights who
portray the interaction among straight, gay, and bisexual men in
interracial groups (*The Toilet, Short Eyes,* and *Streamers*), we have
yet to explore the dynamics of sexual difference among men of
color. *Yankee Dawg* affords this opportunity, one rarely in published plays. Even though racial identity is the originating point of
conflict, gender codings appear to subsume it by the end of the play.
Gotanda dramatizes, as have many white male-cast playwrights before him, that sexual orientation and gender can dominate issues of

race when a man comes to terms, through conversation, with his personal identity. The evidence is in the plays' discourse coherence.

As Vincent enters into greater "Asian American consciousness" in act 2, his connection to his racial community strengthens. He lessens the power of the dominant culture to marginalize him, since he places himself as subject in the "sameness" of his own racial culture. As we have seen repeatedly, however, that which disrupts the sameness among men is one's sexual orientation.[7] If he is rejected by his own race because he is gay, Vincent resumes his position as the doubly marginalized. Act 2 focuses on the conflict of personal identity that a doubly marginalized person experiences after he "overcomes" one of his marginalizing features. As Vincent demands the freedoms that are inherent in one's claiming responsibility for one's racial self, he frees himself to confront remaining personal marginalization that keeps him from being more wholly identified. It is a risk for him to engage this final confrontation, since he jeopardizes his part in an otherwise harmonious racial community. In his efforts to foreground the social pressures thrust upon the doubly marginalized male, Gotanda reaches deep into the heart of the problematic representation of characters in the male-cast play. Although Gotanda is not altogether successful in dramatizing Vincent's struggle (Kissel; Winer), Frank Rich's assertion that the concern with sexual issues "plunge[s] the play into ideological overload" is not necessarily on target (1989). From the perspective of this study, Gotanda's dramaturgy reconfirms the pattern of discourse coherence that has characterized much of the canon: issues of gender and sexual orientation lurk beneath issues of race, ethnicity, class, and religion.

In the final sequence of act 2—scene 3, interlude 7, scene 4— Gotanda's characters complete the cycle of personal transformations that is the dramatic through line in *Yankee Dawg*. Scene 3, the men's eighth conversation, is personal and confessional: Bradley admits that he is not above taking stereotyped minority roles, while Vincent admits that his sexual relationships are unconventional. Bradley rightly assumes they are same-sex relationships, yet the still-closeted Vincent refuses to claim them as such, even upon hearing Bradley speak supportively of homosexuality (46– 47). Not until scene 4, six months later, when the men converse for the last time, does each explicitly accept responsibility for his actions: Bradley announces that he has in fact taken a racist acting role; Vincent reveals that he has not only turned down a racist part in order to accept a role in an Asian-American-identified film (49), but that he has "been seeing more of [his] friend . . . Kenneth" (48). Over the course of their one-year relationship, the two men switch roles. Vincent becomes more like the Bradley of a year earlier—racially proud, confident in acknowledging his intimacies, and secure in his self-definition—while Bradley becomes more like the earlier Vincent—compromised, deluded, and driven to secure employment despite personal costs. By breaking the unity of time in his play, Gotanda dramatizes characters' personal growth over time; in this way, the nonrealist structure accommodates their convenient reversal.

One critical approach is to read *Yankee Dawg* as a bildungsroman in which Gotanda dramatizes the educations of Vincent and of Bradley. By the conclusion of his lessons, which are marked by the discourse coherence in each scene, Vincent is sensitized and radicalized to the politics of race, gender, and sexual orientation. He becomes empowered across time. In time, therefore, he becomes a suitable mentor for the increasingly wayward Bradley, a real-life (rather than cinematic) father role model to Bradley's son (49). And Vincent's transformation is well timed. Despite his earlier role as the older man's self-identified teacher, Bradley yields to the dominant culture's mythologies primarily because he perceives a lack of committed, believable Asian American role models. He, like the former, unenlightened Vincent, gets his nose fixed and accepts racist, stereotypical roles (48–50). He becomes, in Vincent's words, "a driven, ambitious, self-centered asshole" (45). Vincent's earlier warning—that Bradley "d[id]n't know" (26), had not experienced social and economic pressures that can submerge one's self-definition—is realized.

But the characters in *Yankee Dawg* do not "self destruct," as James Moy contends, "at the very moment of their representation, leaving behind only newly disfigured traces" (55). While Bradley appears to "succumb to Chang's fate," Bradley also converses at the end with a Vincent Chang who is no longer a "fated" man, but rather one who begins to take responsibility to define himself truthfully—as a gay Asian American. Bradley is made aware of just how powerful such self-identification can be when he witnesses the transformation in Vincent's character (49). Bradley finally has an elder role model in Vincent, and he is "deeply moved" by this recognition (50). Gotanda ends his play at this specific point of recognition in his characters' conversation, one all the more significant—if one positions the play within the male-cast canon—

because it occurs between a straight male and a gay male. Gotanda achieves his dramaturgical goal of presenting two men who "in some way . . . see into each other's souls" (qtd. in Rothstein). Unlike the roles they play in racist Hollywood, Vincent and Bradley become for one another "human beings with honest emotions" (F. Rich 1989). They certainly do not remain "as one-dimensional," as Barnes argues, "as they were at the beginning" of the play (1989). Reciting before Bradley his well-known Sergeant Moto monologue, which structurally links two of his previous private moments (interludes 1 and 7) with this public expression, Vincent soon drops his stereotypic, cinematic Asian voice in favor of his own passionate one in order to claim his right to be heard for who he really is: "Why can't you hear what I'm saying? Why can't you see me as I really am?" (50). Vincent achieves a kind of freedom by transforming the words of a fictional character into a personalized statement before another person. He unites word and deed into self-knowledge. In going public, albeit before only one person, Vincent claims both his racial and his sexual identities as his own.

Unlike Moy, who criticizes Gotanda's Asian Americans as characters "marginalized, desexed, and made faceless . . . [and] constitut[ing] no threat to Anglo-American sensibilities" (55), I suggest that the playwright succeeds in dramatizing the communicative process by which one claims not only racial but sexual identity. This does not imply that Gotanda's dramaturgy is unproblematic. "Gotanda's play would probably express his ethnicity better," as Michael Feingold notes, "if he would stop announcing it and put it into dramatic motion instead." Nonetheless, Gotanda accomplishes a great deal in dramatizing, through colloquial and poetic languages, Vincent's story of personal evolution. "Gotanda is to be commended," as Jan Stuart recognizes, "for attempting to measure the full depth of personal identity, beyond ethnic origin, that must be compromised for public consumption in *and* out of Hollywood." Vincent's story is about choice and change—the choice one has to change, to come out and embrace "otherness" as an empowering source of self-identity, personal truth, and "dignity" (26).

In *Yankee Dawg,* the dignified individual is the one who articulates his desire to be heard for who he really is. The play's emphasis on the intersection between racial and sexual tensions that one experiences when coming to terms with his individualization is an uncommon feature in a male-cast play. This feature, virtually unnoticed by critics, is all the more noteworthy because *Yankee Dawg You Die* involves minority characters whose fictional lives currently remain underpublished, and therefore invisible. Whereas Gish Jen asks, "Are Asian-American writers the only hope for new forms of characterization?" Gotanda establishes an important foundation for the dramatic reconstruction of male representation, most critically for Asian American men, but also for other minority men and for all men who interact among themselves.

Family Business, Dick Goldberg

In *Family Business,* Dick Goldberg uses realist structure to challenge the conventional representation of men who are blood relatives. Just as the gay lovers and friends formed one kind of male family in Morris's *If This Isn't Love!* and Swados's *A Quiet End,* so Goldberg's men test the boundaries of love in their male family as they confront what it means to be a brother. Goldberg centers on ailing Isaiah Stein's four Jewish sons, who, in the aftermath of Isaiah's death (which concludes act 1), redefine their relationships in a new, fatherless world. The author accommodates the men's personal transformations by breaking the unities of time and action during his "realist" three-act play.

Set in the Beverly, Massachusetts, home of the Steins, *Family Business* takes place over one month in 1974. Act 1 deals mainly with the family's business issues; act 2, which occurs one week after Isaiah's death, shifts focus to the business of family issues; and act 3, three weeks later, highlights each individual's personal business. The progression of the play's discourse coherence reflects this thematic shift in focus from family business to private, personal business. In act 1, the Steins primarily engage in social dialogue. The father and sons initiate eleven conversations, more than half of them focusing on eighteen-year-old Jerry, an energetic, college-bound wise guy. The remaining conversations consist of combinations of the other family members: seventy-four-year-old Isaiah; thirty-five-year-old Bobby, manager of the family toy store and sports enthusiast, who still grieves for the unexpected death of his fiancée; thirty-two year-old Phil, a Harvard-educated psychologist, husband, father, and director of a lucrative foundation; and twenty-eight-year-old Norman, a bachelor who attends Salem State College as a returning student, having worked for years in the family business. Phil is the only brother who no longer lives in the childhood home.

The central event of act 1 is Isaiah's meeting with his two eldest sons, Bobby and Phil, to discuss the recent alterations in his will. Prior to this conversation, the family's social dialogue juxtaposes two common features, the masculine ethos and the absent woman, with a thematic of male difference in sexual orientation that transgresses that dialogue. This transgression momentarily lifts the talk into personal dialogue; it subsides just as quickly back into social dialogue, however, as soon as another character disrupts the personal dialogue. Much of the social dialogue focuses on Jerry, aligning him with the masculine ethos. Whether father, brothers, or Jerry himself speak about the youngest Stein, Jerry is coded as self and subject, as the normal, active, heterosexual boy among other straight men. His relatives see Jerry as one of their heterosexual family; he is the one who gets "laid every fucking night" (Goldberg 18).[8] The young man encourages this image through jocular talk and other behavior, coding his speech with predictable topics, including his sexual conquests of various women and his interest in sports.

What exposes this construction of Jerry's identity is Norman's interjection of personal dialogue very soon after the play begins, an unusual intrusion into men's social dialogue. Goldberg even directs Norman's moment of self-assertion to be spoken in a whisper: "My gay little brother—I wonder what father would do if I told him you were gay?" (13). But Jerry blithely strips Norman of power over him by threatening his otherwise passive sibling with images of his own masculine shortcomings. The men return to social dialogue when Bobby reenters their conversation, as he casually refers to the absent woman who is Jerry's alleged date for the evening. Lies and half-truths again characterize the social dialogue, a feature that intensifies as the conversations progress. The family's dialogue remains social from this point on until the final moments of Isaiah's meeting with the older sons.

While relying upon the masculine ethos and male mythologies for perpetuating their social dialogue, the Steins depend even more noticeably on specific, repeated references to absent women. In terms of its discourse coherence, act 1 of *Family Business* is structured like the plays analyzed in chapter 1. A man speaks about himself through an absent woman and through that association identifies himself. The women to whom the Steins repeatedly refer are a cluster of Virgin/Goddesses in misogynistic roles (Case 1988, 6): Ruth (Phil's wife), Alice (Bobby's deceased fiancée), Margaret (the housekeeper), Jerry's fictitious big-breasted dates, and, of course, the beloved matriarch, Miriam. Goldberg's play begins, in fact, with Isaiah's drowsy direct address to his dead wife,

"Miriam . . . Miriam" (5). She frames act 1's action and discourse coherence, since Isaiah is motivated by his desire to honor his wife's wishes. Responding to his sense of the absent woman's commands, Isaiah changes his will. "I had to work out something that would seem right to Miriam," Isaiah admits. "I had to do right by her" (26). The action of act 1, therefore, is prompted by the absent woman's influence on the lives of this family of men. The Other still has power in the Stein household. Or rather, how the men *perceive* the Other orchestrates their communication—absent women are a constant topic of conversation.

In the "plain talk" of business (25), Isaiah informs Bobby and Phil of the new legal dispersal of his nearly one-and-a-half-million-dollar estate: Bobby and Norman receive joint title to the house and the store; Phil collects all stocks that will be held in trust for his foundation; and Jerry, who will be accountable to Bobby and Phil's trusteeship, receives cash from the savings and insurance. Bobby has no objection to the content of the new will, but Phil challenges his father's wisdom. He does so, however, without fully disclosing his reasons. Phil's efforts to get ready cash from his father's estate provide the main action line for the remainder of the play; his reasons surface only at the conclusion. Long before that disclosure, however, Phil angers his father to the point of causing Isaiah to threaten to cut him out of the will, which in turn prompts his son to neglect to get emergency medical treatment for Isaiah when his condition appears fatal. Only one week after Isaiah's death, Phil conspires to secure cash from his father's estate by blackmailing his younger brother and lying to his remaining siblings.

In terms of the discourse coherence in act 1, the dialogue shifts from social to personal during Isaiah's dispute with Phil. The honesty is raw and painful between the ill father and his healthy son, not unlike the directness that characterizes the conversations between ill Max and healthy Jason in *A Quiet End*. In both instances, the dramatic space is infused with an awareness of man's mortality. The characters' attitudes toward one another substantially differ, however, and that difference is evident in what the men say to one another. Unlike Swados's Max and Jason, who easily engage personal dialogue, Goldberg's father and son exchange metalinguistics that foreground their strained communicative relationship. "[T]hat's what we're talking about, isn't it" (27), Phil generally queries, to which Isaiah replies periodically, "I don't know what you're talking about" or "You know what I'm talking about" (28). "Why don't you ever listen to what I say? To what anybody says?" the anxious psychologist confronts his father, "You only hear and see what you want" (29). With this last hurtful remark centering on their failure to understand one another, Isaiah succumbs to the evening's animosities and prepares to depart for his room.

It is not certain that Phil loves his father, especially when greed drives him to deny Isaiah medical attention. "Don't play games with me," Isaiah chastises Phil, to which Phil replies, "[Y]ou're using [Miriam as] a way of dealing with guilt" (28). Phil's subsequent dialogue—which is articulate, truthful, and confrontational in its psychological and emotional complexity—is uncommon for a straight, sober, unconfined character: "I'll be honest with you. I want money. I need money. I have obligations" (29).

Isaiah: I don't see that I can do anything besides what I've already told you.
Phil: Which satisfies something within you. . . .
Isaiah: You want me to die, don't you.
Phil: I don't know.
Isaiah: What kind of an answer is that?
Phil: An honest one. And I guess I really shouldn't expect you to be able to deal with it.

(29)

Their social dialogue revealed for its apparent worthlessness, the elder Steins conclude their mutual power plays over one another. The family's business now yields to "family" business, as Isaiah goes off to die.

Isaiah does not understand what has motivated one of his sons to knowingly hurt his father so deeply—nor is he aware that Phil consciously acts to assist him in dying. He also goes to his grave with the illusion that his youngest son embodies the social codes of the all-American dream boy: intelligent, attractive, well liked, promising, and straight. The truth is no character is comfortable with or confident of his sense of identity at the end of act 1. Each constructs a persona based upon illusions, yet each gradually becomes aware of the dangers of such constructions. Nonetheless, they maneuver into new positions of power in act 2.

Ending their mourning period for Isaiah after the traditional one-week shiva, the Stein brothers pursue their goals through manipulations of social and personal dialogues. Phil's scheming eventually causes each Stein to clarify his immediate goals. The details of family matters are now the pressing business at hand. This business underscores the complications behind the brothers' personal issues: Bobby wants to sell the house to be free of his emotionally claustrophobic past; Norman wants to remain in the house, surrounded by memories of his dear, dead mother and buoyed by visions of family togetherness; Jerry wants to move out so that he can more easily negotiate his double life as a gay man; and Phil wants cash to ease his financial anxieties. Of the four brothers, Bobby is the most consistently honest. He is also the least complicated—his desires up front, his biases well known, his manner usually straightforward; he is agreeable without being a pushover. Jerry, Norman, and Phil are more complex individuals, as each lies and role-plays his way into and away from the others' business.

There are three dyadic conversations at the heart of act 2, of which the latter two are personal dialogues. The first talk between Jerry and Phil, however, is social dialogue. Self-disclosure is absent from the exchange. In this initial talk, the brothers strictly discuss business. Yet each has a hidden agenda that bars him from being truthful with the other. Trustee Phil asks Jerry, his financial charge, if he will loan him thirty-five thousand dollars, but he is not honest about how he plans to use the money. Jerry counters this request, mentioning that he plans to help finance a friend's downtown club; he does not tell Phil that his friend is his lover, David (33). "I really think I ought to think about it," Jerry admits, to which Phil responds approvingly, "You've talked enough business for one night" (35).

In the second conversational dyad, Phil and Norman discuss Jerry. The youngest brother and absent women remain the predominant topics of most Stein discussions. This critical feature of the play's discourse coherence now reveals multiple layers of "otherness" in the men's dialogue and characters. First, the most obvious level of otherness is the actual reference to absent women; again, Miriam is the primary topic. Second, Norman talks with Phil as the son who has taken on his mother's role in the family; he has become, as Bobby pigeonholes him, "a nice Jewish lady" (17). While Norman's choices and remarks in act 1 allude to this role-playing, its codings are unmistakable during Phil and Norman's interchange (as well as during the act's third dyad, when Norman speaks to Bobby about his strongly Oedipal love for his mother). Norman conducts the shiva "the way Mama would have wanted" (35); he believes that Jerry is "not ready to handle [financial] responsibility" (36); he believes that Jerry is "better off staying right where he is for a few years," where "someone [can] look after him";

and later, he even remarks that Jerry "doesn't know anything about cooking and cleaning" (54). Norman wants desperately to mother his brother in the family house. He wants to be responsible for Jerry's well-being, to provide him with the nurturance and protection of which Jerry was deprived at an early age when Miriam died.[9] And he urgently wants to keep the family house ("You don't understand," Norman later appeals to Bobby, "I need it" [41]). In the absence of a real woman from the Stein's dramatic interaction, Norman takes on several conventional social codes attributed to the female Other: he expresses his affinity for a domestic life, his preference for the woman's traditional role in relationship to child, family, and home, and his willingness to privilege other men's authority over his own. Although confident in his ability to assume the role of Other, Norman nonetheless insists that his choices are not odd: "I just don't like people saying I'm—I'm different" (41).

During the act 2 intermission of the New York production of *Family Business,* I overheard two separate conversations in which spectators discussed Norman as a closeted homosexual. A straight man in American drama is rarely represented as having a favorable relationship to domestic life—and certainly, by cultural standards, no single male character who is approaching thirty is both domestically oriented and straight.[10] In straight Norman, the socially unconfident man who relies upon the singles dance at the center for meeting people (17), Goldberg presents a seldom-dramatized male character, who represents the extreme differences that exist among heterosexual men. As a striking counterpoint to (homosexual) Michael's unconscious plight in Mort Crowley's *The Boys in the Band,* Norman consciously chooses to become what "Mama would have wanted" (35). Norman is the heterosexual who is "other," and he is no less "real" because his choices are unconventional. This brings us back to the Stein brother who is the more conventional dramatically coded "other" in the semiotic of maleness—gay Jerry.

While sharing drinks with Phil, Norman confides that Jerry is gay. "I don't have anything against the way anybody wants to lead his life," Norman remarks during their personal dialogue. "But I think he may be hurting himself" (36). Norman exposes Jerry's sexuality to Phil strictly for his own selfish ends; he wants at least one of Jerry's trustees to support his efforts to keep Jerry at home. And while Norman's reactions to Jerry's sexuality are not without homophobic overtones, the more reclusive, asocial brother seems to want Jerry to stay not just because he thinks it would be better for the young man (i.e., it would "straighten" him out), but because he does not want to be left alone. Norman is comfortable with himself only if he cares for and serves others.

Phil, in contrast, realizes that he can blackmail Jerry. Knowledge of Jerry's homosexuality is the missing piece in Phil's scheme of greed. In a display of Machiavellian obsession, Phil exploits one of the most fragile tenets of personal dialogue for his own selfish gain. Slipping comfortably back into social dialogue with Norman, Phil knows that he can force Jerry to give him the money he needs. Phil has no boundaries. He knows no loyalty to a brother; he certainly feels none toward one who is "other" at a time when that otherness can be used to his advantage. Phil promptly concludes his conversation with Norman, pleased that he has the necessary ammunition with which soon to engage in battle with Jerry, whose money is the victor's prize.

After Norman and Bobby complete the third dyad, in which they discuss their conflicting, personal feelings about a possible sale of the house, Phil and an "ashen" Jerry reenter the living room and reintroduce the topic of business (42). This group talk concludes act 2. Jerry tells Bobby that he wants to loan the thirty-five thousand dollars to Phil and that he needs Bobby's cosignature to legalize the payment. Through numerous twists and turns of the argument, Bobby refuses this transaction. Phil, he says, is the sibling who "goes through money that [Bobby] worked [his] ass off for" (40). "You're not letting your personal feelings about me get in the way, are you," Phil challenges Bobby, who replies, "What the hell do you mean—personal feelings? . . . I like you fine. You're my brother" (44). The four brothers vacillate between the social dialogue of business transactions and the personal dialogue of emotional confrontations and deep-seated feelings. "You don't want me to have the money. You don't want me to have anything you don't have. Like a nice house . . . or a wife . . . or anything" (45), Phil ruthlessly insults his older brother, pointedly tossing the treasured icons of the American masculine ethos into their talk. Bobby remains calm amid Phil's tirade, claiming that he is "honestly . . . trying to . . . approach this thing sensibly. So there are no hard feelings afterwards."

Realizing that he is on the verge of losing his battle for Jerry's money, Phil activates the final strategy of his blackmailing scheme. He has previously coerced Jerry into insulting Bobby, his "main man" (12), with personal attacks; should Jerry fail to humiliate Bobby into an agreement, then Phil will reveal Jerry's homosexuality to the oldest brother. A sense of Phil's desperation is heightened all the more when one recalls that Norman confided to Phil that knowledge of Jerry's homosexuality "would kill" Bobby (since Bobby still has some investment in the masculine ethos). In response, Phil lied, "My solemn promise; nothing to Bobby" (39). Phil violates personal dialogue by using information about another person, shared in confidence, to exploit that person for his own ends. And so, a terrified Jerry, believing that his sexuality will be exposed to his favorite brother, uncharacteristically attacks Bobby: "I hate you! Why do you have to be like Pop!... You're Bobby—dumb, old Bobby. Who never was good for anything... and never will be" (47). But just as quickly as Jerry speaks these lies, he retracts them: "It's not true. I don't mean it.... He made me say it." Jerry, finally, will not betray himself as he taps into a power that his remaining three brothers have only to imagine.

The dialogue and action now quickly conclude the act: Jerry identifies himself as a gay man; Bobby responds by violently assaulting Jerry (and not Phil, the blackmailer!) as he hits and punches the young man; Jerry chastises Norman for breaking the confidence of their personal dialogue; and Bobby declares Phil the victor of this family battle: "[Y]ou won.... Take the faggot's money" (48). The male nuclear family is shattered by homophobia.

Whereas the escalation of the violent, uncooperative communication is common in male-cast plays (the circumstances that precipitate the violence are not unlike *The Toilet* or *Streamers*), a transformation occurs in Jerry that distinguishes him from other men who are bashed. Jerry does not capitulate to his attacker(s). In fact, he faces the other men in the group more honestly than at any other time in his life. He seizes the moment to take complete responsibility for his self-identity. He moves to a level of personal dialogue that is truthful: "I'm getting out of here and moving in with my friend, my friend David. You know what he is, Bobby?... Just like me.... [Y]ou're going to hear it, and you're going to live with it. Cause that's what little Jerry is and he likes it" (48). In taking the risk to claim his truth and thereby to relinquish any wish to have this truth accepted, let alone understood by other men, Jerry denies the power of his listener to pass judgment on him.

Through his self-identification as "other," Jerry is released to claim himself as subject. He reverses the dynamic typically experienced by male characters who voice personal feelings when among men; he does not accept that another man's maleness is more appropriate, is more acceptable than his own. At least he forces his brother to hear him articulate personal truths. The words free Jerry. At the end of their battle, the Stein boys are forced to see that the "other" is a brother. He lives at home among men. They are also left to question if "everything is not going to be all right" again (48). In Goldberg's play, the "other" no longer denies his rights or his voice among men. Like Piñero in *Short Eyes'* epilogue, Goldberg provides an opportunity for his characters to understand difference. In act 3, he dramatizes the rare portrait of men who struggle to live responsibly with difference, once difference is truthfully revealed to them. Goldberg, like Piñero, breaks realist form to do so: he interrupts the unity of time between his dramatization of the men's violence and his rendering of their movement toward understanding. In other words, playwrights consistently present male characters who require time in order to understand, to reconcile their relationship to the "other"; few dramatize men who experience this behavioral insight at the (same) time as the precipitating crisis.

Three weeks after he assaults Jerry, Bobby completes his move from the family house. In the opening moments of act 3, Bobby takes time from his packing to speak frankly with Norman about his future at the house. "What do you need this place for," the older brother asks Norman. "What are you going to do... [w]ith your time?" Norman's repeated response: "I don't want to talk about it" (51–52). Norman is evasive for two reasons. One is practical, the other psychological. Norman expects Jerry's lover to arrive shortly to discuss (at Norman's invitation) the possibility of Jerry's and his moving back into the family house. Yet also, Norman does not want anyone to challenge his fantasy: namely, that he possesses enough of the absent woman's nurturing power to reunite the now fragmented Stein family. After all, they *are* a family of brothers who may, again, need a place where "everybody gets together" (51). "You know how much our being a family meant to her. I mean that's... that's what she lived for" (14). And while the house is a symbol of the family, Norman draws his daily strength to go on, even to fantasize, from his presence in—and his ownership of—the actual place. This brother who is "other," who is the stage embodiment of the absent woman, lives for the house and its possibilities as he envisions his mother lived for them. Like the conventional, heavily coded female Other, Norman is the coded object who is defined according to his relationship to the male subject and his needs.

Soon after Bobby's departure, David arrives. Norman and his younger brother's lover interact awkwardly, their social dialogue marked by clumsy questions and answers that pretend to polite conversation. Norman, who supposedly has not "done a dishonest thing in [his] whole fucking life" (40), continues to tell little white lies in order to project an image of sibling harmony. However, he eventually gets the courage to move into personal dialogue: he asks David to move into the family house with Jerry; David rejects his offer and confirms that Jerry is expected momentarily "to talk with [Norman], to explain why [the lovers] can't do it" (55). Hurt and embarrassed, Norman leaves the room.

It is important to David and Jerry that they confront Norman in person (and not simply on the telephone [55]). Valuing the appropriateness of face-to-face conversation, the lovers anticipate that such self-disclosing talk can just possibly help to minimize inevitable personal hurt—especially when the participants bring complex emotional and psychological issues to the exchange.[11] But the pair do not have the chance to engage Norman, since Jerry's arrival at the house overlaps with Bobby's return to complete the move of his furniture. David leaves the Stein home to return to the apartment he shares with Jerry, leaving the hostile brothers together for the first time since the violent attack.

The interaction between Bobby and Jerry is among the most poignant in the male-cast canon. It demonstrates the power struggle, often realized metalinguistically, between speaker and listener as their positions alternate in conversation. Goldberg provides a rare opportunity to observe the progression of male verbal and nonverbal dynamics of disconnected personal dialogue. While the brothers communicate cooperatively, they strain to distinguish their responsibility toward one another. Their talk is infused with personal risk, singular claims of responsibility, and the power of individualization—all vital features in men's communication committed to the understanding of differences and to self-identification. I quote liberally, since their unrelenting, intense conversation captures so many of the codes and thematics evidenced throughout this study. It is useful now to let the flow of the dialogue speak for itself and to listen for the echoes to previously analyzed plays. This is the personal level of conversation weeks after the eruption of violence. Violence and silence, therefore, precede this sustained self-disclosing dialogue of personal business:

Bobby: Will you listen to me?
Jerry: If you have something to say.
Bobby: I wish I understood.

Jerry: You wish you understood what?
Bobby: Why you are what you are.[12]
Jerry: [*Turns to exit.*] Fuck off, mister.
Bobby: Let me finish. I don't understand but I want you to
          know that I'm going to try....I need some time to
          pull it all together. I'm asking you for that time....I'm
          asking you to try to understand me.
Jerry: I'll do my best.
Bobby: Jerry, don't say it that way.
Jerry: How do you want me to say it?
Bobby: LIKE YOU MEAN IT.

(56–57)

Self-assured in the truth of his own identity, yet bitter and hurt
over Bobby's previous rejection of him, Jerry has no ground to trust
Bobby. Bobby is aware of this fact:

Jerry: What are you reading into me? What do you see in
          me?...Why don't you just say it?...
Bobby: It takes more than a few weeks to unlearn thirty-five
          years of something.
Jerry: And I don't think that you can.

(58)

Here, Bobby voices his willingness to question the authority
of the masculine ethos. His effort certainly differs from that of most
straight characters, including Roma in *Glengarry Glen Ross,* Sherman and Boyd in *At the Club,* Ora in *The Toilet,* Longshoe in *Short
Eyes,* and even Peter in *The Zoo Story.* But Jerry cannot trust
Bobby's claims to change, as their verbal sparring gets more abusive, threatening to thrust them once again into the violent grip of
uncooperative communication. Bobby momentarily loses his re-
straint as he speaks about slapping Jerry around again, "to try to
knock some sense" into him (58). This hint of violence only
strengthens Jerry's case against Bobby's sincerity and ability to
change. It also reinforces his commitment to personal dialogue
rather than verbal abuse or physical violence. "Go ahead, Bobby,
that's what you're good at," Jerry taunts. "You could get in a lot of
good belts....Or are you afraid that you'd kill me this time....Two
minutes ago you were begging forgiveness...ten seconds ago you
wanted to beat up the fairy. I don't trust you, Bobby, it's as simple
as that."

Bobby backs Jerry up against the wall as he tells the young man to strike him, as if a reciprocated act of violence will make Jerry happy and get them back to "ground zero" with one another (58). Yet, words (as was the case with their earlier physical violence) are unable to break down the barrier between the two men and reground their relationship:

Jerry: I don't think I want to touch you.... Get away from me! Get out of my life!

Bobby: I love you.... What do I have to do to make you believe it?

Jerry: Ain't no way.

Bobby: Why? Answer me that and I'll leave you alone for good.

Jerry: I don't have to....

Bobby: Well, then you'll just have me hanging around....

Jerry: Don't come near me, Bobby.

Bobby: Then you come to me.

Jerry: No! [*Slowly Bobby moves toward Jerry and embraces him. Jerry simply allows this to happen. After a long moment, Bobby lets him go. Without saying anything, Bobby turns and exits.*]

(58–59)

Jerry exits soon after. In stark contrast to the tragic silence that links Peter and Jerry in *The Zoo Story,* a silence of relief, renewal, and survival accompanies this connection between Bobby and Jerry.

Goldberg's act 3 portrait of Bobby is an extraordinary representation of a straight white male. Rather than diluting Bobby's efforts to reconnect with Jerry with some romantic notion about filial bonding or ethnicity (since Jews are frequently represented in literature as closely bonded people),[13] one must initially position Bobby among classic American characters who are subject to, and often aggressively supportive of, rigid gender codings. Bobby liberates himself from these shackles, however, in his reconciliation with Jerry. In his willingness to be vulnerable, Bobby speaks personally and truthfully; he acknowledges that constructive, meaningful connections can exist between people who are different from one another. For a heterosexual white male to try actively to connect with a marginalized male is for the former not only to embrace the difference within himself (that is, to acknowledge his own

211

"otherness," individualization) but also for him to lose cultural power within the coded patriarchal hegemony.

In a remarkable moment, Bobby eventually combines the language of love with appropriate, nonerotic physical reinforcement. Bobby realizes that any attempt to connect through words alone is futile. Only a physical action as intense and deliberate as his earlier physical violence can penetrate Jerry's ironclad defenses. Showing Jerry, and himself, that he can assume responsibility for his words, Bobby acts truthfully by touching his brother. Few straight white characters speak as honestly and lovingly as does Bobby Stein; even fewer embrace their relatives, let alone a friend or stranger, as a sign of compassion, concern, or reconciliation. Like Jerry and Norman, Bobby becomes one of the "other" men in the male-cast canon.

Goldberg makes a rare dramaturgical choice in male representation through Bobby's transformative story. The playwright dramatizes before the spectator the open-ended process by which male characters can move from violent uncooperative communication to nonviolent personal dialogue. In doing so, Goldberg enlivens men who know that they "can't be like [they] were before" (14). The playwright also invigorates the realist structure with male representation beyond the conventional boundaries—a space where characters are released into a world of individualization. Men's lives change, and these lives necessarily differ from man to man. As another Jew, Coney, wisely tells his Christian friend, Mingo, in Arthur Laurents's *Home of the Brave:* "I *am* different. Hell, you're different! Everybody's different. But so what? It's OK because underneath, we're guys!" (164). This coexistent relationship between sameness and difference is a fact of human existence. Yet the necessity to recognize and respect difference from man to man is a pivotal attribute for male-cast characters—for without it, the individualization of a character cannot survive.

Family Business ends as the remaining bothers reconcile. Phil comes to Norman to ask if he and his family can move back home. He is bankrupt, with nowhere else to go. In a swift flood of final confessions (which much too conveniently tidy up the loose ends in this otherwise well-made play), repentant Phil confesses *his* love for Norman and in turn wins Norman's acceptance. Phil secures a roof over his head, as Norman secures a family in the house. Evoking the maternal wisdom and personal dignity of Linda Loman in *Death of a Salesman,* Norman acknowledges that the Steins loved one another "as much as [they] could" (61). Having masterminded the callous destruction of the bachelors' home, Phil also witnesses the real pain of separation among those who genuinely cared for each other. Phil comes to recognize the emptiness of his disconnected life and the real illusions that threaten his own survival. Like a child, he returns "home" to root himself anew in a kind of innocence and genuineness that frees him to confront the business of his own self-identity. In *Family Business,* only the power of individualization frees a man to connect, personally and meaningfully, with other men.

The words and deeds that remain with the spectator, however, are not these final ones that neatly wrap up the plot. The memorable ones are those that are most faithful to human experience. They are captured in the power of Bobby's repeated "I love you" to Jerry, fortified by his unexpected, silent embrace of the young man. In the relationship between Bobby and Jerry, Goldberg succeeds in dramatizing a penetrating, self-disclosing verbal and physical dimension of communication that is sadly underrepresented in the male-cast canon. His characters' man-to-man talk and physical embrace are believable, desirable, and undeniably commendable acts between male characters.

What has yet to be dramatized, however, is the occurrence of this dynamic level of talk and action when three or more characters are present—that is, when men are *among* themselves.

American Buffalo, David Mamet

Written within two years of one another, David Mamet's *American Buffalo* and Goldberg's *Family Business* have more in common than initially meets the eye and ear. Each is in the well-made, realist tradition. Within acts, each abides by the unities of place and action. Both dramatize the talk of men in groups rather than limiting their characters to dyadic conversations. And despite their different backgrounds—Goldberg's men are wealthy, educated, articulate, professional, while Mamet's men are poor, uneducated, inarticulate, working-class—the two sets of characters value talk among themselves, albeit for different ends. "What I write about is what I think is missing from our society," Mamet asserts. "And that's communication on a basic level" (qtd. in Lewis and Browne 69).

In *American Buffalo,* Mamet dramatizes men's struggle to communicate meaningfully, as they flip-flop between social and personal dialogue, a dynamic not unlike the Steins' discourse in *Family Business.* Mamet's and Goldberg's characters' dialogue is vividly distinct, however, from that of characters who are either obsessed with social dialogue (as in *Glengarry Glen Ross,* for instance) or instantly comfortable with personal dialogue (as in *A Quiet End*). Social and personal dialogues coexist with one another, often in a seemingly contradictory relationship, as a kind of sociopersonal talk. Mamet's sociopersonal talk is a rare feature for a male-cast play without the aid of alcohol and drugs. Mamet's men engage "[t]alk as action...not passive reportage but an active agent in shaping the world and the terms of human relationships.... Conflict may be at the heart of dramatic action but the heart of conflict is talk" (King 539).

American Buffalo is first and foremost a play about how American males talk and what American males have to say to one another. It is only appropriate that a play about communication generates a lot of talk about itself. Over the last forty years, few American plays have provoked as much criticism and commentary as has *American Buffalo*. Its author, with his many interviews and personal essays, himself contributes to the ongoing discourse. The critical appraisal of *American Buffalo* has been just that—an evolving discourse that has moved from earlier, unfavorable critiques of the play as plotless and formless (Clurman; Gill 1977; Rogoff 1977) to favorable reassessments that cite the play's linguistic innovation (Bigsby 1985, 1992; Gussow 1980; Kerr 1981) and cultural resonances—whether they be economic (as an indictment of capitalism: Bigsby 1985, 1992; Demastes; Schlueter and Forsyth), social (Herman; Hubert-Leibler), or metaphoric (Bigsby 1985, 1992; Carroll; Schlueter and Forsyth). While the various Marxist-material-ist-mad-metaphysical-metaphorical readings of the play are customary, few consider the value of its assessment from the position of its gender codings among men. Mamet's unconventional handling of standard elements in a realist play—language, characters, and action—receives acclaim for its sparse, neonaturalist dramaturgy. When viewed within the conventions of male-cast drama, however, the uniqueness of his dramaturgy is less obvious than critics usually understand. Examined for the progression of its discourse coherence—the dynamics of the men's sociopersonal talk and its topic selections (not to be confused with its "realism" [S. Gale; Mamet 1986])—*American Buffalo* offers an atypical representation of men among themselves.

While critics readily acknowledge the quality of relationships among Mamet's characters (S. Gale; Herman; Hubert-Leibler; Schvey), they choose not to identify the frame of their relationships

214

as a male "family." Nearly fifteen years after the play's premiere, however, the playwright himself invited a rethinking of his drama. In 1988, Mamet remarked, "*American Buffalo* sneakily enough, is really a tragedy about life in the family—[it] is really the play [of mine] which is closest to *Death of a Salesman,* though it's something I only realized afterwards" (1988, 93). (Several years earlier, Christopher Bigsby anticipated Mamet's observation, suggesting offhandedly that "in a sense, [the characters] form a kind of family" [1985, 84]). From this perspective, the male characters in *American Buffalo* join the men previously discussed in *If This Isn't Love!, A Quiet End,* and *Family Business* to dramatize a third type of male family, one composed neither of homosexuals nor blood relatives, but rather unrelated straight men who, presumably, are single. It is with Mamet's blessing, therefore, that one considers *American Buffalo* within the American dramatic tradition of realist domestic drama and all its codings. But it is a domestic play with only male characters.

American Buffalo is set in a junk shop owned and managed by Don Dubrow, a man in his late forties. The plot is uncomplicated. Don has his "gopher," Bobby, spy on a former customer whose coin collection the two men plan to steal (Mamet 1976, 1).[14] The customer previously purchased a buffalo-head nickel from Don for ninety dollars. Don assumes that the collector exploited his ignorance of the coin's value, so he plots to reclaim the coin and others of value. In hearing this plan, Teach, Don's "friend and associate" (1), convinces Don to let him be his partner in crime rather than young Bobby, an unreliable recovering junkie. In return, however, Teach must agree to let Fletcher, another of Don's buddies, participate in the heist. In act 2, Teach returns to the junk shop nearly twelve hours later, having overslept the scheduled time for the burglary. The frustrated robbers, Don and Teach, are interrupted by Bobby, who tells them that Fletcher was mugged and is now in the hospital. Suspicious of and enraged by this report, Teach viciously attacks Bobby; Don hits Teach in response; and Teach then ravages the shop with a pig iron. Amid the rubble, finally, Don "restores the solicitude toward Bobby we noticed in Don at the start of the play" (Barbera 273).

Since the "plot" of the play is primarily talk about an inaction (i.e., the robbery), the characters' conversations take on singular importance. Characters reveal through language their relationships to one another, as well as their own natures to themselves. Talk as action (Don tells Bob that "[a]ction talks" [4]) and the revelations that accompany talk are at the heart of *American Buffalo*. Mamet "shift[s] from a sort of Aristotelian philosophy that argues humans reveal themselves through their actions," William Demastes suggests, "to one that argues humans reveal themselves through speech" (68). Don, whom Mamet identifies as the play's protagonist (1986, 76), participates in each of the twelve conversations that structure the play. His voice, in all its contradictions, centers the men's discourse. Seven of the characters' talks are dyads, while five are triads. Among the former, Don has his most involved conversations with Teach. He has only three, relatively brief conversations with Bobby. Two of these talks (one opens act 1, the other concludes act 2) frame *American Buffalo*. They also reinforce Mamet's intention that Don and Bobby's relationship be pivotal to the play's communicative dynamics and meaning. For this reason, Don and Bobby's initial conversation, which is sociopersonal, establishes not only the parameters of the play's discourse coherence, but the issues that evolve into the play's thematics.

During the opening conversation, Don and Bobby combine the usual topics of social dialogue—the mechanics of their business arrangement and absent women or men—with a more personal topic: the nature of friendship. This combination of discourses, a sociopersonal level of speaking, is significant for two reasons. First, it simply yet succinctly distinguishes between the topical features in social and personal dialogues. When, for example, Don talks about the heist or when Bobby reports on his spying adventures, the men's dialogue is clearly social in its focus on business concerns. When Don talks to Bobby about the young man's need to maintain good eating habits, to take vitamins, and to take better care of himself "for [his] own good" (9), their dialogue is personal in its parent-to-child-like concern with self-inquiry and evaluation. "As in the father-son relationship," Pascale Hubert-Leibler notes, Don's "exercise of power is mitigated by feelings of solicitude and love, and a real concern for the other's well being" (562). Second, a character's sociopersonal dialogue outlines the features that characterize his social identity, in direct contrast to those that individualize his personal, self-disclosing identity. When speaking about business to Bobby, for instance, Don is direct, assertive, and no-nonsense, while Bobby remains attentive, flexible, and eager to do a good job. When speaking about personal matters, the older man is compassionate, concerned, and helpful, while Bobby is needy, responsive, and appreciative.

In a key illustration of the dynamics in Mamet's sociopersonal dialogue, Don reminds his young charge, "I'm trying to teach you something here" (4), as he goes on to identify the critical differences between business-based and friendship-based relationships. "[B]usiness is.... [p]eople taking *care* of themselves," Don asserts. "'Cause there's business and there's friendship ... and what you got to do is keep clear who your friends are, and who treated you like what. Or else the rest is garbage, Bob, because.... [t]hings are not always what they seem to be" (7–8). Speaking from a philosophical position not unlike the title character's in Mamet's later work, *Edmond,* Don maps out the boundaries of the play's discourse coherence and thematic focus. Don's conversations throughout the play test his own hypothesis that "things are not always what they seem to be." Don, whom Mamet sees as a tragic hero, is tempted by a force within himself that is materialized in Teach.[15] This force tries to influence Don to favor business over friendship. Driving *American Buffalo* forward is the temptation of Don Dubrow through (Teach's) *language.* And it is the characters' fluctuating reliance upon sociopersonal language that shapes the play's discourse coherence. This frame, however, finally favors personal dialogue as Don realizes that, in Mamet's words, "rather than his young ward needing lessons in being an excellent man, it is he himself who needs those lessons" (1988, 94).

The play's first triadic and dyadic conversations (the latter between Don and Teach) focus on typical topics in social dialogue: a shared activity (their card game of the previous evening) and absent women (specifically Ruthie and Grace, who are friends with this trio of men). Yet, when speaking alone to Don, Teach chooses to dwell on the absent women, believing that Ruthie won the recent card game because she cheated, with Grace's help. Teach complains that he does not "like the way they're treating [him]" (11), especially since he naturally assumes that they are friends (10). "This hurts me in a way I don't know what the fuck to do" (11), Teach confides; "there is not one loyal bone in that bitch's [Ruthie's] body" (14). Employing a sociopersonal rhetoric to comment further on Ruthie's actions—which are tied up with the business of money—Teach distinguishes, supposedly for Don's benefit, between business and friendship: "We're talking about money for chrissake, huh? We're talking about cards. Friendship is friendship, and a wonderful thing, and I am all for it. I have never said different, and you know me on this point. Okay. But let's just keep it *separate* huh, let's just keep the two apart, and maybe we can deal with each other like some human beings" (15). Teach agrees with

Don that business and friendship are separate things, but neither man has yet to articulate clearly what constitutes friendship—except that it is *not* business. The closest that either man comes to this naming is when Don speaks personally to Bobby in the play's opening talk; here, Don's words are action—his action talks—as he reveals his friendship through the content and quality of what he says.

Like Samuel Beckett's men before them, Don and Teach talk to pass time. After momentarily exhausting the topic of absent women, the men face a "long pause" of silence (16). Whereas such moments in other male-cast plays might lead to verbal abuse or physical violence (that is, rejection of further social dialogue), Mamet's men revert to the most basic social dialogue: "So what's new?" Teach asks. "Nothing," replies Don. "Same old shit, huh?" "Yup," Don answers. And so the men talk about Teach's missing hat (an echo of Lucky's hat in *Waiting for Godot*); Fletcher, the absent man whom they are waiting for (another Beckett allusion);[16] objects from the Chicago 1933 World's Fair that Don sells; cards; and the weather. It never crosses the mind of either man to engage any broad or controversial, yet potentially personal, topics such as sex, race, ethnicity, class, politics, or religion. Although the absent woman remains a dependable topic, the two men monitor the often blurred boundaries between business and friendship, since any topics they discuss are automatically coded according to one of these two polarities.

The personal stakes between Don and Teach increase when Teach realizes that he is excluded from Don's plan to do a business "thing with the kid" (25). In the third dyadic talk in act 1, Teach is desperate to get business details about the "thing" from an unforthcoming Don: "I'm making conversation. . . . I'm just asking for talk" (26). Don finally gives in. Through social dialogue, he tells Teach the story of the coin collector and his unexpected, pricey purchase of Don's buffalo nickel. The narrative momentarily turns personal, however, as Don touches on the class distinctions between the collector and himself. "He comes in here like I'm his fucking doorman" (31), Don bitterly recalls, as he tells Teach that Bobby and he will be robbing the man's home later this same day. It is at this point that the play's discourse coherence takes a turn, in favor of sociopersonal dialogue that Teach now, also, fully engages. Upon hearing that Don is using Bobby to do the heist, Teach manipulates the topics of business and friendship through sociopersonal dialogue in an effort to change Don's mind.

Teach assumes that Don chooses Bobby for reasons based only in friendship. He knows that he must convince Don to separate friendship from business if Don intends this job to be completed successfully. Teach also knows that if he can replace Bobby, he will strengthen his ties of friendship to Don. After Teach gets what he wants, he uncharacteristically says to Don, "I like you like a brother" (45). Paradoxically, therefore, business and friendship are not always unrelated. But in order to succeed at business, from Teach's perspective, one must initially demand from one's partner something distinctly different from friendship. Business requires, as it were, nonfriendship, nonloyalty (34). Business requires that partners maintain social and not self-disclosing identities between themselves; to expose the latter to others is simply "not good business" (63). And finally, business requires one's unwavering commitment to the capitalist ethos that, in its codings, is a near replica of the masculine ethos.

The vigorous, impressive feature of Mamet's dialogue (and what some might call his genius) is the choreography of language as Teach convinces Don to drop Bobby. Mamet's method is to stress the social dimension of Teach's sociopersonal dialogue, to emphasize why Don cannot "afford to take the chance" with Bobby (35). Teach never forgets that he is talking business, or social dialogue, with Don. However, he skillfully and selectively draws from the codings in personal dialogue to capitalize on the sentiments (and power) of friendship that he knows underlie Don's (his listener's) fundamental communicative dynamic. Uniting features of the two dialogues, with emphasis on the *socio*personal, Teach appeals to the Don who is a gendered, culturally coded male—one who prefers material success over the male bonding of friendship. This is the kind of talk that Teach knows the two men understand: "We both know what we're saying here" (34)—to "take the time to go first-class" (37). And so Teach, with confidence and bravado, warns Don, "This loyalty. This is swell. It turns my heart the things that you do for the kid.... All I mean, a guy can be too loyal, Don. Don't be dense on this. What are we saying here? Business" (34). Bobby is, after all, the kid in this male family, and the robbery is clearly an adults-only, parental job.

When Bobby returns a second time from the restaurant with the men's coffee, Don lies to him about the scheduled robbery. "I was thinking, you know," Don tells the young man, "[w]e might hold off on this thing" (41). Don is so influenced by Teach's position that he is disloyal to Bobby. He cannot even tell Bobby that he has been dropped from the robbery team. By lying to Bobby about their business in the name of business, Don violates a vital premise of their friendship, of their personal relationship—that is, he violates their trust. "The business ethic is vicious enough *in* the business world," Demastes surmises, "but it alters those in it to the point that they adapt it to *all* situations" (79). And as Mamet himself concludes, "[T]here are no extenuating circumstances for supporting the betrayal of a friend" (1986, 76).

Act 1 ends as Teach and Don privately discuss business in order to "make up rules" for the evening's burglary (47). Although he is "hurt" but not "mad" that Don wants Fletcher on their "team" for "depth" (52, 54, 51), Teach agrees to the plan since they are "talking business" (52). "It's good to talk this stuff out" (47), Teach instructs an equally incompetent Don. "You *have* to talk it out. Bad feelings, misunderstandings happen on a job." In act 2, Don is able to understand the value of friendship, "family," and "home" only after Teach and he, ironically, really *do* "talk it out" about "fuckin' business" (55). Only when the two men freely respond through personal discourse to bad feelings and misunderstandings about their bungled job is Don able to differentiate between his true feelings for Bobby and Teach.

At the opening of act 2, Don is alone in the junk shop waiting for Teach and Fletcher, both of whom are late for the scheduled heist. Bob, however, shows up to talk business with Don; he needs cash in order to buy a buffalo-head nickel from "some guy" (69). As the two men speak in circles about the relative value of this latest coin, Teach enters the room and interrupts their social dialogue. He is upset about being late for the robbery (his watch broke), Fletcher's absence, and Bobby's unexplained presence in the junk shop. Before Don dismisses Bobby, Teach once again demeans the young man to his face. Yet, as in previous instances throughout their dialogues, Teach immediately apologizes to Bobby and to Don for speaking harshly: "I'm sorry. I spoke in anger. I'm sorry, I'm sorry. (Everybody can make mistakes around here but me.) I'm sorry, Bob.... [*To Don.*] So what do you want me to do? Dress up and lick him all over?" (65). Teach knows that his business partner, Don, disapproves of any personal insults directed at Bobby. Although Don has been disloyal to Bobby in their business arrangement, he still protects his young charge from outsiders whose words intend to humiliate the inarticulate recovering junkie. And Don seems to be all the quicker to rise to Bobby's defense in light of his own frustration at Teach (and Fletcher) for botching the robbery. The seeds of nonbusiness talk are already sprouting in this first of two triadic conversations to occur in the act.

Alone and waiting for Fletcher, Teach and Don pass the time by repeating previous remarks about absent people: Bobby, Fletcher, Ruthie, and the intended crime victim. With very little new to say to one another, Teach uses this opportunity to reimpose his capitalist notions on Don, ones shaped by self-interest, exploitation of others, and, implicitly, disregard for friendship. "You know what is free enterprise," Teach asks Don. "The freedom . . . Of the *Individual* . . . To Embark on Any Fucking Course that he sees fit . . . In order to secure his honest chance to make a profit" (72–73). In the canon of male-cast plays, characters who embrace this capitalist ethos do so not as the individual whom Teach evokes, but rather as the socially constructed Man whose actions are mirrored by many men in the capitalist patriarchal system. Teach is not the individual he thinks he is—and, consequently, he has no idea what it means for an individual to have freedom. As he ironically admits to Don, who wants to know "what makes [him] such an authority on life," Teach responds, "[T]he way I've lived it."

Don:	Now what does that mean, Teach?
Teach:	What does that mean?
Don:	Yes.
Teach:	What does that *mean*?
Don:	Yes.
Teach:	Nothing. Not a thing.

(74)

Teach is all business talk and nothing more.

Bored and angry at their wait, Teach eventually tries to convince Don to break the deal with Fletcher—since he did so with Bobby—so that the two of them can get on with the robbery. Teach is desperate to connect with Don to validate his own existence. He knows that the two of them can move forward as a "team" only if he successfully disconnects Don from Fletcher (51). To do this, he must tarnish Fletcher's image as an appropriate business partner, just he has previously done with Bobby. But Teach also knows that Don is loyal to Fletcher in ways that are similar to his (albeit now-contested) loyalty toward Bobby, loyalty that bespeaks friendship. As part of his strategy, therefore, Teach even suggests that Fletcher is an "animal" who might single-handedly try to execute the robbery (75). Don rejects Teach's conjecture. Still bothered by his dismissal of Bobby from the game plan, Don honors his commitment to another friend, the smarter, skilled Fletcher. By doing so, the shop owner demonstrates that his commitment to others is not always corruptible. Don's unbusinesslike behavior, in Teach's estimation, is a clear sign of favoritism toward Fletcher and lack of trust in Teach (79). Discouraged, a self-absorbed Teach begrudgingly returns to social dialogue, as he discusses the robbery's mechanics with a now cautious Don.

Moments before Bobby returns unexpectedly to the junk shop, Teach activates sociopersonal dialogue in an irrevocably vicious strategy to discredit Fletcher in Don's eyes; it is a strategy that he will eventually use against Bobby in final desperation. "The man is a cheat," Teach says of Fletcher (80), and his most recent display of dishonesty was during the previous evening's card game. Don immediately rejects this accusation, only to be chastised by Teach in return: "You live in your own world, Don. . . . You can't take the truth. . . . And you don't know what goes on." "This is nothing but poison," Don exclaims, as he works against this final temptation to discredit all that he knows and trusts Fletcher to be. "Don't fuck with me [about Fletcher]," Don warns, to which Teach assuredly replies, "I don't fuck with my friends, Don. I don't fuck with my business associates. I am a businessman, I am here to do business, I am here to face facts" (83). Deliberately blurring the distinctions between friends and business associates in his sociopersonal dialogue, Teach once again attacks the foundation upon which Don establishes personal relationships. If Fletcher cheats at cards, then there is no reason to believe that he is honest when Don leaves him alone in the junk shop or when the two engage their friendship away from business interests. Teach momentarily shakes Don's confidence in his judgment, his perceptions of reality, and his evaluation of character. Yet Don now knows the challenge directly before him: to take responsibility to uncover whether Teach's "poison" is fact or fiction. Enter Bobby, again.

Typical of the metalinguistic features that characterize the tension in the men's dialogue throughout *American Buffalo*, Bobby mentions repeatedly that he has "*got* to talk to Donny" because he has something to "tell." Teach, in response, reiterates that Don "does not want to talk to [Bobby]." "You do not have to do anything that we tell you that you have to do," Teach reminds the young man, unaware that his language now contradicts his intentions (87). Words alone fill the space in the junk shop, words disconnected from context and meaning. Capturing some meaning to their conversation, however, Bobby tells the others that Ruthie and Grace told him that Fletcher is in the hospital. Unable to verify the accident, Donny begins to suspect that Bobby may be involved in a covert business deal with Fletcher, one that is to undermine Don's planned robbery. Teach has encouraged Don to be suspicious of both Fletcher and Bobby, and the fruits of his effort appear to be ripening.

Teach now takes complete control in directing the discourse. For all intents and purposes, Don works for Teach at this point. Teach's strategy is to move aggressively, sure in his own assumptions. He insists that Bobby "understands" that they "want some answers" (93). He reminds the young man that "loyalty does not mean *shit* a situation like this" since they are talking "business" and not "friendship." As if judge and jury, Teach demands that Bobby tells them "what is going *on* . . . and everything [he] know[s]" (94). Don, listening attentively to the testimony, fears that his friends may well be cheating on him, as Teach had warned him. "I can't believe this," Don says to himself, as Bob goes on to claim, "I don't know anything."

Bob's admission that he lacks (certain) knowledge and that he is unable to articulate in sociopersonal dialogue something of value that will satisfy Teach triggers, from Teach's point of view, a breakdown in their cooperative communication. Clearly, Bobby did not understand (or so Teach thinks) that he must know *something* and that he must find the language to describe that which he knows. Don also appears to side with Teach in the latter's efforts to get information from Bobby. Failing to find the words, because there are no words to convince Teach that he is telling the truth, Bobby is the victim of the play's first full-blown violent action as "Teach grabs a nearby object and hits Bob viciously on the side of the head" (94). Once again, violence combines with uncooperative communication to echo a conventional feature of all-male interaction. As realized in other male-cast plays, this combination is coded into the discourse coherence. From this perspective, therefore, Teach's violence is a semiotic feature of men's dramatic interaction, not simply "a thematic necessity" (Demastes 81), a component of Teach's "paranoid narrative" (Bigsby 1985, 80), or the only source of "tension" that is available to "the stupid" (Crouch 1981). After this burst of violence, Bobby witnesses Donny's capitulation to Teach's behavior. "[W]e don't want to hit you," the older man consoles, "we didn't want to do this to you" (95). Don, in effect, condones the violence against his friend, all in the name of business.

Before uncooperative communication has the opportunity to overwhelm the men's interaction, the telephone rings. Mamet, like so many playwrights of male-cast plays, depends upon the telephone to redirect the interaction out of violent behavior and back into (socio)personal dialogue. And, of course, an absent woman inserts her presence into the action: Ruthie provides the information that the men are otherwise trying to beat out of each other. Appearing to call deliberately to derail Teach's control over Don (which of course, is not the case), Ruthie confirms that Fletcher is indeed in the hospital. Thus, in one phone call that confirms a particular truth, all of the conflicts that hound Don after his initial sociopersonal dialogue with Bobby—the suspicion of betrayed friendships, the violations of personal trust, and the act of irrational bloody violence—serve only to demonstrate just how far Don strays from who he is and from what he values. Teach's temptation of Don (or Don's self-deception) comes nearly full circle as the tempter confesses, "[W]e're fucked up here" (97), which only prompts Don to regain control of his "house" and begin to take care of first things first, as friendship dictates: to see that the "kid" gets to a hospital for proper medical attention (98).

But since Teach has no strings on anyone's friendship, he reminds Don (by way of racist, misogynistic associations), "I am not your nigger. I am not your wife" (98). He contentiously pulls both men back into business talk, in which Bobby, not Teach, is still the "other." Despite Don's forceful protestations that "this is over," the explosive Teach retorts, "No, it's not.... *I'm* in this. And it *isn't* over." After all, Teach believes that every day on the streets he "put[s his] dick on the chopping block" for Don and their business (103). In their linguistic commerce, Teach believes that Don *owes* him. So, Teach bombards Bobby with unrelenting questions about the buffalo-head nickel. Bobby finally admits that he bought the coin from a collector "for Donny" (99). Teach automatically assumes that the kid junkie is lying; Teach is unable (or unwilling) to reason the rest of the scenario—Bobby used the money he borrowed earlier to purchase and thereby replace Don's other coin, doing so because Don is his friend. Rather, in flashing verbal abuses, Teach attacks Don who, unbeknownst to Teach, has now reasoned through Bobby's action: "You *fake*. You fucking *fake*. You fuck your friends. You *have* no friends.... You seek your friends with *junkies*. You're a joke on this street, you and him" (100–101). Teach's tirade, as Henry Schvey explains, "contains, despite its self-serving aspects, a considerable measure of truth. Only at this point does Donny see Teach clearly as the deceiver he is" (83).

Teach's verbal abuse prompts two reactions—one physical violence, the other personal dialogue—from the men who are friends: Don attacks Teach, after which Bobby confesses a lie to Don.[17] Each reaction in its own way defends friendship over business. First, Don acknowledges that Bobby did not lie about Fletcher; Bobby has, in fact, been loyal to the code of friendship. For good or ill, Don comes to understand, friends like Bobby and Fletcher can also be partners in business. Under Teach's manipulative power, however, Don willingly allows himself to deny that which he knows. Although Don appears ready to accept responsibility for the error of his ways, his words are ineffectual: he fails to convince Teach to leave the junk shop. True to the structural conventions of the realist male-cast play, Don resorts to physical violence, as he attacks his enemy, naming Teach for what he is: "You stiff this one, you stiff that one . . . you come in here, you stick this poison in me" (101). Out of selfishness and greed, Teach poisons Don's values with suspicion and distrust toward personal relationships. Other private relationships threaten any individual gain that Teach stands to achieve should he become both a business partner and friend of Don. Thus, Teach creates absolutes out of half-truths. He assumes anything about Bobby and articulates it *if* it serves his purpose to poison Don's mind about Bobby (or Fletcher). But Don calls Teach's bluff: "You make life out of garbage." Don realizes that Teach animates lies and fears to deceive him into turning on his friends. But more importantly, Don knows that he *chose* to believe Teach and thereby betray Bobby—and herein lies Don's conflict in consciousness as well as his reaffirmation of the values he hopes to reestablish. His immediate goal is to rectify his flawed judgment.

Observing Don's outburst of violence, ostensibly in defense of their friendship, Bobby demands that Don hear his confession. The young man, in his characteristically inarticulate speech, admits to Don that he has been lying not only about the whereabouts of the coin collector but about the possibility of the robbery at all. From Bob's admission, Don reasons that the young man borrowed their money earlier in order to buy another buffalo-head nickel. Bob intended that this gesture compensate for his friend's earlier loss and overcome the shop owner's desire for revenge via a heist (which Bob knew could not take place because he had fabricated its possibility). "Even Bobby," as Benedict Nightingale notices, "re-pay[s] Donny's kindness with betrayal" (1983, 3)—but it is a be-trayal intended to save Don from his worst side: revenge. Bob lies about business throughout the day's various conversations in order to please his friend: he tells Don what the shop owner wants to hear, or so Bobby assumes, and does not tell him anything that jeopardizes his cover—that is, until Bobby accepts that only a "shit" perpetuates a lie to a friend (102). The motivations behind Bobby's and Teach's words and actions toward Don, therefore, dif-fer dramatically.

Despondent and angry at these latest revelations, which cast him as a manipulative villain, Teach responds by "trashing the junk shop" (103), a kind of home and sanctuary for the three men. Teach no longer knows his position in this room, so he moves to destroy what he cannot have. If he cannot have business, friend-ship, or a space of his own, then no one else can have them either. Once again, destruction and violence surface as man's means to strike back at the chaos of his own making. Teach's verbal, "wild accusations," Jeanette Malkin concludes, are "almost metaphysical, decrying the grotesque and violent disparity between human needs—contact, communication, comprehension—and the moral and verbal poverty that prohibit their attainment" (154). Ironically, Teach's axiomatic litany—there is "No Right And Wrong. The World Is Lies. There Is No Friendship" (103)—is disproved in Don and Bobby's relationship. While Teach's "Whole Cocksucking Life" may be without morals, truth, and bonding, Don comes to under-stand and realize that he shares some semblance of morals, truth, and bonding with Bobby. His life has some individualization, some personal meaning, that he jeopardizes when he lets Teach's "poi-son" overcome him. Unlike Teach, who believes that "there is nothing out there" (104), Don moves to create "something of worth" (Barbera 273) in his relationship with Bob that will sustain them, whether they are inside or outside their junk shop home.[18]

Don realizes the freedom inherent in self-definition before he takes Bobby to the hospital (which, in and of itself, is yet another sign of the shop owner's willingness to care for another man, unlike Peter, for instance, who abandons Jerry in *The Zoo Story*). In a brief, private moment with the injured, bleeding Bobby, Don ac-knowledges in personal dialogue the completeness of what he has just experienced. He values loyalty and truth in a friend—in a "family" member—and Bobby, Don comes to understand, embodies these qualities in the often contradictory context of their relationship. Don also claims responsibility for his words and deeds. Consequently, he regains his initial dynamic with Bobby, one Mamet identities as critical to (ethical) survival: "[O]nce you step back from the moral responsibility you've undertaken, you're lost. We have to take responsibility" (qtd. in Wetzsteon). The world of *American Buffalo* is not, finally, as Hersh Zeifman suggests, "literally ruthless and graceless" (129); it is a world in which charity and responsibility can be, and are, present.

In one of the more primitive, yet strikingly compassionate scenes of bonding between characters in American male-cast drama, Mamet represents the natural simplicity that can accompany a man's expressions of profound feelings and insights. Mamet's play of talk ends neither in violence nor in business, but in sparse, personal dialogue:

Don: Bob. I'm sorry.
Bob: What?
Don: I'm sorry.
Bob: I fucked up.
Don: No. You did real good.
Bob: No.
Don: Yeah. You did real good. [*Pause.*]
Bob: Thank you.
Don: That's all right. [*Pause.*]
Bob: I'm sorry, Donny.
Don: That's all right. [*Lights dim.*]

(106)

Don's and Bob's talk is finally based in self-awareness. It is open and sincere, and not "pointless words of apology and forgiveness," as Malkin argues (154). Their attempt through language to fill a "missing intimacy" (Bigsby 1985, 22) is an uncommon feature in male-cast drama. It is a particularly unique communicative interaction for (white) heterosexual male characters, made all the more paradoxical in its inarticulate, fragmented presentation. The men in this "straight family" are noticeably less comfortable with language than are their familial counterparts: the gay men in *If This Isn't Love!* and *A Quiet End* and the blood relatives in *Family Business*. But Mamet's men finally do speak frankly, and in doing so, each takes the necessary risk and responsibility toward the individualization of his identity and toward his relationships.

The language of *American Buffalo*—despite (or perhaps because of) its metalinguistic circularity, semantic gaps, vulgarity, and urban rhythms—is actually one of the more articulate, direct representations of straight male communication committed to (so-cio)personal dialogue. Mamet's men's talk is not marked by the "self conscious analysis [and] debate" (Jacobs 55) that is prevalent in the personal dialogue of Goldberg's and Swados's characters. Yet Mamet succeeds in presenting a progressive portrait of men who come to value their relationship to one another and to speak of that value. Mamet achieves one of his immediate artistic goals, to "tear down . . . some of the myths about this country" (1988, 96), here accomplished in his representation of a male relationship that defies, ever so briefly, powerful gender codings.

Mamet's men, Don in particular, are not simply "losers" (Barbera 273) and "mediocrities" (Hubert-Leibler) in an "offensive piece of writing" (Gill 1977). They demand that the truths of their unconventional, unmythic lives and relationships be taken seriously, not evaluated simply as a "metaphoric heap of junk" (Schlueter and Forsyth 499), nor as "broken and useless as the cast-off objects which surround them" (Malkin 154). Very few critics address the poignant relevancy of the organicism that characterizes Don and Bob's relationship, especially as it is captured in their final talk. Nightingale rightly valorizes it, nonetheless, as "one of the most touching and pregnant moments in contemporary drama":

> On the face of it, nothing happens. . . . But actually something rather momentous *has* happened. These people sense it, and so perhaps can we. David Mamet has asked the most crucial question any drama could pose—do values exist?—and quietly and unsentimentally answered in the affirmative. All in a small, unpretentious play involving small, unpretentious people and set in a junk shop. (1983)

Mamet has written a play not only of "intellectual content" (Barbera 275), but of social content: he dramatizes the potential for meaningful relationships between men despite the stifling power of gender codings that would deny such connections. Mamet's men, dangerously close to remaining in the world of *The Zoo Story*, take a decisive step away by the end of their talks. Despite their uneasiness with language, Mamet's men come to understand the value in human connection as well as to respect and desire such connections within the male community. For this reason, Bigsby's assessment falls short of recognizing the achievement of Mamet's characters: "At the very center of [Mamet's] work is his recognition of a failure of will, imagination, and courage" (1985, 70). Within the final conversations in *American Buffalo,* Mamet's men struggle against this tendency, as they do successfully animate their will, imagination, and courage. Their struggle is evident in the progressive dynamics of the characters' dialogue, which in turn structures the play's discourse coherence. They briefly crack the code of the semiotic of maleness in their conversation. Don and Bobby come a long way, given who they are and "given the moral inversions of the world they inhabit" (Bigsby 1985, 84). Through sober, personal talk, they *choose* to regain a moral grounding in their individualization, in their friendship, and just possibly, in a world in which the gender system codes men such as themselves as the marginalized "other"—men who are what Don and Bobby have the potential to become.

The discourse coherence in male-cast "family" dramas represented here by *If This Isn't Love!, A Quiet End, Family Business,* and *American Buffalo* is similar to that which structures the mixed-cast play in American domestic realism. American family dramas in the well-made play tradition favor personal dialogue. Morris, Swados, Goldberg, and Mamet draw from the structural and characterological traditions particular to mixed-cast family dramas, yet in doing so they dramatize, paradoxically, *un*characteristic representations of men among themselves. As gender-coded subjects, the protagonists in each of these plays transcend (to varying degrees) the linguistic and behavioral limitations imposed upon them by social codings—by the semiotic of maleness. While they initiate personal dynamics despite the pressure and assumptions of gender codings, they nonetheless do so in the context of standard familial codings. Arguably, familial codings—as defined within the conventional features of American domestic realism—are those that finally shape the men's (personal) discourse. Thus, male-cast plays in which the dramatis personae are not family for one another are a distinctive litmus test (again, as established with the traditions of American dramaturgy) of man's ability to take responsibility for his words and deeds, and thereby for his self-identity.

That Serious He-Man Ball, Alonzo D. Lamont, Jr.

It should come as no surprise that there are very few published, nondomestic, noninstitutional all-male plays whose discourse coherence is shaped by personal dialogue. The exceptions include a great many plays cast with characters who drink alcohol or take other drugs. One recent realist play, however, establishes new standards for the nonfamilial male-cast drama, Alonzo D. Lamont, Jr.'s *That Serious He-Man Ball.* This play, like the nonrealist *Yankee Dawg You Die,* is cast exclusively with men of color who are not blood relatives. Each play also dramatizes the progressive dynamics of male discourse from social dialogue to personal dialogue, revealing in language the complicated intersection between race and gender when men of color speak among themselves. Yet, unlike Gotanda's play and all other full-length plays covered in this study, Lamont's two-act work adheres perfectly to the neoclassic unities. It provides, therefore, a rare opportunity to hear extended conversation in a group of men and to see how they interact in a noninstitutional setting over an uninterrupted period of time without drinking or taking drugs.[19]

Lamont insists that issues of race and gender, as well as class, intersect in his representation of African American men. This trio of codings, race, class, and gender, recall the dramatic tensions created in earlier male-cast plays by minority writers, such as *The Toilet* and *Short Eyes.* Whereas differences in characters' sexual orientations are central to the primary conflict in Baraka's and Piñero's plays, that is not the case in Lamont's drama. The earlier writers present sexual and gender codings that subsume racial and class differences, but Lamont focuses on their convergence as his characters move from cooperative to uncooperative communication, only to engage, finally, in self-disclosing dialogue. His characters' concluding words, nonetheless, are like those of so many men throughout the male-cast canon: they challenge the rigid gender codings that keep men from becoming their own self-identified subjects. Gender codings distinguish the real Man from the male "other," a distinction that, for all intents and purposes, is eventually color-blind.

That Serious He-Man Ball is set in a basketball court in a suburban playground during the summer of 1985. Three straight African American friends, each in his late twenties, come to play basketball as part of a seasonal ritual they have maintained since their high school days. Their interaction is, in fact, both male "tradition at play" (Lamont 1989, 5)[20] and a manifestation of their desire to reclaim what Cokes experienced in *Streamers* as the unproblematized infantile self. Jello is a fiction writer with a graduate-school degree. He is single and still lives at home with his parents while writing stories and working odd jobs, the latest being at a convenience store. Sky is also single, and he works as a minority employment counselor, dedicated to finding jobs for African Americans. Twin is the only one who works in the dominant culture's professional system. Married to a white Jewish woman, Twin is an up-and-coming employee at Xerox Corporation, where, for unexplained reasons, he recently turned down a promotion. From the perspective of economics and the characters' class struggle, Lamont's play is a "caste drama," as Sam Shirakawa suggests, that "challenge[s] the notion that we are a classless society" (35).

It is not coincidental that Lamont dramatizes the lives of three middle-class African Americans nearly twenty years after their coming of age. After all, historic events and political movements of the turbulent 1960s—the Civil Rights Act (1964), the Voting Rights Act (1965), and the Civil Rights and the nationalistic Black Power movements—were to revolutionize the lives of African Americans, just as comparable events and movements, such as feminism and gay liberation, were to change the lives of other marginalized peoples. Lamont focuses on minority males whose adult lives benefit from these earlier social and political actions, the lasting effect of which, however, is now seriously questioned. The playwright dramatizes unsettling competition among such men, as each measures his successes and failures, own values, and self-identity against the other men's social achievements and personal selves in white-controlled, capitalist America. The men are at crossroads in their lives. The judgments they pass on one another become judgments upon themselves.

The discourse coherence in act 1 initially mirrors that which structures most male-cast plays: social dialogue centered on either discussions of employment or absent women. At first, Lamont's characters "are possessed by male cut-up activity" (1), shooting baskets while verbally jousting among themselves. They are "gloriously chauvinistic," quick with "nasty male chuckles" (2) and "male mirth" (3) as they affirm for each other their shared identities as gender-coded Men. They do so by talking about their sexual prowess and conquest of women. Jello is the first to brag about his male dominance over the female Other, proudly claiming that his "sticky wicket" (1) was recently "drained to the bone" by "Ms. Femme" (3). Here and throughout the play, the men engage in a verbal banter akin to the dozens (which nearly always demeans absent women). Much of the play is, according to Gordon Rogoff, "an eloquently vulgar expression of male sexism" (1987, 128): Jello boasts of his conquest of Annette, Sky gloats about Shaleeka (6),

231

and Twin tolerates cracks about his "connubial bliss" and lack of "nut" from his wife (18, 22). The play's unique contribution to the representation of men is, in fact, the dialogue's eventual subversion of its vulgarity about the Other to focus more truthfully on the difference within.

Lamont creates a distinctive rhetorical strategy in *He-Man Ball:* a "Black Idiom" that Phillip Brian Harper describes as a "vocal affirmation of conscious black identity" combined with an "articulate verbal performance in the accepted standard dialect of the English language" (120, 121).[21] This strategy, nonetheless, parallels language usage and topic selections within the semiotic of maleness; it does not disrupt the discourse coherence that characterizes male-male dramatic talk. Initially, the cooperative communication varies from explicit, streetwise sex talk to general remarks that reflect more complicated syntactical constructions, sophisticated vocabularies, and figurative imagery than are usually apparent in men's talk. The friends' early comments on the basketball court sound a bit strained and the voices are undifferentiated, a product of the playwright's self-conscious efforts to mesh naturally occurring dialogue with thematic concerns. The result occasionally smacks of what Allan Wallach calls "basketball court debate" (1987). But it is not the "pretentious jargon" that Mel Gussow cites in his dismissal of the drama (1987). Rather, the three friends enjoy their play with language as they move effortlessly from inflated Elizabethan-like rhetoric to street jargon, archaic diction, and unembellished prose. "The languages of the play," opines Patrick Gaffney, "crackle with an idiomatic electricity, a beat more hypnotic than rap and more meaningful than the blues." In an observation one might also make about Mamet's salesmen in *Glengarry Glen Ross,* Rogoff concludes, "Words, finally, are the only defense these men have against their overwhelming impotence. Everything fails them except their language" (1987, 128).

The obvious, public impotence facing Lamont's characters is identified in act 1: each man has a disturbing, unfulfilled relationship to the business world (9). Each man's private impotence, however, is not revealed until the conversation advances to unqualified personal dialogue in act 2. It is at this latter point that *He-Man Ball* dramatizes unconventional male interaction. Much of the dialogue in act 1 recalls the sociopersonal talk that characterizes *American Buffalo.* What distinguishes Lamont's talk, however, is that the characters attack one another, especially on the issue of employment. Lamont's men constantly defend themselves against one another; they repeatedly switch their subject and object positions in relation to each other. Rarely is one able to sustain an offensive (that is, subject) position. Just as the men are on the court to compete in one-on-one basketball, so they engage in one-on-one verbal battles. These battles are designed to separate the men from the boys in two realms: capitalist, white America and its equally coded (inclusionary) counterpoint, the African American community. Through social dialogue the friends confront one another about their professional status; yet they also invite personal feelings about that status when one acknowledges that his race has a profound impact on opportunities and success. The cycles of socio-personal dialogue in act 1 focus on employment and race. The personal dialogue in act 2 focuses on issues of gender and male identity. This progression, however, exists within the semiotic of maleness; hence, it is disrupted by scattered outbursts of verbal and physical violence.

Immediately after the men refer to absent women, Twin arrogantly passes judgment on the questionable value of his two buddies' career choices. They suffer "'employment mockery,'" Twin chides, because of "silly male pride" (6), an accusation that could be applied to Twin himself. Jello's efforts to "change topics" (5) fail as Twin resists. Having achieved success through "hard work," Twin criticizes college-educated Jello for his self-indulgence in living off his parents in order to support his efforts to be a writer; he also criticizes Sky for devoting years to secure work "for the brothers and sisters [while] things don't seem to be getting any better" (5) as they wait to be "free at last" (11). He reminds Jello and Sky that he continues "to hold the door open" at Xerox for them should these "talented young black men" want to secure real, financially rewarding jobs (7). Yet both Sky and Jello "love everything" about their work (5, 8), a claim Twin cannot make. Jello knows that Twin's "personal turf" is not untroubled, despite the latter's unconscious projection of himself as a black role model to the boys from the neighborhood (7).

Twin, who dislikes Jello's often "serious and sociological" stories about African Americans (10), limits his ties to his racial community to embrace the financial rewards of white corporate life. He constructs seemingly impenetrable boundaries around his social identity in order to function among whites, or "Master Chuckie," as Jello calls them (20). In contrast, Sky is wholly identified with his racial community, although his boundaries appear to be less rigidly maintained than Jello's. That is, in his ten-year commitment to his race through his work at the association, Sky achieves a kind of social and personal freedom. Nonetheless, Twin disregards the value both Sky and Jello place on racial identification, as he accentuates their economic instability. He challenges the value of their choices, which, in his estimation, undercut their claims to manhood. Yet Sky and Jello distinguish themselves from Twin by remaining outside the latter's predominantly white world. Within the masculine ethos, however, both males are diminished among men by their weak earning power. Twin's statements heighten the group's devisiveness, leading to the first physical battle of the day, between Sky and Jello, both of whom turn to their basketball prowess to heal their damaged egos. Through athletics, the men hope to regain self-pride.

"The atmosphere turns serious" as Sky and Jello face-off (14). Throughout their interaction, the men compete athletically as a physical, nonverbal arena where they can exhibit their virility. Preceding the basketball challenges, Twin appears to be the least damaged by the men's talk about jobs. However, the court action tips the balance in Sky's favor. Sky claims the first victory, blocking Jello's shot and knocking him to the ground; Sky's second victory is over Twin, who also falls victim to the counselor's aggressive fouls. Twin, however, calls Sky on his illegal moves, only to have his now confident opponent call him a "loser" (15).

Twin's response to the label is pivotal to the play's discourse coherence and ensuing action. It signals the end of the first cycle of sociopersonal dialogue. Out of fear that others just might view him as a loser—and that he might think of himself as one—Twin turns the tables on Sky by returning to the topic of employment. According to Twin's defense, no one is a loser who "works" (15); a real loser is not the man who fails to make a basket or to block a shot, but rather the man who is financially insecure. "More power to you," Sky replies, as he underscores Twin's vulnerability in the face of blurred differences between "breadwinning capabilities" (16) and winning at hoops. All three men are engaged in power plays that challenge their self-worth and self-identity, yet they resist moving beyond a sociopersonal level of dialogue. They are still content to attack each other through their talk about jobs and performances on the court. Jello finds himself mediating rising tensions between Sky and Twin. But when the job talk and basketball play get too close to troubling, intimate issues, the trio retreats back to the topic of absent women.

Lamont's men reconnect with one another in their heterosexual power over the female Other. They do so throughout act 1 to avoid the most threatening level of communication, personal dialogue, which demands that each man declare his identity, his "otherness," as the decisive step toward self-definition. The second cycle of sociopersonal dialogue begins, therefore, immediately after the completed first cycle. The men talk about absent women, then return to the topic of employment—this time, Jello presses Twin to discuss his salary and rejection of promotion—and finally, another face-off on the basketball court (Sky, again, is the winner over Twin). These cycles shape the discourse coherence of act 1. The final cycle, however, propels the communication into another dynamic level. In doing so, the cycle foreshadows a unique correlation between content and form in a male-cast play, which materializes in the thematics and structure of act 2.

Still focused on absent women, the trio recalls the 1960s and 1970s, when the "political manifesto" expected African American men to reject the "ole nasty white woman" as a "symbol of Western decadence and beeeeee-u-tay" (25, 24). As a result, African American "brothers" lay macho claim to an exploitative kind of intimacy with their "sisters" (25) of the kind analyzed by Michele Wallace, all in the name of Black Power. But the Reagan years, with their racist, sexist elitism, submerge human rights in favor of white capitalist enterprise and affluence. The result for African American men is to become the object of hate, to become an essential "other":

Sky: Nowadays . . . white women hate us.
Jello: Sisters hate us!
Twin: Talk is: we hate us!
Sky: Talk is: *everybody hate us*!

(25)

But the trio's reading of history, as well as their grappling with personal bitterness, finds a scapegoat outside of themselves:

Sky: Let me recite human betterments achieved from the black revolutionary movement. . . . [A]nd least we forget—[*Pauses.*] we got your *feminism*!
Jello: [*Ancient black sage*]: "Feminism"! Why, reason brothers can't get no jobs now is feminism. Affirmative action spelled sideways is feminism. . . . [*Grabs crotch.*] I sez: time to spread some this here "masculism" smack dab into that *femmy-nism*!

(26)

Unwilling to accept feminism as the reason African American male's class struggle was derailed, Twin reaffirms that he "paid his dues" in the white work world and now "want[s] [his] money's worth" (26). For Twin, the black revolutionary movement deteriorated because the strategies of its grassroots organizations—he cites the Urban League, the Black Caucus, and the NAACP—failed to reorder the white system and redistribute its power base (27). Twin no longer believes that change will occur; any attempts to work within the system for African American rights and power are doomed. Sky, on the other hand, firmly believes that racially identified groups "are still in the game," a sign that better days are still ahead for African Americans who work from within the system in order to dismantle it.

Anticipating the characters' extended engagement of personal dialogue (now seething below the surface of their sociopersonal dialogue), an agitated Twin names race and gender codings as the persistent frame that threatens to marginalize the men doubly. While his remarks echo the DuBoisian description of the African American's "double consciousness" (3–4), his word choice also heightens the significance of gender codings as applied to American men: "I deal with truth," Twin claims. "We living a double hustle. . . . Be a black man, then a man" (27). But Sky rejects this position. Hoping to deflect the mounting tension between the assimilationist and nationalist, Jello tries to get the two men to play basketball. Yet their physical competition only extends their verbal battle. Somewhere, somehow, each man wants to win something, and if he fails through talk, then he will try physical challenge. Anxious to assert his claim to manhood in front of his racial likenesses, Sky does his "man-thing" (28)—he bets Twin that he can sink five consecutive baskets. Sky is confident that his "system," at least on the court, will work (29). But it does not, and Twin secures the ball.

Refusing to give the ball to Sky (who has just failed to shoot his way into momentary manhood), Twin capitalizes on the symbolic resonance of his friend's unimpressive athletic display to express the deeper rage he feels as an African American male: "When do we become real men on this planet?" (29). Twin is angry that his two friends do not share his outrage at the failed revolution, a failure that signaled the African American males' return to "Chuckie's" world and rules. Paradoxically, Twin is more immediately dependent upon the white system than either Sky or Jello. His rage, therefore, while directed at his friends, is actually directed at himself. Unconscious at this point, however, that self-hatred motivates his feelings, Twin displaces his emotions onto Sky in a tirade of verbal abuse. This ignites a brutal phase of uncooperative communication as the men verbally and then physically assault one another. Racist, misogynistic, and homophobic references characterize the escalation in the men's emasculating, uncooperative exchange:

Twin: Let me read you what your problem is, he-man.... You think you still black. I think you a pussy.

Sky: Wifey done pussywhipped your brain as well as your dick....

Twin: Your shit's a fake, man! It don't count for nothing! ... You been raped Sky! Swallowed alla Chuckie's program! [*Throws ball hard at Sky.*] Just a dickless, black eunuch with your cheeks spread all open! [*Sky moves to Twin. Jello restrains him, moves him back as Twin advances.*]

Sky: You a big punk, gettin' humped in your face—gaggin' on it. Bet precious wifey don't never gag—she sucks down hard, don't she?

Twin: Let him go—I'ma give it to him real sweet! [*Pulls shorts down.*] C'mon daddy, spread 'em for me—open your black ass and take it! Take it all bitch!

(30–31)

Chaos ensues. Sky attacks Twin and punches are thrown among the trio. "Quickly, the fight turns more to wrestling than boxing" amid a "flurry of movement" (31). (Ideologies of gender traverse race and class structures, argues Robert Staples, when the social codings of masculinity decisively contribute to the construction of men's identity [7–35]. For this reason, most men—and black men, in particular, proposes Kobena Mercer [via Staples's argument]—not only internalize "patriarchal definitions of male power as brute force" but, by doing so, they perpetuate "the patriarchal legitimation of male violence" [Mercer and Julien, 116, 117]).[22] The act ends with the three sprawled on the court, breathing heavily, and then falling into silence.

Act 1 mirrors without deviation the progression of discourse coherence, from social (or sociopersonal) dialogue to violence, that structures the paradigmatic male-cast plays in this study. As determined by the semiotic codings that characterize the dramaturgy of the realist male-cast play, act 2, then, is distinguished by its reli-

237

ance upon personal dialogue. Indeed, after their explosion of violence followed by extended silence, the men talk again soon after
the opening of act 2. Their momentary social dialogue, however,
quickly transforms into confrontive, personally challenging interaction. And their first topic? To talk about the violence that just
occurred. "It was hostile, to be sure," remarks Twin. Sky concludes, "It builds up, what can you say. Leave it at that" (33). Sky's
comment is a direct analogue to the semiotic system of communication among men: just as the men's behavior builds up to a violent
eruption, so the discourse coherence in male-cast plays builds up
to violence after social dialogue is exhausted. "What can you say"
Sky asks, when verbal communication collapses? You can say nothing. For Lamont's characters, as for most men in the male-cast
canon, physical violence fills in the space and action when words
disappear. Sky later remarks, "Started to stew, happen to anybody"
(46). Yes, violence does happen often according to the canon's
dramaturgical conventions of discourse coherence. But his observation cannot be universally applied; surely other masculinities exist
in which violence is not a defining feature or an approved choice.
There is a gap between realist drama and the lived experience it
purports to mimic.

Since it adheres to the neoclassic unities, Lamont's full-length
play stands as a seamless example of the progression of discourse
coherence in American male-cast drama. If its representation of
men among themselves in act 1 remains conventional, in act 2
Lamont creates an unusual correlation between content and form,
one that materializes, paradoxically, in the name of feminism and
the structures of feminist discourse.

"There is no real love for women in this play," Abiola Sinclair
suggests (30). Yet, men's love for women is a complicated issue in
Lamont's drama. It resists black-and-white readings, as it were, especially when it comes to the assessment of what is or is not
authentic in the world of the play. The men do know, however,
that their hostility toward one another is real. And they also know
that women often confront their anger differently than do men.
Rather than resorting to violence, "the ladies handle [hostility]
quite the reverse," Jello mockingly comments. "They have—that—
goddamn—feminism" (34).

> Twin: The ladies, my good men, sit down and let all that
> "sisterhood" pour out like some grand spiritual—
> "upchuck."

Jello: And we've just seen how the brotherhood operates. At least feminism has mystique. Masculism is—

Sky: Masculism is nothing but an *e-rect* penis. Period.

Twin: The ladies may go about it funny. But they do go about it.

Jello: Maybe it's their lot in life.

Sky: Think so?

Twin: Maybe it's ours.

(34)

Here, early in act 2, the men begin to talk more seriously about women. While their love for women remains problematic and unspoken, Lamont's characters appear, in spite of their persistent macho posturing, to respect women's relationships among themselves. Rarely do men in male-cast plays speak even slightly admiringly of women's communications. Twin's observation that women "do go about it," therefore, is uncommon for two reasons. First, the remark appears to recognize that men may have something to learn from the alternative choices, encouraged by feminism, which most women allegedly exercise when faced with conflict; and second, a man articulates this position while in the company of other men and it goes unchallenged by the listeners. From this point on, the dialogue in *He-Man Ball* is essentially personal talk. Without identifying this dynamic of conversation as one that feminism encourages among people, the men nonetheless proceed to engage it. The men's self-disclosure, for the sake of empowerment through individualization, is, in fact, condoned by feminism. It is *not* a traditional masculinist action. Nor is the moment of its feminist leaning wholly unlike the stimulating effect that gay men have on personal confession in such plays as *Streamers, A Quiet End,* and *Family Business;* in this regard, feminism parallels homosexuality as a stimulus of self-disclosing dialogue. Here, thematics and language converge. Yet at critical junctures through the rest of the play, the men retreat into very Male, nonfeminist actions, only to return to personal dialogue.

Two cycles of communicative dynamics occur in act 2. In the first, Jello and Twin confront one another with a frankness rare for male characters. "I try and communicate," Jello tells his friend, who refuses to respond to Jello's work, creative writing; "I need to be thought of" (36). Jello confronts Twin with his persistent absence in Jello's creative life, after which Twin chastises his friend generally for his lack of steady employment, and specifically for his arrogant unwillingness to engage the politics of publishing. "I have value and substance in my life, dammit! But if I tried to put all of that in front of your face," Jello challenges, "you wouldn't know how to handle me! Not at close range!" Addressing one of the play's major thematics—man's desire, yet often eventual failure, to connect personally—Jello bravely questions Twin, "You ever express any interest of a personal nature?" (37). Frustrated at his inability to reach Twin through the power of personal dialogue, Jello projects his anger onto a one-on-one basketball challenge against Sky.

Jello now joins Sky and Twin as an instigator of physical violence; he becomes one of the boys. Upset that neither buddy desires to "reach for [him]. . . . reach in and pull [him] the fuck *out!*" (39), Jello plays out his frustration. He flattens Sky when the latter shoots, prompting both to throw punches. Sky injures his ankle, whereupon he expresses his desire for revenge in homophobic terms: "Lemme hit that simple faggot!" Jello remains at the center of the storm, however, in his fury that his friends refuse to take him seriously. "You can't be one of the brothers and get where you want to go," Twin ominously concludes, as he repeats, again, what Jello calls Twin's "bourgeois rap" (41). According to Twin, a man of color cannot embrace his difference and still succeed within the system of white patriarchal power. Jello is troubled, nonetheless, that his buddies refuse to acknowledge a power that resides within each of them—despite their racial positioning in the dominant culture—if they respect their individual differences. But Jello himself has yet to be generous toward the other men in his estimation of their choices and needs. He reserves his understanding (if he is to extend it at all) until he confronts Twin with his own dishonesty. Twin has yet to address why he turned down a job promotion. "[W]ere you ever going to tell us the truth?" Jello menacingly inquires (41). Twin's personal dialogue completes the first round of communicative dynamics (personal talk, violence, personal talk) in act 2.

Lamont's men know that a precious price is paid each time they fragment their identities into racial, class, or gender features. Loyalty to one's race surfaces again as a topic when Jello exposes the facts of Twin's recent, disturbing "business" (43): Twin not only turned down a promotion and raise, he supported a white employee over another African American as a replacement candidate. Reminiscent of black-on-black racism in Charles Fuller's *A Soldier's Play,* Twin judges harshly his fellow African American:

"He wanted to bring his street-corner act into my territory, he was raggedy." What Twin really wants to discuss are his own needs as an African American struggling in a white world. Jello's badgering eventually breaks down the barriers that Twin has constructed to protect himself. "They sucked all the black out of me," Twin explodes. "It gets tired being 'representative' of my goddamn race all day long!" (44). Twin is exhausted by the "double hustle" of struggling to "[b]e a black man, then a man" (27). He fears that he is token, a well-paid "slave . . . [who] bit into the whole apple pie" (43). He anticipates, yet fears, that his inner "system" for survival is doomed to an early "death" (44). Twin screams in recognition that he is a *black* man struggling, as does any man of color in America, to succeed within, yet against, a formidable racist system whose homogeneous construction of whiteness depends upon racial erasure. In the business of America, the "other" must mimic the (white) subject; the "other" must perform sameness. Yet, as traumatic as it is for him, Twin bears his personal truth before his friends. He takes responsibility for his feelings and for their articulation. His talk ushers in what will become the final cycle of the men's personal interaction, one that moves from issues of racial identity to the struggles generated by gender constructions.

Before engaging this last communicative cycle, the trio exhausts itself with wild basketball antics reminiscent of "Globetrotter" play (45). The role each adopts in relation to his friends is mirrored in his role on the basketball court: Sky "love[s] to leap" regardless if his moves are offensive or defensive; Twin, a defensive man, loves to "block shots"; and Jello, an offensive "runn[er]," yearns "to feel the wind in [his] face." These men—who live and dream to leap, block, and run—suspect that they have lost not only the "fun" that their physical play once had for them (46), but also the security and authority (as well as mindlessness) of the nonjudgmental homosocial bonding they once shared. After all, Jello and Twin have just challeged each other through talk in an unusually confrontational manner for two straight males. Each man fears the consequences of his self-disclosing dialogue because such expressions have yet to be viewed as sources of empowerment. Each man fears that he may embody, and therefore represent, a failed black man as well as a failed Man.

Jello, acting as the conscience of the trio, now provokes the final revelations of the men's talk toward Sky. Not one of the friends is free this particular day from self-examination and truth telling. Only if they express their inner selves to one another, transgressing the boundaries of the gendered male persona, do the men have choice to self-identify. Sky remains so aggressively well defended that his "manhood got everybody beat" (39). Jello tempts Sky, however, to "take the gloves off," to be less competitive and "Rigid! Rigid! Rigid!" (46, 47). Sky is the most politically black-identified male in the play and also the most rigid in his masculinity; Wallace remarks that black macho and black nationalist struggles "automatically... devalue the contributions of women, as well as gays or anybody else who doesn't fit the profile of the noble warrior" (xx). Sky is determined to link his blackness to his masculinity at all costs. As Isaac Julien notes, for the "black masculinist, hard representation is what's important in articulating polemics against racism and institutionalized racism. But if we're actually trying to create a discussion among ourselves or trying to show another kind of representation, it's important to portray the kind of construction of black masculinity that *is* something very fragile and vulnerable" (hooks and Julien 1991, 177).

An unrelenting battle of personal dialogue ensues, nonetheless, as each man again confronts the dynamics of his race and gender codings in relation to his choice of employment. A man's choice of work, in Lamont's play, is the dominant sign of who the man is. It must be reinscribed because of "the bourgeois myth that a man's value is determined by his job" (Gaffney). In this last communicative cycle, the characters penetrate below that choice to reveal deeper truths about their identities. In the play's closing moments, each character becomes more than the sum total of his socially encoded job.

After Jello criticizes him for "perpetuating this civil-rights fraud" at his agency, Sky condemns Jello for self-indulgent writing that has "nothing to say to black folk" (48). "You could never tell me this, could you?" the writer challenges his friend. Again, Jello voices the need for candid interaction if these men are to face their fears and move on toward personal growth and, quite possibly, meaningful social contribution. "You don't have to like [my work]," Jello clarifies. "Just respect it!" This plea for respect is pivotal in diminishing the frustration that each man feels. Each one inwardly desires the respect of his peers, respect that appreciates the value of individualization, or the difference within. Accordingly, each man attacks "man-to-man" the others' most vulnerable spot—the spot most in need of respect. Not surprisingly, it involves absent women, the recurring topic that precedes men's uncensored expression of personal feelings.

Quick to divert attention from himself, Sky expresses his disdain for Twin's marital choice, "some Jew-ey JAP princess" who "took all the male outta [Twin's] system" (48, 49). Race and gender again converge through the transference of the men's personal feelings onto the absent woman. Implying that Twin's marriage only heightens his capitulation to the codes of the white system, Sky suggests that Twin turned down the promotion because he was unable to manifest "the only truth in this life"—to "hold onto [his] balls" (49). To Sky, Twin is in an emasculating relationship with a castrating white "Jew babe"; he insists on linking race and gender expectations in his attack. Although Sky browbeats Twin with accusations of racial disloyalty, and then (hetero)sexual failure, Twin staunchly defends his choices as his own. "Caught with the truth," Twin admits that he "didn't want the embarrassment" associated with his being the "representative" African American in an otherwise humiliating situation. Sky insists that Twin refused because he thought he could not do the job, that he did not have the "balls" to accept the challenge. Twin, however, forcefully claims that he *chose* not to accept the promotion, and that choice implies that he is not committed to a repressive, depersonalized frame of male achievement. In this interaction, Twin reveals that he is still adjusting to thinking about and accepting himself outside the codings inherent in the dominant male ethos. Despite Sky's adamant appeal to Twin's allegiance to such codes, Twin freely chooses to articulate his desire to disengage from them. While he does so with hesitation and concern for his future, he nonetheless takes a decisive action against the gender expectations in American culture.

During Sky's inquisition, Jello "paces around the court" (49), a repetitive movement that recalls Jerry's activity around the bench in *The Zoo Story*. As with Albee's deeply troubled character, who verbally explodes once he perceives that he is misunderstood, Jello responds to Sky's self-confident grilling of Twin. Sky, after all, skirted by Jello's earlier efforts to understand Sky's competitiveness, his tension, and his anger—feelings that now can be seen to degrade the trio's interaction. I quote at length to illustrate the rapid shift as the characters move from issues of race and gender to issues of gender and sex—all by way of the absent woman. Misogynistic and homophobic references are frequent, along with an appeal to a sense of violence and hypermasculinity:

Jello: [*Moves into Sky's face.*] You tense, Sky. [*Pauses.*] Tense
        'cause I'm this close to where our sex hangs, 'cause I'm

getting inside your sex, man. I am climbing all the way inside where you live and where you breathe.... I've been talking to your ladies, Sky.

Sky: That's your jag, ain't it lover-man? They tell you something juicy. I'm a fag. Got AIDS. My dick small—

Jello: No you hundred percent man, all right. They told me how you do it to 'em, Sky. How you always so ruff and ready.... Same way you are with your ho's you are with us—pounding away—pounding—them—us doesn't matter to you.

Sky: Catty bitch mutha—

Jello: Wanna pump your manhood into everybody—don't know how to be easy, do you?!

Sky: Somebody need to pump some into you, missy!...

Jello: Your ladies told me how you hit it! All the time—hard! Harder!... [*Slams his fist into his palm, over and over, voice breaking.*] This you—a dick with no brains—no feel—no touch!

(50–51)

Jello confronts Sky with the ungenuineness of their male relationship, as well as with his lack of connection to women. This link between problematic homosocial behavior and misogynistic attitude and conduct is striking. Here, the quality of the interaction, as influenced by Sky's behavior, is considered to be no more meaningful than are Sky's encounters with his "ho's." Jello names "feel" and "touch" as the emotions and gestures missing from the men's interaction—their inability to feel anything deeply toward the other, their resistance to touch truly one another's lives. Each of the men, Jello suggests, is merely an object to be used, abused, and discarded by other men, all in the name of a coded, color-blind manhood.

Jello implicitly validates feeling and touching in the establishment of any meaningful relationship. Nonetheless, he identifies male-male interaction as the site where men's characters, their senses of identity, are most clearly defined. Accordingly, men's characters can alter radically, and more truthfully, *if* men are available to change—or to express their difference within—while in the company of other men. Lamont's play suggests, therefore, that the dynamics men share among themselves foreshadow and influence their dynamics with women. Men who abuse men will surely abuse women in comparable ways.

"What's it take for you to *get it!*" Jello asks Sky, after the two men once again physically attack each other (51). The interplay between taunting, physical violence, and the outpouring of a man's repressed, intense emotions is vivid. At this fever pitch, the personal dialogue is entirely focused on the individuals' inner lives. They no longer refer to absent women as a topic through which to talk indirectly about themselves. They are finally at the raw, unprotected core of their beings. Jello solidifies this communicative dynamic by boldly, directly demanding, "*LOOK—AT—ME—MAN!*" (52), to which Sky responds by spitting at Jello. Again, a longer quotation preserves the rhythm of the final confrontation of the play, one that crescendos to verbal and emotional heights rarely dramatized when straight, sober, noninstitutionalized men are among themselves. Through language, Jello strikes back at the gender construction of maleness that operates unrelentingly to keep the men from experiencing their individualizations, their differences within:

Jello: *LOOK—AT—ME*! [*Face to face.*] It's fear! fear! It's in you, it's in Twin, it's in me! [*He, too, near tears, explodes.*] GOD DAMN THE WHOLE—FUCKIN'— WORLD—JESUS, IT'S IN ME!

Sky: Yeah, it's in you—it's in him—the both of you lost it! Not Sky. Sky kept his manhood!

Twin: [*Grabs him by the throat.*] FUCK YOUR FUCKIN' MAN- HOOD, LOOK—AT—US! [*Sky tosses Twin aside, stands atop him. Twin makes to struggle, Sky keeps him down.*]

Sky: You wish you remembered what manhood was! Jew babe throw *you* on the bed, spread *your* legs, don't she! Y'all got so *integrated* you forgot manhood is *all* we got left! . . . SKY HUNG TOUGH! SKY IS SOLID! [*Sky pulls back for a haymaker punch, all cry out, one after another, Jello's cry crescendoes.*] SKY IS SOLID!

Twin: LOOK AT US!

Jello: WE'RE AFRAID! [*He breaks away.*]

Sky: [*Haymaker frozen in place.*] I—DON'T—BREAK!

Jello: *WE ARE—AFRAID!* [*Pause. Sky now overcome, bravado lost.*]

Sky: [*Speaks through sobs.*] Sky—don't—[*Whispers.*] Sky. . . . [*Sky breaks. Bends to his knees in tears.*]

(52)

245

The silencing of language leads to tears. Jello has reached into himself, as well as into the others, to "pull out" their fear (51). Each man is overwhelmed, silenced, and humbled. He releases, in effect, the lies of manhood in favor of the realities of individualization. Recalling the stages of the hero's journey in classical tragedy, the men purge themselves after their recognition of truth, of a knowledge deeper than they had previously imagined. Amid the men's "huddled" mass (53), Rogoff rightly points out, "one of those rare theatrical moments when idea and gesture become one" transpires (1987, 126). Jello offers a wet cloth to Sky, only to have Sky knock it away. "Jello retrieves cloth, offers it again. Sky takes no notice. Jello presses it to the back of Sky's neck. Sky makes to knock it away, instead looks at Jello" (53).[23]

After this ritualistic, baptismal moment when the wet cloth passes among themselves, the men verbally acknowledge that their strategy for survival has "gotta be different" than what they have recently, and always, enacted (53). They enliven and commit to an atypical male presence. This type of representation is, according to Julien, the most threatening for contemporary spectators: it invites the audience to "look in a different way" (hooks and Julien 1991, 177). Embedded in the extension and acceptance of Jello's simple gesture is one of the play's profound images and messages. "It's painful to open oneself up to feelings," Keith Antar Mason notes. "It's even more frightening to communicate them to someone" (qtd. in Breslauer). Men who can extend comfort to and receive comfort from other men not only diminish the power of fear in their lives but replace that fear with an understanding of the human need for connection, compassion, and support. Individual empowerment aligned with self-realization resides in such understanding. Unconnected to other men, man, in his isolation, suffers deadening fear. Connected, man can more effectively defy, if not overcome, his fears because he knows that he is loved and supported by a community. Lamont's men come to understand this "game plan" for survival as they act upon their knowledge through both deed and words: "In here. Us," Jello wisely councils, motioning to the trio. "Here on out . . . let's be some human muthafuckas, OK?" (53).

In *That Serious He-Man Ball,* a man's differences distinguish him from all others in whose image he thinks to see himself—in whose image he presumably shares sameness. Lamont's men fight and verbally beat themselves to reach the center of their souls. They turn inward to return outward again to the world beyond their immediate interaction with a redefined sense of community and personal identities. Such journeys occur in precious few male-cast plays. In Lamont's drama, three men are "hangin'" with one another (54), despite their profound disappointment, in hopes of bettering their lives as friends, brothers, lovers, husbands, sons, fathers, workers—as humans. "We humanize what is going on in the world and in ourselves by speaking of it," Hannah Arendt reminds us, "and in the course of speaking of it we learn to be human" (25). Like Miguel Piñero, David Rabe, Robin Swados, Philip Kan Gotanda, Dick Goldberg, and David Mamet, Alonzo Lamont presents men whose dynamic interaction works toward dismantling the coded myth, the semiotic of maleness, that men among themselves have nothing important—nothing of personal value—to say to one another.

Other American men who are committed to individualization amid human interaction await the dramatic representation of their lives. There are other diverse portraits of men's lives to be represented in the American male-cast canon, multiple subjectivities that defy the conventional, undynamic representation of men that has dominated the realist canon for a century. Some of these alternative masculinities are beginning to reach the stage and the published page. One hopes that the liberation of the dramatic imagination in respect to realist male-cast plays is an achievement of this century. Should this occur, then surely new models for the representation of men among men will greet us—as well as challenge us—in twenty-first-century American drama.

Epilogue

Beyond Power Plays:
Men, Sexism, Feminism, and Representation

Race, sexual orientation, and gender intersect at the thematic core of male-cast plays. Since the overwhelming majority of published realist male-cast plays are white authored and white cast, race has rarely been an explicit issue in the canon for much of this century. Quite simply, white men among themselves represent racial privilege in American culture; their skin color does not set them up as "other" men, therefore race is not one of the features that limits their access to cultural power. What does influence a white man's access to power, however, is his affinity to the gender-coded masculine ethos. For this reason, the character who is not heterosexual represents the most extreme male "other" to inhabit a white male-cast play. At this point in the history of representation in the American male-cast drama, a white character's sexual orientation, his relationship to nontraditional masculinities, and to a lesser extent his class, inform the social and personal tensions in the dramatic dialogue of white men.

In the dramatic representation of men among themselves, characters privilege specific topics as they move from social to personal dialogue. Across the century, men's topics within personal dialogue are consistent: they privilege gender difference as the most deeply provocative topic, more so than race or class. The majority of published male-cast plays, regardless of their racial composition, indicate, therefore, that men who discuss race and class will eventually progress to gender *if* their dialogue exhausts the former two topics. They approach gender from the perspective of their own "difference" in the social construction of male gender, confronting the possible existence of their own difference within.

These observations are drawn from the published canon of predominantly white male-cast plays. Any comprehensive theoretical positions, therefore, must remain qualified because minority plays are underrepresented. As Valerie Smith correctly suggests, "Textually grounded future work needs to be done ... on the way constructions of masculinity affect the experience of race, and the way that connection is represented in literature" (1989, 68). Nonetheless, most minority realist plays that are published appear finally to privilege gender issues when the casts are men of the same race.

Over the last ten to fifteen years, however, several interracial male-cast plays have been produced (a few have also been published) that privilege racial issues. Even more recent, and equally significant in terms of diversification within the canon, is the appearance of the interracial drama not set in confining institutions. Consider, for example, Kevin Heelan's *Distant Fires,* the 1986 winner of the Dramatist Guild/CBS, Inc., New Plays Competition, which had its New York premiere in October 1991. Set in the present on the upper floor of a Maryland building-construction site, *Distant Fires* focuses on a five-man crew of Anglo and African American cement layers who come face to face with the intersection of racial and gender tensions when a black man and a white man are pitted against one another for a job promotion.

Foos, a volatile African American crew member, speaks graphically and eloquently about racism in *Distant Fires.* His drunken monologue at the end of act 1 is particularly poignant in its depiction of the oppression that the African American man suffers under the authoritative charge of white America. While listening to Foos's narrative, one is reminded of Frederick Douglass's description in his *Narrative* of his feelings regarding the pivotal, physical battle with his white master, Mr. Covey: "You have seen how a man was made a slave," Douglass reminds his reader, "you shall see how a slave was made a man. ... This battle ... revived within me a sense of my own manhood" (97, 104). After physically beating Mr. Covey, Douglass is never again whipped in his life. Only upon taking violent physical action against his oppressor does Douglass "free" his *male* identity; he can finally manifest a long desired self-confidence in his manhood. While his skin color remains the sole determinant of his oppression as a slave-object-"other" in a racist culture, Douglass's gendered identity as a man and subject appears to transcend such a culture—or at least to coexist with it—as it allows him to take on the valued identification of Man within a sexist, gender-coded culture.[1] While neither Foos's talk nor the dramatized the-

matics of *Distant Fires* explicitly engages the slave/man duality
that was Douglass's sense of self, characters of color may nonetheless experience the object/subject crisis at the volatile intersection
of race and gender-sex. Based upon my findings from the published
canon, I suggest that gender codings may well underlie the discourse coherence in noninstitutional plays, like *Distant Fires,* that
are interracial in their dramatis personae. This certainly appears to
be the case for all remaining published male-cast plays that fall
outside of this criterion. Only the examination of a considerable
number of yet-to-be produced or published interracial male-cast
plays, however, can provide documented evidence to substantiate
such a claim.

White authors, in general, continue to ignore race issues when
writing male-cast plays. Furthermore, white authors—Heelan excluded—rarely write interracial-cast plays set in nonconfining institutions, let alone plays cast exclusively for men of color. For this
reason, the relatively few published plays written by people of
color for men of color become, unfairly, the representative works
of their particular racial community. It is a kind of critical token-
ism, by default, in American theater. Whether intended or not to
be works dealing primarily with racial issues, these plays nonetheless are filtered first through the lens of race. As Suzan-Lori Parks
comments on the dominant culture's tendency to enclose minority
writers into "little circles of possibilities": "I really get a little ill
when people use only my African-Americanness to talk about my
plays. For instance, lots of people try to look at my work solely in
terms of racism. There's a whole other thing going on that they
don't see—that they *refuse* to see" (37).

Recent male-cast plays by people of color also indicate that
characters' gender identifications—that is, what it means to the
males to be Men in America—dynamically intersect and often col-
lide with their racial identifications. More often than not, however,
the discourse coherence in these plays indicates that while race
may be the dominant topic in men's personal dialogue, it eventually yields to issues of gender before talk terminates. Although the
dramatic feature of gender identity characterizes much of the male
representation written by white authors, this does not mean that
minority plays that also deal with gender issues are capitulating to
or assimilating white issues (that is, that gender identity is somehow only of concern to white culture). Nor does this observation—
nor for that matter, do any of this study's findings—suggest an

insensitivity to those authors who are "committed to resisting politics of domination" embedded in racism and sexism, as discussed by critic bell hooks, a resistance that must "not promote an either/or competition between the oppressive systems" (1990, 64). Rather, the semiotic of maleness in the male-cast canon reveals that regardless of the authors' individual, distinguishing features, playwrights consistently dramatize a *sequential relationship* among the intersecting topics of race, sexism, and gender when men speak.

While they may not be intended by the authors as representative minority dramas, Gotanda's *Yankee Dawg You Die* and Lamont's *That Serious He-Man Ball* are written by men of color and are to be cast exclusively with nonwhite actors. Each play dramatizes men of color who engage personal dialogue in an effort to better understand their inner, raging tensions between their private and public self's racial and gender identifications. These plays are the progeny of such earlier (albeit multiracial-cast) dramas as Baraka's *The Toilet,* Piñero's *Short Eyes,* and Rabe's *Streamers,* which share similar race and gender thematics. Just as Twin expresses in *That Serious He-Man Ball* sentiments not unlike those of abolitionist Douglass—"Be a black man, then a man" (27)—most characters of color in published plays experience themselves, and speak of themselves, in a similar fashion: first as racial beings, then as gendered beings. In realist male-cast plays, therefore, men speak of their identity through a linear construction that takes shape as the play's discourse develops. For example, Twin's naming of himself only reinforces what this study suggests: that there is a relationship between realist dramatic structure and the male representation that is or can be created within that structure. Twin's self-definition—which is one of the split selves in the African American community of this play—distinguishes the intersection between race and gender that is presented throughout the canon as the primary feature in men's lives. It also suggests a *sequencing* of topics within men's communicative interaction: first race, then gender. This pattern, one can argue, is driven by sexist ideology and practice. Although bell hooks is addressing specifically the African American community with her remarks, they are nonetheless applicable to *all* men when one discusses representation in the male-cast canon: "Until black men can face the reality that sexism empowers them despite the impact of racism in their lives, it will be difficult to engage in meaningful dialogue about gender" (1990, 75). In an art-life crossover, the male-cast canon illuminates hooks's insight:

the ongoing struggle when men are among themselves in drama is to "engage in meaningful dialogue about gender."

One of the intentions of this study is to locate in dramatic art those cultural phenomena that incorporate, if not outrightly interrogate, men's gender issues: the women's liberation movement, the Civil Rights and Black Power movements, gay liberation, and the multiple incarnations of a men's movement. Realist male-cast plays, in particular, offer different writers' perspectives on the dynamics of men's interaction. They provide an actual cultural artifact from which discussion about men's lives can ensue. Male-cast plays can serve as a foundation for an ongoing public discourse about the impact of social change on men's thinking and feelings. They can also stimulate a vital opportunity for one to imagine "other" representations of men—to imagine men's cultural and personal differences.[2] In this regard, drama returns to its original function, serving as a place for a community to come together to better understand its relationship to its individual members and to its world. Here, the role of the spectators is vital to the quality of the public discourse fostered by the performance. Spectators provide the necessary link between the page, stage, and street in their reactions to dramatic renderings of male communication and interaction. They bring the experience of their private and public lives to bear on the dramatic story of American men. Their reactions and comments, if heard or recorded, can stimulate a circuit of interchange, of communication, that keeps the discourse on men's lives immediate within the culture. In this way, the dynamic between life and art becomes unfixed and fluid, as public discourse on and about art (and vice versa) informs the collective consciousness—in this case, focused on gender issues. Herein lies a valuable interaction that spectators (and their diverse experiences) and the authors of realist male-cast plays have only begun to explore. The radical revisioning of language within the structure of realist drama—which the majority of critics speak of as a hopeless, fixed system, outdated in its sexist and racist premises—resides at the heart of such fluid, imaginative interchanges. Just as cultural systems are altering, so, too, can realist dramatic systems that purport to capture society. Realism can be "politically effective," as Dorinne Kondo argues, if it engages the "urgent project" of recognition of a diversity of subjects; these subjects, in turn, capture a more "authentic" relationship that can exist between life—including the "'reality' of marginal peoples"—and its representation in art.

As has been demonstrated, the published male-cast canon presents men who talk through social to personal dialogue (usually with varying degrees of violence occurring between the two) in order to individualize and decode their socially constructed gender identities. Accordingly, two prominent features of male-male interaction come into focus, sometimes in actual terms (usually at the end of the play) but in any case always underneath the dramaturgy of male-cast plays. First, as a play's discourse progresses during personal dialogue toward the topic of gender, the absent woman as Other resurfaces as a reference point. She is central to any definition of the gender system and its codings. She is coded as "not male," one who is Other than the idealized embodiment of the masculine ethos.

But further on, as the male character begins to engage in personal conversation when among men, his individualization marks him also as an "other," as one who fails (or refuses) to embody the mythic ideal of maleness. For a man to self-identify, therefore, is to name himself as "other." And in his otherness, the male character, at least by cultural definition, is read as a more femalelike presence. This "female" presence is embodied in the male character who distances himself from the dominant, impersonal masculine ethos and thereby becomes a facilitator of personal communication. In this regard, the second striking feature that not only underlies realist male-cast plays but in fact determines their structure via their discourse coherence, is an obligatory female-associated *presence.* Examples of such a presence include Prentice in *At the Club,* Erie in *Hughie,* Juan in *Short Eyes,* all the men in *A Quiet End,* Bobby in *Family Business,* and Jello in *That Serious He-Man Ball.*

In its most obvious manifestations, the "other" is apparent in four recognizable constructions: (1) in a character's discussion of himself (often implicit within his talk) as not-Other or as dissimilar from the absent woman; (2) in his explicit reference to the absent woman, who is the coded Other; (3) in his engagement of (to the possible point of mimicking) the absent woman's voice; or (4) in his individualized embodiment of the spirit of the female Other and her ethos through his personal refusal to embrace wholly the coded masculine ethos and its attendant mythologies. The potential authority of this "female" figure is so powerful that its absence or degree of presence is in fact the *primary* determinant of the success or failure (in Elamian and Gricean terms as outlined in the introduction) and *quality* of male characters' communication. The more prominent the female-associated presence is in a male-cast play, the more likely it is that male characters will engage in and sustain personal dialogue.

If this gender polarity and its attendant social codings impact so substantially on the construction of realist male-cast plays—and in particular, on the characters' discourse coherence—do they also influence the structure of realist mixed-cast and female-cast plays? Are gender codings a driving force behind the structuring of characters' talk in all American realist drama? Since limited research has been done in the area of discourse analysis and gender codings, one can only speculate.[3] Further research may reveal whether or not the presence of the "other" is, in fact, the *underlying structural device* in the entire canon of American realism. If this is so, then it is possible to consider an alternative theory of the construction of American dramatic realism based on gender codings.

It is crucial to reiterate that if personal dialogue is thought of as "speech of otherness"—that is, talk that identifies the speaker as one who challenges the social construction of male identity—then a man who engages personal dialogue is necessarily vulnerable to a listener's rejection of his position, particularly if the listener adheres to the principles inherent in the masculine ethos. At this point, it is useful to recall the discussion of *The Toilet* (chap. 2), in which racial issues come to exist on the edges of the play's personal dialogue, while homophobia—and implicitly, misogyny—reside at the heart of the text. The critical clash over the meaning of *The Toilet*, over the author's intentions, only heightens the play's significance; no other male-cast play analyzed here has generated such extreme, impassioned readings from its critics. In and of itself, this diverse critical reaction lends support to the notion that, within the theoretical frame of this study, Baraka's play epitomizes the (underlying) dramaturgy of twentieth-century American male-cast plays through its stark, heightened representation: whereas its development of discourse coherence is conventional, its full-blown dramatic exploration of the intersection of race, sexism, sexual orientation, and gender—the most volatile topics in men's talk—reveals, in a noninstitutional setting, the ongoing, conflicted state of American culture's collective (un)conscious.

When Baraka's Karolis demands personal dialogue, when he individualizes himself in the presence of a group of males who are obsessed with maintaining the power allotted their masculine social identities, he is persecuted for constructing a self through *language* that aligns him with the "other." As imposed upon them by the construction of gender identity in American culture, men who are vulnerable, whether emotionally, psychologically, or physically, are labeled as less than the desired Man. In American popular thinking, for a man to be weak and vulnerable is to categorize him as feminine, as an "other." It is a homophobic and misogynistic perspective. The dramaturgical significance and social poignancy of Baraka's text, therefore, are that it reflects the specific thematic that underlies realism's positioning and appropriation of the Other, and that it illuminates a prominent, intensely contested issue since modern feminism: America as a misogynistic culture. And in this gender-based circuit of cultural codings, women and homosexuals share the position of the coded Other. Thus, realist male-cast drama is essentially a misogynistic, homophobic canon. A male character's conflict between social talk and personal talk, between violent action and nonviolent behavior, between a social role and individualization, is rooted in his attitude toward the Other, in his attitude toward women. The point is that traditional male-cast plays exist for the sole purpose of furnishing a very specific definition of maleness: in this kind of play, Men are defined as not-Woman.

And so the American male-cast drama and the culture of which it is a part appear to be at a critical impasse. The plays continue to reinforce the notion that men among themselves, and in particular straight men among themselves, are unequivocally driven by socially constructed gender codings, that they are violent, that they are resistant to if not incapable of personal interaction, and that they are untouched by feminism. These features, I should add, surface in recent unpublished (yet produced) male-cast plays written by both men and women.[4] But while realist drama appears forthright about *its* vision of men among themselves, American culture activates a less decisive—certainly more diversified—picture of men. It is a composite that outrightly rejects the determinist position that "all men are the same," and more pointedly, that feminism has not had an impact on American men's lives.

To some, it may well be news that men among themselves in life have not spoken the same language for some time now. Certainly, many men continue to engage in myth-driven talk and action. But many do not. For these men, feminism has provided encouragement to challenge the constraints of gender codings. In our society today, a man either supports antisexist ideology and practice or he does not. Yet, despite the clarity of this choice, men frequently sit on the sexist fence, weighing their feminist allegiances on an issue-to-issue or relationship-to-relationship basis. Upon choosing (or not) the type of feminism he advocates (based on his awareness of the various and often conflicting kinds of feminism that are practiced), an American male establishes an identity that either does or does not align him with the traditional masculine ethos and its attendant mythologies. (A man's relationship to feminism, of course, remains essentially different from a woman's relationship; patriarchal power, after all, is male-centered power.)

While the majority of men (may) appear unmoved by or resistant to feminist advances, many other men have heeded the feminist call to question socially constructed gender identities. Just as all women do not consider themselves feminists, so all men do not consider themselves antifeminists. Within such flexible, gendered spaces of identification, personal, communal, and cultural change reside. hooks, for instance, has forcefully argued for an alliance between the racially specific community of African American feminists and African American male supporters of feminism (1984, 67–81; 1990, 65–77); it is to be hoped that such an alliance of women and men may occur in American culture at large. Feminism is certainly, as Michael Kimmel says, "the most important political ideology to challenge men's power over women, and some men's power over other men" (66). Changes brought about through feminist thinking and behaving will affect the diversity of representations of men dramatized in male-cast plays.[5]

The male character who understands, who "gets" feminism to the point of its informing his self-identity, represents the most innovative characterization that can be achieved in today's male-cast drama. As this study demonstrates, there are ample numbers of plays that present men among themselves who do not understand feminism, because they are either unsympathetic toward or unaware of feminist goals. These plays are constructed in such a way as to affirm the male/female power dichotomy of Self/Other, subject/object; their discourse coherence and male representations are undynamic in addressing male diversity. For a male character to "get" feminism is for him to understand the extent to which America is a misogynistic culture. Its male-dominant culture is steeped in contradiction as it extends rights to the Other, while it remains completely threatened and intimidated by the potential power of the Other. Arguably misogyny may well lie at the heart of racism, as we have seen it fester at the heart of homophobia.[6] For a male character to "get" feminism, therefore, is for him *to begin* to "get" racism and homophobia. One must first deeply understand the workings of misogyny before one can begin to understand the complexities inherent in racism and homophobia, the other systems of domination under consideration here.[7]

The stages of a male character's developing consciousness in realist drama—the stages of Western men's developing consciousness in real life, for that matter—are not random. As repeatedly demonstrated in male-cast plays, the male character's awareness of and conflict with the Other is the starting point of every play. Only through the course of the play does the Other, *initially* coded as Woman, begin to redefine itself as *men's* differences among themselves—that is, when men see each other as "other" relative to each one's distinguishing features, including sexual orientation, race, ethnicity, and class. As the male character defines his relationship to the absent Other and what she represents to him—all of which is explicit or implicit in his dialogue and actions—he begins to identify his sexual politics. These politics indicate his relationship to women, to men, and finally to sexism. Just as feminism is a politics of the Other (in Beauvoirian terms) as subject *and* object, so the male-cast play illuminates, essentially, a politics of the Self as subject *and* object. Only recently has a feminist voice in male-cast drama, usually written by playwrights who are of color or gay or both, begun to influence noticeably the plays' form and content—to offer diverse visions of the subject's politics.

The male-cast canon has precious few plays that include male characters for whom feminism has naturally, and not just polemically (or begrudgingly), informed their way of life. For a writer to consider that a character may have a supportive relationship to feminism appears to be a key to unlocking the writer's imagination when it comes to the representation of men among themselves. A whole new world of original, diverse voices is waiting to speak its unconventional male dialogue. Such voices will necessarily demonstrate, and thereby validate, the real fluidity to gender codings that American feminist Margaret Fuller advocated in 1843: "Male and female . . . are perpetually passing into one another. . . . There is no wholly masculine man, no wholly feminine woman" (43). And although a fluid male voice has yet to enter fully into the American dramatic idiom, it does exist in many different manifestations in American life. To dramatize the diversity of men's lives, the range of their masculinities, would constitute a challenging act in American male-cast drama.

The cast of that future drama has long been assembled. We await the start of this new play.

Notes

Introduction

1. Speaking of gay men as "differently masculine" (356), Ken Corbett suggests that "homosexuality is a differently structured masculinity, not a simulated femininity or nonmasculinity" (347). "The gay man's experience of gender," Corbett argues from a clinical perspective, "does not rest on a binary tension modeled on heterosexual masculinity and femininity" (349), a position David Bergman cites in his critique of gay self-representation in American literature (26–43).

   With respect to *all* men and women (as represented within literary texts), however, I suggest throughout this study that if gender is viewed as a fluid construct, then all men are necessarily differently masculine from each another, just as all women are necessarily differently feminine from each another. Within any given man, the masculine coexists with the feminine, and within any given woman, the feminine coexists with the masculine. Or, as Linda Bamber explains it, "the Otherness of the feminine [is] in the consciousness of individual men. . . . [and] the masculine Other is in the consciousness of women" (11). One's individualization, therefore, is partially determined by the unique variation of these coexisting gender codes that he or she embodies. See also Butler 1990.

2. Chaudhuri uses "difference within" to refer to culture, yet the term is also applicable to gender. Chaudhuri acknowledges Barbara Johnson's discussion of "difference as a suspension of reference" (328), illustrated in the writings of Zora Neale Hurston, as a precursor to her own notion of difference within. For Chaudhuri, "[T]he drama of immigrants . . . furnishes more and more examples of what a truly differential interculturalism will look like. Its ultimate subject will be, I suspect, the distinction between two kinds of difference: one *between,* the other *within*" (196–97). See Michele Barrett for a discussion of the different meanings of the concept of difference, particularly as they

apply to the recognition of "'the differences within' the idea of woman" (37). Barrett's definitions more closely relate to my immediate interest in gender, but, unlike Chaudhuri's more appealing, non-gender-specific "personalist terrain" (199), they remain focused only on women's experience. Undoubtedly the distinction between "difference" and "power," which indicates, to Barrett, a hierarchical construct that privileges some women over other women, is the same distinction that privileges all men over all women, despite any of their shared differences (e.g., race, class, ethnicity, sexual orientation). There has been no discussion of what the "difference within" the idea of man might do to challenge the traditional notions upon which distinctions between difference and power are based. What happens, therefore, if we imagine a dialogue of difference that includes men, male difference, and the "difference within" the idea of men?

3. This figure refers to all modes of male-cast drama: realist, nonrealist, and monodramas. Over three hundred texts written in the latter two modes are published.

4. In her provocative essay, "Looking for Mr. Bovary," Lavonne Mueller acknowledges that few women playwrights "invent" (that is, imagine and write) "strong" male characters (and, I might add, male-cast plays); "today's most successful women's plays have no male characters at all." "[E]ntering the male psyche is generally not prevalent among women writers in general and women playwrights in particular," remarks Mueller.

> If, indeed, there are plays the public expects a woman to write, subtle as this expectation may be, then this "feminine timidity" could become a self-fulfilling prophecy. If a man wrote a definitive portrait of a woman—a *Madame Bovary*—then potentially there is a woman who can write and will write the "Bovary" of a man. Somehow, the climate for women who write has to be made more accepting by the public, critics, and women themselves.

5. Among the plays set in domestic spaces that are cast with straight characters are William Inge's *The Call,* Jason Miller's *That Championship Season,* and John Ford Noonan's *Some Men Need Help.* Gay plays in domestic settings include Victor Bumbalo's *Kitchen Duty* and *After Eleven,* Robert Chesley's *Jerker, or the Helping Hand,* Mart Crowley's *The Boys in the Band,* Terrence McNally's *The Lisbon Traviata,* Sidney Morris's *If This Isn't Love!* and Robert Patrick's *T-Shirts* and *The Haunted Host.*

6. Rosen draws this conclusion from an analysis of ten European texts and four American, all written by males. The European texts have mixed casts and nonrealist structures. Of the American texts, three are

written in a realist mode, and two (*The Brig* and *Streamers*) are male-cast plays.

7. Among the more familiar male-cast plays set in hospitals are Juan Shamsul Alám's *Accession*, Tom Cole's *Medal of Honor Rag*, Corinne Jacker's *Terminal*, and Ronald Ribman's *Cold Storage*; in prisons, Alám's *God's Children*, David Montreal's *Cellmates*, Miguel Piñero's *Short Eyes*, Ribman's *The Poison Tree*, Martin Sherman's *Bent*, John Wexley's *The Last Mile*, and Carlota Zimmerman's *Man at His Best*; and in military camps, Kenneth Brown's *The Brig*, Charles Fuller's *A Soldier's Play*, Robert Hock's *Borak*, Arthur Laurents's *Home of the Brave*, and David Rabe's *Streamers*.

There are no American male-cast plays like Peter Weiss's mixed-cast *Marat/Sade*, for example. American theater has yet to portray mad men among sane men in a civilian institutional system and the struggle for control between them, a major theme of mixed-cast plays set in asylums. There are three qualified male-cast asylum plays, however: Robert W. Masters's *The Window*, James McLure's *Pvt. Wars*, and Arthur Miller's one-act play *The Last Yankee*. In a ward room in a mental hospital, patients interact in *The Window*. McLure's play, according to the text, is set in an Army veteran's hospital; Christopher Bigsby calls the setting a "mental hospital" (1992, 260). *The Last Yankee* (produced at New York's Ensemble Studio Theatre, June 1991) is set in the waiting room of an institution, where two men, who are not patients, converse. Among the topics the men discuss are their wives (the play's absent women) who are patients in the asylum. In January 1993, Manhattan Theatre Club premiered Miller's revised text of *The Last Yankee:* a two-act, mixed-cast play (the wives are present on stage during the second act).

8. Occupational dramas include plays set in police stations, Thomas Babe's *A Prayer for My Daughter*, Arthur Kopit's *The Questioning of Nick*, and Tom Topor's *Answers*; courtrooms, Saul Levitt's *The Andersonville Trial*, Herman Wouk's *The Caine Mutiny Court Martial*, and Larry Atlas's *Total Abandon*; physicians' offices, Charles Dizenzo's *The Last Straw*; teachers' offices and academic institutions, Bill Cain's *Stand-up Tragedy*, Martin Duberman's *Metaphors* and *The Colonial Dudes*, and Robert Marasco's *Child's Play*; business offices, Clay Goss's *Of Being Hit*, Mamet's *Glengarry Glen Ross*, Dennis McIntyre's *Established Price*, and Murray Schisgal's *The Flatulist*; and clerics' quarters, Leo Brady's *Brother Orchid*, Bill C. Davis's *Mass Appeal*, and Emmet Lavery's *The First Legion*. A hotel room is the setting for the traveling salesmen in Tennessee Williams's *The Last of My Solid Gold Watches*.

Examples of plays set in nonprofessional work environments include the industrial factory of Martin Flavin's *Amaco*, the construction sites of Kevin Heelan's *Distant Fires* and David Ives's *Mere Mortals*, the railroad tracks of David Henry Hwang's *The Dance and the Rail-*

road, the junk shop of Mamet's *American Buffalo* and the ship deck of his *Lakeboat,* the garage of Gary Richards's *The Root,* the freight elevator lobby of David Therriault's *Floor above the Roof,* and the newspaper's reel room in James Yoshimura's *Union Boys.* The blue-collar characters in these plays are often immigrants or men of color or both.

9. A distinguishing characteristic of the male-cast canon is, indeed, its persistent portrayal of American men as drinkers, if not drunks. Consider, along with J. Miller's *That Championship Season,* such plays as Davis's *Mass Appeal,* Heelan's *Distant Fires,* Louis LaRusso's *Lampost Reunion,* Stephen Mack Jones's "The American Boys," McLure's *Pvt. Wars,* McNally's *The Lisbon Traviata,* Noonan's *Some Men Need Help,* Patrick's *T-Shirts,* Jeff Stetson's *Fraternity,* Candido Tirado's *First Class,* and Jane Willis's *Men without Dates.* American men as drug users, captured in Patrick's *The Haunted Host,* are also portrayed in Babe's *A Prayer for My Daughter,* Alan Bowne's *Forty-Deuce* and *A Snake in the Vein,* Ed Bullins's *Salaam, Huey Newton, Salaam,* Crowley's *The Boys in the Band,* and Therriault's *Floor above the Roof.*

A point of interest: Eugene O'Neill's *The Iceman Cometh,* according to Thomas B. Gilmore, is American drama's foremost example of the "anatomy of alcoholism and a distinction between alcoholics and drunks" (15). Getting drunk and revealing pipe dreams go hand in hand in O'Neill's play. While frequently thought to be male cast, O'Neill's three-act play set in Harry Hope's bar is mixed cast. See Gayle Austin for a discussion of the significant, brief presence of three women in the predominantly male setting (30–37).

10. A notable exception is McNally's *The Lisbon Traviata.* The kind of violence featured in the play, however, depends solely upon which performance or published version of the script one refers to: Stephen either contemplates, but does not act upon, killing his lover Mike with a pair of scissors at the play's end (Promenade Theatre, New York, October 1989; McNally 1990) or he kills Mike with the same scissors (McNally 1988; Manhattan Theatre Club, New York, May 1989; Mark Taper Forum, Los Angeles, November 1990). Although the reality of domestic violence in gay or straight relationships is indisputable, I find it curious that while such violence is rarely portrayed between gay men, it is portrayed in the first commercially successful American gay male-cast play (i.e., the Off-Broadway run of McNally's play at Second Stage) to reach a popular audience since Crowley's *The Boys in the Band,* produced Off Broadway in 1968.

McNally's earliest published version of *The Lisbon Traviata* (1988) harkens back to Edward Albee's *The Zoo Story,* the pivotal male-cast play, at least within this study's scope (see chap. 2), which dramatizes unconditionally man's failure to connect nonviolently with another man as well as man's inability (or unwillingness) to understand another man's personal needs. McNally presents men who are very different, initially, from Albee's Jerry and Peter. Stephen and Mike are neither strangers to one another nor incapable of speaking personally when in one another's company. Their love and concern for each other are evident, yet these feelings, in and of themselves, do not make a healthy marriage. What happens in McNally's "operatic" play of "big passions" is the triumph of irrationality and violence in a relationship between two men who know one another, individuals who are highly articulate and sensitive to interpersonal dynamics. Love fails to spare the lives of two men who "love" each other; only through death (at least from Stephen's point of view) can a deeper connection between men be accomplished. While McNally struggles "to write a play that demonstrates what might be called the operas of everyday life," says David Román, he "fails to let his characters, gay men in the midst of an epidemic, recognize that opera is opera and everyday life something much more negotiable than . . . Stephen can fathom" (310). McNally's play, therefore, actually recycles a very familiar structural pattern that dominates male representation. His characters mimic the construction of male identity and discourse coherence that their creative forefathers established: American men's inability to sustain nonviolent interaction. From a different perspective, Román, who positions McNally's men solely within gay male representation, argues that the "instability of McNally's text, evident in its various editions, suggests the difficulties of staging gay relationships and friendships, but even more points to McNally's struggle with the available discursive means of staging gay relations, gay subjectivity, and death in the late 1980s" (307).

11. Representative of the many multidisciplinary approaches to the study of gender, according to somewhat arbitrary but useful subdivisions, are the writings of Hélène Cixous; Michel Foucault; Luce Irigaray; Julia Kristeva; Monique Wittig; Joseph Boone, Barbara Johnson, Nancy K. Miller, Toril Moi, Eve Kosofsky Sedgwick (feminist literary theory); bell hooks, Kobena Mercer, Cherrie Moraga, Valerie Smith, Gayatri Chakravorty Spivak (studies in world majorities and colonialism); Ed Cohen, Lee Edelman, Diana Fuss, Michael Moon (gay and lesbian studies); Peggy Reeves Sanday, Carol MacCormack and Marilyn Strathern (anthropology); Ruth Bleier, Evelyn Fox-Keller, Donna Haraway, Suzanne Kessler and Wendy McKenna (biology and the history of science); Catherine MacKinnon (law); Jessica Benjamin, Carol Gilligan, Richard Isay (psychology); Nancy Chodorow, Barbara Ehrenreich, David Reisman, Gayle Rubin, Lynne Segal, Lionel Tiger (sociology); Joan Scott, Elizabeth Fox-Genovese (history); Judith Butler (philosophy); Dierdre Burton, Deborah Tannen (linguistics); Wendy Brown, Kathy Ferguson (political science); Teresa de Lauretis, E. Ann Kaplan, Tania Modleski, Laura Mulvey, Kaja Silverman (cinema studies); Sue-

Ellen Case, Elin Diamond, Jill Dolan, Lynda Hart, Peggy Phelan, David Román, David Savran (theater and performance studies); and Robert Bly, Warren Farrell, Herb Goldberg, Sam Keen, Peter Middleton, Joseph Pleck, Victor Seidler, Robert Staples, John Stoltenberg ("men's studies").

12. Sanday notes, however, that Beauvoir's "universals were based on her acceptance of Lévi-Strauss's and Hegel's views regarding deep structures of the human mind" (1990, 2).

13. Distinguishing between Self and Other, Beauvoir defines "[t]he category of the *Other* is as primordial as consciousness itself. In the most primitive societies, in the most ancient mythologies, one finds the expression of a duality—that of the Self and the Other. This duality was not originally attached to the division of the sexes; it was not dependent upon any empirical facts" (xvi).

14. It should be noted that several scholars, while examining speech acts (i.e., how sentences function in communication), apply speech act theory (which, according to Norma Rees, provides "a framework for analyzing speaker interactions and how listeners derive them" [199]) to literary discourse, including some discussions of drama. See Ohmann 1971, 1973; Searle 1975a, 1975b; R. Gale; and Urmson.

15. H. P. Grice goes on to distinguish four categories (and their specific maxims, such as "be truthful," "be relevant," "be clear,") that produce results in agreement with the Cooperative Principle; echoing Kant, he calls these categories "Quantity, Quality, Relation, and Manner" (45–46). For each maxim informing talk exchanges, Grice also marks corresponding analogues in the sphere of transactions that are not talk exchanges. Together, a maxim and its analogue support a range of "implicatures," which Grice defines as that which is "implied, suggested [or] meant" within conversation rather than said directly (43). These maxims, analogues, and implicatures yield conversational results in lived experience in accordance with the Cooperative Principle.

16. Elam illustrates his point by referring to Sam Shepard's *The Tooth of Crime,* demonstrating that it is better ordered and more coherent than a transcript of an actual café conversation. Elam then identifies the major ways in which dramatic exchange differs systematically from any real-life equivalent: syntactic orderliness, informational intensity, illocutionary purity, and floor-apportionment control (180–82).

17. While there is limited scholarship that explores the relationship between dramatic dialogue and dynamics of conversation in real life (Elam; Kane), the value of analyzing dialogue in naturalistic drama from a realistic, or mimetic, position has been challenged theoretically (Hornby). This critical debate strongly suggests, nonetheless, a possible overlapping between distinct dramatic and language theories that critique mimetic doctrine. Leading the way in identifying this theoretical relationship are stylistic analysts, such as sociolinguist Deirdre Burton,

who uses "discourse-analysis findings to explain effects in simulated talk," or play talk, "to suggest modifications and innovations in the analysis of spoken discourse," or real talk (168). "A rigorous and comprehensive analysis of dialogue style," Burton says, "must be able to draw on a rigorous and coherent theoretical and descriptive framework for the analysis of all naturally occurring conversation" (ix); to attain these goals, one must accept, however, that "any central, basic model of theatre interaction must have [realism] as its first paradigm" (174). This assertion provides a useful base from which to analyze the relationship of dialogue to discourse.

If one accepts that a critical, concentric relationship exists between the systematic codes of drama and its dialogue, on the one hand, and lived experience and its speech, on the other, then Burton's work, as well as that of other stylistic analysts working on fictional and realistic speech (Fowler; Freeman; Halliday 1966, 1967, 1973; Page; Uitti; Widdowson), is quite useful to the literary critic of dramatic texts. Likewise, other areas of language inquiry—specifically philosophy of language, including its pragmatic and speech act theories, and conversation analysis—provide insights into discourse formation that further illustrate how knowledge of spoken discourse can illuminate certain aspects of the workings of written and spoken dialogue. Each of these language disciplines also contributes to a more broadly based semiotic approach to drama that further reveals that dialogue, like discourse, is characterized by a shared concern "with the processes of signification and with those of communication" (Elam 1). Once semiotics is engaged as a critical mode of inquiry, the dialogue within the text is "restored to its place" as one feature of "one system among the systems of the whole of the performance" (Pavis 29).

18. The remaining levels of textual coherence that usually constrain dramatic dialogue are proairetic, referential, discourse, logical, rhetorical (or stylistic), and semantic coherence (Elam 182–84).

19. The study of a text's proairetic coherence, argues Elam, focuses on how its dialogue functions as a linguistic interaction. "Dialogue in the form of both the speech acts performed through it and the extralinguistic actions reported by it" manifests the drama's proairetic dynamic; "this imposes a strict temporal ordering and underlying action structure on the process of speech acts" (182–83).

20. Please note that, in general, I do not discuss gestural language in this study of published dramatic *texts*. While a critical component of theatrical production, gestural language—gesture, movement, face-to-face behavior, facial expression, and other nonverbal cues—is often determined by directors and actors and not by playwrights. Although gestural language accompanies verbal expression, its absence from the written text makes it nearly impossible to mark without imposed critical interpretation. I do, however, refer to such language when the text

explicitly foregrounds it. I discuss, in particular, silence and physical violence. But on the whole, this study concentrates on dramatic and dialogical structure, a focus that readers of published texts can investigate on their own; the study does not emphasize theatricality since to do so would shift its focus to the complex theatrical production of communication (i.e., interpretation and reception) among text, performance, and spectators.

21. My definition of *personal dialogue,* which acknowledges an absent author, necessarily differs from that which Sue-Ellen Case defines as part of women's "Personal Theatre":

> [P]ersonal dialogue is created by partners in production rather than by an absent author who designs it for production in front of a reading or listening audience. It is a dialogue built on mutuality and intersubjectivity, eliminating any sense of formal distance or representation. Personal dialogue is not removed from life, so it operates not by mimesis but by enactment. It is an engaged dialogue, rooted in everyday life, rather than a mimetic dialogue, aimed at lasting repetition. (1988, 46)

22. Since only published texts are analyzed in this study, a play title cited in the introduction is followed by the date of its original publication.

23. The position of women as (articulated) objects in male-cast drama is not unlike the representation of women in Renaissance male-authored drama: male actors speak the male playwrights' words that are written for female characters. Along this same line, I am aware of my own subject position in this study when I discuss absent women—when I claim to speak about or on behalf of voiceless female characters. My remarks, therefore, cannot help but capture moments when criticism and theory do the same thing that male-cast plays do: subject women to the power of male authority and privilege.

Since this study of realist male-cast drama focuses on the talk exchanges between men and the "realist" representations of men and masculinities that occur in American drama, I maintain parameters regarding these plays (and their productions) that are "realistic": I necessarily assume that male actors are the intended speakers for the male characters. Certainly a consideration of cross-gender casting (i.e., a nonrealist choice for casting a realist play) would contribute a fascinating and useful dimension to deconstructing the actions and dialogue of men among themselves, and to illuminating more sharply the codings that operate in a gendered dramatic system. My immediate interest remains, nonetheless, focused on "realist" representation and the conditions under which this specific portrayal can be explored most "faithfully."

24. "Uncooperative" communication, if positioned within Searle's speech act theory, can occur when a character voices intentions that are not picked up by any listener, making any coherent, unified speech act impossible (1975a, 59–61).

Chapter 1

1. The world premiere of Mamet's (b. 1947) play, under the direction of Bill Bryden, was in September 1983 at the Cottlesloe Theatre at the Royal National Theatre in London. This production went on to win for Mamet the Olivier award, England's prestigious theater honor. The American premiere, directed by Gregory Mosher, was at Chicago's Goodman Theatre in February 1984; this production opened on Broadway at the John Golden Theatre in March 1984.

2. For example, in her otherwise very useful analysis of *Glengarry Glen Ross* and *American Buffalo,* Jeanette Malkin remarks that Mamet's "surface realism . . . is implicitly critical of a society, a social ethos, and a political system which can produce such a debased verbal—and moral—existence" (145). In both plays, Malkin continues, "the 'male' world of business manipulation intermingles with the values of male friendship; and in the distortion of both—business ethics and personal loyalty—Mamet offers a sharp criticism of the moral disintegration of a capitalist society" (147). While this general reading of the plays is certainly defensible, it neglects to make explicit the connection among the *gender* features of its own observations: the social ethos is a masculine ethos; the debased verbal existence is men's verbal interaction; the world of business manipulation is a "male" world; the distortion of friendship occurs in male friendship; and so forth. Like many critics, Malkin chooses not to draw attention to the feature of gender that, perhaps, most significantly determines the plays' action and the characters' dialogue: *Glengarry Glen Ross* and *American Buffalo* focus only on men among themselves.

3. Mamet's is not a quintessential male-cast play, however, in that a typical feature in this canon, alcohol and drug use, is not specified. As he is about to launch into his Glengarry Highlands sales pitch, Roma offers to purchase a "couple more" drinks to share with Lingk (50). This gesture is within moments of the end to act 1, scene 3. Whether or not the men drink throughout the scene is not indicated; this activity remains a director's decision.

4. Hersh Zeifman suggests a gendered reading behind "Always be closing," one that might also

stand as Mamet's credo in *Glengarry*. For Mamet has once again "closed" this play about American business to women, excluding the "feminine" and its reputed values from the sphere of dramatic action; once again there is no place for such values in a world ruled by machismo. As in [*American Buffalo*], women haunt the margins of the text but never break through to the stage. (132)

Although Zeifman rightly cites the significance of Jinny Lingk to the action in *Glengarry,* he underestimates the profound, practical influence that absent women in both *Glengarry* and *American Buffalo* have upon onstage dialogue and actions, as well as the presence of the feminine in some men's words and deeds. The absent woman, therefore, has more than "metaphorical import" (Zeifman 133) in Mamet's all-male setting. Analysis of discourse coherence is one method that reveals the absent woman's considerable impact on the plays' form and content.

5. Consider, for example, the talk between Anglo Americans in such plays as Preston Jones's *The Last Meeting of the Knights of the White Magnolia* and James McLure's *Lone Star,* the African Americans' conversations in Alonzo Lamont's *That Serious He-Man Ball* and OyamO's *Let Me Live,* the Latinos' dialogue in Candido Tirado's *First Class,* the talk of interracial groups in James Yoshimura's *Ohio Tip-Off,* Miguel Piñero's *Short Eyes,* and David Rabe's *Streamers,* and (while occurring much less frequently than in the preceding male groupings) the talk of some gay characters in such plays as Mart Crowley's *The Boys in the Band* and Victor Bumbalo's *Kitchen Duty.*

6. Mamet defines a "gang comedy" as a play "about revealing the specific natures and the unifying natures of a bunch of people who happen to be involved in one enterprise. . . . Because [*Glengarry Glen Ross*] is a comedy as opposed to a tragedy, or even a drama, the confrontation is between individuals and their environment much more than between individuals opposed to each other" (1988, 92).

7. Moss's response to Aaronow is, according to Anne Dean, "the ultimate betrayal of the trust implied in ordinary conversation; Aaronow is designated as a criminal simply because he 'listened'" (201).

8. "Monologue is, after all, the consummate sales pitch: not only does it preclude interruption, but it allows the speaker to appear 'personal' and 'confessional' even when (s)he is only acting" (Geis 1992, 60).

9. Consider Malkin's perceptive analysis as to *why* all Mamet's men "partake of the same inarticulate obscenities, the same limited vocabulary and repetitive jargon" that "almost seem to *precede* [the men], and to mold them" (160). As Malkin argues, the men

seem reduced to the words at their disposal or to what Benjamin Lee Whorf calls the "patternment," the unconscious structures of their specific language and thought-world. These patterns, according to Whorf, are pre-conscious and culturally determined: ". . . significant behavior is ruled by patterns from outside the focus of personal consciousness." Whorf opposes "patternment" (structuring) to "lexation" (word choice), arguing that the former "always overrides and controls" the latter [Whorf 256–58]. . . . Mamet's emphasis on rhythm, on the aural patterning of speech which enables the characters to ignore lexical contradictions, even nonsense, seems to intuitively translate Whorf's ideas into concrete prose—and is cardinal to the production of a sense of determinism in his plays. (160)

If one analyzes Mamet's language within the context of the semiotic of maleness and discourse coherence, however, a more comprehensive pattern arises, one that reveals a conscious choice by Mamet to structure the language of male characters according to a rigid semiotic system based upon gender codes. Gender codes that operate on characters' (playwrights') word choices appear to determine more profoundly the patternment, if you will, in male characters' talk than the characters' rhythms and aural patterns. The "sense of determinism" that Malkin finds in the language of Mamet's plays is actually a conventional feature of male-male dialogue in the male-cast canon. Also see Whorf.

10. See, for example, Thomas Babe's *A Prayer for My Daughter,* Robert Marasco's *Child's Play,* and Dennis McIntyre's *Established Price.*
11. Compare Levene's to Bob and Michael's metatheatrics in Bumbalo's *Kitchen Duty.* Rather than attempting to distinguish themselves from "other" men through role-playing (as in Levene's case), Bob and Michael "act out" a ritual fantasy between leather master and his slave, complete with requisite costuming, dialogue, and behavior, not only to create the desirable illusion of becoming men "other" than themselves but to celebrate their own identities as "other" men—as gay men—on the margins of the dominant culture.
12. For example, consider Prentice's assertion of Hyacinth's voice in the early-twentieth-century play *At the Club* by Alice Gerstenberg (the next play analyzed in this chapter) or the three men's varied voices in D. B. Gilles's more recent full-length work, *Men's Singles.*
13. This is comparable to the moment in act 2, previously discussed, when Moss (desiring actual conversation) interrupts Levene's performance.
14. This sexist, homophobic, ageist attitude is not unlike the racist, sexist, and homophobic stance of the bigoted Coach in Jason Miller's *That Championship Season.* Coach, the quintessential white extremist, warns his former team of white basketball players to beware of "niggers," "kikes," "Jews," "queers," "commies," and "bitches." "We are the country, boys, never forget that, never. . . . But no dissension. We stick together" (18).
15. Here, I refer to "symbolic order" within a Lacanian framework and the "social codings of gender" within a Beauvoirian context. Addressing the origins of the (Lacanian) symbolic order, Jill Dolan remarks that

Lacanian psychoanalysis [is] an articulation of the Oedipal crisis in terms of language and cultural meanings. The penis becomes the phallus in Lacanian theory—the organ comes to represent cultural information. The pre-Oedipal realm is Lacan's Imaginary, where the child exists before language acquisition in sensual unity with his mother. The recognition that the mother lacks the phallus persuades the child to ally himself with the father and accede to his rightful place in the phallologocentric order. The mirror stage is Lacan's term for this scene of sexual differentiation, the entry into a polarized gender structure, and into an articulation of subjectivity within language.

Phallologocentricism organizes phallic authority in language, and the phallus becomes the symbolic object of exchange in a family and social system that denies women agency. The phallus passes through women and settles upon men. (11–12).

See also Rubin, 191–92.

16. Although I have selected works by a woman (Gerstenberg) and a gay man (Morris) to illustrate plays whose discourse coherence focuses on the absent woman, the authorship of this type of play is neither gender inflected nor gay inflected. Throughout the century, heterosexual male playwrights have also used this form; see, for example, Eugene O'Neill's *A Wife for a Life* and Gilles's *Men's Singles*.

17. For biographical overview on Gerstenberg (1885–1972) see M. Atlas; Hecht. For bibliographical information see Coven (89–92). *At the Club* (copyright 1925; first published 1930) premiered at the Ravinia Workshop (Ravinia, Illinois), under the direction of Lionel Robertson, sometime between 1925 and 1930 (specific date unknown); subsequent performances include those in May 1957 by the Alice Gerstenberg Experimental Theatre Workshop (founded by Paul Edward Pross and Otto E. Anderson) during its inaugural season in Chicago. In honor of Gerstenberg's contributions to Chicago theatrical life, the Workshop was dedicated to the critique of plays in playwriting clinics, as well as to workshop productions of plays before select audiences and in the larger theatrical market.

18. Along with *Overtones,* Gerstenberg wrote three additional female-cast dramas; among her fifteen female-cast comedies are *Where Are Those Men, Fourteen, Mah-Jongg, Mere Man,* and *Time for Romance.*

19. Gerstenberg advances the technical apparatus through which the textual presence of the absent woman increases, adding the device of actual phone conversations to the telegrams, photographs, and letters that embodied the absent woman, Yvette, in O'Neill's *A Wife for a Life.* As a point of interest, the telephone is frequently used by characters in male-cast plays (usually to advance plot): men speak to absent women (as in Sidney Morris's *If This Isn't Love!*); men speak to absent

men (as in Bumbalo's *Kitchen Duty* and Robert Patrick's *The Haunted Host*); or men who are in realist split scenes (i.e., they are visible to the spectator but not to one another) speak to men (as in Joe Cacaci's *Old Business* and Robert Chesley's *Jerker*–in both plays, all dialogue is spoken over telephones).

20. The Sherman-Hyacinth-Prentice—or the husband, the (absent) wife, and her lover—triangle is actually a dramatic convention in male-cast drama, beginning as early as O'Neill's *A Wife for a Life* (written in 1913). Within these plays, the absent woman is seen from two dichotomous perspectives. The men's dialogue about the absent woman, in turn, generates the plays' main conflict.

21. This power is manifested in a range of characters who appear in humorous as well as serious plays, or movements within such plays, throughout the male-cast canon. For instance, Ora embodies a comparable, aggressive male voice in Amiri Baraka's *The Toilet*, a play written forty years after *At the Club* and discussed in detail in chapter 2. While not intended for comic relief but rather to heighten dramatic tension, Ora's voice dominates the selection and maintenance of social dialogue and, eventually, of violence in Baraka's text. Vocal males of Boyd's and Ora's type—ones who aggressively adhere to the social and gender codings that privilege them in either the white patriarchy (as in Boyd's case) or in their immediate group of minority men (as in Ora's)—effectively inhibit the topic selections within men's interaction.

22. Sidney Morris's (b. 1929) *If This Isn't Love!* under the direction of Leslie Irons, premiered at New York City's Shandol Theatre in April 1982. The show ran for eight months and over 180 performances, making it one of the most successful, long-running plays to date for its producers, The Glines (who would go on to produce Harvey Fierstein's Tony Award–winning *Torch Song Trilogy* on Broadway in 1983). Among Morris's produced plays are *A Gallery of Characters*, *A Pocket Full of Posies*, *Exorcism of Violence*, *Last Chance at the Brass Ring*, *The Six O'Clock Boys*, *The Demolition of Harry Fay*, *Video's Child*, *Uncle Yossil: A Mystery*, and another successful male-cast play, *The Wind beneath My Wings*. Morris has also written the book for the AIDS musical *We've Got Today*. For additional background information on American gay theater history see Clum 1992; Shewey.

23. Samuel L. Kelley's *Pill Hill* is the most recent full-length male-cast play to utilize a format similar to Morris's decade structure in *If This Isn't Love!* Kelley's play focuses on the impact of time and change on the relationships among the same six African American men: act 1 is set in 1973, act 2 in 1978, and act 3 in 1983.

It should also be noted that Robert Patrick has written a series of seven one-act plays, each in a different setting with different characters, which together trace the romantic comedy of gay male love from decade to decade, starting with the 1920s and ending with the 1980s. Collected under the title *Untold Decades,* six of these "gay history plays" are male-cast while *Pouf Positive,* a monodrama set in the 1980s, features a man with AIDS. About this suite of plays, Patrick remarks: "My theme here is the effects of repression upon the noble spirit, and I picked the stories to trace it. I know ten thousand more gay stories, have told a lot of them, and will tell, I hope, many more. I'll get to the slumber parties and gay synagogues, believe me" (1988, xvi).

24. Adam and Eric's coded language also has historical resonance for an entire community: even though Morris's play was written during the 1980s, act 1 (and much of act 2) captures a milieu represented by other gay playwrights writing before the 1980s. As such, the coded social dialogue of Morris's characters in act 1 resembles, for example, the language of the men in Crowley's *The Boys in the Band,* Bumbalo's *Kitchen Duty,* and Patrick's *The Haunted Host.* Like a good bit of the dialogue in these earlier plays, the discourse coherence in act 1 acknowledges the power of the absent woman and the masculine/feminine model of behavior.

25. In the semiotic of gay maleness in drama, there seems to be a relationship between the facts that the primary absent woman is the mother and that the favored setting is domestic. An Oedipality, if you will, of the domestic space appears to be operating in the dramatic codes. Although her remarks specifically address the "notion of the domestic household" in the black straight community, bell hooks's insights, through their inversion, possibly explain why "the domestic household" might *appeal* to authors when they construct gay characters. According to hooks, the domestic household is "the place where sex and desire end, so that one is always moving outside to try to reconnect with some site of pleasure and sexual ecstasy" (hooks and Julien 179). By inverting hooks's paradigm of the straight household, many playwrights focusing on gay characters appear to recreate the domestic setting for male-male interaction as an Oedipal space—a "site of pleasure and sexual ecstasy."

26. Although this bodily contact is homoerotic in intent, it should be noted that most nonviolent bodily meetings (homoerotic or nonerotic) between male characters (whether they be gay, straight, or bisexual) are followed by hitherto unexpressed personal dialogue. Consider, for example, the intimate dialogue that follows the nonviolent physical interaction between the straight characters in Corinne Jacker's *Terminal;* the gay and straight characters in Dick Goldberg's *Family Business;* and the gay characters in Terrence McNally's *The Lisbon Traviata.*

27. "The state plays a decisive role in regulating a hegemonic heterosexual masculinity," argues Lynne Segal.

The labelling and policing of gay men is one obvious way of constructing a compulsory and dominant heterosexual masculinity: a masculinity defined through difference from, and desire for, women; a masculinity depicted as sexually driven and uncontrollable in its relentless pursuit of women—in perpetual contrast to the depiction of the passive and restrained sexuality of the "gentle sex." (98–99)

Along with his victimization by homophobic laws, Adam also alludes to the racism he feels as a Jew in America. Although Adam struggles to empower himself through his acceptance of his identity as a gay Jew (acts 2 and 3), his deepest struggle is with his homosexuality. This latter topic dominates his conversational contributions.

28. It should be noted that in American drama, gay characters continue to be presented stereotypically as eager, uninhibited conversationalists in social and personal dialogue.

Chapter 2

1. Whereas no one has previously discussed *Hughie* and *The Zoo Story* within the context of male-cast plays and the semiotic of maleness, critics have analyzed the plays together in terms of their shared focus on storytelling (see Harvey) and their general structural technique and style (see Krafchick).

2. Many one-, two-, and three-act plays cast with three or more male characters do not limit their dramatic conflicts to characters' uncooperative communication. Qualified exceptions include, as we shall see, Amiri Baraka's *The Toilet* and Israel Horovitz's *The Indian Wants the Bronx*. In Horovitz's play, two American men verbally and physically threaten a non-English-speaking character for the play's duration. As in Baraka's text, Horovitz's play involves two or more characters who engage in social dialogue and thereby communicate cooperatively; however, they focus their talk on the debasement of an essentially non-communicative, onstage character. This topic leads to the verbal abuse of and physical violence toward the male victim by the remaining men.

3. On the other hand, silence is not an uncommon feature in non-American male-cast plays, especially in the works of Samuel Beckett and Harold Pinter.

4. Eugene O'Neill (1888–1953), who won the Nobel Prize for Literature in 1936 and three Pulitzer Prizes, originally projected *Hughie* as one of a series of eight plays to be called *By Way of Obit*. Although he outlined some of the other plays, he died before the series was completed. *Hughie* is the only one-act play O'Neill wrote after 1919, and it is also the author's last completed work before his death. The world premiere of *Hughie,* under the direction of Bengt Ekerot, was in Sep-

tember 1958 at the Royal Dramatic Theatre in Stockholm, Sweden. *Hughie*'s premiere followed the posthumous world premieres of two other O'Neill masterpieces at the same theater: *Long Day's Journey into Night* (January 1956) and *A Touch of the Poet* (March 1957). The English-speaking world premiere, directed by Fred Sadoff, was in London, July 1963, with Burgess Meredith as Erie. The United States premiere, with Jason Robards as Erie under the direction of José Quintero, was at the Royale Theatre, December 1964. The first major revival of the play was in February 1975 at New York's John Golden Theatre, where Ben Gazzara played Erie.

5. O'Neill worked with this technique as early as 1926 in *Strange Interlude*.

6. See Ronald Ribman, *Cold Storage*. The deadliness of silence and the struggle to defeat it through personal dialogue are central ideas in this two-act play. Like O'Neill's Erie, Joseph Parmigian tries to engage a resistant listener, Richard Landau, in conversation. He does so as a survival tactic. Unlike O'Neill's Charlie, hostile Landau does respond to Parmigian:

> Parmigian: Tell me about all those places, Landau.
> Landau: It's just something to talk about, just something else to talk about isn't it?
> Parmigian: Tell me about Madrid, Landau. Tell me about the restaurant in Madrid.
> Landau: Tell me about anything that isn't silence is what you mean! My life to fill your silence! You're interested in anything that isn't silence!
>
> (1978, 54)

By the end of the play, however, Landau appreciates the necessity of "anything to stay alive" (61). For these two men, personal dialogue overcomes silence and secures their momentary connection with one another. As Landau tells Parmigian, "In talking to you I am very aware of that [need for connection in order to survive]" (61).

7. Looking at *Hughie* "not within the context of O'Neill's career but within the larger framework of modern drama in general," Susan Harris Smith suggests that unqualified, optimistic readings of the play "miss the ironies implicit in the resolution, reduce the hard-won symbiosis to easy, transfiguring redemption, and fix the play in a nineteenth-century reconciliatory mode" (170). Foregrounding these features in her analysis, Smith concludes that "all the evidence suggests that O'Neill would have moved naturally into post-modern dramaturgy. *Hughie* is a compelling example of the direction he might have taken." Note Harris's explanation and outline for a postmodern production of *Hughie* (178).

8. LeRoi Jones (b. 1932) has used the African name Amiri Baraka ("blessed prince") in his civil and literary life since 1968. Baraka allegedly wrote *The Toilet* in six hours. "[I]t came so much out of my memory, so exact," commented the playwright. "Just like I was a radio or something and zoom! I didn't have to do any rewriting" (qtd. in Stone). According to Henry Lacey, *The Toilet* was first presented in 1961 by the Playwright's Unit of Actor's Studio in an Off-Broadway production (34). The Grove Press edition of the play, however, notes its premiere in a double bill with *The Slave* at St. Mark's Playhouse, New York City, December 1964; the play, directed by Leo Garen, ran for over one hundred performances. In January 1965, a New York District Attorney's office turned down a city request to bring obscenity charges against *The Toilet*.

   A 1965 West Coast production of *The Toilet* received an even more hostile reaction than the East Coast production, with which it was running concurrently. Originally set to open at the Las Palmas Theatre in Los Angeles, *The Toilet* was forced to move to another space after the theater owner refused the production based upon the play's objectionable language and its characters' urination while on stage. Director Burgess Meredith finally opened his show, along with *Dutchman,* on 24 March 1965 at Warner Playhouse. On 25 March, the Los Angeles vice squad closed down the show, having taken tape recordings of *The Toilet*'s dialogue to prove that it was obscene. By 5 April 1965, the *Los Angeles Times* and the *Hollywood Citizen-News* had decided that they would no longer accept ads for the play's promotion.

   For background information on the history of African American theater, see Abramson; Haskins; Hay; Hill; Mitchell; Sanders; Edward G. Smith; and M. Williams.

9. Richard Cooke, for example, argues that *The Toilet* is a "thesis" play in which "white men are either actual homosexuals or at least ineffectual, and the strength of the world belongs to the Negro." George Oppenheimer's critique suggests that the "young Negroes [are] little better than savages." Paul Witherington reads the text as a "ritual . . . [an] adolescent exorcism of the maternal" (159), to which Robert Tener adds that it is a ritual focused on "the black male intellectual and his relationship to his black brothers in a white society" (208). Owen Brady finds meaning in the play's "transformation of African tradition and blackness itself by American experience[, which] is the cause of the boys' cruelty" (71). And finally, Theodore Hudson cites "love" as the play's "universal" subject. Yet, according to Hudson, "The fact that the love in this play is homosexual. . . . [and] biracial is irrelevant. . . . race does not control the narrative line and the play's inherent drama" (159).

10. Uncooperative communication is common throughout twentieth-century American drama. Consider, for instance, the prolonged abuses in

Bill Cain's *Stand-up Tragedy*, Israel Horovitz's *The Indian Wants the Bronx*, Miguel Piñero's *Short Eyes*, David Rabe's *Streamers*, Martin Sherman's *Bent*, and John Voulgaris's *Best Friends*; the sporadic physical and verbal harassments in Thomas Babe's *A Prayer for My Daughter*, Martin Duberman's *The Electric Map*, Clay Goss's *Homecookin'*, Lyle Kessler's *Orphans*, Alonzo Lamont's *That Serious He-Man Ball*, Robert Marasco's *Child Play*, John Ford Noonan's *Some Men Need Help*, Ronald Ribman's *The Poison Tree*, and James Yoshimura's *Union Boys*.

11. Roger Abrahams explains that

> the dozens stands as a mechanism which helps the Negro youth adapt to his changing world and trains him for similar and more complex verbal endeavors in the years of his manhood. The dozens are commonly called "playing" or "sounding," and the nature of the terms indicates the kind of procedure involved; "playing" illustrates that a game or context is being waged, and "sounding" shows that the game is vocal. It is, in fact, a verbal context which is an important part of the linguistic and psychosocial development of the Negroes who indulge in this verbal strategy. . . . "Sounding" occurs only in crowds of boys. (1962, 209)

The most frequent objects of insult in dozens are women and human sex organs. Its two goals, writes O. Brady: "to humiliate your opponent through verbal wit or to anger him to the extent that he will fight back physically" (70). The roots of contemporary rap are in the dozens.

12. O. Brady believes that Jones's imaginary one-on-one basketball game creates a "true image of black life"; this activity, along with playing the dozens, contribute to the realistic dramatization of the "life rhythms of the black American culture" (73).

13. A striking manifestation of Richard Isay's view, as theorized within the black (gay or straight) community, is offered by Reginald T. Jackson:

> For gay tops, what is really being used to define a real man isn't his penis but his alignment with the sexism and misogyny of other straight black men in the community. The worst thing in the black community you can be considered is a "bottom," not because you are gay but because you are considered equal to or less than a woman. In fact, some gay butch tops get even more respect than straight men. After all, the ultimate supermachismo thing a man can do to another man is get his behind. Having the ability to take another man's manhood blots out the negatives of being a homosexual, and awards one with social identity, stature in both gay and straight communities, and a sense of respect—the real key to manhood. (51)

14. Kimberly Benston, Lloyd Brown, and Lacey are among the few critics of *The Toilet* who discuss in a nonracist, direct (i.e., nonmetaphoric) critique the play's handling of sexuality and gender issues. However, in "American Sexual Reference: Black Male," Baraka, himself, leads the way for spectators to interpret white gay Karolis as the embodiment of the black man's primary enemy—or what Michele Wallace calls Baraka's "struggle of black against white . . . the super macho against the fags" (63). In Baraka's words: "Most American white men are trained to be fags. . . . They devote their energies to the nonphysical, the nonrealistic, and become estranged from them. . . . The purer white, the more estranged from, say, actual physical work. . . . Can you, for a second, imagine the average middle class white man able to do somebody harm? . . . Do you understand the softness of the white man, the weakness" (1966b, 216–18). The playwright's sexist, racist, and homophobic sentiments are elaborated upon by Eldridge Clever in *Soul on Ice*: Black male homosexuality is informed by a racial death wish.

Since the early 1970s, Frances Cress Welsing has promoted the notion, as Michael S. Smith argues, that "queerness comes from the white man and, therefore, is contrary to African self-empowerment" (78). Welsing, a psychiatrist formerly of the Atlanta Center for Disease Control, writes that her treatment of all black male patients—

whether their particular disorder be passivity, effeminization, bisexuality, homosexuality or other—is to have them relax and envision themselves approaching and opposing, in actual combat, the collective of white males and females. . . . As a people, we will need increasingly strong men because we can expect that white males, driven into homosexuality from their sense of weakness compared to the world's majority of colored men, also will move towards others (non-whites), which is always an attempt to compensate for the awareness of true weakness. Black male bisexuality and homosexuality has been used by the white collective in its effort to survive genetically in a world dominated by colored people. (91–92)

O. Brady remains the most outspoken critic of *The Toilet* to link the play's codings of whiteness, femininity, homosexuality, and America to a transformational semiotic and thematic in opposition to African tradition (which, to Brady, adheres to compulsory heterosexuality) and blackness.

15. Consider, for example, the range of hostile interactions between gay and straight characters in Babe's *A Prayer for My Daughter*, Duberman's *The Electric Map*, Dick Goldberg's *Family Business*, Goss's *Homecookin'*, Rabe's *Streamers*, and Ribman's *The Poison Tree*.

16. The critics assign contrasting meanings to the names Foots and Ray according to their position on the play's sexual and racial politics. For Lacey, as an example, Foots "implies a plodding, lock-stepped entanglement" that indicates the young man's surrender "to the gang's debased concept of manhood." Ray, on the other hand, "implies freedom and the light of the spirit, able to shine only when free of the restraining pressures of the group" (37). For Werner Sollors, however, "[T]he identity of a down-to-earth 'Foots' [is] more desirable than that of the lofty 'Ray,' who has removed himself from his ethnic reality. For, if the 'love story' is a sentimentalization of 'Ray,' the 'black-and-white story' is a bitter acceptance of Foots" (107). And finally, O. Brady believes that "Ray Foots's tragic fate is to be ever divided between his identity as a member of a black community and his individual preference, the love of a white boy. He is forever Foots and forever choosing to be Ray" (76–77). In support of Brady's reading, Leslie Sanders notes that "the black characters know him as Foots, and both the white characters call him Ray" (136). Sanders's criticism of the play, among the most blatantly homophobic, concludes: "The tragedy for Ray Foots is that the Ray part of his personality can only be shared with whites, a sharing that takes the shape of an obscene interaction. . . . Neither the activities of Foots and his gang nor Ray's private acts are a model for the expression of humanity" (136). By equating the black gang's games of the dozens (and, one might well add, their subsequent activities of physical violence) to (interracial) homosexuality—an "obscene interaction"—Sanders offers a disturbing, problematic explanation for the intersection of race, gender, and sexuality in the play.

17. To suggest yet another angle on the complicated issue of race and sexuality, consider the young (straight) men's homophobia within M. S. Smith's analysis of Afrocentricity ("an ideology based on the concept of Africa as the point of reference for all activities in which African people engage. . . . Afrocentrism is a conscious response to European cultural domination" [30]):

> Too many of the purveyors of Afrocentric theory spout mindless homophobic nonsense which only serves to alienate productive Black women and men, who are gay, from our home community. Such homophobia also risks conferring on heterosexual Black men a weak definition of manhood based on not being a faggot. This is the hegemonic white male's definition of himself as *not the other*— not a woman, not a Black, and not a queer. And that way of thinking is clearly *not* Afrocentric: The heterosexual Black man would be centering himself around what he is *not,* as opposed to what he *is*." (31)

See also hooks 1989, 120–26.

18. Critics often analyze this moment as Foots's "baptism" while disagreeing as to its meaning. For example, O. Brady argues that "Ora displaces Ray Foots as the natural leader of the boys by baptizing him into white American citizenship and simultaneously excommunicating him from the black freedmen" (70). In an opposing view, Witherington concludes, "Ora's gesture and the ritual of exorcism are undercut as Jones shows that the baptism actually signifies Foots's mature victory . . . over his own divided self," a "'baptism' into Ray, his more humane half" (162).

19. In contrast to his racist, homophobic writings of the 1960s, Baraka offers (and apparently unintentionally so) a vision of interracial desire at the end of *The Toilet* that presents, paradoxically, what Isaac Julien calls (in relation to the radical, interracial images in his films) "an exciting new way of uncovering various taboos in black politics or black cultural representation" (hooks and Julien 1991, 171). Among these taboos, according to bell hooks:

> how can we [blacks] name the black desire of the white body without reinscribing the idea of black self-hatred or distaste for the black body? . . . According to the crude nationalism, the decolonized black subject should only have a love object who's black. It's hard for us to formulate paradigms of interracial desire that aren't about the self-hating black man who's looking to the white Other for some kind of glorification or betterment. (hooks and Julien 1991, 170–71, 174)

Baraka's final image of Foots and Karolis, I believe, represents an early stage in the formulation of just such a paradigm—despite what may have been the author's intention.

In 1971, Baraka disavowed any allegiance to this final image, as he spoke of his embarrassment at the play's ending: "When I first wrote the play, it ended with everybody leaving. I tacked the other ending on; the kind of social milieu that I was in, dictated that kind of rapprochement. It actually did not evolve from the pure spirit of the play. I've never changed it, of course, because I feel that now that would only be cute" (Watkins 26). Baraka is "wrong in implying that 'that kind of rapprochement' should be read 'racial rapprochement,'" concludes Lacey, a position with which I concur. "Were Karolis black or Ray white, the play would carry the same thematic weight. . . . A measure of the writer's total involvement in his milieu is seen in his ability to populate his works with blacks and whites, even in conflict, and yet not be obsessed with race as central theme" (38).

While I question the playwright's retrospective logic in explaining the play's conclusion, the dramatic image of black and white embrace remains, nonetheless, as revolutionary a dramatic action today as the

279

playwright considered the political ideologies and agenda in his revolutionary plays of the 1960s. Certainly within the semiotic of maleness evident in the play's, as well as the male-cast canon's, discourse coherence, this action *does* evolve out of the dialogue and violence that precede it.

20. The world premiere of Albee's (b. 1928) play was at the Schiller Theatre Werkstatt in Berlin, Germany, in September 1959. *The Zoo Story's* first American performance, directed by Milton Katselas and with George Maharis as Jerry and William Daniels as Peter, was in January 1960 at the Provincetown Playhouse, New York City; it was on a double bill with the American premiere of Samuel Beckett's *Krapp's Last Tape,* directed by Alan Schneider. Christopher Bigsby calls *The Zoo Story* "the most impressive debut ever made by an American dramatist" (1992, 131).

21. Mickey Pearlman argues that Albee presents in *The Zoo Story* "all stereotypical characterizations of women . . . [who] emerge full force, tumbling into the hostile atmosphere of Albee's anti-female universe" (183–84). Thus, the play "enlarges the endless canon of plays, stories, and novels that agonize over the predicaments of men by further diminishing the emotional, sexual, and spiritual needs of women" (187). While not diminishing Pearlman's concern for the text's exact references to women, I would suggest that this observation has less to do with what the men have to say specifically about absent women than it does with the conversational dynamics created between men who experience one another in the absence of females. In this light, any references to women—whether complimentary or not—are part of a patterned discourse coherence existing within men's dialogue in drama.

22. Unless they are violent in their intentions (as are the males in *The Toilet* and Horovitz's *The Indian Wants the Bronx*), or under the influence of alcohol or drugs (as are the men in Jason Miller's *That Championship Season* and Voulgaris's *Best Friends*), or engaged in sports (as are the men in Lamont's *That Serious He-Man Ball*), straight male characters seldom make physical contact with one another in American drama. Most certainly, nonviolent contact is rare if the straight men are strangers; exceptions usually occur only if the men, regardless of their sexual orientation, are drawn to one another erotically, as in Babe's *A Prayer for My Daughter,* Neal Bell's *Raw Youth,* Robert Patrick's *T-Shirts,* and Rabe's *Streamers.*

It should be noted that this physical interaction between Peter and Jerry is overlooked by critics who identify Jerry as a homosexual. Rather, they base their arguments on sexual allusions in Jerry's discourse. See Rutenberg 27–28; Brustein 21–22; Driver 275; Hirsch 14, 120–21; Kostelanetz 62–70; Sarotte 134–36. According to Sarotte, "Albee has vehemently denied any homosexual interpretations of his plays, and in particular he has refuted Kostelanetz's analysis" (136).

23. Criticizing Jerry's curtain speech, Brian Way remarks:

> This sudden reversion to a faith in the validity of traditional explanations makes previous events in the play seem arbitrary in a wholly unjustifiable way.... [B]ecause of this misguided attempt to exploit the advantages both of the theatre of the absurd and of realism, *The Zoo Story* misses the greatness which at times seems so nearly within its grasp. (40)

On the contrary, *The Zoo Story* dramatizes identifiable dynamics of male communication that progress from their social dialogue. Although I find the speech to repeat points that already have been dramatized sufficiently, it does clarify any ambiguities that may remain for the spectator. Nevertheless, Jerry's personal dialogue, following an act of violence, is faithful to the discourse coherence in dialogue between men. It is, perhaps, the "reality of the absurd" that is inherent in this entire progression of male dialogue that Way, regretfully, misses. Rather than exploiting the advantages of absurdism and realism, Albee masterfully exposes their implicit coexistence in respect to the dynamics of male dramatic dialogue.

24. See, for example, Sam Shepard's *4-H Club*. In their realistic kitchen setting, Shepard's three male characters live and play like animals. Surrounded by garbage, the men pass time in an eccentric manner: excessively eating apples, engaging in ritualistic movements, and playacting. Male chaos invades the traditionally tranquil domain of the female-coded domestic space. Eventually, these "monkeys," like Albee's characters, physically confront one another through Shepard's conceptualization of man's inherently uncivilized, animalistic nature. The play's broad themes include America's social rituals (of daily living and playing), American imperialism and commercialism, male aggression, the relationship between language and violence, the nature of power, and the tensions between man's primitive and social selves.

Chapter 3

1. For additional information on Puerto Rican American theater, as well as on the theater of other Latino cultures—including Cuban American, Dominican American, Columbian American, and Mexican American, see Antush; Brokaw; Huerta; Kanellos; John C. Miller; and Pottlitzer. Regarding post–*Short Eyes* theatrical involvement for some members of The Family, see Antush 14. See Blau for insights into the all-male Family's offstage relationships while performing *Short Eyes*.

2. The original production of Piñero's (1947–88) play opened in January 1974 at Riverside Church in New York City and then moved to the

Public Theater. In May 1974, *Short Eyes* moved again for an extended run at Lincoln Center's Vivian Beaumont Theatre.

After his success with *Short Eyes*, Piñero went on to receive the prestigious Hull-Warriner Award from the Dramatists Guild, an Emmy Award for his script *Lonely Lives*, Rockefeller and Guggenheim grants, and critical praise for his script of the film version of *Short Eyes* (1977), directed by Robert Young. Among Piñero's other plays are *Cold Beer, Eulogy for a Small Time Thief, Irving, A Midnight Moon at the Greasy Spoon, Paper Toilet, Sideshow, The Sun Always Shines for the Cool, Tap Dancing and Bruce Lee Kicks,* and the male-cast play, *The Guntower.*

3. Consider how the codings of Cupcakes's physical appearance and his function inside the all-male prison's sexualized-genderized matrix are not unlike the codings of drag performers' appearance and their function inside the sexualized-genderized world of cross-dressing balls as discussed by Peggy Phelan (93–111). The balls, according to Phelan, are "masquerades of absence and lack which enact the masochistic power and genuine pleasure of symbolic identification so crucial to both capitalism and erotic desire" (94). In Piñero's prison, however, the men's (initial) symbolic identification of Cupcakes as Other—as Woman—creates a dynamic whereby the young man is then perceived as either a masquerader (a subject) of "absence and lack" (i.e., a masquerader of the Other) or as a present "other" (i.e., a [male] object). When positioned by the prison inmates in this latter "real" role, Cupcakes is most susceptible to rape.

4. Depending upon the context within which it exists, the male body takes on distinctive features in institutional settings. For instance, in Kenneth Brown's *The Brig*, set in a World War II marine detention camp, the body is subject to task completions, humiliation, and abuse. In *Short Eyes*, the body is subject to the pain of violence as well as the pleasure of sex. In hospital or hospice settings such as in Corinne Jacker's *Terminal* and Robin Swados's *A Quiet End*, the body is subject to excruciating pain of physical malady and the comfort of nonsexual physical contact with other bodies.

5. Refer to chapter 2, notes 14 and 17 for related commentary on the racist, homophobic position that El Raheem articulates.

6. According to David Bergman, "Prisoners engaged in intramale sexual acts may avoid the label of homosexual, provided that they are confined to single-sex institutions and that upon release they revert to heterosexual relations" (28). Bergman, citing Bruce Jackson's study, "Deviance as Success," suggests that

> [m]ale prisoners divide themselves sexually into three groups: queens, those who are homosexual outside of prison; studs, those who while in prison play the inserter role with other men; punks,

those who while in prison play the receptor. If asked, studs and punks, in this system, say they play their roles because they are denied access to women. Jackson argues, however, that many of "those argot-role actors . . . would very much like to be homosexual outside, but they just *did not know how*" (260, Jackson's italics). According to Jackson, "prison was the only place they had a moral structure that permitted them to be acting-out homosexuals, a place where there was a grand body of folk culture that legitimized their behavior" (261). Consequently, these men often commit crimes immediately after their release so that they can be returned to prison where they may reenter their desired sexual roles. "By adopting the convict stigma they were enabled to act out the homosexual roles without any of the attendant stigma they would have suffered (and self-applied) in the free world" (261). Their male egos can better accept being criminal than being gay. (Bergman 28–29)

7. Piñero's gloss of *program*:

The do's and don'ts of prison life. Programs are ethnically determined: they are different for whites, black, Puerto Ricans, etc. Programs are not enforced by prison authorities; they are determined by the prisoners themselves. The program for the whole prison population regulates the way in which members of different ethnic groups relate to one another in specific situations. It rigidly governs who sits with whom in the mess hall; where people sit in the auditorium; who smokes first; etc. It is the first thing a prisoner learns when he enters an institution. Failure to follow the program is a sure way to have trouble with fellow inmates and will result in physical reprisals—sometimes death. (1975, 125–26)

8. In linking one's intentionality behind homosexual rape and "racial retaliation" to the humiliation of "the victim in a display of power and domination," Ariel Ruiz explains Paco's actions toward Clark within a "complex web of ethnic, sexual, and political interactions" (97):

It should not be surprising, therefore, that where the social significance of a man is reinforced by his sexual dominion over his peer, the desire for power implicit in the attacks we are discussing may be explained by the desire of the inmate called 'minority' to affirm his self-esteem constantly denigrated by the contempt in which the predominantly white society hold him" (98).

Ruiz's "complex web" seems to underestimate the fact that Paco's wish to violate Cupcakes against his will doubly marginalizes his racial brother, also as "the victim in a display of power and domination." Finally, in Paco's own words (and ethos), Anglo American Clark and Puerto Rican American Cupcakes are, in the end, nothing more than "faggots": sexual objects to be penetrated.

9. Within the male-cast canon, and in particular plays that are set in confining institutions, it should be noted that men's (gang) rape fantasy of the absent woman is not unusual. From David Rabe's *Streamers,* Juan Shamsul Alám's *God's Children,* and John DiFusco's *Tracers* to James McLure's *Lone Star* and *Pvt. Wars,* male characters talk about their actual seduction of, or their rape fantasies of women. Their descriptions can occur during either social or personal dialogue.

10. Candido Tirado's insightful, disturbing play for two men, *First Class,* is a recent example of the semiotic of maleness operating in male-cast plays whereby homophobic dialogue (interspersed with misogynistic references to absent women) precedes either talk of or actual violence. Tirado closes each of his two acts according to this pattern. The set of each act centers on a bench in a New York City traffic island (which serves as a metaphor for Puerto Rico), an image that recalls the primacy of the isolated Central Park bench in *The Zoo Story.* Within moments of the end of act 1, Apache (a veteran gang leader) humiliates his younger stepbrother, Speedy (a former convict), by reminding him that "in jail [Speedy] gave up [his] ass if somebody raised their voice." "I ain't a faggot," Speedy replies, "I was gang raped. Like we used to do to Debbie." "Debbie liked it," Apache responds. "Maybe you did too," which prompts Speedy to pull a knife on Apache. "The first thing I'm going to teach you about fighting is not to talk so much," Apache, now armed with a chain, warns the "faggot whore"; Speedy counters with "your mother was a whore." The men now drop their weapons, each ready for a fist fight, to "[d]ie like a man" (101–2). The act ends as Speedy leaves the scene, responding to the car horn of one of his gang members.

Six months later, at the conclusion of act 2, Speedy asks Apache, "Am I a man?" and then he describes in detail how "they took [his] manhood" during the prison rape. Apache replies, "It takes more than a tight asshole to be a man" (115). Picking up chains and planks, the men commit to their "last fight" against the enemy gang (117). The play ends as the two pledge to stay together after this last battle. Their unconditional acceptance of one another, therefore, is predicated on their defense of the (traffic) island home—the violent defense of the (Albeeian) bench.

11. Thanks to Joseph A. Boone for this insight.

12. Rabe's (b. 1940) *Streamers* received its world premiere at the Long Wharf Theatre, under the direction of Mike Nichols, in January 1976. Including three of the original cast members, Nichols's second production of *Streamers* opened Off-Broadway, at Lincoln Center's Mitzi Newhouse Theatre, in April 1976.

13. See, for instance, Charles Fuller's *A Soldier's Play,* Arthur Laurents's *Home of the Brave,* and Celeste Bedford Walker's *Camp Logan,* or such nonrealist military plays as DiFusco's *Tracers,* Quincy Long's *The Virgin Molly,* and Stephen Mack Jones's *Back in the World.*

14. See William Herman for one of the few discussions of *Streamers* to focus on the importance of gender and sexual issues in the play as they relate specifically to men who are in the military. Notice the role of the absent woman in this scenario. "What is at stake in *Streamers,*" Herman argues,

> is what is at stake for men who leave civilian life to go to war.... The army, which needs a psychologically stable group of men in order to function properly, is by its nature responsible for disorientations and instability. That is, a heterosexual male entering the army gives up not only his physical safety but also the psychologial safety that lies in the confirming rituals of his gender. Without the protection of those rituals, for which women are necessary, his unconscious emotional organization is subjected to the strains of being stimulated by other male psyches, the momentum and angular force of their needs. To protect his heterosexuality he needs to hold back. For the homosexual male, entering the army is also the occasion for a loss of confirming gender rituals, for which other homosexual males are necessary. He too is subject to the pull of other male psyches. To protect his homosexuality he needs to press its claims. (103)

In general, Herman's theory on heterosexuals' and homosexuals' psyches and behaviors in the military is one of many that surfaced during the congressional debates on the legal status of self-identified gays and lesbians in the U. S. military (which currently bans homosexuals) in 1993. Some of these alternative theories, obviously, disagree with Herman's assertion.

15. See, for example, Bill C. Davis's male-cast play *Mass Appeal,* which focuses on the conflict of a seminarian's bisexuality. The characters in the play perceive even their metalinguistic dialogue as too damaging and risky to sustain, as the priest and his student struggle to talk about whether or not they can or should talk about the student's sexuality.

16. Race and racism are often the principal issues in the historically based military plays of African American writers. See, for example, Fuller's *A Soldier's Play* and Walker's *Camp Logan.*

17. The reverse situation is never acknowledged in male-cast plays as a possible sexual, erotic development for a man: a homosexual who gets "hooked" on bisexuality or heterosexuality.

18. This rite of male passage is not uncommon in male-cast plays. See, for example, McLure's *Pvt. Wars,* when Silvio takes Gately out of the veteran's hospital to pick up girls.

19. As illustrated recently by Carlota Zimmerman's *Man at His Best,* on-stage erotic action between an interracial male couple occurs only in plays set in confining institutions. Zimmerman's play is a penetrating look at a relationship between two men in prison: Skyler, a white murderer, and Dean, a black hustler. Through fifteen scenes, Sky and Dean engage in various games of sexual fantasy: one is always designated the (female) Other who is the object of the (male) Self's domination, seduction, and humiliation. Nearly all of the men's metatheatrics of power and sex are fantasized within a heterosexual context that not only appropriates straight culture to legitimize their behavior but also affirms (albeit graphically) the function of the absent woman in male characters' relationships. Adhering to the semiotic of maleness, however, Zimmerman's play—and, in particular, its discourse coherence—offers a too familiar resolution between men (i.e., in terms of its violence). Overcoming their verbal and physical abuse of one another, Sky eventually admits that he loves Dean. Just after the words "I love you" come out of his mouth, Sky kisses Dean—and then proceeds to strangle him to death.

20. See Philip Kolin for *Streamers'* stage history; Kolin documents the wide range of critics' and audiences' reactions to the play's closing violence (65–77).

21. *Streamers* are parachutes that fail to open. Any alternative lyrics are sung to the melody of Stephen Foster's "Beautiful Dreamer."

22. The American premiere of Swados's (b. 1953) play was at the International City Theatre in Long Beach, California, under director Jules Aaron, in January 1986; the British premiere, directed by Noel Greig, was at London's Offstage Theatre, February 1986. Subsequent productions include those at the American Repertory Theatre in Amsterdam (director, Robin Swados; September 1986); Repertory Theatre of St. Louis (director, Sam Blackwell; October 1987); Theatre Off Park in New York City (director, Tony Giordano; May 1990); and PlayWorks Theatre in Philadelphia (director, Leland Hoffman; October 1993). In his introduction to *Gay and Lesbian Plays Today,* which includes *A Quiet End,* Terry Helbing speaks of Swados's play (as well as the other plays in the anthology) as offering an alternative to the "dick-wiggling theatre" tradition of early gay drama (x). Helbing praises *A Quiet End* for its themes of "human interaction, friendship, and simply caring" (xi). As such, the play offers an "important slice . . . of contemporary gay life as expressed in the theatrical idiom" (xiii).

23. See, for example, the quality of Steven's life in the absurd-realist *Terminal* by Jacker or Landau's and Parmigian's lives in the realist *Cold Storage.* Although Ribman's *Cold Storage* is not a male-cast play (one woman speaks briefly at the beginning and conclusion of act 1), I find the play quite revealing in its commitment to and development of personal dialogue between men.

24. One exception occurs between the straight men in *Terminal*'s conclusion: after getting into bed with Oswald, who is naked, Steven kisses Oswald in order to get him to *stop* talking!

25. This picture was not helped by the images in Mart Crowley's successful *The Boys in the Band*. For the gay community, let alone mass culture, to reclaim *The Boys in the Band* from the (historic) jaws of homophobic readings, however, is not to fear the play's representations. Certainly many gay men's lives were and are like some of the characters whom critics of the play consider negative images of gay life. Yet differences exist within any community. *The Boys in the Band* challenges members of the gay community to acknowledge differences among themselves. This issue must be separated out, however, from the larger one of the marketplace: why was *The Boys in the Band*, which ran 1968–70, the first gay male-cast play to become mainstream? What is historically significant about Crowley's work, a fact that reaches beyond a community's exposure to some of its own differences, is the limited representation of homosexuality it presents to a mass audience. For many, *The Boys in the Band* only confirmed the stereotypical image of homosexuals as male others, as objects within the semiotic of maleness: self-pitying, tortured, homophobic alcoholics who, very simply, are not "real" men. Such reactions, while understandable, tend to overshadow any appreciation for the positive images of gay life represented in the play, including lovers Hank and Larry's reconciliation (see Clum 1992, 258) along with Bernard and Emory's caring, supportive friendship. Much depth of character, however painfully exposed and excruciatingly truthful, is revealed in Crowley's play, albeit at the bottom of a glass, at the end of a joint, or over the telephone wires—conventional technical apparati for facilitating self-disclosing dialogue in any American play.

26. Each of the three men links his past sexual behavior to his current health crisis. Each also indicates some regret over that conduct. This is a controversial aspect of the play as it may appear to some that the characters are participating in the "I deserve AIDS" punishment syndrome, one that is finally homophobic. As Douglas Crimp aggressively argues, promiscuity does not kill, diseases do; safe sex is part of the solution in the battle against AIDS. While Swados's characters do not advocate monogamy, they also do not reclaim the possibility of multiple sex partners in the age of safe sex. Safe sex, practiced in any relationship(s) or encounter(s), is a viable sexual-behavioral choice that one can make in an effort to diminish one's potential exposure to viruses.

Acknowledging that Swados's "approach to the disease is decidedly traditional here, with little or no discussion of holistic approaches or organizations like HEAL [a Brooklyn-based organization that advocates alternative nontoxic therapies]," Terry Helbing nonetheless commends the play, for "there is no lack of warmth in Swados's impressive effort" (xii). Swados has written his characters honestly; each appears to accept responsibility for the choices he makes, whether or not his choices are popular, or even the best ones.

27. Self-accepting gay characters in American realist and nonrealist mixed-cast dramas have become a staple of representation on the Broadway stage: from Lanford Wilson's *The Fifth of July* (produced in 1978) and Harvey Fierstein's *Torch Song Trilogy* (1983), to William Hoffman's *As Is* (1985), Richard Greenberg's *Eastern Standard* (1989), and Tony Kushner's *Angels in America: A Gay Fantasia on National Themes* (1993, 1994). Each of these representative mixed-cast plays was critically acclaimed and successful at the box office. No American realist drama cast only with gay male characters has been performed on Broadway. (Note: McNally's *Love! Valor! Compassion!*, which opened February 1995 on Broadway, is nonrealist.)

For a play produced on Broadway, Greenberg's text should be singled out for its original portrait of friendship between gay and straight men. As Frank Rich remarks, "[T]he college-spawned fraternity between Drew [gay] and Stephen [straight]" is "impressively gripping." "Whether engaging in juvenile lockerroom humor or propping each other up in tearful sorrow, these two friends achieve a fluent intimacy that, in my experience, has never previously been alloted to male stage characters of opposite sexual preference" (1988). Whereas Greenberg's achievement in a mixed-cast play of a "fluent intimacy" between men is to be applauded, there has been no American male-cast play on Broadway that has accomplished a comparable communicative dynamic between gay and straight characters.

And in light of this chapter's focus on *A Quiet End,* an AIDS (gay) male-cast play, the dramatization of the impact of AIDS on a gay man's straight friend, with either man being the ill individual, would be an original contribution to male-cast drama—whether on Broadway, Off Broadway, or in the regional theaters. Alám's two-character piece, *Zookeeper* (Latino Playwrights Theatre, New York, 1989), is among the first male-cast plays to focus on gay and straight siblings, one of whom has AIDS. The brothers are Latino.

28. When considering the core of Max and Jason's struggle with death, one is reminded of this interchange between two patients in Jacker's *Terminal:*

Oswald: I can talk about death, cremation, pain, my body, and my blood pressure doesn't change, my pulse remains slow and steady.

Steven: Listen, why don't we talk about something else.

Oswald: You *are* afraid of death. The only way to deal with it is to talk about it.

(25)

While there undoubtedly is truth to the adage, "talking it to death," in Jacker's and Swados's plays the context and specific, but repressed, needs of the participants within that context are the deciding features that stimulate the personal talk.

29. Tony's request echoes the desperate need for conversation expressed by most terminally ill men represented in male cast plays, including Oswald in *Terminal*. See also Parmigian in *Cold Storage*.

30. Whereas Tony and his roommates find it liberating to speak the truth among others who are ill, Landau, in *Cold Storage*, finds such self-disclosure between the sick as "humiliating" (Ribman 1978, 66).

31. As the terminally ill Parmigian says to his fellow patient, Landau, in *Cold Storage*, "It's important that people understand each other." Landau responds: "They understand each other. It just never makes any difference." "So tell me, and we'll see if it makes a difference," Parmigian concludes (Ribman 1978, 58). See also Harvey Fierstein's *Safe Sex*, a nonrealist, noninstitutional play in which two gay lovers, both HIV negative, engage extraordinarily frank, caring, and humorous personal dialogue, as they negotiate the boundaries of their relationship amid the reality of AIDS.

32. In a comparable moment of personal connection for the two straight patients in *Cold Storage*, Parmigian's words to Landau echo Jason's sentiments: "That's it, my friend, laugh a little bit, and while you're laughing I'll wait a little bit longer with you" (Ribman 1978, 69).

33. Joining in on the Crimp side of this debate, whether challenging explicitly *A Normal Heart* or implicitly AIDS plays like *A Quiet End* (which has an entirely different dramaturgical strategy and intention than Kramer's play), Mark Gevisser concludes about

> the direction theatre about AIDS has taken: it veers more toward humanist tragedy—the expression and working through of individual grief—than toward the defining of a collective political and social identity around a common experience of oppression and marginalization. The AIDS crisis is perceived not as a national disaster, but as something that has challenged the little niche professional and creative gay men have carved for themselves within urban bourgeois society. (50–51)

What distinguishes Swados's play from all the mixed-cast examples of AIDS plays cited by Crimp and Gevisser is that *A Quiet End* is a male-cast drama—a dramatic genre characterized by a near monolithic semiotic of maleness operating on its discourse coherence. A playwright would first have to crack the codes of the male-cast plays' semiotic system, because, as the canon now stands, that which marks a male character's social identity exists at a relatively apolitical, status quo level of cultural maintenance. For the writer of a male-cast play,

Swados advances male-male representation simply by dramatizing men's ability to communicate cooperatively (without alcohol or drugs) on a self-disclosing level. It is quite possible that future authors of male-cast plays will write their way through characters' individual grief in order to connect that grief to a collective identity—and thereby formulate a kind of nonbinary activist sociopersonal identity responsive to "a common experience of oppression and marginalization." The male-cast play has yet to explore what happens to (the male) community once one is or all are on the other side of verbalized, nonviolent individualization—once one has or all have recognized the difference within.

34. But as Michael Paller concludes, "[A]long with the increased potency that results when a writer takes on a subject [AIDS] that is not only a pressing social issue but also a painful, personal one, comes an increased risk that the work will not be excellent" (57).

35. Consider the extent to which Terrence McNally's *The Lisbon Traviata* is a current example of a gay play that complicates, yet nonetheless participates in, the continuance of this trend (refer to introduction, note 10).

36. As demonstrated in this study, the discourse coherence in gay male plays (i.e., the dynamics of characters' topic selection) relates to the semiotic of maleness in ways similar to nongay male-cast plays. This observation, as it applies both to the representation of men among themselves and to drama theory, therefore, qualifies Bergman's position on the structure of homosexual discourse: "No doubt, hierarchical forces come to play their part in homosexual relations—homosexuality exists only within the patriarchy—but homosexuality is more notable in the way it resists hierarchies than in the way it bends to them" (31).

37. I would like to reiterate Ronald Ribman's achievement in the nearly all-male *Cold Storage* for his representation of heterosexual men. His characterization of straight male hospital patients and their frank dialogue is as impressive as Swados's handling of the self-disclosing talk among gay men who are ill. Unlike Swados's nonfamilial characters (including healthy Jason), however, Ribman's unrelated men choose not to have any physical contact with one another.

Chapter 4

1. For background information on the history of Asian American theater, including that of Japanese American, Chinese American, Filipino American, Korean American, South Asian American, and Southeast Asian American cultures, see Bigsby 1992, 327–32; Berson; Chin; Houston; Kim; and Wong.

2. Gotanda's (b. 1950) *Yankee Dawg You Die* received its world premiere at the Berkeley Repertory Theatre in February 1988. The production

was subsequently moved to the Los Angeles Theatre Center in May 1988. Gotanda's play received its Off-Broadway premiere at New York City's Playwrights Horizons in April 1989. Sharon Ott directed each of these productions.

Gotanda, who holds a degree from Hastings College of Law, is the recipient of numerous awards, including the National Theatre Artist Grant, Rockefeller Playwright-in-Residence grants, a National Endowment for the Arts Playwriting Fellowship, a McKnight Fellowship, and the Ruby-Yoshino Schaar Playwright Award. In 1989, he was awarded the Will Glickman Playwriting Award for *Yankee Dawg You Die*. Among his other plays are *A Song for a Nisei Fisherman, Bullet Headed Birds, Day Standing on Its Head, Fish Head Soup, The Dream of Kitamura, The Wash,* and the rock musical, *The Avocado Kid.*

3. Since, by definition, nonrealist drama (which includes monologues and monodramas) rejects the neoclassic unities in favor of nonmimetic representation, this study, which is interested in the discourse coherence in plays that adhere, in principle, to realist dramaturgy, does not analyze nonrealist plays. Gotanda's *Yankee Dawg You Die* is analyzed as a representative nonrealist play in order to illustrate the ready link between nonrealist structure and personal dialogue.

However, it should be noted that some nonrealist plays continue to present content that mirrors the historically grounded, conventional representation of men as perpetrators—as well as victims—of social constructions of gender. Consider, for instance, Neal Bell's *Raw Youth,* Harry Gamboa, Jr.'s *Jetter Jinx,* Clay Goss's *Homecookin',* Jon Klein's *T Bone N Weasel,* Arthur Kopit's *The Day the Whores Came Out to Play Tennis,* Quincy Long's *The Virgin Molly,* Peter Parnell's *Scooter Thomas Makes It to the Top of the World,* James Purdy's *True,* Sam Shepard's *4-H Club, Cowboys #2,* and *Geography of a Horse Dreamer,* and Megan Terry's *Keep Tightly Closed in a Cool Dry Place.* Nonrealist structure, therefore, does not guarantee that male characters will engage personal dialogue. Whether portrayed in a realist or nonrealist play, American male characters do not appear to know *how* to talk personally among themselves.

The most radical representations of a male "voice" in American theater today—that is, portraits of men who are capable of personal talk—are to be found in monodramas, which include monologues (based upon fictional as well as nonfictional material) and solo pieces by performance artists. From a historical-canonical viewpoint, however, one cannot help but be struck by the fact that these nonrealist works eliminate the actual dynamic of male characters talking among themselves; the solo character (even one who takes on others' voices) is a true talking head, one who exists outside of human interactive communication. Usually, the monodrama is a character's "conversation" with himself, a means to an end of personal talk, if not personal revelation. Its structural counterpart in nonmonodramas is characters' personal dialogue in plays' discourse coherence.

Among popular American monodramas are those focused on (1) historical, public figures, who are often portrayed by recognizable actors (for example, Henry Fonda as Clarence Darrow in David Rintels's *Clarence Darrow*; Hal Holbrook as Mark Twain in Holbrook's adaptation of Twain's writings, *Mark Twain Tonight!*; Geoffrey C. Ewing as Muhammad Ali in Ewing and Graydon Royce's *Ali*; James Whitmore as Harry Truman in Samuel Gallu's *Give 'em Hell Harry!*; Laurence Luckinbill as Lyndon Johnson in James Prideaux's *Lyndon*; and Robert Morse as Truman Capote in Jay Presson Allen's *Tru*); (2) singular, fictional characters (such as a visionary professor in Maria Irene Fornes's *Dr. Kheal*, a man with AIDS in Jeff Hagedorn's *One*, a jailed Cuban American boat person in Pedro Monge-Rafuls's "Trash," a dying gay diva in Robert Patrick's *Pouf Positive*, a sex-industry employee in James Carroll Pickett's *Dream Man*, a gun salesman in Robert Schenkkan's *The Survivalist*, and a death-row criminal in Shepard's *Killer's Head*); (3) singular, fictional characters who impersonate other voices as part of their narrative (as in Thomas Jones's *The Wizard of Hip*); (4) a single performer whose fictional dialogue incorporates voices not intended to be impersonated by the actor (for example, Shepard and Joseph Chaikin's *Savage/Love*); fictional narratives based on one's autobiographical material (Shepard and Chaikin's *The War in Heaven* and Jean-Claude van Itallie and Chaikin's *Struck Dumb*).

Akin to the male monodrama is the male monologue, which, if manifested in various solo voices, provides the author with an opportunity to represent multiple male subjectivities. Solo performers who act their own pieces base the monologues on (1) diverse male characterizations (for example, Eric Bogosian's *Sex, Drugs, Rock & Roll, Drinking in America, Funhouse, Men Inside, Voices of America*, and *Pounding Nails in the Floor with My Forehead*, David Drake's *The Night Larry Kramer Kissed Me*, and Richard Elovich's *Somebody Else from Queens Is Queer*), or on (2) diverse male and female characterizations (such as Jeffrey Essmann's *Artificial Reality*, Danny Hoch's *Some People*, Michael Kearns's *intimacies* and *more intimacies*, and John Leguizamo's *Mambo Mouth* and *Spic-o-rama*). Several of the aforementioned writers-actors might also be considered performance artists. Often drawing upon fictional as well as autobiographical material, the male performance artist approaches his nonrealist piece as a collage of language, gesture, movement, sound, and visual arts through which he mediates his performance. A recurring motif in many of the male performance artists, whether performing individually or in groups (the latter configuration suggests that *shared* dialogue is a possible structural choice for the writer) is the deconstruction of the socially constructed male identity. The diversity of male representation (and their attendant sexual, racial, and class politics, for instance) are dramatized in such solo or group pieces as Luis Alfaro's *Downtown*; John Fleck's *BLESSED Are All the Little FISHES* and *A SNOWBALL'S CHANCE IN HELL*; Keith Mason's *Pieces Reconstruction DOA* and, for Hittite Empire, *For Black Boys Who Have Considered Homicide When the Streets Were Too Much* and *49 Blues Songs for a Jealous Vampire*; Tim Miller's *Stretch Marks* and *My Queer Body*; Pomo Afro Homos' *Fierce Love: Stories from Black Gay Life* and *Dark Fruit*; Lawrence Steger's *Worn Grooves*; Gay Men's Theatre Collective's *Crimes against Nature*; Dan Kwong's *Tales from the Fractured Tao*; Bill Talen's *American Yoga*; Han Ong's *Symposium in Manila*; and Curtis York's *The Boys in Curtis York*.

And finally, some male writers-performers embrace the monodrama as a structure for first-person autobiographical narrative. Utilizing this format, Spaulding Gray (*47 Beds, Sex and Death to the Age 14, Terrors of Pleasure: The House, Swimming to Cambodia, Monster in a Box, Gray's Anatomy*) is currently America's most widely known autobiographical monologuist. Gray has a one-sided conversation with the noninteractive spectator. His text is scripted, not improvisational; he speaks of events in his life both as factual incidents and as sources of self-reflection. While Gray may alter his vocal delivery to differentiate his voice from that of one of the characters in his narrative, the spectator never loses sight that Gray remains the only speaker in the play. For this reason, Gray's writing and performance blur conventional distinctions between art and life. He makes art directly out of his life, presenting himself as text, as a living artifact. He animates his real life on stage in the name of drama, disregarding fiction per se in favor of first-person nonfiction narrative. His drama (and performance) are best likened to a living journal or diary. In this regard, Gray's pieces are part of a long-standing tradition of male autobiography in American literature: from the writings of John Smith, John Woolman, and Ben Franklin to Frederick Douglass and Henry David Thoreau. Gray's monodramas remain the closest approximation of a (fictional or nonfictional) male's representation of individualization that exists in the American dramatic canon of male-cast plays—simply because they transgress the traditional boundaries between art and life in an attempt to make art and life one.

Gray has not cited any notable detail to personal relationships with men since his early *47 Beds,* a piece that refers to time spent with his father, his brother, Ryan Ryder (a buddy about whom he devotes his longest recollection of an adult male friend in his canon), Arjuna Aziz (a new acquaintance in Mykonos), and Robert, a gay expatriate with whom he has a sexual encounter in Athens; the monodrama also frequently mentions Gray's drinking. In his recent works, such as *Monster in a Box* and *Gray's Anatomy,* Gray depends upon an absent woman (his companion Renee) or a representative of an "institution" (a person he consults for personal matters—his psychiatrist or his eye doctor, for instance—or a person with whom he conducts business) to prompt his self-disclosures. He speaks of no male friends as confidants, as individuals with whom he engages in personal dialogue. Therefore, Gray's "life as art" performance has become peculiarly conventional and formulaic in its choice not to represent man as capable of, let alone desirous of, personal, nonprofessional interaction and dialogue between men. See also Geis 1993, 151–71.

4. Upon highlighting the historical and artistic significance of sansei playwrights like Gotanda and David Henry Hwang, Gish Jen concludes that they "are not only more likely to present Asian-Americans in their work, but to present Asian-Americans who are not of the immigrant generation." An exception in Hwang's canon is his immigrant drama, *The Dance and the Railroad,* set in the nineteenth century. This short play is cast with two men.

5. Additional authors who have written male-cast "history" plays are African Americans Charles Fuller (*A Soldier's Play*), OyamO (*Let Me Live*), and Celeste B. Walker (*Camp Logan*). Also noteworthy is Jeff Stetson's *The Meeting,* a dramatization of a fictional meeting between two prominent figures in the Civil Rights and Black Power movements—Martin Luther King, Jr., and Malcolm X.

6. I stress the men's "apparent power" over women at this moment in the play because the scene ends with Bradley telling Vincent that while he may have "got[ten] the [white] woman" in his film, their interracial kiss has been cut from the edited version currently shown on television (28). This intersection of race and gender establishes the degree of gender-inscribed power the Asian American male can exercise within the dominant culture; it establishes the terms whereby he is framed in the dominant culture's imagery as well as erased (i.e., through male-male violence he can claim his right to the passive [white] Other, but he cannot express, physically and nonviolently, his sexual desire for her before the eyes of America's mass audience).

7. Addressing the complexities that confront gay men of color (and, in particular, men of African descent) in white patriarchical cultures, Kobena Mercer says, "'Self-centredness' is a key characteristic of white sexual politics, or rather, it is an interpretation of the radical slogan 'the personal is political' which is made in an individualistic manner which thus excludes questions of race and ethnicity because it is so preoccupied with the 'self,' at the expense of the 'social' (Mercer and Julien 119). Mercer, along with filmmaker Isaac Julien, suggests that "European culture has privileged sexuality as the essence of the self, the inner-most core of one's 'personality'" (Mercer and Julien 106). His privileging of sexuality, of sexual orientation, therefore, prompts a white gay man to equate "the truth of his identity in his sex." The

critics imply that the white heterosexual also seeks his true identification in the same place. His sexual orientation, then, becomes the primary determinate of self-identity for any white man. By virtue of his whiteness, a white male erases his race as a potentially marginalizing feature of his identity in white patriarchal culture. This is not true for the black man (whether he is straight or gay), Mercer and Julien argue, since, as black homosexuals, their "experience tells [them] that being black is actually more important, more crucial" in defining their oppression, which in turn forms their collective identity, than is homophobia, which in turn forms their self-identity. How true this is for other men of color is uncertain; nonetheless, Gotanda's Vincent appears to fear his homosexuality (and others' homophobia) *after* his racial acceptance (which occurs while he is in the company of another Asian American). Yet, by asserting that white gay racism exists toward gay men of color, Mercer and Julien convincingly position a man's race and ethnicity as his most distinct feature of difference when he is among people whose race *differs* from his own. His skin color, and not his sexual partner, immediately codes him as subject with power or "other" without power within a white dominant culture.

Mercer also acknowledges that while blacks are most deeply oppressed as a race if viewed within the context of white culture, blacks are also aggressively homophobic within their own community (Mercer and Julien 121). "We cannot rationalize the disease of homophobia among black people as the white man's fault," claims Cheryl Clarke, "for to do so is to absolve ourselves of our responsibility to transform ourselves" (197). To the naming of woman as Other, therefore, one must add homosexual as "other." Here, in their mutual privileging of (male) heterosexuality, white and black cultures parallel, as presumably do other American cultures of color (as in the Asian American community, for instance, as suggested by Gotanda's Vincent's sense of his double marginalization). As Clarke concludes in her address to African Americans, a message that also crosses over cultural differences in its liberating vision: "Homophobia is a measure of how removed we are from the psychological transformations we so desperately need to engender" (207).

8. Under the direction of John Stix, Goldberg's (b. 1947) *Family Business* was first produced in 1976 at the Berkshire Theatre Festival in Stockbridge, Massachusetts. In April 1978, *Family Business,* again under Stix's direction, opened at the Astor Place Theatre, New York City. In partial recognition of its year-long Off-Broadway run, Otis Guernsey selected Goldberg's drama as one of ten plays for (excerpted) publication in *The Best Plays of 1977–1978* (two additional male-cast plays were also selected: Thomas Babe's *A Prayer for My Daughter* and David Mamet's *A Life in the Theatre*). *Family Business* was subse-

quently presented on "American Playhouse" (February 1983), starring Milton Berle as the dying patriarch, Isaiah Stein. For this PBS-TV performance, Goldberg added a cantor and two women to the cast.

Prior to the New York production of *Family Business,* Goldberg was the founding director of the American-Jewish Theatre (later renamed the National Jewish Theatre) in Boston. From 1974 to 1978, Goldberg was producer of Stage South, the state theater of South Carolina, located in Columbia. Goldberg's other plays include *Apostle of the Idiot, Black Zion, Comrades,* and *Heart and Soul.* He has also written for television ("Kate and Allie" and "MacGyver") and film (*The Image Maker* [1986]).

9. It should be noted that Norman was driving the car when his mother was killed. He feels responsible for her death, a feeling Isaiah does not discourage.

10. See Sy Syna for a misreading of Norman's character that, in turn, illustrates a typical, clichéd reading of male representation. Syna faults Goldberg for failing to "draw his characters fully": "Jerry, Norman, and Bobby all seem to be aspects of the same homosexual character—the celibate bachelor living at home; the secret gay; and the fussy mother substitute who only wants to keep house." Syna's insensitive, reductionist interpretation of these characters is due, in part, to his privileging conventional gender codings and stereotypes; it is also a reading that smacks of homophobia. While Syna's remarks support the individuals' interpretations that I overheard in the theater lobby, their collective view affirms the extent to which critics and spectators resist alternative dramatic representations of men, especially if the man whose image is being "tampered with" is a white heterosexual.

11. As a vivid counterexample of men's desire to connect personally yet choosing *not* to speak in person, but rather only on the telephone, see Robert Chesley's *Jerker, or the Helping Hand: A Pornographic Elegy with Redeeming Social Value and a Hymn to the Queer Men of San Francisco in Twenty Telephone Calls, Many of Them Dirty.* Bert and J. R. never meet in person in Chesley's play; rather, they come to know one another through the conversation and fantasy of safe, phone sex. While the men's interaction is among the most verbally intimate in theater, it does rely upon the conventional technical feature of the phone conversation as a means to elicit male characters' individualization (and here, their imaginations as well). Therefore, by portraying David and Jerry as eager to engage Norman in face-to-face conversation about difficult personal issues, Goldberg's characters—who, in a sense, reject the telephone as an intermediary—join a select group of men who pursue self-disclosing dialogue in person. Among the most eager and determined characters to pursue in-person self-disclosing dialogue are Ghee and Mead in Harvey Fierstein's *Safe Sex* and the men in Swados's *A Quiet End.*

12. Bobby's difficulty in accepting Jerry's homosexuality is not unlike Alan's response to Hank's homosexuality in Crowley's *The Boys in the Band* (64). Just as Alan cannot believe that Hank, who appears to embody the ideals of the American masculine ethos, is a homosexual, so Bobby, for the same reasons, is shocked at Jerry's admission. As in Alan and Hank's relationship, Bobby's own judgment, ideals, and sexuality are threatened by the naming of Jerry as "other." Bobby considers Jerry to be a mirror image of himself. As Georges-Michel Sarotte concludes, homosexuality "is the most categorical rejection of the American virile ideal, which must of necessity be gained heterosexually. To be a homosexual is to be relegated to nonconformity" (295). By responding to Jerry's homosexuality through "brute force," Bobby demonstrates what Sarotte would call a virile "resistance of homosexual tendencies" feared within himself (78). Along this line of thought, heterosexual white male characters often do find white homosexuals to be the most personally threatening of minorities. Since both sets of men share identical racial identities, each is necessarily privileged within the patriarchal hegemony: each passes within the power structure of the system. The gay male's identity is often not confirmed unless he articulates it. Thus, while straight and gay white men generally enjoy equal access to patriarchal privileges, one embodies the ideals of the American masculine ethos while the other transgresses them. Whereas one's physical presence visibly marks his race, one's sexual orientation is not as easily distinguishable. Influenced by the constraints of gender codings within a homophobic social structure, most Americans assume that a man is heterosexual unless he identifies himself otherwise. When a gay white man outs himself, as it were, he risks becoming the victim of the heterosexual white male's possible homophobia (comparable to the latter's possible racist-sexist-homophobic victimization of all remaining "others"—those over whom *all* white men presumably have cultural privilege). The issue of naming one's self as either straight or gay taps into codings that are gender based within the culture at large (that is, the acceptable parameters of male identification in America) as well as additional codings that are unique within individual racial, ethnic, and religious communities. Different sets of issues from those of the Anglo American may arise, therefore, for the gay African American, gay Latino, gay Asian American, or gay Native American who comes out of the closet within his own racial community. Any gay man of color is doubly marginalized in American culture. With the exception of Gotanda's *Yankee Dawg You Die,* no male-cast plays are published that highlight gay and straight men of color who, together, confront nonviolently the disclosure (or issue) of their sexual differences. (Juan Shamsul Alám's *Zookeeper* is a qualified exception. Carlos, a Puerto Rican American, slaps his younger gay brother, José, who has AIDS, in an effort to make

him to go to a clinic. "You never liked me. You never liked the person I turned out to be," José remarks. "I learned to live with it," replies the older brother, before embracing the crying, ill man and apologizing for his violent action [440].)

13. Speaking on 22 June 1980, at the First Jewish Theatre Conference/ Festival (held at Marymount Manhattan College), Goldberg linked the men in *Family Business* to their Jewish heritage, especially since some of the Steins' concerns reflect, as Goldberg identified, traditional issues often dramatized in contemporary Jewish theater: a Jew's recognition of his "alienation from his past"; a Jew's belief in "social justice"; and a Jew's regard for education. However, in regard to the Jewishness of one's religious observance, only Norman is an obvious devotee. It is possible, therefore, to attribute Norman's penchant for personal discourse to his ardent adherence to the traditions of the Jewish faith; that is, he is personal with others as a reflection of his personal commitment to a religious doctrine. Nonetheless, "Jewishness [is] incidental to the play," Goldberg concluded (much the same way, for example, that Catholicism, one presumes, is incidental to Jason Miller's *That Championship Season*). According to the playwright, the fact that the Steins are Jewish "is not part of the characters' final struggle on stage." From the point of view of this study, therefore, one can consider that the characters connect personally for reasons other than their being Jewish; their Jewishness does not guarantee their participation in personal dialogue.

14. Under the direction of Gregory Mosher, *American Buffalo* was first produced by the Goodman Theatre Stage Two in Chicago, November 1975; the Goodman's twelve-performance showcase reopened at Chicago's St. Nicholas Theatre Company in the same year. Also under Mosher's direction, a production was showcased at St. Clements, New York City, in 1976. *American Buffalo* opened on Broadway at the Ethel Barrymore Theatre in February 1977; the director was Ulu Grosbard.

15. "*American Buffalo* is classical tragedy," Mamet claims,

> the protagonist of which is the junk-store owner who is trying to teach a lesson in how to behave like the excellent man to his young ward. And he is tempted by the devil into betraying all his principles. Once he does that, he is incapable of even differentiating between simple lessons of fact, and betrays himself into allowing Teach to beat up this young fellow whom he loves. He then undergoes, as I have said, recognition in reversal—realizing that all this comes out of vanity, that because he abdicated a moral position for one moment in favour of some momentary gain, he has let anarchy into his life and has come close to killing the thing he loves. And he realizes at the end of the play that he has made a huge mistake, that rather than his young ward needing lessons in being an excel-

lent man, it is he himself who needs those lessons. That is what *American Buffalo* is about. (1988, 94)

16. Distinguishing, finally, between the visions in *American Buffalo* and Beckett's *Waiting for Godot,* Thomas King argues that "Don offers an alternative to the world of Vladimir and Estragon in *Waiting for Godot* where 'nothing is certain.' Nothing is certain in Don's world, but he has found a way to act in that world through his pragmatic use of language" (547).

17. Note how Teach's violent action also activates a repetitive cycle of personal dialogue and violence throughout the remainder of the play. *American Buffalo*'s cyclical discourse coherence is similar to the one dramatized in the institutional plays *Short Eyes* and *Streamers*. This similarity among the three plays supports the contention in chapter 1 that the work environment is not unlike that of confining institutions in terms of its impact on the dynamics in men's conversations.

18. Regarding Teach's condition, Dennis Carroll concludes, "And, though Teach seems to realize that there is emptiness in life, he does not have insights into how he is implicated in this emptiness—as the salesmen of *Glengarry Glen Ross* do. Even as he yearns for contact, he compulsively creates circumstances which ensure that he will live his life in isolation" (35). "Sensitive to others' comments and criticism, Teach is plagued by the constant threat of failure," according to June Schlueter and Elizabeth Forsyth. "Neither real friend nor true businessman, he experiences abrupt mood swings from that of the authoritarian leader to that of the child wounded by imagined offenses. With frantic desperation, Teach's voice pierces the awful silence of the play, filling them, fighting them, with dialogue that betrays how thoroughly money has determined his personal relationships" (498).

19. Compare Lamont's play to other neoclassically structured male-cast plays in noninstitutional settings—Crowley's *The Boys in the Band* or J. Miller's *That Championship Season,* for example—where characters readily engage personal dialogue as they drink or take drugs or both.

20. An earlier version of Lamont's (b. 1953) play premiered in 1983 as part of the New Southern Playwrights Festival in Atlanta. In November 1987, *That Serious He-Man Ball* opened at New York's American Place Theatre; Clinton Turner Davis directed this Off-Broadway production. The version of the play published in *Plays in Process* (1989) and Dramatists Play Service (1992) had been revised by November 1988. Among the recent outstanding regional stagings of the play are the Chicago Theatre Company's production at Parkway Playhouse and the Los Angeles Theatre Center's production, both in April 1990.

Lamont has received playwriting fellowships from the Florida Arts Council and the District of Columbia Commission on the Arts. He currently is Playwright-in-Residence at the University of Maryland–

Baltimore County. Among his other works are *The Black Play, 21st Century Outs, Life Go Boom!* and *Vivisections from the Blown Mind.*

21. Phillip Brian Harper illustrates his critique of language and black speakers who achieve mainstream success in America while maintaining their African American identification through reference to Max Robinson, a popular newscaster who died in 1988 of AIDS. Harper astutely aligns his recognition of the African American's behavioral dichotomy to W. E. B. DuBois's "classic discussion of blacks' 'double-consciousness'—the effect of their inability to reconcile their blackness and their 'American' identity" (136). See also Abrahams 1976; Kochman; Smitherman.

22. A possible motivation for Twin's threatened rape of Sky, a threat that captures the increasingly violent dynamics of their power plays over one another, is suggested by Robert Staples's assessment of a black man's motivation to rape a woman: "For black men, rape is often an act of aggression against women because the kind of status men can acquire through success in a job is not available to them. This act of aggression affords a moment of power, and, by extension, status" (65).

23. Through the character Jello's actions, Lamont creates a redemptive image of black men, not unlike Rochester's actions in Amiri Baraka's [LeRoi Jones] play, *Jello* (1965), a farcical burlesque version of the popular 1950s television series, the "Jack Benny Show." The "humorously 'revolutionary' Rochester," comments Henry Lacey, "represents, of course, the rebellious instinct lurking within the most ostensibly passive black man" (133). Lamont may well be paying homage to Baraka's groundbreaking work(s) of staged black reality in which, as Leslie Sanders remarks, the "images of the Negro . . . either as stereotype or as black bourgeoisie, are redeemed" (156). In *Jello,* "Rochester's actions destroy the script that has become legend in American popular culture," Sanders notes; "his actions and words [also] rewrite the script and reverse the roles . . . Rochester acts the part of the master" (160). At the end of *That Serious He-Man Ball,* Lamont's Jello performs with an authority that recalls the behavior and actions of the earlier African American character in Baraka's *Jello.*

Epilogue

1. See George Cunningham for a different perspective on how Frederick Douglass's historically important *Narrative* provides "a useful place to begin an inquiry into Afro-American subjectivity and Afro-American male subjectivity in particular" (109). Cunningham argues that the "psychosocial context of Afro-American males like Douglass does not place them in the position where the self is equated with masculinity, power, and identity while the other is invariably feminine, dominated, and negated." Therefore, the critic of Douglass must "capture the com-

plexity of the text" by reading simultaneously Douglass's "deconstructive posture toward gender and an exclusionary (white) American genealogy as elements of dominance, and [Douglass's] engendering posture toward [himself] and other black men and women" (111).

2. Briefly, let me mention a selection of "other" men's lives—which cross racial, ethnic, religious, and sexual orientation profiles—that have yet to be dramatized, or are severely underrepresented, in published male-cast plays, excluding monodramas: single, divorced, or widowed men who, as sole parents, are raising either their birth children or adopted children; bisexuals; interracial male friendships that occur outside of confining institutions; interracial male desire; house husbands; men in careers that have traditionally been female identified; working-class men; senior citizens who are not in confining institutions; men who are differently abled; men who are in mental institutions, under the care of other men; class variations among men of color; men in settings that were once male identified but are no longer sex specific (e.g., the military, same-sex colleges, and social organizations); gay or bisexual parenting; straight men among themselves—as well as gay and straight men together—who are comfortable in expressing physical affection toward one another; men who are supportive of feminism; nonviolent men; and men who voice opposition to alcohol and drug abuse. Interesting enough, despite all the culture's attention to the evils of alcohol and drugs, few male-cast plays acknowledge this concern. Finally, there are very few published male-cast plays that focus on the lives of Latinos, Asian Americans, or Native Americans.

3. While no substantial research has been done on discourse coherence in the realist mixed-cast canon, recent feminist criticism has begun to address this issue in the analyses of individual all-female plays. Sue-Ellen Case, for instance, criticizes Marsha Norman's Pulitzer Prize–winning 'night Mother, a play many consider to be a woman-identified play, as "animated by the absent male" rather than by women's subjectivity (1987). Jill Dolan suggests that the play's discourse coherence derives from a failure "to discuss Jessie's dilemma in terms of a wider [patriarchal] social context" (36; emphasis added); that is, the women's talk maintains the characters' positions as objects, not subjects, within a gender-coded dialogue—within a gender-coded realist framework. In this regard, Norman's women speak about themselves, paradoxically, as men among themselves speak about absent women: as articulated objects. As indicated in their speech, they fail to (re)create the female Other as subject. It remains to be seen—certainly in a high-profile production—if a woman can be represented as an "authentic" subject in a realist female-cast play (see Forte). In short, the structure of the published realist female-cast play also appears to be overdetermined by socially constructed gender codings. A qualified exception to this reading, however, is found in realist lesbian plays. Jane

Chambers's *Last Summer at Bluefish Cove,* for instance, is a ground-breaking American realist play in its *resistance* to being overdetermined—in respect to characterization and discourse coherence—by socially constructed gender codings.

4. From 1989 to 1992, I contacted hundreds of American theaters and playwrights in an effort to identify the current state of male representation in unpublished, produced works as well as in unpublished, unproduced plays. I was particularly interested in receiving male-cast plays and monodramas from writers of color; their work, in general, is underrepresented among published plays. Some of these writers and their plays are included in the Selected Bibliography.

Particularly helpful to me in locating emerging playwrights were the publications of Theatre Communications Group and the Non-Traditional Casting Project's 1989 Ethnic Playwrights Listing.

5. For discussions on and examples of the impact of feminism on men's scholarship see Jardine and Smith; Boone and Cadden.

6. "[H]omophobia directed by men against men is misogynistic, and perhaps transhistorically so," argues Eve Sedgwick. "By 'misogynistic' I mean not only that it is oppressive of the so-called feminine in men, but that it is oppressive of women" (1985, 20).

7. From a different perspective, and, with a different emphasis, Michael Kimmel suggests that "gender may be the single most important feature that determines character, surpassing (or underlying) even class and race" (63).

Works Cited

Plays

Male-Cast Plays

Alám, Juan Shamsul. 1984. *Accession*. Family Repertory Company, New York, July.

———. 1993. *God's Children*. *Ollantay Theater Magazine* 1, no. 2:97–139.

———. 1994. *Zookeeper*. In *Nuestro New York*, ed. John V. Antush, 421–41. New York: Mentor.

Albee, Edward. 1961. *The Zoo Story*. In *The American Dream and The Zoo Story*, 11–49. New York: New American Library. Originally published in 1960 by Coward-McCann.

Atlas, Larry. 1981. *Total Abandon*. New York: Samuel French.

Babe, Thomas. 1977. *A Prayer for My Daughter*. New York: Samuel French.

Baraka, Imamu Amiri [LeRoi Jones]. 1966a. *The Toilet*. In *The Baptism and The Toilet*, 33–62. New York: Grove Press. Originally published in 1963 in *Kulchur* 3, no. 9:25–39.

Bell, Neal. 1986. *Raw Youth*. New York: Dramatists Play Service.

Bowne, Alan. 1983. *Forty-Deuce*. New York: Sea Horse Press.

———. 1993. *A Snake in the Vein*. In *Plays in Process* 13, no. 7. New York: Theatre Communications Group.

Brady, Leo. 1940. *Brother Orchid*. New York: Samuel French.

Brown, Kenneth. 1965. *The Brig*. New York: Hill and Wang.

Bullins, Ed. 1991. *Salaam, Huey Newton, Salaam*. In *The Best Short Plays, 1990*, ed. Howard Stein and Glenn Young, 1–14. New York: Applause Theatre Books.

Bumbalo, Victor. 1984a. *After Eleven*. In *Niagara Falls and Other Plays*, 135–81. New York: Calamus Books.

———. *Kitchen Duty*. 1984b. In *Niagara Falls and Other Plays*, 87–134. New York: Calamus Books.

Cacaci, Joe. 1987. *Old Business*. New York Shakespeare Festival's Susan Stein Shiva Theatre, New York, November.

Cain, Bill. 1990. *Stand-up Tragedy*. Criterion Theatre, New York, October.

Chesley, Robert. 1988. *Jerker: Or the Helping Hand*. In *Out Front: Contemporary Gay and Lesbian Plays*, ed. Don Shewey, 449–91. New York: Grove Press.

Cole, Tom. 1977. *Medal of Honor Rag*. New York: Samuel French.

Crowley, Mart. 1968. *The Boys in the Band*. New York: Farrar, Straus & Giroux.

Davis, Bill C. 1981. *Mass Appeal*. New York: Dramatists Play Service.

DiFusco, John. 1983. *Tracers*. New York: Dramatists Play Service.

Dizenzo, Charles. 1970. *The Last Straw*. In *The Last Straw and Sociability: Two Short Plays*, 5–27. New York: Dramatists Play Service.

Duberman, Martin. 1975a. *The Colonial Dudes*. In *Male Armor: Selected Plays 1968–1974*, 17–45. New York: Dutton.

———. 1975b. *The Electric Map*. In *Male Armor*, 95–125.

———. 1975c. *Metaphors*. In *Male Armor*, 1–15.

Falk, Lee. 1971. *Eris*. In *Eris and Home at Six: Two Plays*, 3–42. New York: Dramatists Play Service.

Fierstein, Harvey. 1988. *Safe Sex*. In *Safe Sex*, 25–62. New York: Atheneum.

Flavin, Martin. 1933. *Amaco*. New York: Samuel French.

Fuller, Charles. 1981. *A Soldier's Play*. New York: Samuel French.

Gamboa, Harry. 1985. *Jetter Jinx*. Los Angeles Theatre Center, Los Angeles, October.

Gay Men's Theatre Collective. 1977. *Crimes against Nature*. San Francisco.

Gerstenberg, Alice. 1930a. *At the Club*. In *Comedies All: Short Plays by Alice Gerstenberg*, 147–72. New York: Longmans, Green.

Gilles, D. B. 1986. *Men's Singles*. New York: Dramatists Play Service.

Goldberg, Dick. 1979. *Family Business*. New York: Dramatists Play Service.

Goss, Clay. 1974a. *Homecookin'*. In *Homecookin'—Five Plays*, 15–47. Washington, D. C.: Howard University Press.

———. 1974b. *Of Being Hit*. In *Homecookin'—Five Plays*, 65–80.

Gotanda, Philip Kan. 1991. *Yankee Dawg You Die*. New York: Dramatists Play Service.

Heelan, Kevin. 1993. *Distant Fires*. New York: Dramatists Play Service.

Hock, Robert. 1958. *Borak*. New York: Dramatists Play Service.

Horovitz, Israel. 1968. *The Indian Wants the Bronx*. New York: Dramatists Play Service.

Hwang, David Henry. 1982. *The Dance and the Railroad*. In *The Dance and the Railroad and Family Devotions*, 9–42. New York: Dramatists Play Service.

Inge, William. 1968. *The Call*. In *Two Short Plays: The Call and A Murder*, 3–18. New York: Dramatists Play Service.

Ives, David. 1989. *Mere Mortals*. In *Four Short Comedies*, 53–73. New York: Dramatists Play Service.

Jacker, Corinne. 1977. *Terminal*. In *Night Thought and Terminal*, 19–32. New York: Dramatists Play Service.

Jones, LeRoi. *See* Baraka, Imamu Amiri.

Jones, Preston. 1976. *The Last Meeting of the Knights of the White Magnolia*. In *A Texas Trilogy*, 13–118. New York: Hill and Wang.

Jones, Stephen Mack. 1988. *Back in the World*. Judith Anderson Theatre, New York, October.

———. 1990. "The America Boys." Duplicated.

Kelley, Samuel L. 1992. *Pill Hill*. In *New American Plays 2*, 137–217. Portsmouth, N. H.: Heinemann.

Kessler, Lyle. 1985. *Orphans*. New York: Samuel French.

Klein, Jon. 1987. *T Bone N Weasel*. New York: Dramatists Play Service.

Kopit, Arthur. 1965a. *The Day the Whores Came Out to Play Tennis*. In *The Day the Whores Came Out to Play Tennis and Other Plays*, 97–140. New York: Hill and Wang.

———. 1965b. *The Questioning of Nick*. In *The Day the Whores Came Out to Play Tennis and Other Plays*, 39–54.

Lamont, Alonzo D., Jr. 1989. *That Serious He-Man Ball*. In *Plays in Process* 9, no. 9. New York: Theatre Communications Group.

LaRusso, Louis, II. 1975. *Lampost Reunion*. New York: Samuel French.

Laurents, Arthur. 1946. *Home of the Brave*. New York: Random House.

Lavery, Emmet. 1933. *The First Legion*. New York: Samuel French.

Levitt, Saul. 1960. *The Andersonville Trial*. New York: Random House.

Long, Quincy. 1991. *The Virgin Molly*. In *Plays in Process* 11, no. 11. New York: Theatre Communications Group.

Mamet, David. 1977. *American Buffalo*. New York: Grove Press.

———. 1981. *Lakeboat*. New York: Samuel French.

———. 1984. *Glengarry Glen Ross*. New York: Grove Press. Originally published in 1983 by Grove Press in a limited book club edition.

Marasco, Robert. 1970. *Child's Play*. New York: Samuel French.

Mason, Keith. 1988. *Pieces Reconstruction DOA*. Laguna Poets, Laguna Beach, Calif., January.

———. 1990. *For Black Boys Who Have Considered Homicide When the Streets Were Too Much*. Los Angeles Theatre Center, January.

———. 1992. *49 Blues Songs for a Jealous Vampire*. Alice Tully Hall, New York, July.

Masters, Robert W. 1962. *The Window*. New York: Samuel French.

McIntyre, Dennis. 1991. *Established Price*. Annenberg Center, Philadelphia, October.

McLure, James. 1980. *Lone Star*. New York: Dramatists Play Service.

———. 1990. *Pvt. Wars*. New York: Dramatists Play Service.

McNally, Terrence. 1988. *The Lisbon Traviata*. In *Out Front: Contempo-*

rary Gay and Lesbian Plays, ed. Don Shewey, 355–418. New York: Grove Press.

———. 1990. *The Lisbon Traviata.* In *Three Plays by Terrence McNally: The Lisbon Traviata, Frankie and Johnny at the Clair de Lune, It's Only a Play,* 1–88. New York: Plume.

Miller, Arthur. 1992. *The Last Yankee.* In *The Best American Short Plays, 1991–1992.* ed. Howard Stein and Glenn Young, 132–41. New York: Applause Theatre Books.

Miller, Jason. 1972. *That Championship Season.* New York: Dramatists Play Service.

Montreal, David. 1987. *Cellmates.* In *Cellmates and Que, Como y Cuando,* ed. Juan Villegas, 15–46. Irvine, Calif.: Ediciones Teatrales De Gestos.

Morris, Sidney. 1982. *If This Isn't Love!* New York: JH Press.

———. 1989. *The Wind beneath My Wings.* Courtyard Playhouse, New York, December.

Noonan, John Ford. 1983. *Some Men Need Help.* New York: Samuel French.

O'Neill, Eugene. 1964. *A Wife for a Life.* In *Ten "Lost" Plays,* 209–23. New York: Random House.

———. 1967. *Hughie.* In *The Later Plays of Eugene O'Neill,* ed. Travis Bogard, 259–93. New York: Random House. Originally published in 1959 by Yale University Press.

OyamO. 1991. *Let Me Live.* Houseman Theatre, New York, January.

Parnell, Peter. 1982. *Scooter Thomas Makes It to the Top of the World.* New York: Dramatists Play Service.

Patrick, Robert. 1972. *The Haunted Host.* In *Robert Patrick's Cheep Theatricks,* 297–358. New York: Samuel French.

———. 1979. *T-Shirts.* In *Gay Plays: The First Collection,* ed. William M. Hoffman, 1–46. New York: Avon Books.

———. 1988. *Untold Decades: Seven Comedies of Gay Romance.* New York: St. Martin's Press.

Piñero, Miguel. 1975. *Short Eyes.* New York: Hill and Wang.

———. 1986a. *The Guntower.* In *Outrageous: One Act Plays,* 51–79. Houston: Arte Público Press.

Pomo Afro Homos. 1991a. *Dark Fruit.* Public Theater, New York, December.

———. 1991b. *Fierce Love: Stories from Black Gay Life.* Jessie's Cabaret & Juice Joint, San Francisco, January.

Purdy, James. 1979. *True.* In *Two Plays,* 43–51. Dallas: New London Press.

Rabe, David. 1977. *Streamers.* New York: Knopf.

Ribman, Ronald. 1977. *The Poison Tree.* New York: Samuel French.

Richards, Gary. 1993. *The Root.* Atlantic Theatre Company, New York, March.

Schisgal, Murray. 1980. *The Flatulist.* In *The Pushcart Peddlers, The Flatulist, and Other Plays,* 27–41. New York: Dramatists Play Service.

Shepard, Sam. 1972. *4-H Club.* In *The Unseen Hand and Other Plays,* 201–33. New York: Bobbs-Merrill.

———. 1974. *Geography of a Horse Dreamer.* In *The Tooth of Crime and Geography of a Horse Dreamer,* 83–131. New York: Grove Press.

———. 1976. *Cowboys #2.* In *Angel City, Curse of the Starving Class, and Other Plays,* 227–40. New York: Urizen Books.

Sherman, Martin. 1980. *Bent.* New York: Avon Books.

Stetson, Jeff. 1989. *Fraternity.* Whole Theatre, Montclair, N.J., April.

———. 1990. *The Meeting.* New York: Dramatists Play Service.

Swados, Robin. 1991a. *A Quiet End.* New York: Samuel French.

Terry, Megan. 1966. *Keep Tightly Closed in a Cool Dry Place.* In *Viet Rock, Comings and Goings, Keep Tightly Closed in a Cool Dry Place, and The Gloaming, Oh My Darling: Four Plays by Megan Terry,* 153–98. New York: Simon and Schuster.

Therriault, David. 1984. *Floor above the Roof.* New York: Broadway Play Publishing.

Tirado, Candido. 1991. *First Class.* In *Recent Puerto Rican Theatre,* ed. John Antush, 81–117. Houston: Arte Público Press.

Topor, Tom. 1972. *Answers.* New York: Dramatists Play Service.

Voulgaris, John. 1989. *Best Friends.* Actors' Playhouse, New York, August.

Walker, Celeste Bedford. 1991. *Camp Logan.* Billie Holiday Theatre, Brooklyn, March.

Wexley, John. 1930. *The Last Mile.* New York: Samuel French.

Williams, Tennessee. 1945. *Last of My Solid Gold Watches.* In *27 Wagons Full of Cotton and Other One-Act Plays,* 73–85. Norfolk, Conn.: New Directions.

Willis, Jane. 1985. *Men without Dates.* In *Men without Dates and Slam!* 5–38. New York: Dramatists Play Service.

Wouk, Herman. 1954. *The Caine Mutiny Court Martial.* New York: Doubleday.

Yep, Laurence. 1990. *Pay the Chinaman.* In *Between Worlds: Contemporary Asian-American Plays,* ed. Misha Berson, 175–96. New York: Theatre Communications Group.

Yoshimura, James. 1983. *Ohio Tip-Off.* Center Stage, Baltimore.

———. 1986. *Union Boys.* Yale Repertory Theatre, New Haven, January.

Zimmerman, Carlota. 1991. *Man at His Best.* Playwrights Horizons, New York, October.

Male Monodramas

Alfaro, Luis. 1990. *Downtown.* Highways Performance Space, Santa Monica, November.

Allen, Jay Presson. 1989. *Tru.* Booth Theatre, New York, December.

Bogosian, Eric. 1987a. *Drinking in America.* In *Drinking in America,* 19–72. New York: Vintage Books.

307

———. 1987b. *Funhouse*. In *Drinking in America*, 73–107.

———. 1987c. *Men Inside*. In *Drinking in America*, 109–31.

———. 1987d. *Voice of America*. In *Drinking in America*, 133–47.

———. 1991. *Sex, Drugs, Rock & Roll*. New York: HarperCollins.

———. 1994. *Pounding Nails in the Floor with My Forehead*. Minetta Lane Theatre, New York, January.

Chaikin, Joseph, and Sam Shepard. 1991. *The War in Heaven*. American Place Theatre, New York, April.

Chaikin, Joseph, and Jean-Claude van Itallie. 1992. *Struck Dumb*. In *The Best American Short Plays, 1991–1992*, ed. Howard Stein and Glenn Young, 262–81. New York: Applause Theatre Books.

Drake, David. 1992. *The Night Larry Kramer Kissed Me*. Perry Street Theatre, New York, June.

Elovich, Richard. 1993. *Somebody Else from Queens Is Queer*. *Theater* 24, no. 2:53–66.

Essmann, Jeffrey. 1991. *Artificial Reality*. Perry Street Theatre, New York, April.

Ewing, Geoffrey C., and Graydon Royce. 1992. *Ali*. Actors' Theatre, New York, October.

Fleck, John. 1991a. *BLESSED Are All the Little FISHES*. *Drama Review* 35, no. 3 (fall): 179–91.

———. 1991b. *A SNOWBALL'S CHANCE IN HELL*. Los Angeles Theatre Center, December.

Fornes, Maria Irene. 1971. *Dr. Kheal*. In *Promenade and Other Plays*, ed. Michael Feingold, 59–73. New York: Winter House.

Gallu, Samuel. 1975. *Give 'Em Hell Harry!* New York: Viking Press.

Gray, Spaulding. 1985. *Swimming to Cambodia*. New York: Theatre Communications Group.

———. 1986a. *47 Beds*. In *Sex and Death to the Age 14*, 79–116. New York: Vintage Books.

———. 1986b. *Sex and Death to the Age 14*. In *Sex and Death to the Age 14*, 1–14.

———. 1986c. *Terrors of Pleasure: The House*. In *Sex and Death to the Age 14*, 199–237.

———. 1990. *Monster in a Box*. New York: Grove Press.

———. 1994. *Gray's Anatomy*. New York: Vintage Books.

Hagedorn, Jeff. 1983. *One*. Organic Theatre, Chicago, September.

Hoch, Danny. 1993. *Some People*. P. S. 122, New York, October.

Holbrook, Hal. 1959. *Mark Twain Tonight!* 41st Street Theatre, New York, April.

Jones, Thomas. 1990. *The Wizard of Hip*. New Federal at INTAR, New York, November.

Kearns, Michael. 1993a. *intimacies*. In *Gay and Lesbian Plays Today*, ed. Terry Helbing, 239–52. Portsmouth, N.H.: Heinemann.

———. 1993b. *more intimacies*. In *Gay and Lesbian Plays Today*, 253–69.

Kwong, Dan. 1991. *Tales from the Fractured Tao*. Highways Performance Space, Santa Monica, January.

Leguizamo, John. 1992. *Spic-o-Rama*. Westside Arts Theatre, New York, October.

———. 1993. *Mambo Mouth*. In *Mambo Mouth*, 27–119. New York: Bantam Books.

Miller, Tim. 1991. *Stretch Marks. Drama Review* 35, no. 3 (fall): 143–70.

———. 1994. *My Queer Body*. In *Sharing the Delirium: Second Generation AIDS Plays and Performances,* ed. Therese Jones, 309–36. Portsmouth, N.H.: Heinemann.

Monge-Rafuls, Pedro. 1989. "Trash." Duplicated.

Nishikawa, Lane. 1981. *Life in the Fast Lane*. Asian American Theatre Company, San Francisco.

———. 1989. *I'm on a Mission from Buddha*. Asian American Theatre Company, San Francisco.

Ong, Han. 1992. *Symposium in Manila*. Asian American Theatre Company, San Francisco.

Patrick, Robert. 1988. *Pouf Positive*. In *Untold Decades,* 199–212. New York: St. Martin's Press.

Pickett, James Carroll. 1985. *Dream Man*. Skylight Theatre, Los Angeles, November.

Prideaux, James. 1991. *Lyndon*. Houseman Theatre, New York, February.

Rintels, David. 1975. *Clarence Darrow*. Garden City, N.Y.: Doubleday.

Schenkkan, Robert. 1993. *The Survivalist*. In *Four One-Act Plays by Robert Schenkkan,* 57–67. New York: Dramatists Play Service.

Shepard, Sam. 1976. *Killer's Head*. In *Angel City, Curse of the Starving Class, and Other Plays,* 119–22. New York: Urizen Books.

Shepard, Sam, and Joseph Chaikin. 1984. *Savage/Love*. In *Sam Shepard: Seven Plays*, 319–36. New York: Bantam Books.

Steger, Lawrence. 1990. *Worn Grooves*. Club Lower Links, Chicago, November.

Talen, Bill. 1982. *American Yoga*. Performance Gallery, San Francisco, May.

York, Curtis. 1991. *The Boys in Curtis York*. LACE, Los Angeles, January.

All Other Plays

Baraka, Imamu Amiri [LeRoi Jones]. 1964a. *Dutchman*. In *Dutchman and The Slave,* 1–38. New York: William Morrow.

———. 1964b. *The Slave*. In *Dutchman and The Slave,* 39–88.

———. 1970. *Jello*. Chicago: Third World Press.

Beckett, Samuel. 1954. *Waiting for Godot*. New York: Grove Press.

———. 1960. *Krapp's Last Tape*. In *Krapp's Last Tape and Other Dramatic Pieces,* 7–28. New York: Grove Press.

Behan, Brendan. 1958. *The Hostage.* New York: Grove Press.

Chambers, Jane. 1986. *Last Summer at Bluefish Cove.* New York: JH Press.

Fierstein, Harvey. 1981. *Torch Song Trilogy.* New York: Gay Presses of New York.

Genet, Jean. 1954. *Deathwatch.* In *The Maids and Deathwatch: Two Plays,* 101–63. New York: Grove Press.

Gerstenberg, Alice. 1912. *Where Are Those Men.* Chicago: Dramatic Publishing.

———. 1921a. *Fourteen.* In *Ten One-Act Plays,* 221–41. New York: Longmans, Green.

———. 1921b. *Overtones.* In *Ten One-Act Plays,* 35–65.

———. 1924. *Mah-Jongg.* In *Four Plays for Four Women,* 1–30. New York: Brentano's.

———. 1930b. *Mere Man.* In *Comedies All: Short Plays by Alice Gerstenberg,* 23–39. New York: Longmans, Green.

———. 1941. *Time for Romance.* Chicago: Dramatic Publishing.

Goldberg, Dick. 1969. *Apostle of the Idiot.* Brandeis University, Boston, April.

———. 1970. *Black Zion.* American Jewish Theatre, Boston, November.

———. 1991. *Comrades.* Trustus Theatre, Columbia, S.C., August.

———. 1993. *Heart and Soul.* Theatre-by-the-Grove, Indiana, Pa., July.

Gotanda, Philip Kan. 1979. *The Avocado Kid.* East West Players, Los Angeles, November.

———. 1980. *A Song for a Nisei Fisherman.* Stanford University, Stanford, Calif., November.

———. 1981. *Bullet Headed Birds.* Asian American Theatre Center, San Francisco, January.

———. 1982. *The Dream of Kitamura.* Asian American Theatre Center, San Francisco, January.

———. 1990. *The Wash.* In *Between Worlds: Contemporary Asian-American Plays,* ed. Misha Berson, 29–74. New York: Theatre Communications Group.

———. 1991. *Fish Head Soup.* Berkeley Repertory Theatre, Berkeley, Calif., March.

———. 1994. *Day Standing on Its Head.* Manhattan Theatre Club, New York, January.

Greenberg, Richard. 1989. *Eastern Standard.* New York: Grove Weidenfeld.

Hoffman, William. 1985. *As Is.* New York: Random House.

Jones, LeRoi. *See* Baraka, Imamu Amiri.

Kramer, Larry. 1985. *The Normal Heart.* New York: New American Library.

Kushner, Tony. 1993. *Millennium Approaches.* Part 1 of *Angels in America: A Gay Fantasia on National Themes.* New York: Theatre Communications Group.

———. 1994. *Peristroika*. Part 2 of *Angels in America*. New York: Theatre Communications Group.

Lamont, Alonzo D., Jr. 1979. *The Black Play*. Primary Stage, Atlanta, October.

———. 1985. *21st Century Outs*. Theatre South, Atlanta, January.

———. 1992. *Vivisections from the Blown Mind*. Seven Stages Theatre, Atlanta, August.

———. 1994. *Life Go Boom!* Playwrights Theatre of Baltimore, March.

Mamet, David. 1983. *Edmond*. New York: Grove Press.

———. 1992. *Oleanna*. New York: Pantheon Books.

Miller, Arthur. 1949. *Death of a Salesman*. New York: Viking Press.

Morris, Sidney. 1963. *A Gallery of Characters*. Turtle Bay Music Center, New York, September.

———. 1976. *The Six O'Clock Boys*. Venture Theatre, Los Angeles, November.

———. 1977. *Last Chance at the Brass Ring*. The Glines, New York, March.

———. 1978. *Exorcism of Violence*. Quaigh Theatre–Diplomat Hotel, New York, April.

———. 1979. *A Pocket Full of Posies*. National Art Theater, New York, March.

———. 1983. *The Demolition of Harry Fay*. Shandol Theatre, New York, September.

———. 1987. *Video's Child*. Shandol Theatre, New York, October.

———. 1990. *We've Got Today*. Wings Theatre, New York, February.

———. 1994. *Uncle Yossil: A Mystery*. JCC Theatre, Pittsburgh, May.

Norman, Marsha. 1983. *'night Mother*. New York: Dramatists Play Service.

Odets, Clifford. 1935. *Awake and Sing*. New York: Covici-Friede.

O'Neill, Eugene. 1928. *Strange Interlude*. New York: H. Liveright.

———. 1946. *The Iceman Cometh*. New York: Random House.

———. 1955. *Long Day's Journey into Night*. New Haven, Conn.: Yale University Press.

———. 1957. *A Touch of the Poet*. New Haven, Conn.: Yale University Press.

Piñero, Miguel. 1984a. *Eulogy for a Small Time Thief*. In *The Sun Always Shines for the Cool*, 89–128. Houston: Arte Público Press.

———. 1984b. *A Midnight Moon at the Greasy Spoon*. In *Sun Always Shines*, 46–88.

———. 1984c. *The Sun Always Shines for the Cool*. In *Sun Always Shines*, 5–45.

———. 1986b. *Cold Beer*. In *Outrageous: One Act Plays*, 37–47. Houston: Arte Público Press.

———. 1986c. *Irving*. In *Outrageous*, 83–114.

———. 1986d. *Paper Toilet*. In *Outrageous*, 9–34.

———. 1986e. *Sideshow*. In *Outrageous*, 117–41.

———. 1986f. *Tap Dancing and Bruce Lee Kicks*. In *Outrageous*, 145–60.

Rabe, David. 1973a. *The Basic Training of Pavlo Hummel*. In *The Basic Training of Pavlo Hummel and Sticks and Bones*, 1–111. New York: Viking Press.

———. 1973b. *Sticks and Bones*. In *The Basic Training of Pavlo Hummel and Sticks and Bones*, 113–228.

Ribman, Ronald. 1978. *Cold Storage*. New York: Samuel French.

Shepard, Sam. 1974. *The Tooth of Crime*. In *The Tooth of Crime and Geography of a Horse Dreamer*, 1–82. New York: Grove Press.

Weiss, Peter. 1965. *Marat/Sade*. New York: Atheneum.

Williams, Tennessee. 1947. *A Streetcar Named Desire*. New York: New Directions.

Wilson, Lanford. 1978. *Fifth of July*. New York: Hill and Wang.

Theory and Criticism

Abrahams, Roger. 1962. "Playing the Dozens." *Journal of American Folklore* 75, no. 297:209–20.

———. 1976. *Talking Black*. Rowley, N.J.: Newbury House.

Abramson, Doris. 1967. *Negro Playwrights in the American Theatre, 1925–1959*. New York: Columbia University Press.

Anderson, Mary Castiglie. 1983. "Ritual and Initiation in *The Zoo Story*." In *Edward Albee: An Interview and Essays*, ed. Julian Wasserman, 93–108. Houston: University of St. Thomas Press.

Antush, John V. 1991. Introduction to *Recent Puerto Rican Theatre: Five Plays from New York*, 7–23. Houston: Arte Público Press.

Arendt, Hannah. 1968. "On Humanity in Dark Times: Thoughts about Lessing." In *Men in Dark Times*, 3–31. Trans. Clara Winston and Richard Winston. New York: Harcourt, Brace, and World. Originally published in 1960 by R. Piper.

Atkinson, Brooks. 1960. Review of *The Zoo Story*, by Edward Albee. *New York Times*, 15 January, L37.

Atlas, Marilyn J. 1982. "Innovation in Chicago: Alice Gerstenberg's Psychological Drama." *Midwestern Miscellany* 10:59–68.

Austin, Gayle. 1991. *Feminist Theories for Dramatic Criticism*. Ann Arbor: University of Michigan Press.

Bamber, Linda. 1982. *Comic Women, Tragic Men: A Study of Gender and Genre in Shakespeare*. Stanford: Stanford University Press.

Baraka, Imamu Amiri [LeRoi Jones]. 1961. "Look For You Yesterday, Here You Come Today." In *Preface to a Twenty Volume Suicide Note*, 15–18. New York: Totem Press.

———. 1966b. "American Sexual Reference: Black Male." In *Home: Social Essays*, 216–33. New York: William Morrow.

Barbera, Jack V. 1981. "Ethical Perversity in America: Some Observations on David Mamet's *American Buffalo*." *Modern Drama* 24, no. 3:270–75.

Barnes, Clive. 1976. "David Rabe's *Streamers* in New Haven." *New York Times,* 8 February, sec. 2, 45.

————. 1989. "Big Bark, Not Much Bite." *New York Post,* 16 May, 31.

Barrett, Michele. 1989. "Some Different Meanings of the Concept of 'Difference': Feminist Theory and the Concept of Ideology." In *The Difference Within: Feminism and Critical Theory,* ed. Elizabeth Meese and Alice Parker, 37–48. Philadelphia: J. Benjamins Publishing.

Beaufort, John. 1976. "*Streamers.*" *Christian Science Monitor,* 26 April, 27.

Beauvoir, Simone de. 1953. *The Second Sex.* Trans. and ed. H. M. Parshley. New York: Knopf. Originally published in 1949 by Gallimard.

Beidler, Philip D. 1982. *American Literature and the Experience of Vietnam.* Athens: University of Georgia Press.

————. 1991. *Re-Writing America: Vietnam Authors in Their Generation.* Athens: University of Georgia Press.

Benjamin, Jessica. 1988. *The Bonds of Love: Psychoanalysis, Feminism, and the Problem of Domination.* New York: Pantheon Books.

Bennetts, Leslie. 1988. "Miguel Piñero, Whose Plays Dealt with Life in Prison, Is Dead at 41." *New York Times,* 18 June, sec. C, 32.

Benston, Kimberly W. 1976. *Baraka: The Renegade and the Mask.* New Haven, Conn.: Yale University Press.

Bergman, David. 1991. *Gaiety Transfigured: Gay Self-Representation in American Literature.* Madison: University of Wisconsin Press.

Berkvist, Robert. 1976. "How Nichols and Rabe Shaped *Streamers.*" *New York Times,* 25 April, sec. 2, 12.

Berson, Misha. 1990. Introduction to *Between Worlds: Contemporary Asian-American Plays,* ix–xiv. New York: Theatre Communications Group.

Bigsby, Christopher W. E. 1985. *David Mamet.* New York: Methuen.

————. 1992. *Modern American Drama, 1945–1990.* New York: Cambridge University Press.

Bishop, Ryan. 1988. "There's Nothing Natural about Natural Conversation: A Look at Dialogue in Fiction and Drama." In *Cross-Cultural Studies: American, Canadian, and European Literature: 1945–1985,* ed. Mirko Jurak, 257–66. Ljubljana, Yugoslavia: English Department, Filosofska Fakulteta, Edvard Kardelj University of Ljubljana.

Blau, Eleanor. 1974. "Ex-Convict Actors Find a Way to Give and Gain." *New York Times,* 21 January, L29.

Bleier, Ruth. 1984. *Science and Gender.* New York: Pergamon.

Bly, Robert. 1990. *Iron John: A Book about Men.* Reading, Mass.: Addison-Wesley.

Bogard, Travis. 1972. *Contour in Time.* New York: Oxford University Press.

Bolton, Whitney. 1964. Review of *The Toilet,* by Imamu Amiri Baraka [LeRoi Jones]. *Morning Telegraph,* 18 December, 2.

Boone, Joseph Allen. 1987. *Tradition Counter Tradition*. Chicago: University of Chicago Press.

Boone, Joseph Allen, and Michael Cadden, eds. 1990. *Engendering Men: The Question of Male Feminist Criticism*. New York: Routledge.

Brady, Owen. 1976. "Cultural Conflict and Cult Ritual in LeRoi Jones's *The Toilet*." *Educational Theatre Journal* 28, no. 1:69–77.

Breslauer, Jan. 1991. "Opening Up to Explore Racist, Sexist Topics in 'Howl.'" *Los Angeles Times,* 18 July, sec. F, 6.

Brody, Jane E. 1967. "The Case Is Familiar but the Theatre Is Absurd." *New York Times,* 15 July, L15.

Brokaw, John W. 1983. "Mexican-American Theatre." In *Ethnic Theatre in the United States,* ed. Maxine S. Seller, 335–53. Westport, Conn.: Greenwood Press.

Brown, Lloyd W. 1980. *Amiri Baraka*. Boston: Twayne.

Brown, Wendy. 1988. *Manhood and Politics: A Feminist Reading in Political Theory*. Totowa, N.J.: Rowman & Littlefield.

Brustein, Robert. 1960. "Krapp and a Little Claptrap." *New Republic,* 22 February, 21–22.

Burton, Deirdre. 1980. *Dialogue and Discourse: A Sociolinguistic Approach to Modern Drama and Naturally Occurring Conversation*. Boston: Routledge & Kegan Paul.

Butler, Judith. 1988. "Performance Acts and Gender Constitution: An Essay in Phenomenology and Feminist Theory." *Theatre Journal* 40, no. 4:519–31.

———. 1990. *Gender Trouble: Feminism and the Subversion of Identity*. New York: Routledge.

Camillo, Marvin Felix. 1975. Introduction to *Short Eyes,* by Miguel Piñero, vii–xiii. New York: Hill and Wang.

Carpenter, Fredric. 1979. *Eugene O'Neill*. Boston: Twayne.

Carroll, Dennis. 1987. *David Mamet*. New York: St. Martin's Press.

Case, Sue-Ellen. 1987. "The Personal Is Not the Political." *Art & Cinema* 1, no. 3:4.

———. 1988. *Feminism and Theatre*. New York: Methuen.

Chaudhuri, Una. 1991. "The Future of the Hyphen: Interculturalism, Textuality, and the Difference Within." In *Interculturalism and Performance,* ed. Bonnie Marranca and Gautam Dasgupta, 191–207. New York: Performing Arts Journal Publications.

Chin, Frank, et al., eds. 1974. *AIIIEEEEE! An Anthology of Asian-American Writers*. Washington, D.C.: Howard University Press.

Chodorow, Nancy. 1978. *The Reproduction of Mothering: Psychoanalysis and the Sociology of Gender*. Berkeley and Los Angeles: University of California Press.

Christiansen, Richard. 1988. "*Yankee Dawg You Die* Bridges Two Worlds of Asian Actors." *Chicago Tribune,* 23 September, sec. 2, 2.

Christie, N. Bradley. 1988. "David Rabe's Theatre of War and Remembering." In *Search and Clear: Critical Responses to Selected Literature and Films of the Vietnam War,* ed. William J. Searle, 105–15. Bowling Green, Ohio: Bowling Green State University Popular Press.

Cixous, Hélène. 1981. "Laugh of the Medusa." In *New French Feminisms,* ed. Elaine Marks and Isabelle de Courtivron, 245–64. New York: Schocken Books.

Clarke, Cheryl. 1983. "The Failure to Transform: Homophobia in the Black Community." In *Home Girls: A Black Feminist Anthology,* ed. Barbara Smith, 197–208. New York: Kitchen Table–Women of Color.

Cleaver, Eldridge. 1968. *Soul on Ice.* New York: McGraw-Hill.

Clum, John. 1989. "A Culture That Isn't Just Sexual: Dramatizing Gay Male History." *Theatre Journal* 41, no. 2:169–89.

———. 1992. *Acting Gay: Male Homosexuality in Modern Drama.* New York: Columbia University Press.

Clurman, Harold. 1977. "American Buffalo." *Nation,* 12 March, 313.

Cohen, Ed. 1992. *Talk on the Wilde Side: Toward a Genealogy of Male Sexualities.* New York: Routledge.

Cohn, Ruby. 1971. *Dialogue in American Drama.* Bloomington: Indiana University Press.

Cooke, Richard. 1964. Review of *The Toilet,* by Imamu Amiri Baraka [LeRoi Jones]. *Wall Street Journal,* 18 December, 14.

Corbett, Ken. 1993. "The Mystery of Homosexuality." *Psychoanalytic Psychology* 10, no. 3:345–57.

Coven, Brenda. 1982. *American Women Dramatists of the Twentieth Century: A Bibliography.* Metuchen, N.J.: Scarecrow.

Cranny-Francis, Anne. 1990. *Feminist Fiction: Feminist Uses of Generic Fiction.* New York: St. Martin's Press.

Crimp, Douglas. 1987. "How to Have Promiscuity in an Epidemic." *October* 43:237–70.

Crouch, Stanley. 1980. "Black Theatre: In the Heart of Our Complexities." *Village Voice,* 9 June, 81.

———. 1981. "The Bison Cometh." *Village Voice,* 10 June, 94.

Cunningham, George P. 1989. "'Called into Existence': Desire, Gender, and Voice in Frederick Douglass's *Narrative* of 1845." *Differences* 1, no. 3 (fall): 108–36.

Dean, Anne. 1990. *David Mamet: Language as Dramatic Action.* Rutherford, N.J.: Fairleigh Dickinson University Press.

de Lauretis, Teresa. 1987. *Technologies of Gender.* Bloomington: Indiana University Press.

Demastes, William. 1988. *Beyond Naturalism: A New Realism in American Theatre.* Westport, Conn.: Greenwood Press.

Diamond, Elin. 1989. "Mimesis, Mimicry, and the 'True-Real.'" *Modern Drama* 32, no. 1:58–72.

Disch, Thomas M. 1988. Review of *The Cocktail Hour, Tea with Mommy and Jack, Spoils of War,* and *Eastern Standard. Nation,* 12 December, 661–64.

Dolan, Jill. 1988. *The Feminist Spectator as Critic.* Ann Arbor: UMI Research.

Douglass, Frederick. 1960. *Narrative of the Life of Frederick Douglass, An American Slave,* ed. Benjamin Quarles. Cambridge: Harvard University Press, Belknap Press. Originally published in 1845 by the Boston Anti-Slavery Office.

Driver, Tom F. 1961. "The American Dream." *Christian Century,* 1 March, 275.

DuBois, W. E. B. 1903. *The Souls of Black Folk.* Chicago: A. C. McClurg.

Easthope, Anthony. 1985. *What a Man's Gotta Do.* London: Paladin.

Edelman, Lee. 1994. *Homographesis: Essays in Gay Literary and Cultural Theory.* New York: Routledge.

Egri, Peter. 1979. "The Use of the Short Story in O'Neill's and Chekhov's One-Act Plays: A Hungarian View of O'Neill." In *Eugene O'Neill: A World View,* ed. Virginia Floyd, 115–44. New York: Frederick Ungar.

Ehrenreich, Barbara. 1983. *The Hearts of Men: American Dreams and the Flight From Commitment.* Garden City, N.Y.: Anchor.

Elam, Keir. 1980. *The Semiotics of Theatre and Drama.* New York: Methuen.

Esslin, Martin. 1969. *The Theatre of the Absurd.* Garden City, N.Y.: Doubleday.

Farrell, Warren. 1986. *Why Men Are the Way They Are: The Male-Female Dynamic.* New York: McGraw-Hill.

Feingold, Michael. 1989. "Rife in the Theatre." *Village Voice,* 23 May, 98.

Felski, Rita. 1989. *Beyond Feminist Aesthetics: Feminist Literature and Social Change.* Cambridge: Harvard University Press.

Ferguson, Kathy. 1993. *The Man Question: Visions of Subjectivity in Feminist Theory.* Berkeley and Los Angeles: University of California Press.

Floyd, Virginia. 1985. *The Plays of Eugene O'Neill: A New Assessment.* New York: Frederick Ungar.

Forte, Jeanie. 1989. "Realism, Narrative, and the Feminist Playwright: A Problem of Reception." *Modern Drama* 32, no. 1:115–27.

Foucault, Michel. 1979. *Discipline and Punish.* Trans. Alan Sheridan. New York: Vintage Books.

———. 1980. *An Introduction.* Vol. 1 of *History of Sexuality.* Trans. Robert Hurley. New York: Vintage Books.

Fowler, Roger. 1986. *Linguistic Criticism.* New York: Oxford University Press.

Fox-Genovese, Elizabeth. 1991. *Feminisms without Illusions: A Critique of Individualism.* Chapel Hill: University of North Carolina Press.

Fox-Keller, Evelyn. 1984. *Reflections on Gender and Science.* New Haven, Conn.: Yale University Press.

Fredman, Shelly R. 1988. *"A Quiet End* Marks a New Beginning." *Advocate,* 19 January, 36.

Freedman, Samuel. 1985. "The Gritty Eloquence of David Mamet." *New York Times Magazine,* 21 April, 32.

Freeman, Donald C. 1970. *Linguistics and Literary Style.* New York: Holt, Rinehart and Winston.

Fuller, Margaret. 1843. "The Great Lawsuit: Man versus Men, Woman versus Women." *Dial* 4:1–47.

Fuss, Diana. 1988. *Essentially Speaking: Feminism, Nature, and Difference.* New York: Routledge.

Gaffney, Patrick. 1988. *"Serious He-Man Ball:* A Meaningful but Angry Game." *Creative Loafing* (Atlanta), 25 June.

Gale, Richard M. 1971. "The Fictive Use of Language." *Philosophy* 46, no. 178:324–40.

Gale, Steven. 1981. "David Mamet: The Plays 1972–1980." In *Essays in Contemporary American Drama,* ed. Hedwig Bock and Albert Wertheim, 207–23. Munich: Max Hueber Verlag.

Geis, Deborah R. 1992. "David Mamet and the Metadramatic Tradition: Seeing 'The Trick from the Back.'" In *David Mamet: A Casebook,* ed. Leslie Kane, 49–68. New York: Garland.

———. 1993. *Postmodern Theatric(k)s.* Ann Arbor: University of Michigan Press.

Gelb, Arthur. 1960. "Dramatists Deny Nihilistic Trend." *New York Times,* 15 February, L23.

Gelb, Arthur, and Barbara Gelb. 1962. *O'Neill.* New York: Harper and Row.

Gevisser, Mark. 1990. "Gay Theatre Today." *Theater* 21, no. 3:46–51.

Gill, Brendan. 1976. "Trilogy's End." *New Yorker,* 3 May, 76–77.

———. 1977. "No News from Lake Michigan." *New Yorker,* 28 February, 54.

Gilligan, Carol. 1982. *In a Different Voice: Psychological Theory and Women's Development.* Cambridge: Harvard University Press.

Gilmore, Thomas B. 1987. *Equivocal Spirits: Alcoholism and Drinking in Twentieth-Century Literature.* Chapel Hill: University of North Carolina Press.

Goldberg, Herb. 1979. *The New Male: From Self-Destruction to Self-Care.* New York: William Morrow.

Grice, H. P. 1975. "Logic and Conversation." In *Speech Acts,* ed. Peter Cole and Jerry L. Morgan, 41–58. Vol. 3 of *Syntax and Semantics,* ed. John P. Kimball. New York: Academic.

Guernsey, Otis, ed. 1978. *The Best Plays of 1977–1978.* New York: Dodd, Mead.

Gussow, Mel. 1980. "Al Pacino Puts His Stamp on *American Buffalo." New York Times,* 26 October, sec. D, 3.

———. 1984. "Real Estate World a Model for Mamet." *New York Times,* 28 March, sec. 3, 19.

———. 1987. "Stage: At American Place, *That Serious He-Man Ball.*" *New York Times,* 21 November, L15.

Halliday, Michael Alexander K. 1966. "Descriptive Linguistics and Literary Style." In *Pattern of Language,* ed. Angus McIntosh and M. A. K. Halliday, 56–69. London: Longman.

———. 1967. "The Linguistic Study of Literary Texts." In *Essays on the Language of Literature,* ed. Seymour Chatman and Samuel R. Levin, 217–23. Boston: Houghton Mifflin.

———. 1973. "Linguistic Function and Literary Style." In *Explorations in the Functions of Language,* 103–38. London: Edward Arnold.

Haraway, Donna. 1989. *Primate Visions: Gender, Race, and Nature in the World of Modern Science.* New York: Routledge.

Harper, Phillip Brian. 1993. "Eloquence and Epitaph: Black Nationalism and the Homophobic Impulse in Responses to the Death of Max Robinson." In *Writing AIDS: Gay Literature, Language, and Analysis,* ed. Timothy Murphy and Suzanne Poirier, 117–39. New York: Columbia University Press.

Hart, Lynda. 1989. "Introduction: Performing Feminism." In *Making a Spectacle: Feminist Essays on Contemporary Women's Theatre,* ed. Lynda Hart, 1–21. Ann Arbor: University of Michigan Press.

Hart, Steven. 1986. "The Theme of 'Race' in Inner-City/Prison Theatre: The Family, Inc." *Theatre Journal* 38, no. 4:427–40.

Harvey, Sally. 1991. "O'Neill's *Hughie* and Albee's *Zoo Story:* Two Tributes to the Teller and His Tale." *Journal of American Drama and Theatre* 3, no. 2:14–26.

Haskins, James. 1982. *Black Theatre in America.* New York: Thomas Y. Crowell.

Hay, Samuel A. 1994. *African American Theatre: An Historical and Critical Analysis.* New York: Cambridge University Press.

Hecht, Stuart J. 1992. "The Plays of Alice Gerstenberg: Cultural Hegemony in American Little Theatre." *Journal of Popular Culture* 26, no. 1:1–16.

Helbing, Terry, ed. 1993. *Gay and Lesbian Plays Today.* Portsmouth, N.H.: Heinemann.

Herman, William. 1987. *Understanding Contemporary American Drama.* Columbia: University of South Carolina Press.

Hertzbach, Janet S. 1981. "The Plays of David Rabe: A World of Streamers." In *Essays in Contemporary American Drama,* ed. Hedwig Bock and Albert Wertheim, 173–86. Munich: Max Hueber Verlag.

Hewes, Henry. 1958. "Through the Looking Glass Darkly." *Saturday Review,* 4 October, 27.

Hill, Erroll. 1980. *The Theatre of Black Americans.* 2 vols. Englewood Cliffs, N.J.: Prentice-Hall.

Hirsch, Foster. 1978. *Who's Afraid of Edward Albee?* Berkeley: Creative Arts Books.

hooks, bell. 1984. *Feminist Theory: From Margin to Center*. Boston: South End Press.

———. 1989. *Talking Back: Thinking Feminist, Thinking Black*. Boston: South End Press.

———. 1990. *Yearning: Race, Gender, and Cultural Politics*. Boston: South End Press.

hooks, bell, and Isaac Julien. 1991. "States of Desire." *Transition* 53:168–84.

Hornby, Richard. 1986. *Drama, Metadrama, and Perception*. Lewisburg, Pa.: Bucknell University Press.

Houston, Velina Hasu. 1990. Introduction to *The Politics of Life: Four Plays by Asian American Women*, 1–31. Philadelphia: Temple University Press.

Hubert-Leibler, Pascale. 1988. "Dominance and Anguish: Teacher-Student Relationship in the Plays of David Mamet." *Modern Drama* 31, no. 4: 557–70.

Hudson, Theodore R. 1973. *From LeRoi Jones to Amiri Baraka: The Literary Works*. Durham, N.C.: Duke University Press.

Huerta, Jorge A. 1982. *Chicano Theatre: Themes and Forms*. Ypsilanti, Mich.: Bilingual Press.

Hurrell, Barbara. 1981. "American Self-Image in David Rabe's Vietnam Trilogy." *Journal of American Culture* 4:95–107.

Irigaray, Luce. 1985. *This Sex Which Is Not One*. Trans. Catherine Porter with Carolyn Burke. Ithaca: Cornell University Press.

Isay, Richard. 1989. *Being Homosexual*. New York: Farrar, Straus, Giroux.

Jackson, Bruce. 1978. "Deviance as Success: The Double Inversion of Stigmatized Roles." In *The Reversible World: Symbolic Inversion in Art and Society*, ed. Barbara A. Babcock, 258–75. Ithaca: Cornell University Press.

Jackson, Reginald T. 1992. "On Being a Man." *QW*, 27 September, 50–51.

Jacobs, Dorothy. 1986. "Working Worlds in David Mamet's Dramas." *Midwestern Miscellany* 14:47–57.

James, William. 1902. *The Varieties of Religious Experience: A Study in Human Nature*. New York: Modern Library.

Jardine, Alice, and Paul Smith, eds. 1987. *Men in Feminism*. New York: Methuen.

Jen, Gish. 1991. "Challenging the Asian Illusion." *New York Times*, 11 August, sec. H, 1.

Johnson, Barbara. 1986. "Thresholds of Difference: Structures of Address in Zora Neale Hurston." In *"Race," Writing, and Difference*, ed. Henry Louis Gates, Jr., 317–28. Chicago: University of Chicago Press.

Jones, LeRoi. *See* Baraka, Imamu Amiri.

Kane, Leslie. 1984. *The Language of Silence: On the Unspoken and Unspeakable in Modern Drama*. Cranbury, N.J.: Associated University Press.

Kanellos, Nicholas. 1990. *A History of Hispanic Theatre in the United States: Origins to 1940*. Austin: University of Texas Press.

Kaplan, E. Ann. 1983. *Women and Film: Both Sides of the Camera*. New York: Methuen.

Keen, Sam. 1991. *Fire in the Belly: On Being a Man*. New York: Bantam Books.

Kerr, Walter. 1960. Review of *The Zoo Story*, by Edward Albee. *New York Herald Tribune*, 15 January, 8.

———. 1964. Review of *The Toilet*, by LeRoi Jones. *New York Herald Tribune*, 17 December, 14.

———. 1976a. "When Does Gore Get Gratuitous?" *New York Times*, 22 February, sec. 2, 1.

———. 1976b. "David Rabe's 'House is Not a Home.'" *New York Times*, 2 May, sec. 2, 5.

———. 1981. "Al Pacino's Supercharged *Buffalo*." *New York Times*, 14 June, sec. D, 3.

Kessler, Suzanne J., and Wendy McKenna. 1978. *Gender: An Ethnomethodological Approach*. Chicago: University of Chicago Press.

Kim, Elaine H. 1982. *Asian American Literature: An Introduction to the Writings and Their Social Context*. Philadelphia: Temple University Press.

Kimmel, Michael. 1989. "Of Whales and Men." *Nation*, 10 July, 63–66.

King, Thomas L. 1991. "Talk and Dramatic Action in *American Buffalo*." *Modern Drama* 34, no. 4:538–48.

Kissel, Howard. 1989. "Stereotypes, Second Time Around." *Daily News*, 15 May, 33.

Kochman, Thomas, ed. 1972. *Rappin' and Stylin' Out: Communication in Urban Black America*. Urbana: University of Illinois Press.

Kolin, Philip C. 1988. *David Rabe: A Stage History and a Primary and Secondary Bibliography*. New York: Garland.

Kondo, Dorinne. 1993. "The Narrative Production of 'Home,' Community, and Identity in Asian American Theatre." Paper presented at Eugene Lang College of the New School for Social Research, New York, 26 October.

Kostelanetz, Richard. 1963. "The Art of Total No." *Contact* 2:62–70.

Krafchick, Marcelline. 1986. "*Hughie* and *The Zoo Story*." *Eugene O'Neill Newsletter* 10, no. 1:15–16.

Kristeva, Julia. 1980. *Desire in Language: A Semiotic Approach to Literature and Art*. Ed. Léon S. Roudiez, trans. Thomas Gora, Alice Jardine, and Léon S. Roudiez. New York: Columbia University Press.

Lacan, Jacques. 1985. "God and the Jouissance of Woman. A Love Letter." In *Feminine Sexuality: Jacques Lacan and the "école freudienne,"* ed. Juliet Mitchell and Jacqueline Rose, trans. Jacqueline Rose, 135–48. New York: Norton.

Lacey, Henry C. 1981. *To Raise, Destroy, and Create: The Poetry, Drama, and Fiction of Imamu Amiri Baraka.* Troy, N.Y.: Whitston.

Landry, Donna, and Gerald MacLean. 1993. *Materialist Feminisms.* Cambridge: Blackwell.

Leahey, Mimi. 1982. "The American Dream Gone Bad." *Otherstages,* 4 November, 3.

Lewis, Patricia, and Terry Browne. 1981. "David Mamet." In *Twentieth-Century American Dramatists,* 63–70. Vol. 7 of *Dictionary of Literary Biography,* ed. John MacNicholas. Detroit: Gale Research.

MacCormack, Carol, and Marilyn Strathern, eds. 1980. *Nature, Culture, and Gender.* New York: Cambridge University Press.

MacKinnon, Catherine. 1989. *Toward a Feminist Theory of the State.* Cambridge: Harvard University Press.

Malkin, Jeanette R. 1992. *Verbal Violence in Contemporary Drama: From Handke to Shepard.* New York: Cambridge University Press.

Mamet, David. 1986. Interview by Matthew C. Roudané. *Studies in American Drama, 1945–Present* 1:73–81.

———. 1988. Interview by Henry I. Schvey. "Celebrating the Capacity for Self-Knowledge." *New Theatre Quarterly* 4, no. 13:89–96.

———. 1989a. "In the Company of Men." In *Some Freaks,* 85–91. New York: Viking Press.

———. 1989b. "Women." In *Some Freaks,* 21–26.

Marcus, Laura. 1992. "Feminist Aesthetics and the New Realism." In *New Feminist Discourses: Critical Essays on Theories and Texts,* ed. Isobel Armstrong, 11–25. New York: Routledge.

Marranca, Bonnie. 1977. "David Rabe's Viet Nam Trilogy." *Canadian Theatre Review* 14 (spring): 86–92.

McDonough, Carla. 1992. "Every Fear Hides a Wish: Unstable Masculinity in Mamet's Drama." *Theatre Journal* 44, no. 2:195–205.

McKelly, James C. 1987. "Ain't It the Truth: *Hughie* and the Power of Fiction." *Eugene O'Neill Newsletter* 11, no. 1:15–19.

Mercer, Kobena, and Isaac Julien. 1988. "Race, Sexual Politics, and Black Masculinity: A Dossier." In *Male Order: Unwrapping Masculinity,* ed. Rowena Chapman and Jonathan Rutherford, 97–164. London: Laurence and Wishart.

Middleton, Peter. 1992. *Inward Gaze: Masculinity and Subjectivity in Modern Culture.* London: Routledge.

Miller, John C. 1987. "Cross-Currents in Hispanic U.S. Contemporary Drama." In *Images and Identities: The Puerto Rican in Two World Contexts,* ed. Asela Rodriguez de Laguna, 246–53. New Brunswick, N.J.: Transaction Books.

Miller, Nancy K. 1988. *Subject to Change: Reading Feminist Writing.* New York: Columbia University Press.

Miller, Peter. 1989. "Relationships, Reviewers, and That Backroom Scene:

An Interview with Harvey Fierstein." *New York Native,* 27 February, 22–23.

Mitchell, Loften. 1967. *Black Drama: The Story of the American Negro in the Theatre.* New York: Hawthorn Books.

Modleski, Tania. 1991. *Feminism without Women: Culture and Criticism in a "Postfeminist" Age.* New York: Routledge.

Moi, Toril. 1994. *Simone de Beauvoir: The Making of an Intellectual Woman.* Cambridge: Blackwell.

Moon, Michael. 1991. *Disseminating Whitman: Revision and Corporeality in Leaves of Grass.* Cambridge: Harvard University Press.

Moraga, Cherríe, and Gloria Anzaldúa, eds. 1983. *This Bridge Called My Back: Writings by Radical Women of Color.* New York: Kitchen Table Press.

Moy, James S. 1990. "David Henry Hwang's *M. Butterfly* and Philip Kan Gotanda's *Yankee Dawg You Die:* Repositioning Chinese American Marginality on the American Stage." *Theatre Journal* 42, no. 1:48–56.

Mueller, Lavonne. 1993. "Looking for Mr. Bovary." Paper presented at the annual meeting of the Association for Theatre in Higher Education, Philadelphia, 5 August. Duplicated.

Mulvey, Laura. 1975. "Visual Pleasure and Narrative Cinema." *Screen* 16, no. 3:6–18.

Nightingale, Benedict. 1983. "*American Buffalo* Proves Its Quality." *New York Times,* 6 November, sec. 2, 3.

———. 1984. "Is Mamet the Bard of Modern Immorality?" *New York Times,* 1 April, sec. H, 5.

Novick, Julius. 1984. "Mamet." *Village Voice,* 3 April, 89.

Ohmann, Richard. 1971. "Speech, Action, and Style." In *Literary Style,* ed. Seymour Chatman, 241–54. London: Oxford University Press.

———. 1973. "Literature as Act." In *Approaches to Poetics,* ed. Seymour Chatman, 81–107. New York: Columbia University Press.

Oppenheimer, George. 1964. Review of *The Toilet,* by Imamu Amiri Baraka [LeRoi Jones]. *Newsday,* 17 December, sec. C, 28.

Page, Norman. 1973. *Speech in the English Novel.* London: Longman.

Paller, Michael. 1990. "No 'Mere' Completion: Theatre in the Age of AIDS." *Outweek,* 4 July, 57–59.

Palmer, Paulina. 1989. *Contemporary Women's Fiction: Narrative Practice and Feminist Theory.* Jackson: University Press of Mississippi.

Parks, Suzan-Lori. 1991. Interview by Cathy Madison. "Writing Home." *American Theatre* 8, no. 7:36–38.

Pavis, Patrice. 1982. "Discussion on the Semiology of Theatre." In *Languages of the Stage: Essays in the Semiology of the Theatre,* 25–35. New York: Performing Arts Journal Publications.

Pearlman, Mickey. 1989. "What's New at the Zoo? Rereading Edward Albee's American Dreams(s) and Nightmares." In *Feminist Rereadings of American Drama,* ed. June Schlueter, 183–91. Cranbury, N.J.: Associated University Press.

Phelan, Peggy. 1993. *Unmarked: The Politics of Performance.* New York: Routledge.

Platinsky, Roger. 1989. "The Politics of Gender in Miguel Piñero's *Short Eyes.*" Paper presented at the annual meeting of the Modern Language Association, Washington, D.C., 30 December.

Pleck, Joseph. 1981. *The Myth of Masculinity.* Cambridge: MIT Press.

Pottlitzer, Joanne. 1988. *Hispanic Theatre in the United States and Puerto Rico.* New York: Ford Foundation.

Quintero, José. 1964. "Eugene O'Neill's Monologue for Two." *New York Herald Tribune Magazine,* 20 December, 27.

Radovich, David. 1991. "Man among Men: David Mamet's Homosocial Order," *American Drama* 1, no. 1:46–60.

Raleigh, John Henry. 1965. *The Plays of Eugene O'Neill.* Carbondale: Southern Illinois University.

Rees, Norma. 1978. "Pragmatics of Language." In *Bases of Language Intervention,* ed. Richard L. Schiefelbusch, 191–268. Baltimore: University Park Press.

Reisman, David. 1953. *The Lonely Crowd.* New York: Anchor.

Rich, Frank. 1984. Review of *Glengarry Glen Ross,* by David Mamet. *New York Times,* 26 March, sec. C, 3.

———. 1988. Review of *Eastern Standard,* by Richard Greenberg. *New York Times,* 28 October, sec. C, 3.

———. 1989. "Two Asians and Hollywood's Bias." *New York Times,* 15 May, sec. C, 13.

Rich, J. Dennis. 1979. "Exile without Remedy: The Later Plays of Eugene O'Neill." In *Eugene O'Neill: A World View,* ed. Virginia Floyd, 257–76. New York: Frederick Ungar.

Rogoff, Gordon. 1977. "Albee and Mamet: The War of Words." *Saturday Review,* 2 April, 37.

———. 1987. "The Overcoming Game." *Village Voice,* 1 December, 126.

Román, David. 1992. "'It's My Party and I'll Die If I Want To!': Gay Men, AIDS, and the Circulation of Camp in U.S. Theatre." *Theatre Journal* 44, no. 3:305–27.

Rose, Jacqueline. 1982. "Introduction–I and II." In *Feminine Sexuality: Jacques Lacan and the "école freudienne,"* ed. Juliet Mitchell and Jacqueline Rose, trans. Jacqueline Rose, 1–57. New York: Norton.

Rosen, Carol. 1983. *Plays of Impasse: Contemporary Drama Set in Confining Institutions.* Princeton: Princeton University Press.

Rothstein, Mervyn. 1989. "A Playwright's Path to His Play." *New York Times,* 7 June, sec. C, 17.

Roudané, Matthew C. 1986. "Public Issues, Private Tensions: David Mamet's *Glengarry Glen Ross.*" *South Carolina Review* 19, no. 1:35–47.

Rubin, Gayle. 1975. "The Traffic in Women: Notes on the 'Political Economy' of Sex." In *Toward an Anthropology of Women,* ed. Rayna R. Reiter, 157–210. New York: Monthly Review Press.

Ruiz, Ariel. 1992. "Raza, sexo y politica en *Short Eyes* de Miguel Piñero." *Americas Review* 15, no. 2 (1987): 93–102. Trans. Paul Budofsky. Duplicated.

Rutenberg, Michael. 1969. *Edward Albee: Playwright in Protest.* New York: Drama Book Specialists.

Sanday, Peggy Reeves. 1981. *Female Power and Male Dominance: On the Origins of Sexual Inequality.* Cambridge: Cambridge University Press.

———. 1990. Introduction to *Beyond the Second Sex: New Directions in the Anthropology of Gender,* ed. Peggy Reeves Sanday and Ruth Gallagher Goodenough, 1–19. Philadelphia: University of Pennsylvania Press.

Sanders, Leslie. 1988. *The Development of Black Theatre in America: From Shadows to Selves.* Baton Rouge: Louisana State University Press.

Sarotte, Georges-Michel. 1978. *Like a Brother, Like a Lover.* Trans. Richard Miller. Garden City, N.Y.: Anchor-Doubleday.

Savran, David. 1988. *In Their Own Words: Contemporary American Playwrights.* New York: Theatre Communications Group.

———. 1992. *Communists, Cowboys, and Queers: The Politics of Masculinity in the Work of Arthur Miller and Tennessee Williams.* Minneapolis: University of Minnesota Press.

Scheibler, Rolf. 1973. "*Hughie:* A One-Act Play for the Imaginary Theatre." *English Studies* 54, no. 3:231–48.

Schlueter, June, and Elizabeth Forsyth. 1983. "America as Junkshop: The Business Ethic in David Mamet's *American Buffalo.*" *Modern Drama* 26, no. 4:492–500.

Schor, Namoi. 1992. "Feminist and Gender Studies." In *Introduction to Scholarship in Modern Languages and Literatures,* 2d ed., ed. Joseph Gibaldi, 262–87. New York: Modern Language Association.

Schvey, Henry I. 1988. "The Plays of David Mamet: Games of Manipulation and Power." *New Theatre Quarterly* 4, no. 13:77–89.

Schwenger, Peter. 1979. "The Masculine Mode." *Critical Inquiry* 5, no. 4:621–33.

Scott, Joan. 1988. *Gender and the Politics of History.* New York: Columbia University Press.

Searle, John. 1969. *Speech Acts.* London: Cambridge University Press.

———. 1975a. "Indirect Speech Acts." In *Speech Acts,* ed. Peter Cole and Jerry L. Morgan, 59–82. Vol. 3 of *Syntax and Semantics,* ed. John P. Kimball. New York: Academic.

———. 1975b. "The Logic of Fictional Discourse." *New Literary History* 6:319–32.

———. 1975c. "Speech Acts and Recent Linguistics." In *Developmental Psycholinguistics and Communication Disorders,* ed. Doris Aaronson and Robert W. Rieber, 27–38. New York: Academy of Sciences.

Sedgwick, Eve Kosofsky. 1985. *Between Men: English Literature and Male Homosocial Desire.* New York: Columbia University Press.

———. 1990. *Epistemology of the Closet.* Berkeley: University of California Press.

Segal, Lynne. 1990. *Slow Motion: Changing Masculinities, Changing Men.* New Brunswick, N.J.: Rutgers University Press.

Seidler, Victor J. 1989. *Rediscovering Masculinity: Reason, Language and Sexuality.* London: Routledge.

Sheaffer, Louis. 1973. *O'Neill, Son and Artist.* Boston: Little, Brown.

Shewey, Don. 1988. Introduction to *Outfront: Contemporary Gay and Lesbian Plays,* xi–xxvii. New York: Grove Press.

Shirakawa, Sam H. 1987. "Original Caste Drama." *Theatre Week,* 14 December, 32–35.

Silverman, Kaja. 1992. *Male Subjectivity at the Margins.* New York: Routledge.

Sinclair, Abiola. 1987. "*That Serious He-Man Ball* at American Place Theatre." *New York Amsterdam News,* 28 November, 30.

Smith, Edward G. 1983. "Black Theatre." In *Ethnic Theatre in the United States,* ed. Maxine S. Seller, 37–66. Westport, Conn.: Greenwood Press.

Smith, Michael. 1964. Review of *The Toilet,* by Imamu Amiri Baraka [LeRoi Jones]. *Village Voice,* 31 December, 79.

Smith, Michael S. 1991. "African Roots, American Fruits: The Queerness of Afrocentricity." *Outweek,* 27 February, 30.

Smith, Susan Harris. 1989. "Actors Constructing an Audience: *Hughie*'s Post Modern Aura." In *Eugene O'Neill and the Emergence of American Drama,* ed. Marc Maufort, 169–80. Atlanta: Rodopi.

Smith, Valerie. 1987. *Self Discovery and Authority in Afro-American Narrative.* Cambridge: Harvard University Press.

———. 1989. "Gender and Afro-Americanist Literary Theory and Criticism." In *Speaking of Gender,* ed. Elaine Showalter, 56–70. New York: Routledge.

Smitherman, Geneva. 1977. *Talkin and Testifyin: The Language of Black America.* Boston: Houghton Mifflin.

Sollors, Werner. 1981. "Amiri Baraka (LeRoi Jones)." In *Essays on Contemporary American Drama,* ed. Hedwig Bock and Albert Wertheim, 105–22. Munich: Max Hueber Verlag.

Spivak, Gayatri Chakravorty. 1987. *In Other Worlds: Essays in Cultural Politics.* New York: Methuen.

Staples, Robert. 1982. *Black Masculinity: The Black Male's Role in American Society.* San Francisco: Black Scholar.

Stoltenberg, John. 1989. *Refusing to Be a Man: Essays on Sex and Justice.* New York: Meridian.

Stone, Judy. 1964. "If It's Anger...Maybe That's Good." *San Francisco Chronicle,* 23 August, sec. TW, 39.

Stuart, Jan. 1989. "Quiet Riot." *Seven Days,* 31 May, 53.

Sullivan, Kathy. 1988. "Albee at Notre Dame." In *Conversations with Edward Albee,* ed. Philip Kolin, 184–89. Jackson: University Press of Mississippi.

Swados, Robin. 1991b. Discussion with author. New York City, 18 June.

Swan, Jon. 1960. Review of *The Zoo Story,* by Edward Albee. *Villager,* 21 January, 44.

Syna, Sy. 1978. Review of *Family Business,* by Dick Goldberg. WNYC-TV, 31 May.

Tannen, Deborah. 1990. *You Just Don't Understand: Women and Men in Conversation.* New York: Ballantine Books.

Taubman, Howard. 1964. Review of *The Toilet,* by Imamu Amiri Baraka [LeRoi Jones]. *New York Times,* 17 December, L51.

Tener, Robert. 1974. "The Corrupted Warrior Heroes: Amiri Baraka's *The Toilet.*" *Modern Drama* 17, no. 2:207–15.

Tiger, Lionel. 1970. *Men in Groups.* New York: Vintage Books.

Uitti, Karl D. 1969. "The Linguistic Point of View." In *Linguistics and Literary Theory,* 193–242. Englewood Cliffs, N.J.: Prentice-Hall.

Urmson, James O. 1972. "Dramatic Representation." *Philosophical Quarterly* 22, no. 89:333–43.

Wahls, Robert. 1974. "Piñero: Prison, Parole, and a Prize." *New York Daily News,* 2 June, sec. 3, 1.

Wallace, Michele. 1990. *Black Macho and the Myth of the Superwoman.* New York: Verso. Originally published in 1979 by Dial Press.

Wallach, Allan. 1987. "Basketball as a Metaphor." *Newsday,* 20 November, sec. 3, 15.

———. 1988. "If the Play Can Be Described in One Sentence, That Should Be Its Length." In *Conversations with Edward Albee,* ed. Philip Kolin, 130–35. Jackson: University Press of Mississippi.

Watkins, Mel. 1971. "Talk with LeRoi Jones." *New York Times Book Review,* 27 June, 4.

Watt, Douglas. 1976. "Power from Up North." *New York Daily News,* 9 February, 25.

Way, Brian. 1975. "Albee and the Absurd: *The American Dream* and *The Zoo Story.*" In *Edward Albee: A Collection of Critical Essays,* ed. Christopher W. E. Bigsby, 26–44. Englewood Cliffs, N.J.: Prentice-Hall.

Weeks, Jeffrey. 1985. *Sexuality and Its Discontents.* London: Routledge & Kegan Paul.

Welsing, Frances Cress. 1991. "The Politics behind Black Male Passivity, Effeminization, Bisexuality, and Homosexuality (August 1974)." In *The Isis Papers,* 81–92. Chicago: Third World Press.

Werner, Craig. 1978. "Primal Screams and Nonsense Rhymes: David Rabe's Revolt." *Educational Theatre Journal* 30, no. 4:517–29.

Wetzsteon, Ross. 1976. "David Mamet: Remember That Name." *Village Voice,* 5 July, 101.

White, Edmund. 1991. "Out of the Closet, onto the Bookshelf." *New York Times Magazine,* 16 June, 22.

Whorf, Benjamin Lee. 1956. *Language, Thought, and Reality.* Cambridge: MIT Press.

Widdowson, H. G. 1975. *Stylistics and the Teaching of Literature.* London: Longman.

Williams, Mance. 1985. *Black Theatre in the 1960s and 1970s: A Historical-Critical Analysis of the Movement.* Westport, Conn.: Greenwood Press.

Winer, Laurie. 1989. "*Yankee* Dawg." *Wall Street Journal,* 20 May, sec. A, 20.

Witherington, Paul. 1972. "Exorcism and Baptism in LeRoi Jones's *The Toilet.*" *Modern Drama* 15, no. 2:159–63.

Wittig, Monique. 1981. "One Is Not Born a Woman." *Feminist Issues* 1, no. 2:47–54.

Wolf, Jeanne. 1988. "Jeanne Wolf in Conversation with Edward Albee." In *Conversations with Edward Albee,* ed. Philip Kolin, 110–20. Jackson: University Press of Mississippi.

Wong, Sau-ling Cynthia. 1993. *Reading Asian American Literature: From Necessity to Extravagance.* Princeton, N.J.: Princeton University Press.

Worth, Katharine. 1981. "Edward Albee: Playwright of Evolution." In *Essays on Contemporary American Drama,* ed. Hedwig Bock and Albert Wertheim, 33–53. Munich: Max Hueber Verlag.

Zeifman, Hersh. 1992. "Phallus in Wonderland: Machismo and Business in David Mamet's *American Buffalo* and *Glengarry Glen Ross.*" In *David Mamet: A Casebook,* ed. Leslie Kane, 123–35. New York: Garland.

Zimbardo, Rose A. 1975. "Symbolism and Naturalism in Edward Albee's *The Zoo Story.*" In *Edward Albee: A Collection of Critical Essays,* ed. Christopher W. E. Bigsby, 45–53. Englewood Cliffs, N.J.: Prentice-Hall.

Zinman, Toby Silverman. 1990. "Search and Destroy: The Drama of the Vietnam War." *Theatre Journal* 42, no. 1:5–26.

Selected Bibliography of
Additional Male-Cast Plays and Monodramas

The selected bibliography, along with the plays and monodramas cited in the book, provides a general overview of the range of works that compose the male-cast canon. It is a supplementary, not comprehensive, listing. Certainly, some of the following authors have written or have had produced male-cast works that are not specified here; other authors of male-cast plays or monodramas may not be listed at all. In either case, the omissions are unintentional: either I am unaware of specific works or I am restricted by incomplete information about known works.

The following realist and nonrealist plays and monodramas share several distinguishing features. All are written for the stage by playwrights who live in the United States (although the United States may not be the writers' country of origin). All have gender-specific casts: the characters are men, the majority of whom are American. (It is possible, however, that a male character or actor may impersonate a woman within a given segment of a piece listed.) Unlike the thirteen plays analyzed in this study, not all of the following works are set in the United States. And finally, when a play's production is cited (because its text is not published), I have tried, whenever possible, to identify the premiere performance; each performance date, however, is the earliest that I was able to verify.

Male-Cast Plays

Adler, Robert, George Bellak, and Louis N. Ridenour. *Open Secret*. New York: Samuel French, 1947.

Aguelrros, Jack. *Awoke One*. Ensemble Studio Theatre, New York, May 1992.

Alám, Juan Shamsul. *Bullpen*. South Street Theater, New York, June 1980.

———. *Define Struggle*. Henry Street Settlement, New York, June 1983.

Albee, Edward. *Fam and Yam*. In *The American Dream, The Death of Bessie Smith, Fam and Yam*, 79–87. New York: Dramatists Play Service, 1962.

329

Allen, Woody. *Death Knocks.* In *Getting Even,* 31–41. New York: Samuel French, 1966.

Apple, Gary. *Black and White.* In *Plays for an Undressed Stage,* 23–32. New York: Samuel French, 1979.

———. *Do.* In *Plays for an Undressed Stage,* 15–21.

Ardrey, Robert. *God and Texas.* In *The Best One-Act Plays of 1943,* ed. Margaret Mayorga, 9–28. New York: Dodd, Mead, 1944.

Ariza, René. *The Meeting.* In *Cuban Theater in the United States,* ed. Luis F. González-Cruz and Francesca M. Colecchia, 62–63. Tempe, Ariz.: Bilingual Press, 1992.

Arnold, C. D. *Dinosaurs.* In *The Dinosaur Plays,* 57–73. New York: JH Press, 1981.

———. *Downtown Local.* Theatre Rhinoceros, San Francisco, 1979.

———. *A Night in the Blue Moon,* 9–27. New York: JH Press, 1981.

Arnold, John. *Doubles.* California Playwright's Festival, Sacramento, 1978.

Arroyo, Rane. *Sex with the Man on the Moon.* 2nd Mainline Artist Colony Festival, Grapeville, Pa., 1991.

Arzoomanian, Ralph. *The Tack Room.* In *The Best American Short Plays 1992–1993,* ed. Howard Stein and Glenn Young, 17–36. New York: Applause Theatre Books, 1993.

Babb, Roger. *Tro.* Downtown Art Company, New York, April 1994.

Ball, Alan. *Bachelor Holiday.* In *Five One Act Plays by Alan Ball,* 20–49. New York: Dramatists Play Service, 1994.

Banacki, Raymond. *Boys' Night Out: A Date with Pip; Dial-a-Hero; The Dating Game.* Lesbian and Gay Community Center, New York, April 1987.

———. *Maybe That's Because I Love You.* Playbox, New York, February 1971.

Baraka, Amiri. *The Death of Malcolm X.* New York: Grove Press, 1971.

Barton, Lee. *Nightride.* Van Dam Theatre, New York, November 1971.

Beach, Lewis. *Brothers.* In *Four One-Act Plays: The Clod, A Guest for Dinner, Love among the Lions, and Brothers,* 77–96. New York: Brentano, 1921.

———. *A Guest for Dinner.* In *Four One-Act Plays,* 23–51.

Beckman, Jules, Jess Curtis, and Keith Hennessy. *Mandala.* New Performance Gallery, San Francisco, 1988.

Beim, Norman. *The Deserter.* In *Off-Off Broadway Festival Plays, Series Three,* 2–24. New York: Samuel French, 1978.

Bent, Norman A. *Phonecall from Sunkist.* In *One Act Plays for Acting Students,* 163–71. New York: Samuel French, 1987.

Bettenbender, Benjamin. *Scaring the Fish.* INTAR Theater, New York, October 1993.

Bevan, Donald, and Edmond Trzcinski. *Stalag 17.* New York: Dramatists Play Service, 1951.

Birimisa, George. *Pogey Bait.* Las Palmas Theatre, Hollywood, 1977.

Bittermna, Shem. *Ten Below.* WPA Theater, New York, June 1993.

Blessing, Lee. *The Authentic Life of Billy the Kid.* New York: Samuel French, 1979.

———. *Cobb.* New York: Dramatists Play Service, 1988.

———. *Lake Street Extension.* New York: Dramatists Play Service, 1991.

———. *Oldtimers Game.* New York: Dramatists Play Service, 1988.

———. *A Walk in the Woods.* New York: New American Library, 1988.

Bob & Bob. *Deluxe.* HERE, New York, April 1994.

Booth, Eric. *Metamorphosis: A Slice of Black Gay Life.* Producers Club, New York, January 1990.

Borland, Hal, and Phil Dunning. *What Is America.* New York: Samuel French, 1943.

Bozzone, Bill. *Breakdown.* In *Buck Fever and Other Plays,* 31–54. New York: Samuel French, 1986.

———. *The Experts.* Judith Anderson Theater, New York, March 1991.

Brass, Perry. *All Men.* American Renaissance Theatre, New York, 1987.

———. *Bar None.* Lionheart Gay Theatre, Chicago, 1990.

———. *Disco.* Meridian Gay Theatre, New York, 1984.

———. *Here, There, and Yonder: Another Temporary Assignment; After the Café Antoine; Chrome Morning.* Meridian Gay Theatre, New York, 1984.

Broadhurst, Kent. *The Habitual Acceptance of the Near Enough.* New York: Dramatists Play Service, 1983.

Bromberg, Conrad. *Transfers.* In *Transfers,* 3–20. New York: Dramatists Play Service, 1970.

Brown, Albert. *Buddy and the Echoes.* In *Six New Plays for Boys,* 49–59. New York: Samuel French, 1938.

———. *Father and Son.* In *Six New Plays for Boys,* 95–104.

———. *How'd You Guess It?* In *Six New Plays for Boys,* 79–94.

———. *On a Night Like This!* In *Six New Plays for Boys,* 27–47.

Brown, Arch. *Brut Farce.* Actors' Outlet Theatre, New York, July 1985.

———. *Samson.* Gay Theatre of New York, New York, 1984.

———. *Two Married Men.* Gay Theatre of New York, New York, 1981.

Brown, Carlyle. *The Little Tommy Parker Celebrated Colored Minstrel Show.* New York: Dramatists Play Service, 1992.

Bruno, Anthony. *Sole Survivor.* Courtyard Playhouse, New York, February 1989.

Budde, Jordan. *Fraternity.* Colonnades Theatre, New York, March 1984.

Bullins, Ed. *The Man Who Dug Fish.* New Dramatists, New York, 1970.

Bumbalo, Victor. *Show.* In *Tough Acts to Follow,* 59–68. San Francisco: Alamo Square Press, 1992.

Cachianes, Ed. *Everybody Knows Your Name.* Producers Club, New York, May 1990.

331

Cadman, Larry. *Peace in Our Time.* In *Off-Off Broadway Festival Plays, Eighteenth Series,* 17–31. New York: Samuel French, 1994.

Caldwell, Ben. *All White Caste.* In *Black Drama Anthology,* ed. Woodie King, Jr., and Ron Milner, 389–97. New York: Columbia University Press, 1972.

——. *Birth of a Blues!* In *New Plays for the Black Theatre,* ed. Woodie King, Jr., 37–44. Chicago: Third World Press, 1989.

——. *Prayer Meeting.* Newark, N.J.: Jihad Productions, 1968.

Calhoun, Matthew. *Money.* In *One Act Plays for Acting Students,* 37–53. New York: Samuel French, 1987.

Callahan, George. *Afraid of the Dark.* Boston: Baker's Plays, 1936.

Carlino, Lewis John. *High Sign.* In *Two Short Plays: High Sign and Sarah Sax,* 3–27. New York: Dramatists Play Service, 1962.

Casner, Howard. *The Kindness of Strangers.* Common Theatre, Chicago, 1990.

——. *The Venery of Larks.* Common Theatre, Chicago, 1989.

Castro, Edward. *Brothers.* In *The Best One-Act Plays of 1950–1951,* ed. Margaret Mayorga, 181–99. New York: Dodd, Mead, 1951.

Censabella, Laura Maria. *Abandoned in Queens.* Theatre Row Theatre, New York, June 1991.

Chesley, Robert. *Arbor Day.* Chelsea Gay Association Theater Project, New York, 1982.

——. *The Deploration of Rover.* In *Hard Plays/Stiff Parts,* 137–47. San Francisco: Alamo Square Press, 1990.

——. *Hell, I Love You.* Theatre Rhinoceros, San Francisco, 1980.

——. *Hold.* In *Hard Plays/Stiff Parts,* 149–57.

——. *Night Sweat.* In *Hard Plays/Stiff Parts,* 9–69.

——. *Somebody's Little Boy.* Theatre at 224 Waverly Place, New York, April 1991.

——. *(Wild) Person Tense (Dog).* In *Hard Plays/Stiff Parts,* 125–35.

Chomont, Kenneth L. *Letter of the Law.* Lesbian and Gay Community Center, New York, 1992.

——. *Night Out.* Lesbian and Gay Community Center, New York, October 1992.

——. *Things to Be Done.* Stage/Bound Productions, New York, August 1992.

Clarvoe, Anthony. *Pick Up Ax.* New York: Broadway Play Publishing, 1991.

Coles, Robert. *Cute Boys in Their Underpants.* Vortex Theatre Company, New York, 1992.

Conkle, E. P. *Muletail Prime.* In *The Best One-Act Plays of 1950–1951,* ed. Margaret Mayorga, 67–82. New York: Dodd, Mead, 1951.

Connelly, Marc. *The Traveler.* New York: Dramatists Play Service, 1926.

Corrie, Joe. *Hewers of Coal.* Boston: Baker's Plays, 1937.

Costello, Ward. *A Wake for Me and Thee.* In *The Best One-Act Plays of*

1948–1949, ed. Margaret Mayorga, 89–115. New York: Dodd, Mead, 1949.

Crabtree, John. *Landscape with Male Figures.* Courtyard Playhouse, New York, December 1990.

Csontos, David. *One-Liners.* The Glines, New York, 1977.

Curzon, Daniel. *Celebrities in Hell.* Theater Off Park, New York, 1991.

———. *Last Call.* One Act Theatre Company, San Francisco, 1980.

———. *S&M.* Theatre at 224 Waverly, New York, April 1991.

Day, Gary L. *No Apologies.* Laetus Theater Group, Philadelphia, 1988.

———. *Spring Eternal.* Walnut St. Theatre Studio 3, Philadelphia, 1991.

Dean, Philip Hayes. *Paul Robeson.* In *Black Heroes: Seven Plays,* ed. Errol Hill, 277–351. New York: Applause Theatre Books, 1989.

del Valle, Peter. *Lovers.* TOSOS Theatre Company, New York, 1974.

Dempsey, David. *It Ain't Brooklyn.* In *The Best One-Act Plays of 1944,* ed. Margaret Mayorga, 13–31. New York: Dodd, Mead, 1945.

DiMurro, Anthony. *Moe Green Gets It in the Eye.* RAPP Arts Center, New York, May 1991.

Duberman, Martin. *The Recorder.* In *Male Armor: Selected Plays 1968– 1974,* 71–94. New York: Dutton, 1975.

Dulack, Tom. *Incommunicado.* New York: Dramatists Play Service, 1990.

Dunster, Mark. *Red.* New York: Linden Publishers, 1979.

Edmonds, Randolph. *Everyman's Land.* In *Shades and Shadows,* 133–40. Boston: Meador Publishing, 1930.

———. *The Phantom Treasure.* In *Shades and Shadows,* 159–71.

———. *Yellow Death.* In *The Land of Cotton and Other Plays,* 180–204. Washington, D.C.: Associated Publishers, 1942.

Elias, Isidore. *Goods.* In *Off-Off Broadway Festival Plays, Sixteenth Series,* 193–230. New York: Samuel French, 1992.

Elliott, Paul. *Ledge, Ledger, and the Legend.* Chicago: Dramatic Publishing, 1972.

Eulo, Ken. *Final Exams.* Courtyard Playhouse, New York, 1977.

Feiffer, Jules. *The Dicks.* In *Off-Off Broadway Festival Plays, Ninth Series,* 1–17. New York: Samuel French, 1984.

Ferzacca, John B. *The Failure to Zig-Zag.* New York: Samuel French, 1978.

Fierstein, Harvey. *Freaky Pussy.* New York Theatre Ensemble, New York, 1974.

———. *Manny and Jake.* In *Safe Sex,* 1–24. New York: Atheneum, 1988.

Finch, Robert. *Dark Rider.* Evanston, Ill.: Row, Peterson, 1952.

———. *From Paradise to Butte.* Evanston, Ill.: Row, Peterson, 1952.

Finley, Mark, and Peggy Platt. *Knockin' Em Dead at the Limbo Lounge.* TUGS Cabaret, Seattle, June 1991.

Foote, Horton. *The One-Armed Man.* In *The Tears of My Sister, The Prisoner's Song, The One-Armed Man, and The Land of the Astronauts,* 47–61. New York: Dramatists Play Service, 1983.

Ford, Frank. *Lucifer at Large*. Boston: Baker's Plays, 1948.

Foster, Andrew. *Chemical Reactions*. In *The Best Short Plays 1989,* ed. Ramon Delgado, 153–73. New York: Applause Theatre Books, 1989.

Freeman, Aaron. *Do the White Thing*. Organic Theater, Chicago, November 1989.

Gamboa, Harry. *Shadow Solo*. Hispanic Urban Center, East Los Angeles, September 1982.

Gardner, Herb. *I'm with Ya, Duke*. Ensemble Studio Theatre, New York, May 1994.

Gardner, Layce. *The Savage God*. Celebration Theatre, Los Angeles, 1991.

Geoghan, Jim. *Only Kidding!* Garden City, N.Y.: Fireside Theatre, 1990.

George, Charles. *Final Performance or the Curtain Falls*. New York: Dramatists Play Service, 1960.

Gerber, John. *Dress Reversal*. Chicago: Dramatic Publishing, 1934.

Giantvalley, Scott. *Fracture*. Fifth Estate Theatre, Los Angeles, 1985.

Gibson, Preston. *The Suicides*. New York: Samuel French, 1929.

Gilles, D. B. *The Legendary Stardust Boys*. New York: Dramatists Play Service, 1981.

Gilroy, Frank D. *A Way with Words*. Ensemble Studio Theatre, New York, May 1991.

Gilroy, Tom. *American Lesion: Collateral Damage and Microwave Recipes*. Playground Theater, New York, May 1993.

Glassman, Bruce. *Strikes*. Pearl Theatre, New York, July 1989.

Glines, John. *Body and Soul*. Courtyard Playhouse, New York, June 1991.

———. *Chicken Delight*. Courtyard Playhouse, New York, January 1991.

———. *Men of Manhattan*. Courtyard Playhouse, New York, June 1990.

———. *Murder in Disguise*. Courtyard Playhouse, New York, June 1992.

———. *On Tina Tuna Walk*. Courtyard Playhouse, New York, July 1988.

Goluboff, Bryan. *Big Al*. In *Big Al and My Side of the Story,* 5–24. New York: Dramatists Play Service, 1993.

———. *My Side of the Story*. In *Big Al and My Side of the Story,* 25–47.

Gonzalez-Scherer, Silvia. *Border*. Aquijon II Theater Company, Chicago, September 1992.

———. *Boxcar*. Original Theatre Works, Cerritos College, Norwalk, Calif., June 1991.

———. *T*. Aquijon II Theater Company, Chicago, September 1992.

Goss, Clay. *Andrew*. In *Homecookin'—Five Plays,* 49–64. Washington, D.C.: Howard University Press, 1974.

Gower, Douglas. *Daddies*. New York: Dramatists Play Service, 1983.

Graham, Bruce. *Belmont Avenue Social Club*. New York: Dramatists Play Service, 1993.

Granger, Percy. *Leavin' Cheyenne*. In *Three Plays by Percy Granger,* 49–73. New York: Samuel French, 1982.

Gray, Amlin. *How I Got That Story*. New York: Dramatists Play Service, 1981.

Greco, Stephen, and J. B. Hamilton. *Gulp!* The Glines, New York, April 1977.

Green, Paul. *Hymn to the Rising Sun.* New York: Samuel French, 1936.

Gross, Alan. *The Man in 605.* New York: Samuel French, 1979.

Hagedorn, Jeff. *Crusaders.* Lionheart Theatre, Chicago, 1987.

Hailey, Oliver. *Picture.* In *Picture, Animal, and Crisscross,* 5–22. New York: Dramatists Play Service, 1970.

Hall, Richard. *Prisoner of Love.* In *Three Plays for a Gay Theater,* 107–43. San Francisco: Grey Fox Press, 1983.

Hamilton, Wallace. *A Month of Fridays.* Lambda Theatre Group, New York, 1973.

Hanley, William. *Whisper into My Good Ear.* In *Whisper into My Good Ear and Mrs. Daly Has a Lover,* 5–42. New York: Dramatists Play Service, 1963.

Harrington, Laura. *Women and Shoes.* Actors Theatre of Louisville, Louisville, 1983.

Harris, Bill. *Up and Gone Again.* In *Roots and Blossoms: African American Plays for Today,* ed. Daphne Williams Ntiri, 161–86. Troy, Mich.: Bedford Publishers, 1991.

Harrity, Richard. *Hope Is the Thing with Feathers.* New York: Dramatists Play Service, 1949.

Hart, Joseph. *Hit and Run.* In *The Best Short Plays 1985,* ed. Ramon Delgado, 177–207. Radnor, Pa.: Chilton Book Company, 1985.

Haubold, Cleve. *Tattoo.* New York: Samuel French, 1972.

Hawkins, John. *Crossing the Line.* The Glines, New York, 1978.

Heelan, Kevin. *Heartland.* New York: Samuel French, 1980.

———. *Split Decision.* New York: Samuel French, 1979.

Heide, Robert. *American Hamburger.* Theatre for the New City, New York, 1976.

———. *The Bed.* Caffe Cino, New York, 1965.

———. *West of the Moon.* New Playwright's Theatre, New York, 1964.

Herlihy, James Leo. *Bad-Bad Jo-Jo.* In *The Best Short Plays 1971,* ed. Stanley Richards, 133–54. Radnor, Pa: Chilton Book Company, 1971.

Higgins, David. *Partners.* In *The Best Short Plays 1984,* ed. Ramon Delgado, 61–92. Radnor, Pa.: Chilton Book Company, 1984.

Hoffman, Phoebe. *Undertones.* New York: Samuel French, 1925.

Holder, Laurence. *When the Chickens Come Home to Roost.* New Federal Theater, New York, July 1981.

Holt, Stephen. *Men.* WPA Theatre, New York, 1974.

Holtzman, William. *San Antonio Sunset.* In *The Best Short Plays 1989,* ed. Ramon Delgado, 27–51. New York: Applause Theatre Books, 1989.

Horovitz, Israel. *The Former One-on-One Basketball Champion.* In *The Great Labor Day Classic and The Former One-on-One Basketball Champion,* 25–53. New York: Dramatists Play Service, 1982.

Howe, Carroll V. *The Long Fall.* In *The Best One-Act Plays of 1949–1950,* ed. Margaret Mayorga, 279–96. New York: Dodd, Mead, 1950.

Huey, Tom. *It Ain't the Heat, It's the Humility.* In *The Best Short Plays 1983,* ed. Ramon Delgado, 89–104. Radnor, Pa.: Chilton Book Company, 1983.

Hunter, Paul. *Happy New Era.* The Glines, New York, October 1977.

Ingham, Robert E. *A Simple Life.* In *Four New Yale Playwrights,* ed. John Gassner, 85–152. New York: Crown Publishers, 1965.

Ingraffia, Sam. *Chateau Rene.* In *Off-Off Broadway Festival Plays, Fifteenth Series,* 4–38. New York: Samuel French, 1991.

Jannuzzi, Luigi. *A Bench at the Edge.* In *Off-Off Broadway Festival Plays, Sixth Series,* 43–79. New York: Samuel French, 1982.

Jessup, Cortland. *congressional AID.* Chez La Roe, New York, June 1990.

———. *Midnight Floral Service.* La MaMa La Galleria, New York, April 1991.

Johnson, Francine. *The Right Reason.* In *Roots and Blossoms: African American Plays for Today,* ed. Daphne Williams Ntiri, 255–62. Troy, Mich.: Bedford Publishers, 1991.

Jones, Silas. *Cowboys and Indians.* Inner City Theater, Los Angeles, 1986.

———. *Night Commander.* Inner City Theater, Los Angeles, 1985.

Joselovitz, Ernest. *Righting.* New York: Dramatists Play Service, 1977.

———. *Sammi.* New York: Dramatists Play Service, 1975.

Kalcheim, Lee. *Friends.* Judith Anderson Theater, New York, June 1989.

Kaplan, Barry Jay. *Going Places.* HOME for Contemporary Theatre and Art, New York, May 1989.

———. *Life in Positano.* HOME for Contemporary Theatre and Art, New York, April 1991.

Kaplan, Carol. *Sitting Man.* Pacific Theatre Ensemble, Los Angeles, February 1993.

Katz, Jonathan Ned. *Comrades and Lovers.* SAME, Atlanta, 1991.

Kaufman, George. *If Men Played Cards as Women Do.* New York: Samuel French, 1926.

———. *The Still Alarm.* New York: Samuel French, 1925.

Kearns, Michael. *Myron, a Fairy Tale in Black and White* In *Sharing the Delirium: Second Generation AIDS Plays and Performances,* ed. Therese Jones, 55–85. Portsmouth, N.H.: Heinemann, 1994.

Kelly, Tom. *Paradise Divided.* New City Theatre, Seattle, 1986.

Kicks, Otto. *When Men Reduce as Women Do.* New York: Samuel French, 1948.

Kimberly, Michael. *Almost an Eagle.* New York: Samuel French, 1978.

Kluger, Steve. *Bullpen.* New York: Samuel French, 1982.

Kopit, Arthur. *Indians.* New York: Samuel French, 1969.

———. *Sing unto Me through the Open Windows.* In *The Day the Whores Came Out to Play Tennis and Other Plays,* 55–77. New York: Hill and Wang, 1965.

336

Korder, Howard. *The Facts*. In *The Pope's Nose,* 11–20. New York: Dramatists Play Service, 1991.

———. *Imagining "America"*. In *The Pope's Nose,* 7–10.

———. *Lip Service*. In *Lip Service and The Middle Kingdom,* 15–52. New York: Samuel French, 1985.

Kronengold, A. J. *Tubstrip*. Mercer Arts Center, New York, 1973.

Kuczewski, Ed. *Queer Things: A Lecture-Demonstration with Slides,* The Glines, New York, November 1976.

Lang, William. *Final Play*. Chicago: Dramatic Publishing Company, 1977.

Laurents, Arthur. *Loss of Memory*. In *The Best Short Plays 1983,* ed. Ramon Delgado, 203–17. Radnor, Pa.: Chilton Book Company, 1983.

Lebow, Barbara. *Trains*. Berkshire Theatre Festival, Stockbridge, Mass., July 1991.

Lee, Maryat. *Four Men and a Monster*. New York: Samuel French, 1969.

Leokum, Arkady. *Enemies*. In *Friends and Enemies,* 3–25. New York: Samuel French, 1966.

———. *Friends*. In *Friends and Enemies,* 27–68. New York: Samuel French, 1966.

Levine, Ross. *A Change from Routine*. In *Off-Off Broadway Festival Plays, Eighth Series,* 63–76. New York: Samuel French, 1984.

Lewis, William. *Trout*. In *The Best Short Plays 1989,* ed. Ramon Delgado, 225–44. New York: Applause Theatre Books, 1989.

Lim, Paul Stephen. *Figures in Clay*. Louisville: Aran Press, 1992.

Long, Katharine. *Unseen Friends*. New York: Samuel French, 1980.

Lum, Darrell H. Y. *My Home Is Down the Street*. Kumu Kahua, Hawaii, 1987.

Magowan, Stephen. *Altar Boys*. Theatre Four, New York, 1979.

Mamet, David. *The Disappearance of the Jews*. In *Three Jewish Plays,* 3–27. New York: Samuel French, 1987.

———. *The Duck Variations*. In *Sexual Perversity in Chicago and Duck Variations,* 71–125. New York: Grove Press, 1978.

———. *A Life in the Theatre*. New York: Grove Press, 1983.

———. *The Luftmensch*. In *Three Jewish Plays,* 35–42.

———. *Prairie du Chien*. In *Short Plays and Monologues,* 23–39. New York: Dramatists Play Service, 1981.

———. *Shoeshine*. In *Short Plays and Monologues,* 47–57.

———. *Where Were You When it Went Down*. Ensemble Studio Theatre, New York, May 1991.

Margulies, Donald. *Space*. In *Pitching to the Star and Other Short Plays,* 51–58. New York: Dramatists Play Service, 1993.

Masterson, Kelly. *Touch*. American Ensemble Company, New York, 1987.

Mauriello, David. *How Many Tomorrows*. Courtyard Playhouse, New York, April 1990.

McKinney, Gene. *When You're by Yourself, You're Alone*. New York: Samuel French, 1974.

McLaughlin, Rosemary. *The Second Coming of Joan*. Waterfront Ensemble at the Raft, New York, 1990.

McNally, Terrence. *Botticelli*. In *Sweet Eros, Next, and Other Plays*, 1–16. New York: Random House, 1969.

———. *Love! Valour! Compassion!* Manhattan Theatre Club, New York, October 1994.

Mearns, Robert. *Now Departing*. In *Off-Off Broadway Festival Plays, Ninth Series*, 45–65. New York: Samuel French, 1984.

Metcalfe, Stephen. *Sorrows and Sons*. In *Sorrows and Sons*, 7–28. New York: Samuel French, 1986.

———. *Spittin' Image*. In *Sorrows and Sons*, 29–51.

Meyers, Patrick. *Feedlot*. New York: Dramatists Play Service, 1984.

———. *K-2*. New York: Dramatists Play Service, 1983.

Miller, Tim, and Doug Sadownick. *Buddy Systems*. P.S. 122, New York, June 1985.

Milligan, Jason. *The Best Warm Beer in Brooklyn*. In *New York Stories: Five Plays about Life in New York*, 25–59. New York: Samuel French, 1991.

———. *Instincts*. In *Southern Exposure: Five Plays about Life in the South*, 35–52. New York: Samuel French, 1990.

———. *Nights in Hohokus*. In *New York Stories*, 97–124.

———. *Shoes*. In *New York Stories*, 7–24.

———. *Shore Leave*. In *Cross Country: Seven More One-Act Plays*, 51–65. New York: Samuel French, 1993.

Mirrione, James. *If DuBois Were Dead*. Press Theatre, New York, June 1990.

———. *Men in Blue*. Press Theatre, New York, June 1990.

Monge-Rafuls, Pedro. *Noche de Ronda (Night of Serenades)*. New York: Gay and Lesbian Community Center, February 1991.

Moore, Christopher. *The Last Season*. Double Image Theatre, New York, April 1990.

Mori, Brian Richard. *Dreams of Flight*. New York: Dramatists Play Service, 1984.

Mueller, Lavonne. *Five in the Killing Zone*. In *WomensWork: Five New Plays from the Women's Project*, ed. Julia Miles, 175–252. New York: Applause Theatre Books, 1989.

———. *Warriors from a Long Childhood*. Theatre Four, New York, 1979.

Murray, Robert. *The Good Lieutenant*. In *Four New Yale Playwrights*, ed. John Gassner, 183–235. New York: Crown Publishers, 1965.

Nelson, Richard. *Jungle Coup*. In *Plays from Playwrights Horizons*, 237–72. New York: Broadway Play Publishing, 1987.

Neu, Jim. *Dark Pocket*. La MaMa Club, New York, March 1994.

O'Dea, John B. *Where E'er We Go*. In *The Best One-Act Plays of 1943*, ed. Margaret Mayorga, 57–74. New York: Dodd, Mead, 1944.

O'Donnell, Jack. *Practice.* Perry Street Theatre, New York, June 1980.

O'Keeffe, A. A. *Slip Ahoy.* In *The Best One-Act Plays of 1944,* ed. Margaret Mayorga, 101–26. New York: Dodd, Mead, 1945.

O'Leary, Thomas. *The Park.* Samuel Beckett Theatre, New York, 1990.

Oliensis, Adam. *Ring of Men.* Ensemble Studio Theater, New York, May 1993.

Olive, John. *Minnesota Moon.* In *The Best Short Plays 1982,* ed. Ramon Delgado, 211–34. Radnor, Pa.: Chilton Book Company, 1982.

O'Neill, Eugene. *Shell Shock.* In *Complete Plays of Eugene O'Neill, 1913–1920,* 1:655–72. New York: Library of America, 1988.

Osborn, Murray. *Men and Boys.* Cubiculo, New York, May 1990.

OyamO. *Angels in the Men's Lounge.* Ensemble Studio Theatre, New York, July 1992.

———. *The Breakout.* Manhattan Theatre Club, New York, 1975.

———. *Every Moment.* Eureka Theatre, San Francisco, 1986.

———. *Out of Site.* In *Black Theatre Magazine* 1, no. 4 (1970): 28–31.

———. *Place of the Spirit Dance.* African-American Cultural Center, New Haven, Conn., 1980.

———. *The Thieves.* Black Arts Festival, Seattle, 1970.

———, *Willy Bignigga.* Henry St. Settlement's New Federal Theatre, New York, 1970.

Page, Elizabeth. *Aryan Birth.* In *The Best American Short Plays 1992–1993,* ed. Howard Stein and Glenn Young, 179–91. New York: Applause Theatre Books, 1993.

Pape, Ralph. *Girls We Have Known.* In *Girls We Have Known and Other One Act Plays,* 5–40. New York: Dramatists Play Service, 1984.

Patricca, Nicholas A. *The Decline of the West.* Commons Theatre, Chicago, 1983.

———. *Dream Machine,* Lionheart Theatre, Chicago, 1985.

Patrick, Robert. *Bill Batchelor Road.* In *Untold Decades,* 53–91. New York: St. Martin's Press, 1988.

———. *Blue Is for Boys.* Theater for the New City, New York, 1983.

———. *Bread Alone.* Wings Theatre, New York, 1985.

———. *Evan on Earth.* California's Own Theatre Company, Sacramento, 1991.

———. *Fairy Tale.* In *Untold Decades,* 167–98.

———. *Fog.* In *Untold Decades,* 145–66.

———. *Fred and Harold.* In *Robert Patrick's Cheep Theatricks,* 57–66. New York: Samuel French, 1972.

———. *Let Me Not Mar That Perfect Dream.* Theater for the New City, New York, 1988.

———. *Odd Number.* In *Untold Decades,* 93–144.

———. *One of Those People.* In *Untold Decades,* 1–19.

———. *Preggin and Liss.* In *Robert Patrick's Cheep Theatricks,* 231–45.

———. *The River Jordan.* In *Untold Decades,* 21–52.

———. *Sit-Com*. Out and About Theatre, Minneapolis, 1980.

———. *Un-tied States*. Changing Scene, Denver, 1990.

———. *The Way We War*. Theatre at 224 Waverly, New York, April 1991.

Pereiras García, Manuel. *Bebo and the Band*. INTAR Laboratory, New York, 1986.

———. *First Vows*. Theatre for the New City, New York, May 1986.

———. *The Two Caballeros of Central Park West*. WOW's June Bust Festival, New York, June 1987.

Pérez, Héctor. *Perhaps the Marshland*. In *Cuban Theater in the United States,* ed. Luis F. González-Cruz and Francesca M. Colecchia, 167–83. Tempe, Ariz.: Bilingual Press, 1992.

Philip, Michel. *Mourning*. Fifth International Conference on AIDS, Montreal, 1989.

Pielmier, John. *The Boys of Winter*. Biltmore Theater, New York, December 1985.

Pierce, Carl Webster. *The Laziest Man in the World*. New York: Samuel French, 1923.

Pietri, Pedro. *Happy Birthday, M. F.* Nuyorican Poets Café, New York, April 1991.

Pintauro, Joseph. *Birds in Church*. In *Plays by Joe Pintauro,* 171–78. New York: Broadway Play Publishing, 1989.

———. *Charlie and Vito*. In *Cacciatore,* 9–24. New York: Dramatists Play Service, 1981.

———. *Frozen Dog*. In *Plays by Joe Pintauro,* 83–94.

———. *Men without Wives*. In *Plays by Joe Pintauro,* 53–60.

———. *Pony Ride*. 47th Street Playhouse, New York, September 1987.

———. *Rosen's Son*. In *Plays by Joe Pintauro,* 43–51.

———. *Uncle Chick*. In *Plays by Joe Pintauro,* 109–17.

Pitcher, Oliver. *The One*. In *Black Drama Anthology,* ed. Woodie King, Jr., and Ron Milner, 243–51. New York: Columbia University Press, 1972.

Povad, Reinaldo. *South of Tomorrow*. In *La Puta Vida (This Bitch of a Life) Trilogy,* 13–42. New York: Samuel French, 1988.

Powers, Verne. *Minor Miracle*. Evanston, Ill.: Row, Peterson, 1950.

Pressman, Kenneth. *Steal the Old Man's Bundle*. In *The Best Short Plays 1971,* ed. Stanley Richards, 171–96. Radnor, Pa.: Chilton Book Company, 1971.

Purdy, James. *Clearing in the Forest*. Northridge, Calif.: Lord John Press, 1980.

———. *What Is It, Zach?* Herbert Berghof Studio Theatre, New York, 1979.

Ramos, Alfonso Peña. *Gun Shopping*. University of California–Irvine, 1989.

Rankin, Rick. *Attack of the Zombie Backup Singers*. Alice B. Theatre, Seattle, 1988.

Rawls, Glenn. *Earl, Ollie, Austin & Bill*. Courtyard Playhouse, New York, February 1993.

Real, Philip. *Breathing Room*. Theatre Rhinoceros, San Francisco, 1977.

Reddin, Keith. *Throwing Smoke*. In *Desperadoes, Throwing Smoke, and Keyhole Lover*, 27–46. New York: Dramatists Play Service, 1986.

Reed, John. *Freedom*. In *The Provincetown Plays: Second Series*, 69–93. Great Neck, N.Y.: Core Collection Books, 1916.

Reyes, Guillermo. *Farewell to Hollywood*. Love Creek Theater Festival, New York, 1992.

Richards, Stanley. *District of Columbia*. In *Black Theatre, USA: Forty-Five Plays by Black Americans, 1847–1974*, ed. James Hatch, 432–36. New York: Free Press, 1974.

Robertson, Lanie. *The Curing of Eddie Stoker*. Penndragon Productions, Philadelphia, 1975.

Rubin, Rich. *That Al Pacino Look*. Theatre at 224 Waverly, New York, April 1991.

Rutherford, Stanley. *Tongue Dance*. Off Ramp, San Francisco, 1985.

Ryan, James. *Iron Tommy*. Ensemble Studio Theatre, New York, May 1992.

St. Germain, Mark. *Camping with Henry and Tom*. Berkshire Theatre Festival, Stockbridge, Mass., July 1993.

Sambol, Paul. *My Hero*. Westbeth Theatre Center, New York, May 1991.

Santa Vicca, Ed. *Natural Causes*. Cleveland Public Theatre Festival, Cleveland, 1987.

Sater, Steven. *Last Winter*. In *Hawaii Review* 16, no. 1 (winter 1991–92).

Schenkkan, Robert. *Intermission*. In *Four One-Act Plays by Robert Schenkkan*, 35–52. New York: Dramatists Play Service, 1993.

———. *Lunch Break*. In *Four One-Act Plays by Robert Schenkkan*, 21–34.

Schisgal, Murray. *Closet Madness*. In *Closet Madness & Other Plays*, 5–34. New York: Samuel French, 1984.

———. *74 Georgia Avenue*. In *Man Dangling*, 37–61. New York: Dramatists Play Service, 1984.

———. *The Rabbi and the Toyota Dealer*. In *Closet Madness & Other Plays*, 35–57.

Schlick, Frederick. *Bloodstream*. Boston: Baker's Plays, 1934.

Schmidt, Ed. *Mr. Rickey Calls a Meeting*. New York: Samuel French, 1989.

Schotter, Richard. *Taking Stock*. New York: Samuel French, 1985.

Shanley, John Patrick. *A Lonely Impulse of Delight*. In *Welcome to the Moon and Other Plays*, 33–38. New York: Dramatists Play Service, 1985.

Shepard, Sam. *Forensic and the Navigators*. In *The Unseen Hand and Other Plays*, 155–76. New York: Bobbs-Merrill, 1972.

———. *The Unseen Hand*. In *The Unseen Hand and Other Plays*, 1–32.

Shepard, Sam, and Joseph Chaikin. *Tongues*. In *Sam Shepard: Seven Plays*, 299–318. New York: Bantam Books, 1984.

Sherman, Martin. *Passing By*. In *Gay Plays*, ed. Michael Wilcox, 1:99–120. London: Methuen, 1984.

Shine, Ted. *Shoes*. In *Contributions*, 27–48. New York: Dramatists Play Service, 1970.

Shiomi, Rick. *Play Ball*. Pan Asian Repertory Theatre, New York, February 1989.

Shockley, Ed. *Badman*. Gettysburg College, Gettysburg, Va., 1990.

Shore, Joseph, and Richard Lincoln. *The Soldier Who Became a Great Dane*. In *The Best One-Act Plays of 1946–1947*, ed. Margaret Mayorga, 203–24. New York: Dodd, Mead, 1947.

Silverman, Judd Lear. *Correct Address*. In *Off-Off Broadway Festival Plays, Seventeenth Series*, 33–58. New York: Samuel French, 1993.

Silverstein, Shel. *Dreamers*. In *The Best American Short Plays 1992–1993*, ed. Howard Stein and Glenn Young, 211–21. New York: Applause Theatre Books, 1993.

Sorkin, Aaron. *Hidden in This Picture*. In *The Best Short Plays 1990*, ed. Howard Stein and Glenn Young, 141–68. New York: Applause Theatre Books, 1991.

Spenser, Stuart. *Cash*. Ensemble Studio Theatre, New York, May 1983.

———. *The Last Outpost at the Edge of the World*. Ensemble Studio Theatre, New York, May 1987.

Stein, Mark. *The Groves of Academe*. In *The Groves of Academe and The Plumber's Apprentice*, 5–30. New York: Dramatists Play Service, 1982.

Sulsona, Michael. *Dudes*. 45th Street Playhouse, New York, 1985.

Swet, Peter. *The Interview*. New York: Dramatists Play Service, 1975.

Tasca, Jules. *Cannibalism in the Cars*. In *Five One-Act Plays by Mark Twain*, 30–41. New York: Samuel French, 1976.

———. *Hardstuff*. In *The God's Honest, An Evening of Lies*, 19–28. New York: Samuel French, 1987.

———. *Inflatable You*. In *Romance Ranch*, 23–31. New York: Samuel French, 1991.

———. *Penance*. In *Romance Ranch*, 81–90.

———. *Support Your Local Police*. In *Five One-Act Plays by Mark Twain*, 42–59.

Taylor, Dominic. *Baychester Avenue—The Bronx*. Playwrights Center, Chicago, November 1993.

Taylor, Hiram. *Man of My Dreams*. Gay and Lesbian Center, New York, 1989.

———. *Members*. Syracuse University, Syracuse, N.Y., 1974.

Thomas, Tom. *The Interview*. New York: Samuel French, 1975.

Thompson, Ernest. *The Constituent*. In *Answers*, 29–44. New York: Dramatists Play Service, 1980.

———. *The One about the Guy in the Bar*. Ensemble Studio Theatre, New York, 1987.

Tolan, Peter. *Best Half Foot Forward*. In *Stay Carl Stay, Best Half Foot Forward, and Pillow Talk*, 43–64. New York: Dramatists Play Service, 1989.

————. *Pillow Talk*. In *Stay Carl Stay, Best Half Foot Forward, and Pillow Talk*, 65–89.

Tradup, Troy. *The Desired Effect*. Unicorn Theatre, Minneapolis, 1991.

————. *Truth and Beauty*. Unicorn Theatre, Minneapolis, 1992.

Tuotti, Joseph Dolan. *Big Time Buck White*. New York: Grove Press, 1969.

Van Duzer, Michael. *Hopeful Romantic*. Celebration Theatre, Los Angeles, 1991.

van Itallie, Jean-Claude. *Final Orders*. In *Early Warnings*, 21–37. New York: Dramatists Play Service, 1983.

Vargas, Fred Rohan. *Fly a Kite*. A Theatre at Studio R, New York, April 1982.

Vetere, Richard. *Gangster Apparel*. Judith Anderson Theater, New York, February 1991.

Wade, Stephen. *On the Way Home*. American Place Theater, New York, May 1993.

Wall, John. *Hot Little Island*. Wings Theatre Company, New York, January 1992.

————. *The Naked Corpse*. Wings Theatre Company, New York, 1992.

Wallace, Robert. *No Deposit No Return*. WSDG Theatre, New York, 1975.

Ward, Bruce. *Paint by Numbers*. 78th St. Theatre Lab, New York, 1983.

Ward, Richard Heron. *An Experiment in Fear*. New York: Samuel French, 1937.

Wesley, Richard. *The Past Is the Past*. In *The Past is the Past and Gettin' It Together*, 5–17. New York: Dramatists Play Service, 1979.

White, Kenneth. *Freight*. In *The Best One-Act Plays of 1946–1947*, ed. Margaret Mayorga, 19–50. New York: Dodd, Mead, 1947.

Wilde, Percial. *Salt for Savor*. In *The Best Short Plays of 1953–1954*, ed. Margaret Mayorga, 107–27. New York: Dodd, Mead, 1954.

Wildman, Paul G. *A Personal Thing*. New York: Samuel French, 1975.

Williams, Gerald Ray. *Maurice Galba*. University of Oklahoma, Norman, 1978.

Willis, Jane. *Slam!* In *Men without Dates and Slam!* 39–59. New York: Dramatists Play Service, 1985.

Wilson, August. *The Janitor*. In *Short Pieces from the New Dramatists*, ed. Stan Shervin, 81–82. New York: Broadway Play Publishing, 1985.

Wilson, Doric. *Forever After*. New York: JH Press, 1980.

Winters, Marian. *All Saint's Day*. In *A is for All*, 67–91. New York: Dramatists Play Service, 1968.

Witten, Matthew. *The Deal*. New York: Dramatists Play Service, 1990.

Wolf, Henry, and Ken Wolf. *My Father, My Son*. South Street Theater, New York, September 1990.

Worcester, Lawrence G. *Below Zero*. Boston: Baker's Plays, 1941.

Wright, Bil. *Mother Father Lover Man*. In *Tough Acts to Follow*, 121–27. San Francisco: Alamo Square Press, 1992.

Yellow Robe, William, Jr. *Wink-Dah.* American Conservatory Theatre Lab, San Francisco, 1988.

Yeomans, Cal. *Richmond Jim.* Theatre Rhinoceros, San Francisco, 1979.

Young, Andrew. *The Execution.* Kraine, New York, January 1994.

Young, Stanley. *A Bunyan Yarn.* In *The Best One-Act Plays of 1945,* ed. Margaret Mayorga, 113–35. New York: Dodd, Mead, 1946.

Male Monodramas

Alden, Jerome. *Bully: An Adventure with Teddy Roosevelt.* New York: Crown Publishers, 1979.

Ameen, Mark. *Seven Pillars of Wicca-Dick: A Triumph.* Duality Playhouse, New York, 1991.

Araiza, Albert Antonio. *Meat My Beat.* Celebration Theatre, Los Angeles, 1990.

Ariza, René. *Declaration of Principles.* In *Cuban Theater in the United States,* ed. Luis F. González-Cruz and Francesca M. Colecchia, 67–71. Tempe, Ariz.: Bilingual Press, 1992.

Belovitch, Brian. *Boys Don't Wear Lipstick!* Charles Ludlam Theatre, New York, May 1994.

Bogosian, Eric. *Notes from the Underground.* P.S. 122, New York, February 1993.

Bosgang, Jeremiah. *Hollywood Hustle.* Soho Rep, New York, May 1994.

Bromberg, Conrad. *Doctor Galley.* In *Transfers,* 41–64. New York: Dramatists Play Service, 1970.

Bullins, Ed, and Idris Ackamoor. *American Griot.* Black Theater Festival, Winston-Salem, N.C. 1991.

Bullock, Ken. *My Life Is a Show.* P.S. 122, New York, July 1993.

Burghardt, Arthur, and Michael Egan. *Frederick Douglass . . . through His Own Words.* St. Marks Playhouse, New York, May 1972.

Burnside, Chris. *Fort Head, One Gay Journey through the Vietnam Era Military.* Dixon Place, New York, December 1993.

Busch, Charles, and Kenneth Elliot. *Après Moi, Le Déluge.* In *Tough Acts to Follow,* 27–32. San Francisco: Alamo Square Press, 1992.

Cale, David. *Deep in a Dream of You.* Goodman Studio Theater, Chicago, January 1991.

———. *The Nature of Things.* Perry Street Theater, New York, March 1990.

———. *Somebody Else's House.* P.S. 122, New York, May 1994.

Carter, Randolph. *I Saw a Monkey.* Cherry Lane Theatre, New York, 1968.

Cayler, Tom, Kay Cummings, and Clarice Marshall. *Men Die Sooner.* HOME for Contemporary Theatre and Art, New York, October 1986.

———. *The Rat Piece.* La MaMa E.T.C., New York, November 1987.

Chandler, Charlotte, and Ray Stricklyn. *Confessions of a Nightingale.* New York: Samuel French, 1987.

Chesley, Robert. *A Dog's Life.* Chelsea Gay Association Theater Project, New York, 1982.

Curzon, Daniel. *One Man's Opinion.* Theatre Off Park, New York, 1991.

Duckworth, Stuart. *Slo-Pitch.* Theatre Uprising, Long Beach, Calif., 1987.

———. *Valdez Coho.* Primary Stages, New York, 1993.

Edwards, Gus. *Ain't No Other City Like It.* In *Lifetimes on the Streets.* Theater Four, New York, April 1990.

———. *Black Is Black.* In *Short Pieces from the New Dramatists,* ed. Stan Shervin, 19–21. New York: Broadway Play Publishing, 1985.

———. *A Garden in the City.* In *Lifetimes on the Streets.*

———. *Lifetime on the Street.* In *Lifetimes on the Streets.*

———. *New Ice Age.* In *Short Pieces from the New Dramatists,* 22–23.

———. *Sorry to Disturb You.* In *Lifetimes on the Streets.*

———. *Streetwalker.* In *Lifetimes on the Streets.*

———. *War Story.* In *Lifetimes on the Streets.*

Elward, James. *Passport.* In *Friday Night,* 23–38. New York: Dramatists Play Service, 1969.

Foster, Emmett. *Emmett: A One Morman Show.* Public Theater, New York, 1983.

Gordone, Charles. *Gordone is a Muthah.* In *The Best Short Plays 1973,* ed. Stanley Richards, 189–208. Radnor, Pa.: Chilton Book Company, 1973.

Greenberg, Albert. *Blonde Like You.* Solo Mio Festival, San Francisco, 1991.

Greenspan, David. *Republican Ascendency and the Nomination of Warren G. Harding for President.* Soho Rep, New York, June 1994.

Hale, Darel. *Favorite Places.* Apollo's Mice, Los Angeles, 1989.

Hampton, Aubrey. *Mixed Blood.* Gorilla Theatre, Tampa, 1989.

Handler, Evan. *Time on Fire.* Second Stage Theatre, New York, May 1993.

Hartman, Jan. *Samuel Hoopes Reading from His Own Works.* In *The Best Short Plays 1978,* ed. Stanley Richards, 329–46. Radnor, Pa.: Chilton Book Company, 1978.

Hennessy, Keith. *The King Is Dead.* Highways Performance Space, Santa Monica, 1991.

———. *Sacred Boy,* Theatre Artaud, San Francisco, 1990.

Hockenberry, John. *Spoke Man.* American Place Theatre, New York, February 1994.

Holsclaw, Doug. *Don't Make Me Say Things That Will Hurt You.* Josie's Cabaret & Juice Joint, San Francisco, 1990.

———. *The Life of the Party.* Theatre Rhinoceros, San Francisco, 1986.

———. *Tattoo Love.* Josie's Cabaret & Juice Joint, San Francisco, 1991.

Horovitz, Israel. *Spared.* In *Stage Directions and Spared,* 25–48. New York: Dramatists Play Service, 1977.

Houck, Billy. *One Beer Too Many.* In *One-Act Plays for Acting Students,* 209–13. New York: Samuel French, 1987.

Hoyle, Geoff. *The Convict Returns.* Berkeley Repertory Theatre, Berkeley, 1992.

Indiana, Gary, Ron Vawter, and Jack Smith. *Roy Cohn/Jack Smith.* Wooster Group Performance Garage, New York, 1992.

Jay, Ricky. *Ricky Jay and His 52 Assistants.* Second Stage, New York, January 1994.

Jenkin, Len. *Highway.* In *Limbo Tales,* 5–16. New York: Dramatists Play Service, 1982.

———. *Hotel.* In *Limbo Tales,* 21–37.

———. *Intermezzo.* In *Limbo Tales,* 17–20.

Jenkins, Ken. *Cemetery Man.* In *Rupert's Birthday and Other Monologues,* 53–67. New York: Dramatists Play Service, 1985.

———. *Chug.* In *Rupert's Birthday and Other Monologues,* 21–38.

Kane, John. *The Other Side of Paradise.* Kaufman Theater, New York, March 1992.

Kearns, Michael. *ROCK.* Highways Performance Space, Santa Monica, April 1992.

———. *The Truth Is Bad Enough.* Cast Theater, Los Angeles, September 1983.

King, Larry L., and Ben Z. Grant. *The Kingfish.* Houseman Theater, New York, March 1991.

Kling, Kevin. *Home and Away.* Second Stage, New York, July 1991.

———. *Twenty-One A.* New York: Samuel French, 1989.

Korder, Howard. *The Laws.* In *The Pope's Nose,* 7–10. New York: Dramatists Play Service, 1991.

Kornbluth, Josh. *Red Diaper Baby.* Second Stage, New York, April 1992.

Lane, Eric. *Lights along the Highway.* One Dream Theatre, New York, August 1993.

Leary, Denis. *No Cure for Cancer.* New York: Anchor Books, 1992.

Lecesne, James. *Word of Mouth, the Story of a Human Satellite Dish.* La MaMa E.T.C., New York, November 1993.

Levitt, Saul. *Lincoln.* Brooklyn Academy of Music, New York, June 1992.

Linney, Romulus. *Gold and Silver Waltz.* In *Pops,* 34–39. New York: Dramatists Play Service, 1987.

———. *Martha Miller.* In *Short Pieces from the New Dramatists,* ed. Stan Shervin, 45–46. New York: Broadway Play Publishing, 1985.

Luczak, Raymond. *The Rake.* Lower Levels of Society, New York, June 1992.

Macdonald, James G. *Big Frame Shakin'.* Ensemble Studio Theater, New York, November 1991.

Mamet, David. *Mr. Happiness.* In *The Water Engine and Mr. Happiness,* 69–82. New York: Samuel French, 1978.

———. *A Sermon.* In *Short Plays and Monologues,* 41–46. New York: Dramatists Play Service, 1981.

Margulies, David. *George Washington Dances.* Ensemble Studio Theatre, New York, February 1992.

Margulies, Donald. *Zimmer.* In *Pitching to the Star and Other Short Plays,* 79–95. New York: Dramatists Play Service, 1993.

McIntyre, Dennis. *The Boyfriend.* In *Short Pieces from the New Dramatists,* ed. Stan Shervin, 59–60. New York: Broadway Play Publishing, 1985.

McMahon, Jeff. *City of God.* Bessie Schonberg Theater, New York, December 1993.

Miller, Tim. *Naked Breath.* Echo Theater, Portland, Oreg., February 1994.

———. *Postwar.* Dance Theatre Workshop, New York, January 1982.

———. *Sex/Love/Stories.* P.S. 122, New York, December 1992.

———. *Some Golden States.* Edge Festival, San Francisco, October 1987.

Mydlack, Danny. *That's Natural.* P.S. 122, New York, December 1991.

Nesmith, Eugene. *Black Male Characters.* Theatre Row Theatre, New York, June 1991.

Nigro, Don. *Nightmare with Clocks.* In *Cincinnati and Other Plays,* 31–45. New York: Samuel French, 1989.

O'Keefe, John. *The Man in the Moon.* In *Shimmer & Other Texts,* 57–66. New York: Theatre Communications Group, 1989.

———. *The Promotion.* In *Three Short Pieces.* P.S. 122, New York, December 1993.

———. *Shimmer.* In *Shimmer & Other Texts,* 1–38.

———. *Sunshine's Glorious Bird.* In *Three Short Pieces.*

———. *Vid.* Berkeley Repertory Theatre, Berkeley, 1991.

Ong, Han. *Corner Store Geography.* Joseph Papp Public Theater, New York, December 1992.

Palminteri, Chazz. *A Bronx Tale.* Playhouse 91, New York, November 1989.

Paraiso, Nicky. *Asian Boys.* P.S. 122, New York, June 1994.

Patricca, Nicholas. *Frankie.* Randolph Street Gallery, Chicago, 1987.

———. *Niki.* Randolph Street Gallery, Chicago, 1987.

Patrick, Robert. *One Person.* In *Robert Patrick's Cheep Theatricks,* 157–72. New York: Samuel French, 1972.

Patterson, Stephen. *Boo!* Musical Theatre Works, New York, February 1993.

Pickett, James Carroll. *Bathhouse Benediction.* Actors Playhouse, Los Angeles, January 1984.

Pintauro, Joseph. *Uncle Zepp.* In *Cacciatore,* 43–47. New York: Dramatists Play Service, 1981.

Quinn, Colin, and Lou DiMaggio. *Sanctifying Grace.* Irish Arts Center, New York, June 1994.

Rappaport, Stephen. *The Chocolate Quarry.* Solo Mio Festival, San Francisco, 1991.

Rice, Howard. *Tradition 1A.* In *Off-Off Broadway Festival Plays, Fourteenth Series,* 31–53. New York: Samuel French, 1989.

Robinson, Matt. *The Confessions of Stepin Fetchit*. American Place Theater, New York, March 1993.

Rosenblatt, Roger. *And*. American Place Theater, New York, March 1992.

———. *Bibliomania*. American Place Theater, New York, October 1993.

———. *Free Speech in America*. American Place Theater, New York, November 1991.

Saunders, Dudley. *Birdbones*. The Kitchen, New York, January 1994.

Scheffer, Will. *The Falling Man*. Ensemble Studio Theatre, New York, May 1994.

Schein, David. *Out Comes Butch*. In *West Coast Plays* 17–18 (1985): 19–37.

Schisgal, Murray. *The Old Jew*. In *Five One-Act Plays,* 99–110. New York: Dramatists Play Service, 1968.

Schulman, Sarah. *1984*. HERE, New York, June 1994.

Sherman, Stuart. *Queer Spectacle*. Performing Garage, New York, July 1994.

Shippy, Kenneth Robert. *So Far, So Good*. Zephyr Theatre, Hollywood, Calif.: July 1990.

Shyre, Paul. *Will Rogers' U.S.A*. Geary Theatre, San Francisco, 1970.

Silverstein, Shel. *The Devil and Billy Markham*. In *Oh, Hell!* 47–79. New York: Samuel French, 1991.

Smith, Roger Guenveur. *Christopher Columbus 1992*. Joseph Papp Public Theater, New York, December 1992.

———. *Frederick Douglass Now*. La MaMa E.T.C., New York, January 1990.

Spring, Barnaby. *The Mayor of Boys Town*. American Place Theater, New York, February 1994.

Stringer, Alan. *Antiphon*. University of New Mexico Experimental Theatre, Albuquerque, 1979.

Talen, Bill. *Cooking Harry*. Cast Theater, Hollywood, Calif., January 1987.

———. *The Pre-Star Condition*. Dance Theater Workshop, New York, January 1985.

———. *The Shape*. Limbo Theatre, New York, October 1985.

———. *Songbirds of Central Nevada*. Intersection Theatre, San Francisco, August 1982.

Tingle, Jimmy. *Uncommon Sense*. American Place Theater, New York, 1993.

Vetter, Kenny. *No Permanent Address*. Performance Gallery, San Francisco, May 1982.

Walker, Phillip E. *Can I Speak for You, Brother?* Memorial Auditorium, University of Illinois, Urbana, 1978.

Walloch, Greg. *White Disabled Talent*. Dixon Place, New York, April 1993.

Ward, Bruce. *Decade*. Living with AIDS Theatre Metro Project, Boston, 1992.

Weiss, Jeff. *And That's How the Rent Gets Paid.* La MaMa, E.T.C., New York, August 1966.

Wilhelm, Le. *Barnacles.* Nat Horne Theatre, New York, May 1991.

Wilson, Lanford. *A Poster of the Cosmos.* In *The Way We Live Now: American Plays and the AIDS Crisis,* ed. M. Elizabeth Osborn, 63–75. New York: Theatre Communications Group, 1990.

Yeomans, Cal. *Poiret in Exile.* Alma Rainbow Productions, San Francisco, 1979.

Zaloom, Paul. *Crazy As Zaloom.* Theatre for the New City, New York, May 1982.

———. *The Fruit of Zaloom.* Theatre for the New City, New York, January 1979.

———. *The House of Horror.* Dance Theater Workshop, September 1988.

———. *My Civilization.* P.S. 122, New York, March 1993.

———. *Zaloominations.* Theatre for the New City, New York, April 1981.

Zimmerman, Paul. *Reno.* Under Acme, New York, September 1987.

Index

Abrahams, Roger, 105, 276n.11, 300n.21
Abramson, Doris, 275n.8
Absent women, in male-cast drama, 1, 8, 18, 42, 49, 50–52, 54–59, 62–68, 70–74, 76, 78, 81–84, 89, 93–94, 106, 109, 119, 135, 137, 140, 156, 164, 179, 182, 201, 204–5, 208, 224, 231, 243, 254, 266n.23, 268n.4, 270n.19, 271n.20, 272n.24, 280n.21, 284nn. 9–10, 286n.19, 294n.3; in misogynistic roles, 18 (definition of), 59–61, 63–64, 67, 72–74, 82–83, 201; in positive roles, 18 (definition of), 59–61, 67–68, 72–74, 83–84. *See also* Topics
Accession (Alám), 261n.7
African American (black), 5, 15, 103–5, 107, 112, 114, 116, 137, 165, 231–33, 235–37, 240, 242, 251–52, 257, 272n.25, 276nn. 11–13, 277n.14, 278n.17, 279n.19, 283n.7, 294–95n.7, 297n.12, 300nn. 21–22, 300–301n.1; as bi-sexual character in male-cast drama, 157, 163, 166; as character in male-cast drama, 5, 17, 20, 75, 102, 105, 109–11, 114, 116, 136–38, 144–45, 148–49, 159, 163, 190, 230–31, 236, 240–43, 250,

268n.5, 271n.23, 275n.9, 282n.5, 286n.19, 300nn. 22–23; as hetero-sexual character in male-cast drama, 111, 114, 152, 231, 234, 282n.5; as homosexual character in male-cast drama, 107, 116. *See also* Race
African American theater, 5, 103, 275n.8, 285n.16, 294n.5. *See also That Serious He-Man Ball; The Toilet*
After Eleven (Bumbalo), 260n.5
AIDS, 3, 73, 174, 178, 179, 181, 184, 185, 186, 244, 271n.22, 272n.23, 287n.26, 288n.27, 289nn. 31, 33, 290n.34, 297n.12, 300n.21
Alám, Juan Shamsul, 261n.7, 284n.9, 288n.27, 297–98n.12
Albee, Edward, 4, 20, 37, 51, 88, 118–19, 122, 124–25, 127, 129–31, 133, 143, 149, 151, 170, 174, 262–63n.10, 280n.20–22, 281nn. 23–24, 284n.10; *The Zoo Story,* 18, 20, 37, 41, 51, 57, 88, 90, 118–31, 133, 140, 142–43, 149, 151, 153, 169, 170, 175, 182, 210–11, 226, 228, 243, 262–63n.10, 273n.1, 280nn. 20–22, 281nn. 23–24, 284n.10

351